GOING TO SCHOOL IN LATIN AMERICA

GOING TO SCHOOL IN LATIN AMERICA

EDITED BY SILVINA GVIRTZ
AND JASON BEECH

The Global School Room
Alan Sadovnik and Susan Semel, Series Editors

GREENWOOD PRESS
Westport, Connecticut • London

Library of Congress Cataloging-in-Publication Data

Going to school in Latin America / edited by Silvina Gvirtz and Jason Beech.
    p. cm. — (The global school room, ISSN 1933–6101)
    Includes bibliographical references and index.
    ISBN-13: 978–0–313–33815–1 (alk. paper)
    1. Education—Latin America—History. I. Gvirtz, Silvina. II. Beech, Jason.
    LA541.G595 2008
    370.98—dc22   2007029311

British Library Cataloguing in Publication Data is available.

Library of Congress Catalog Card Number: 2007029311
ISBN-13: 978–0–313–33815–1
ISSN: 1933–6101

First published in 2008

Greenwood Press, 88 Post Road West, Westport, CT 06881
An imprint of Greenwood Publishing Group, Inc.
www.greenwood.com

Printed in the United States of America

The paper used in this book complies with the
Permanent Paper Standard issued by the National
Information Standards Organization (Z39.48–1984).

10 9 8 7 6 5 4 3 2 1

CONTENTS

SERIES FOREWORD

Over the past three decades, with globalization becoming a dominant force, the worldwide emphasis on schooling has accelerated. However, a historical perspective teaches us that global trends in schooling are by no means a recent phenomenon. The work of neo-institutional sociologists such as John Meyer and his colleagues has demonstrated that the development of mass public education systems became a worldwide trend in the nineteenth century and most nations' schools systems go back significantly further. *The Global School Room Series* is intended to provide students with an understanding of the similarities and differences among educational systems throughout the world from a historical perspective.

Although comparative and international educational research has provided an understanding of the many similarities in school systems across nations and cultures, it has also indicated the significant differences. Schools reflect societies and their cultures and therefore there are significant differences among different nations' school systems and educational practices. Another purpose of this series is to examine these similarities and differences.

The series is organized into nine volumes, each looking at the history of the school systems in countries on one continent or subcontinent. The series consists of volumes covering schooling in the following regions:

North America
Latin America
Europe
Sub-Saharan Africa
North Africa and the Middle East
South Asia

Central Asia
East Asia
Oceania

As the fourth volume in the series to be published, *Going to School in Latin America*, edited by Silvina Gvirtz and Jason Beech, provides an important and timely examination of the educational systems in Latin America, including those in Argentina, Bolivia, Brazil, Chile, Colombia, Costa Rica, Cuba, El Salvador, Mexico, Nicaragua, Paraguay, Peru, and Uruguay. Through the history of the educational systems in each country and an analysis of contemporary systems, the authors provide a rich description of how schooling is related to national culture, religion, identity, social, political and economic structures, and economic development. Moreover, the book illustrates the importance of historical, philosophical, and sociological perspectives in understanding the similarities and differences among societies and their schools. Finally, the book provides everyday examples of what schools in each country are like and how curriculum and teaching practices reflect the larger cultural, social, religious, and historical patterns of each society. Finally, its "day in the life" sections provide rich commentary on what it is like to go to school in these countries.

The editors and authors of each chapter examine a number of important themes, including colonialism, the effects of Western educational models, the cultures, education, and treatment of indigenous peoples, the effects of development and globalization, the tensions between Western educational systems and indigenous conceptions of education, revolutionary and reformist educational movements, and differences among countries with respect to access and opportunity systems.

Going to School in Latin America is emblematic of the series in that it provides students with an understanding that schooling needs to be understood in the context of each local culture, rather than viewed ethnocentrically from a U.S. or Western perspective. We often tend to make broad generalizations about other continents and assume that culture and schooling are uniform across countries. This book demonstrates the importance of examining national systems to uncover differences, as well as similarities.

In *National Differences, Global Similarities* (2005), sociologists David P. Baker and Gerald K. LeTendre argued that the purpose of studying another country's educational systems is to understand worldwide trends in education, as well as national differences. Merry White in *The Japanese Educational Challenge* (1987) argued that the purpose of studying another country's educational system is not necessarily to copy it, but rather to learn from the lessons of other societies, and where appropriate to use these lessons to improve our own schools, but only in the context of our own culture and schools.

Going to School in Latin America provides important illustrations of worldwide trends and national differences, as well as many important lessons.

However, it also cautions us to understand educational systems in the contexts of historical, national, and cultural differences. At a time when policy makers in the United States and elsewhere look to other countries in order to improve student achievement and to remain competitive in the global economy, this book reminds us that national achievement trends must be understood in a historical, sociological, and cultural context.

We invite you to continue to explore schooling around the world, this time in Latin America and then the rest of the world, as subsequent volumes are published.

Alan Sadovnik and Susan Semel

REFERENCES

Baker, D. P. and LeTendre, G. K. (2005). *National Differences, Global Similarities.* Palo Alto: Stanford University Press.

White, M. (1987). *The Japanese Educational Challenge.* New York: The Free Press.

Chapter 1

INTRODUCTION

Silvina Gvirtz and Jason Beech

The aim of this book is to present a history of the educational systems of Latin America. Each of the chapters refers to a specific country within the region, and we have made an effort to include most Latin American countries in order to give a representative sample of the diverse historical experiences that can be found in the region. This book serves as a useful resource for students of education or teachers in different parts of the world who are interested in widening their perspectives on education by learning how the universal problem of educating new generations has been approached in different societies within Latin America. Even though the authors are all highly respected researchers and educators, when commissioning the chapters we asked them to write in a simple way, avoiding technicalities as much as possible, with the aim of providing the reader with a general panorama of the history of schooling in each of the selected countries.

The chapters, which are organized in alphabetical order, have some common characteristics: they all include certain features like a "Day in the Life" that narrates a typical day in the life of a school boy or girl, and a "Timeline" that will help the reader to situate the most important events in the history of each educational system. At the same time, given the huge differences in the social and educational histories of Latin American countries, we have given the authors the freedom to highlight certain periods or themes according to the specificities of each case. For example, the chapters about Bolivia, Mexico, and Peru, where strong and lively indigenous cultures coexist with the Westernized cultures that were born from European colonization, emphasize this cultural clash that continues even 500 years after colonization by the Spanish conquerors—an issue that is given much less space in the Argentine or Uruguayan chapters.

We made an explicit effort to highlight the specificities of each national case, so the reader who is not very familiar with the region is warned against the abuse of stereotypes in understanding Latin America. In other words, we made an effort to avoid the construction of a general comparative history that forces the data in order to provide a false idea of historical coherence. We rather preferred to challenge the reader with the task of trying to put together a jigsaw puzzle in which they do not necessarily have all of the pieces. Thus, in each chapter, we have added a "Resource Guide" that provides a map for those readers who would like to continue exploring within the realms of the history of education of a particular country—after the overview presented in this book. However, we should also be conscious that these oddly-shaped pieces do not necessarily fit together to create a general and coherent history. On the contrary, our histories are full of incoherent discontinuities, comings, and goings. This precaution that we have in the comparative history must be read in a context in which the "history of Latin America" is being revised. The type of history that is being abandoned is one that was aimed at finding common origins, explanations, and coherences, many times ignoring the empirical evidence that showed that a great narrative of a Latin American history cannot be constructed.

However, avoiding a grand history of Latin America does not imply that we deny that the histories of these educational systems have some common characteristics and, especially, some common influences. One of the best books that addressed a general comparative history of education in Latin America is Gregorio Weinberg's classic *Modelos educativos en la historia de América Latina* [*Educational models in the history of Latin America*] (Weinberg, 1995).

These common features in the history of Latin American education are also reflected in the different chapters of *Going to School in Latin America*, albeit with a perspective that emphasizes how each specific educational system has adopted and adapted similar tendencies. The first, and most obvious, commonality rests in the fact that all of the countries included in this book have been colonized by Spain with the exception of Brazil, which was colonized by Portugal. This implied that schools were seen during the colonial period as institutions aimed at civilizing the indigenous people by promoting "European civilization" and Christian doctrine. There is a decisive event in the history of Latin America that defined the philosophical base for this view of education. Since the "discovery" of the Americas, European theologians discussed the nature of the inhabitants of the "New Land." The debate was ended in 1537 when Pope Paul III declared that the indigenous people of the Americas had a soul, were human beings, and, consequently, could not be brought under slavery. This also implied that they were worthy of being converted into Christianity and, of course, that their own religions, cultures, and ways of life should be abandoned, since the European colonizers viewed indigenous cultures as inferior. Several religious orders carried out the civilizing educational enterprise—the Jesuits were the most influential until they were expelled in 1759 from the Portuguese colonies and in 1767 from the Spanish territories. The other major cultural consequence of the Pope's decision was that large numbers of Africans were brought to the Americas as slaves and, in this way, the influence of African cultures added another fundamental trait to the configuration of Latin America.

The leaders of the independence movements in Latin America were fascinated by the Lancaster method that had developed in England, and funded those types of schools in places such as Argentina, Brazil, Chile, Colombia, El Salvador, Uruguay, and Venezuela. Later in the nineteenth century, as nation-states started to consolidate, mass elementary education systems were constructed on the basis of positivistic influences, especially coming from France. In the early twentieth century, the New Education (or Active School) Movement also inspired pedagogical ideas in Latin America, and, since the 1950s, it was mainly international agencies that started having a strong influence on education in the region. Furthermore, the chapters in this book take into account some interesting influences between Latin American countries. For example, the chapters on Costa Rica and Uruguay show how the ideas of the Argentine educator Domingo F. Sarmiento served as inspiration for the construction of those educational systems. Later, the ideas of Paulo Freire have influenced many educational activities in the continent, such as the "popular schools" funded by the rebels during the Civil War in the 1980s in El Salvador.

However, these influences have been interpreted differently in each country, resulting in particular patterns in each of the educational systems discussed in this volume. Thus, although there are some common features to the history of Latin American education, the chapters in this book show that educational developments in Latin America are as varied and diverse as its intriguing cultures. We now invite you to judge for yourself, and enter into the fascinating realms of the history of education in the countries of Latin America.

BIBLIOGRAPHY

Weinberg, Gregorio. 1995. *Modelos educativos en la historia de América Latina* (Buenos Aires: UNESCO-CEPAL-PNUD: A–Z Editora).

Chapter 2

SCHOOLING IN ARGENTINA

Silvina Gvirtz, Jason Beech, and Angela Oria

INTRODUCTION

This chapter offers an overview of the history of education in Argentina. Unfortunately, not much is known about the educational practices of the original inhabitants of the actual Argentine territory. Thus, we will start our historical journey with some notes on education during colonial times and the first decades after independence. Then, we will describe the foundation of the modern educational system in Argentina and provide some data showing the success of this model until the 1950s. The third section presents a brief analysis of the University in Argentina in the first half of the twentieth century, and the fourth part of the chapter examines education during the second half of that century. Then, some comments on the growth of the private sector and the criticisms made of the educational system since the 1980s will be offered before analyzing the reforms that were made in the 1990s. The last section reflects on the latest developments in the Argentine educational system and the opportunities that have been opened up by the new Law of National Education that was passed in 2006.

COLONIAL TIMES AND THE FIRST YEARS AFTER INDEPENDENCE

The Spanish "discovered" the land that is now Argentina in 1516, when the sailor Juan Díaz de Solís entered the Rio de la Plata mistaking it for a passage between the Atlantic and the Pacific Oceans. The city of Buenos Aires was founded in 1536. However, attacks by the indigenous peoples forced the settlers away and the site was abandoned in 1541. A second (and permanent) settlement was established in 1580. Nevertheless, Buenos Aires was quite marginal to the interests of the Spanish Crown at the time. Other cities had been previously founded in what is now northern Argentina: Santiago del Estero, Londres de Catamarca, Mendoza, San Juan, and Córdoba. These settlements were dependent upon the Viceroyalty of Lima in Peru. It was with the creation of the Viceroyalty of Rio de la Plata in 1776 that the city of Buenos Aires adopted a hegemonic political role in the region that continues until the present day (for example, the 2001 census showed that out of 36 million inhabitants of Argentina, 11 million lived in the City of Buenos Aires and its suburbs). As will be shown later, the disputes between the Capital City and the provinces have been a central feature of the political and educational history of the country.

The Spanish (and the Catholic Church) considered education a fundamental part of their colonizing strategies. Religious indoctrination and the legitimation of the sociopolitical system established by colonial institutions and legislation were considered to be the central issues. Several religious orders carried out this task—the Jesuits were the best organized and most influential during the seventeenth and eighteenth centuries. The political and educational strategy of the Jesuits in the colonies was based on two objectives: to use education to indoctrinate the indigenous masses and to prepare young men for their participation in the governing elite. In order to address the second goal, the Jesuits founded the first university in Argentina. This institution, located in the actual Córdoba Province, was created in 1613 as a Jesuit college and became a university in 1622 (Cano 1985).

While learning the principles of Christianity, the few people who went to school were taught how to read, write, and count. They would also receive practical courses to prepare themselves for different trades. Social elites usually provided private tuition for their children. From the mid-eighteenth century, formal education started expanding in all Hispanic America, in part due to the economic development of the region. Schools for learning the "first letters" were founded in convents and, later, the *Cabildos* (a colonial version of municipalities) also became interested in providing education. In 1771, the *Cabildo* of Buenos Aires opened a "School of First Letters" and by 1805, three more were created. These were the first proper public schools; the Cabildos hired the teachers and paid at least partially for their expenses.

The separation of Argentina from Spain took place in 1816. The first decades of independence were characterized by internal conflicts—caused in most cases by the Province of Buenos Aires attempting to prevail over the rest of the provinces. Political instability was constant and it actually reached its peak in 1820 with the dissolution of the newborn National State. Public schools continued to operate under the control of the local Cabildos. By 1812, the City of Buenos Aires had seven of these communal schools (there were separate schools for girls and boys). In 1817, the position of General Director of Schools was created. The first to occupy this position was Saturnino Segurola, who was then replaced by the Englishman James Thompson who is famous for promoting the Lancaster method in Buenos Aires. The use of this method was short-lived.

Meanwhile, in the university, during the independence period, classical studies, such as law, philosophy, and theology, were being questioned and confronted with a utilitarian, rational, and scientific concept of education imported from Western Europe. The educated group of *porteños* (Buenos Aires habitants) who promoted independence thought that the application of these pragmatic ideas would result in the modernization of the colonial social structure. In its *Manifesto*, addressed to all of the countries in the world, the Congress of Tucuman explained that one of the causes for the Declaration of Independence was that due to the action of the Spanish Monarchy: "[T]he teaching of the sciences was forbidden for us, and the only thing we were taught was Latin grammar, ancient philosophy, theology, and civil and canonical jurisprudence" (cited in Tedesco 2003).

In 1815, while the war against the Spanish Army continued, the study plans for the University of Córdoba were reformed and adapted to the new political situation, and strongly influenced by the enlightened ideas (Cano 1985). In 1821, the University of Buenos Aires (UBA) was funded using the Napoleonic Imperial University as a model. The Cabildos were suppressed and primary education went under control and supervision of the University. For the first time, modern philosophy was officially taught in Argentina (Tedesco 2003). The medieval university model inherited from Spain was being abandoned and replaced by the French educational model in an attempt to modernize the colonial society.

Nevertheless, due to political instabilities and internal conflicts during the first decades after independence, educational achievements were weak and fragmented. The rise of Juan Manuel de Rosas as Governor of Buenos Aires in December 1829 brought about hopes of peace and order. He presented himself as "The Restorer" of discipline and traditional values, and as the reverse of the "European elitism," identifying himself with the common man and the *gaucho* (man from the countryside).

As an advocate of the federal scheme, he actively intervened in the political life of the rest of the provinces and opposed cooperating in the elaboration of a constitution. Rosas soon achieved the "sum of public power"; that is, no limits or parliamentary control over his decisions. The persecution of opponents to the "federal government" provoked massive emigration of political exiles. Intellectuals and political exiles advocated education and criticized Rosas's government from their foreign residencies. They expressed their opinions through the press as well as in educational, political, and literary publications. The most salient characters were Esteban Etcheverría, Domingo Sarmiento, Bartolomé Mitre, and Juan Bautista Alberdi—who later returned to Argentina to initiate the process of National Organization.

Between 1828 and 1852, the State's educational budget suffered extraordinary restrictions. The worst moments of the financial crisis coincided with the French blockade of the port of Buenos Aires in 1838. The expected effects of this event (suspension of international sea commerce and sudden fall of tax collection) caused the State to proclaim extreme austerity: education, health, and social care were simply erased from the budget (Newland 1992). From the French blockade onwards, schools had to fund themselves by imposing student fees. The fees were meant to provide for teachers' salaries. Naturally, student enrollments dropped: by May 1840, only four schools remained open out of the eight that operated in 1838. Meanwhile, the imposition of fees in public schools ordered by Rosas resulted in the development and strengthening of the private sector.

The fall of Rosas in 1852 inaugurated what is known in Argentine history as the "Period of National Organization." The first National Constitution sanctioned in 1853 emphasized the role of education for achieving the nation's organization, and established the "right to teach and learn" (Art. 14th). The fifth Article also established that every province must guarantee its own public system of primary education. The road was paved for the construction of a modern educational system in Argentina.

THE FOUNDATION OF THE MODERN EDUCATIONAL SYSTEM

It is now widely accepted that the creation of the Argentine educational system was part of the State-led project aimed at shifting from a "traditional" scattered society to a united "modern" nation integrated with the rest of the world. Within this vision, a "modern" educational system was seen as the most adequate social technology to give rise to cultural unity out of a vast territory with intense regional disparities. This cultural diversity was considered a threat for the central power (Tedesco 2003; Gvirtz 1991). This project required new men and women who would be united by their common feeling of love for the *Patria* (Nation). It was the culture of the elites that was taken as a model for this new vision. Thus, the kind of "ideal" citizen that was promoted was very different from most of the population that inhabited the Argentine territory at that time. The people had to be "converted," and it was through the public primary school that this new vision would be disseminated, homogenizing the population under the new "Argentine culture" (Alliaud 1993).

"Civilización o barbarie" was Sarmiento's slogan, who is considered the founder of the Argentine educational system. Two strategies were mainly used in the quest for civilizing the country: education and the promotion of European immigration (Tedesco 2003). European immigrants were seen as "civilizing" agents that would bring with them their culture, order, and attitude towards work, serving as a model for the Argentine population. As one of the most important Argentine intellectuals of the time, J. B. Alberdi, said: "Each European who arrives at our shores brings more civilization in his habits— which he then communicates to our inhabitants—than many books of philosophy" (quoted in Alliaud 1993, 27).

However, immigrants became another obstacle in the homogenizing project. The newly arrived introduced many different cultural traditions, languages, and values, adding to existing cultural diversity. Thus, the new immigrant groups reinforced the need for a public primary school that would "convert" all of the population into a common culture and guarantee political stability, legitimizing the power of the central State (Alliaud 1993).

In 1884, the National Law of Education was passed, establishing that primary schooling ought to be compulsory, free of cost for the pupils, and that no religious content should be taught in schools. Primary schools expanded rapidly throughout the Argentine territory. The National State exercised a strong control over primary education with the aim of guaranteeing that each and every school in Argentina would work in exactly the same way, offering the same content, at the same time, with the same methods, and using the same didactic materials.

At first, the action of the State was aimed at disciplining the diverse schooling experiences that existed in the Argentine territory. Specifically, since the second half of the nineteenth century, the *Direcciones de Escuelas* of the different provinces and–later–the *Consejo Nacional de Educación* established a number of norms that regulated the finance, structure, and institutionalization of the school system: every school was brought under the control of one of these national or provincial agencies (Newland 1992). By applying this policy, the State successfully disciplined the corporations of educators (both religious and secular) who had been in charge of the education of children until that time.

During the first decades of the twentieth century, the State had a quasi-monopoly over the provision of education in Argentina. The National State and the provincial states (but especially the National State) assumed total responsibility for schooling, excluding the civil society from any participation in these matters. Even though some educational activities were partially left in the hands of the civil society, the State kept a strong control on these activities. For example, most private schools during the first half of the twentieth century were not allowed to award educational credentials and they were thoroughly inspected by state personnel. The state inspector could intervene in the school and even take the place of the principal.

In this way, the Catholic Church was displaced from the public school system. The teaching of the Christian doctrine that had been compulsory in the schools of the colonial period and during the first decades of independence became an extracurricular activity. The Catholic Church seemed to accept the rules of the game and demanded its participation in education within the regulations imposed by the State. It was only between 1943–54 that the Church's demands were heard and the teaching of religion was reintroduced into public schools. However, in May 1955, the Law of Religious Education was repealed. In this same year, a Decree allowed *Colegio El Salvador* and *Inmaculada Concepción de Santa Fe* to issue nationally valid secondary school certificates. These were antecedents of Decree Number 12179 in 1960, which enabled private schools to issue certificates that were recognized as valid by the State (Narodowski and Andrada 2001). This was one of the most relevant historical precedents in the history of private education regulation. Then, following decentralization of curricular design in the 1990s, religion was included as a compulsory subject in the official curriculum of a few provinces.

In the late nineteenth century, the Argentine State had promised to offer quality public education to all the inhabitants of the Argentine territory. Through schooling, the living conditions of each and every one of the Argentines—rich or poor, native or immigrants, men or women—was to be improved.

As part of the policies linked to establishing mechanisms of control over the system, teacher training was organized around a discipline-enforcing model. The State promoted amongst teachers an identity that fundamentally emphasised a political role: to homogenize the population by converting them into a specific culture. However, there was a problem with the State's strategy. The Argentine elite held an ambiguous position towards the culture that should be promoted in schools: they promoted a "European way of life," but at the same time they struggled against the perpetuation of the ways of life of each of the particular foreign communities. Consequently, finding the agents that would transmit the dominant culture, which was foreign to them, was a problem for those in charge of the educational system. It was necessary to create an "army" of specialists that would perform this fundamental task in the nation-building project (Alliaud 1993).

Adopting the French model of the Normal Schools, the State assumed the responsibility for the education of teachers (Gvirtz 1991, 28). The idea was to have educators that were as homogeneous as possible, so that they could be interchangeable and any deviation in the transmission of the unifying culture could be avoided (Alliaud 1993). In 1869, the first Normal School was founded in the City of Paraná. By 1885, the National State had funded eighteen of these teacher training institutions (at least one in each of the fourteen Argentine provinces) (Alliaud 1993, 89–90), and by 1889, there were thirty four Normal Schools in Argentina (Alliaud 1993, 106).

The Normal School was placed as an intermediate institution, standing between primary schools—oriented towards the civilization of the masses, and secondary schools—oriented towards the education of the elite (Gvirtz 1991). Although Normal Schools were legally considered a part of the middle school subsystem, there was a major difference between teacher training institutions and other secondary schools: graduates of secondary schools obtained a baccalaureate and thus could have access to higher education, while graduates of the Normal School were not allowed into higher education (Gvirtz 1991).

Positivism had a strong influence on the kind of education that took place in the Normal Schools. Unquestioned faith in God and in the moral principles of the Church was replaced by secular faith in science and natural laws (Alliaud 1993). Even though the contents of the moral principles of the Church were displaced, its forms were kept. The previously unquestioned love for the Father, the Son, and the Holy Spirit was displaced by love for the school, science, and the *Patria*. Schools became the "temples of knowledge," and teachers became the "priests of civilisation" (Alliaud 1993).

Teachers not only had to transmit certain fundamental knowledge for citizenship (such as, the three Rs), but one of their main tasks was to promote certain norms, values, and principles. Consequently, it was the teacher's moral aptitudes that were given preeminence in the Normal Schools. Emphasis was placed on fostering love for the *Patria*, altruism and generosity, hygiene, good character, and especially "good" habits and a love for order (Alliaud 1993). Additionally, as part of the State's vigilance, the *Consejo Nacional de Educación* was created at the end of the nineteenth century with the aim of legitimizing the knowledge that should circulate in public schools. Textbooks were a central element within this concern. One of the *Consejo*'s specific functions was to "choose and prescribe the textbooks which were adequate for the public schools, favouring their edition and improvements and ensuring their uniform and permanent use" (Law 1420).

From the end of the nineteenth century to 1940, two objectives were salient in the rulings related to textbooks: to guarantee the universal provision of books for all of the school population, and to control the contents of the textbooks that were to be used in schools (Narodowski and Manolakis 2002). The proliferation of school textbooks was seen as generating a great danger: diversity was threatening homogeneity and could result in deviations. This concern dominated the regulations related to textbooks until the 1950s. Although some regulations considered didactical, methodological, and administrative issues, it was the ideological concerns that were salient.

Finally, among so many actions leading to the creation of a structured educational system, a body of agents was organized to supervise, legislate, enforce, and control daily school life. Inspectors centralized these tasks and secured the homogeneity required by the system by ensuring that everyday school practice followed the rules established by the central organs of educational management and governance. According to Pineau, the inspectors' actions were comprised of both inside and outside school activities: they would evaluate the performance of teachers and councils, appoint honorable candidates for those jobs, investigate reasons for educational stagnation, report on findings, review accounting books, and schedule pedagogic conferences for school staff. Outside of school, they would provide lectures for the community on national history, economics, industry, arts, public health as well as other issues, in order to promote the community's "physical, intellectual, and moral development" (Pineau 1997, 65). Additionally, inspectors ought to serve as counselors for teachers and principals.

The policies described above, which centralized most educational power at the national level, endured more than one hundred years of state policies, and only began to be deactivated in the late 1950s (and, as will be shown later, replaced by other state policies). The educational system was extremely successful in attracting most of the school-aged population to primary schools and in

Table 2.1
School-aged Population and Enrollments in Primary Education (1850–95)

	1850	1869	1883	1895
School-aged Population	183,000	403,876	507,769	877,810
Enrollments	11,903	82,679	145,660	246,132
Percentage	6.5%	20.4%	28.6%	28%

Source: Tedesco, 2003.

promoting a national identity. Argentina took a great leap forward from 77.4 percent illiteracy rate in 1869 to 13.6 percent in 1947. In the City of Buenos Aires, for example, as early as in 1930, 95 percent of the population was literate, and 30 percent attended secondary school. We will now analyze in more detail the quantitative expansion of schooling in Argentina between 1850–1955.

Table 2.1 shows the impressive expansion of enrollments that took place since the political situation was stabilized in Argentina (1860s) and at the end of the century. It is also important to note that this expansion took place in a context of significant growth of the school-aged population, rooted in the massive arrival of immigrants. Thus, although 100,000 children were incorporated into schools between 1883–95, the percentage of enrollments dropped. For example, in the City of Buenos Aires, where most of the immigrants stayed, enrollments dropped from 64.6 percent in 1883 to 57.7 percent in 1895 (even though in absolute numbers there was a significant growth).

The expansion of the system was not distributed evenly around the country. In contrast with the City of Buenos Aires, in 1895, in the Province of Corrientes, 16 percent of the school-aged population was enrolled, and in Santiago del Estero only 13.4 percent was enrolled. Other provinces, such as Santa Fe, Entre Rios, Catamarca, and Tucuman had close to 25 percent enrollment, and Mendoza and San Juan were the most advanced with 40 percent and 50 percent of enrollments, respectively (Tedesco 2003). Another issue to consider in the 1890s is that only about 2 percent of the children who started primary education finished it. Furthermore, most of the dropouts took place between the first and the second grades.

By 1914, 48 percent of the school-aged population was enrolled and by 1930, primary schools had incorporated 60 percent to 70 percent of the children in the corresponding age ranges, placing the Argentine educational system amongst the most advanced systems in the world in terms of primary school enrollments. The expansion of the system stagnated from 1930 to 1945, but it gained impetus again with Perón's arrival to power in 1943 and continued in the second half of the century with enrollments of 73.5 percent in 1947, and 80.6 percent in 1960 (Tedesco 2003). Dropouts were still significant. In the 1930s, only 33 percent of the children who started primary school finished it. In the 1940s, the percentage rose to 37.4 percent.

Table 2.2
Enrollments in Secondary Education (1930–55)

Year	1930	1935	1940	1945	1955
Enrollments	85,732	104,862	153,918	201,170	471,895

Source: Adapted from Tedesco, 2003.

Meanwhile, secondary education also grew significantly, but the point of departure was quite different. Since the origins of the educational system, secondary education was aimed at the education of the elites and teacher training in the case of the Normal School that became the option for women of the upper (and later middle) classes. For example, in 1890, 46 percent of enrollments in Normal Schools were concentrated in schools for women (there were separate institutions for men and women); five years later, that number rose to 58 percent, and from 1930–45, 85 percent of Normal School students were women (Tedesco 2003). Total enrollments (including the Normal School) are shown in Table 2.2. The growth was quite steady until 1945, when the Peronist government opened access to post-primary education to the lower classes and enrollments more than doubled in 10 years. Before moving on to the analysis of the Peronist period, a brief analysis of the Argentine university will be offered, emphasizing how the profound social changes that took place in the sociopolitical structures of Argentina in the first decades of the twentieth century impacted on this educational level.

THE ARGENTINE UNIVERSITY AT THE BEGINNING OF THE TWENTIETH CENTURY

One of the main characteristics of the Argentine University until the beginnings of the twentieth century was its close ties with political power. The movement of people between the university and government and from the government to university was very common. Nicolas Avellaneda is a good example of this relation: he was a professor, rector of UBA, a National Minister, and president of the republic. Conflict between the government and the university was almost nonexistent (Cano 1985), and the main objective of higher education was to prepare young men [*sic*] for their entrance into the governing elite (Mollis 1990).

Following Tedesco (1986), it can be said that Argentine education was geared towards the interests of the ruling oligarchy. The ruling group was composed mainly of rich landowners that obtained large benefits from the agro-exporting model of the Argentine economy. Thus, this group was not interested in promoting the economic development of the country through industrialization, but rather, maintaining the status quo (Halperin Donghi 1969). In these circumstances, the expansion of education during the second half of the nineteenth century did not have an economic function: it was driven instead by political motivations (Tedesco 2003). The most coherent kind of education for this objective was encyclopaedism. This type of education, in the Argentine case, did not present any benefits for industrialists since it prepared secondary students for administrative posts in the government or for staying in the university—and later moving to a political career (Tedesco 2003).

During that time, being a doctor—lawyers are also given the title of doctor—was almost indispensable in order to reach the highest political posts: in 1914, between 85 percent and 97 percent of Argentine congressmen had been trained in either law or medicine (Zimmermann 1995). Both of the national universities (Córdoba and Buenos Aires) had three *facultades*: medicine, law, and physics and mathematical sciences. However, 80 percent of the students in 1893 chose medicine or law and the concentration in these disciplines increased to 89 percent by 1898. Meanwhile, scientific studies were, de facto, discriminated against by the policy of the central government, which allocated most of its resources to the traditional disciplines (Tedesco 2003). The posts that required technical skills were occupied mostly by immigrants that did not participate in Argentine political life.[1] For example, in 1895, out of 1,481 engineers, 407 were Argentine and 1,074 were foreigners. In the same year, there were 1,506 lawyers from Argentina while only 200 were foreigners (Zimmermann 1995). Thus, by choosing an encyclopedic education centered in the classic disciplines and discarding instruction geared towards productive activities, the oligarchy that controlled the central government was using education as a means to guarantee the stability of the social order (Tedesco 2003).

Nevertheless, the social structure of Argentina changed extensively between 1880–1920. By 1895, the middle class, which was almost nonexistent before 1860, represented 35 percent of the population of the City of Buenos Aires (Germani 1955). A great number of immigrants—proportionally twice as many as those that reached the United States—had arrived in the country and the process of urbanization had advanced. The policies adopted by the upper class to protect their interests limited the possibilities for the immigrants to buy land. Consequently, most of the newly arrived stayed in the cities, where they had better opportunities, and became an urban and modern middle class. Most of the immigrants did not integrate into Argentina's political life. In this context, the middle class was for many years excluded from national politics. Finally, the "popular class" represented approximately 60 percent of the economically active population. The main characteristic of this highly heterogeneous group was its lack of political power and, by the 1940s, its concentration in urban areas (70 percent) (Bejarano 1969; Halperin Donghi 1969; Di Tella 1969, 1974; Germani 1955).

The spread of humanist-encyclopedic education meant that the middle class began to have access to higher education and demand participation in the country's political life, disputing the power of the ruling elite (Cano 1985; Mollis 1990). The university became one of the arenas for the increasing class struggle. The middle classes continued to press for the democratization of higher education and university enrollments grew rapidly during the first years of the twentieth century (by 362 percent from 1893–1918) (Mollis 1990). Between 1900–1905, UBA students established their own organizations and several strikes and demonstrations were organized in the schools of law and medicine. In 1918, the students of the University of Córdoba began a strike that resulted in the Córdoba Reform.

The students called for the abolition of the monopoly of university governance that rested in the hands of a clique of fifteen academics (Romero 1979). The movement had evident popular support and the sympathy of the new democratic government that represented the middle classes (Schugurensky 1997). As a result, many professors were fired, new ones were appointed and a rector approved of by the students was elected. That same year, to avoid unrest among its students, UBA adopted the principles of the movement: student participation in university government, open enrollment, and academic freedom. The newly founded University of La Plata followed the same path (Romero 1979), and the Córdoba Reform became a model for many universities in Latin America.

The reform defended the idea of a nonutilitarian concept of man. The student was no longer considered as a mere apprentice that collected skills and formulas for the exercise of a profession. *Profesionalismo utilitario* [utilitarian professionalism], which deliberately ignored social problems, was considered to be immoral. Thus, the university's professionalizing role was to be expanded. The university should not only study national problems, such as the economy, social welfare, and abuses of power; rather, it should also take a position on these questions.

Thus, the reform, by promoting a more democratic education, changed many aspects of the educated identity fostered by the university. Nevertheless, its fundamental role—to educate an elite for political action—was not altered. Different actors—the middle classes—now controlled the university. However, it was the encyclopedic university that had opened the opportunity for the middle class to gain access to power, and they were not willing to abandon that kind of education. In order to consolidate their version of democracy, the university should still educate men for political posts, but the opportunity of higher education—and of participating in political life—would now be open to the middle classes.

The advocacy of an encyclopedic education by the middle class was not uncontested. From the 1890s, the oligarchic Conservative group noted the growth in enrollments in secondary education. Although not many students finished secondary school and aspired to attend the university, the presence of middle class students—usually the sons of prosperous immigrants—was already disturbing the monopoly that the traditional upper classes used to have in the university (Tedesco 2003). Thus, there was a series of reform projects from 1890–1916 that promoted the "modernization" of education by dividing secondary instruction into two paths. The modern path, more specialized and utilitarian, was destined for those who were not expected to aspire to become a part of the governing elite, while traditional encyclopedic education was meant for those who would continue into higher education and became part of that elite (Tedesco 2003).

A paradox resulted from the struggle for control of education between the middle and upper classes. While the Conservatives were advocating modernization of education, the middle class was defending the traditional encyclopedic system, arguing that the "modernizing" proposals were oligarchic and discriminatory. Before leaving office, the Conservative government had reformed secondary education, creating the *Escuela Intermedia*, a "professional option" where the students would receive an education that "would make them productively useful and politically neutral" (Tedesco 2003, 283). However, when the Radical government that represented the middle classes rose to power in 1916, it reestablished the traditional curriculum in secondary schools. The middle classes aimed their policies at guaranteeing democratization of access to institutions, which allowed for social mobility, but they never questioned the institutions themselves nor did they review the country's economic policies (Tedesco 2003, 283).

Thus, this overview of the "revolution" that took place in Argentine universities, reflecting the enormous social and political changes that took place in society at large, also helps to understand why basic education remained almost unchanged during such a unstable period: the middle classes that started to challenge the hegemonic power of the landowning elite did not review the educational system. Rather, they aimed their educational policies at maintaining the existing configuration of the system, hoping that it would allow for greater social mobility. It was only after Peron's rise to power in 1943 that a more systematic attempt was made to change the educational system.

PERONISM AND POLITICAL TURMOIL

The next phase of change in the educational system responded to another rupture in social, economic, and political structures in Argentina. These changes started with the world economic crisis in 1930, which resulted in the collapse of the agro-exporting model that had sustained the Argentine economy (Halperin Donghi 1969), and were consolidated between 1943 and 1955. During this period, new actors appeared in the Argentine political scene: the industrial bourgeoisie and the industrial working class (Gvirtz 1991). Under the leadership of these groups, among others, the Peronist government reintroduced democratic elections, gave women the right to vote, and developed a version of a welfare state. Social justice, economic independence, and political sovereignty were the slogans of a regime with a clear national project in which education was ascribed major importance (Gvirtz 1991).

One of the main characteristics of educational policies during the Peronist government was the redistribution of education among the different social groups through a dramatic increase in enrollments, especially at the secondary and university levels where enrollments were doubled and tripled, respectively (Tedesco 2003). There was massive construction and improvement of school buildings, the education budget was significantly increased, and for the first time in Argentine history, a separate Ministry of Education was created (Rein 1998).

The other peculiarity of education policies in this period is what some historians call the "*politization*" of school contents: Peronist doctrine became a compulsory feature in the study programs in all educational levels (Gvirtz 1999). For example, in the Normal Schools, four subjects of "National Doctrine" were included, and consequently 25 percent of instruction time was used in the study of the "achievements" of the Peronist government. In addition, new textbooks based on the ideology of the Peronist Party were incorporated into schools. The figure of Evita, the wife of President Perón that had been named by the National Congress as Spiritual Guide of the Nation, started to occupy a privileged position in school contents. For example, in some first grade textbooks, the traditional phrase "*yo amo a mi mama*" (I love my mom) that was used to teach how to read and write, was replaced by the phrase "*yo amo a Evita*" (I love Evita). In the illustrations, Evita was often drawn with a halo around her head, as if she were a saint. After her death in 1952, the government established that it was compulsory to read her autobiography in all Argentine schools. Even though teachers used several techniques to resist the teaching of Peronist doctrines, the government also had its own strategies to ensure that these themes were included in lessons. First, the government tried to co-opt teachers by giving promotions to those that showed loyalty to the Party. Additionally, those that were not considered loyal were fired (Gvirtz and Narodowski 1998).

Meanwhile, in the University, in 1930 a military coup ended with the democratic period that had started with the Reform. The military government took control of the universities, replacing the authorities with their own. The statutes were modified—suppressing student participation in the government of the institutions—and many professors and reformist students were incarcerated (Mollis, 1990). A new period began that was characterized by a hostile posture of the military governments towards the university (which the military would indefinitely accuse of being subversive centers) and a clear anti-militaristic stance of the students' movements (Romero 1979; Cano 1985).

With Perón's arrival in office in 1946, conflict between the government and university continued. Even though Perón was democratically elected, his government was strongly resisted by the students and university staff. This was reflected in demonstrations, protests against the regime, students' strikes, and takeovers of university buildings. The Peronist regime, wishing to eliminate all pockets of resistance, employed repressive tactics to silence the students and restore calm. Autonomous universities were not consistent with the Regime's policy of political indoctrination. The Peronist government took control of the universities, student organizations were outlawed, and some 1,250 academic personnel were forced out of the institutions and replaced by staff loyal to the Regime. In 1947, a new university law eliminated autonomy, democracy, and student participation. The government was given the right to appoint university authorities and all political activities in the university were banned. Paradoxically, in the 1950s, lessons on "political education" were made compulsory; these were actually lessons in Peronist doctrine (Rein 1998).

Despite the lack of qualitative democracy, university enrollments increased from 51,272 students in 1947 to 143,542 in 1955 (Rein 1998), especially with the decision in 1950 to eliminate tuition fees, which opened the possibility for students with limited financial means to access higher education (Rein 1998). The *Universidad Obrera* (workers' university) was opened as part of the Peronist economic program that promoted industrial development and modernization in order to obtain "economic independence." This institution was founded as the place where the graduates of the vocational high schools that the regime had created could continue their education (Rein 1998). However, the leaders of the military coup that overthrew Perón in 1955 closed the *Universidad Obrera*. It was not reopened until 1959—as the *Universidad Tecnológica Nacional* (National Technology University) (Rein 1998).

With the exception of two brief democratic periods interrupted by military coups, the armed forces took control of the state between 1955–73. In the 1960s and especially in the 1970s, guerrilla groups were formed. In 1976, a new military coup started the darkest period in Argentine history—when state-sponsored violence against citizens resulted in tens of thousands of people made to "disappear." The dictatorship's objective was to discipline Argentine society, and reinstall the values of "order" and respect for hierarchies and authority. However, with five ministers of education from 1976–82, the regime's different leaders did not agree on a clear project for education. Rather, as Tedesco (1983) notes, what was common among the different postures was that which they wanted to destroy.

In this context, the educational policies of the military government were characterized by strong ideological control. This was done through the expulsion of teachers, control over the curriculum and the activities of students and parents, and by regulating the physical appearance of both teachers and pupils (Tedesco 1983). Similarly, the university policy of the new dictatorship had two dimensions, both aiming at the depoliticization of higher education. On one hand, there was physical and ideological repression of everything considered "subversive"—students, teachers, and staff were detained, expelled, or made to "disappear";[2] and texts, courses, theoretical orientations, programs, and whole disciplines were eradicated. On the other hand, the regime tried to reduce the number of students and staff in the universities by establishing entrance examinations, quotas for certain courses, and tuition fees (Balan 1993). As a result, enrollments fell by 25 percent in the first years of the 1980s when compared to the mid-1970s (Balan 1993). In 1983, a new democratic government took office inaugurating the longest democratic period in Argentine history that continues until the present day.

PRIVATIZATION, RECENT CRITICISMS, AND PROPOSALS FOR IMPROVEMENT

Since the 1960s, the most affluent members of society have been moving from the public to the private system. Figure 2.1 shows a significant growth in private enrollments at the primary level in Argentina since the late 1950s. The lowest percentage of private enrollments was in 1941. Since that year, a period of sustained expansion of private enrollments started. The number of students in the private sector increased considerably from fewer than 289,000 pupils in 1967 to almost 717,000 in the mid-1990s—40.3 percent growth in absolute terms.

By 1994, when the proportional growth of private enrollments ended, the private sector represented 21.34 percent of total enrollments at the primary level and 25 percent when all levels are considered, with significant peaks of more than 50 percent and up to 65 percent in urban districts with a high middle-class population, such as Vicente López and San Isidro. In that same year, in Buenos Aires City, 50 percent of the students went to private institutions. However, if only teacher-training institutions are taken into account, enrollments in the private sector were even higher. Additionally, it is interesting to point out that there is a direct (and very strong) correlation between public

Figure 2.1
Private Sector Participation in Total Enrollments: Primary Level

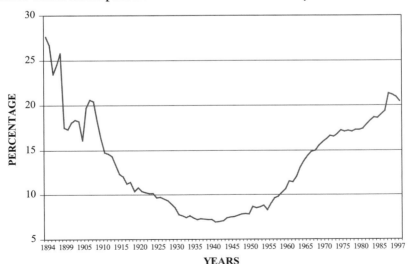

Source: Morduchowicz, et al., 1999.

enrollments and the percentage of the population with "unsatisfied basic needs" (Narodowski and Nores 2000). This means that public schools in Argentina cater mainly to the most economically disadvantaged. Meanwhile, private enrollments are concentrated within the families with the highest incomes. Thus, according to official data, the following conclusion can be drawn: for every ten students that study in private institutions, nine belong to the most economically advanced segments of society. This situation especially affects the big urban centers where the increase in private schools has had the most significant impact.

Finally, another notable feature of the process of privatization that has occurred in Argentine education is that the State subsidizes private schools in two ways. First, some schools receive direct subsidies from the State that permit, at least in theory, a reduction of fees paid by students. In some cases, like in many *escuelas parroquiales* (parochial schools located in economically disadvantaged areas), fees are dropped to an insignificant amount or sometimes even eliminated, offering education at no cost for students' families. However, the State gives "indirect subsidies," when it does not charge any (or some) taxes to private schools. The sums awarded in direct subsidies are significant: for example, in 2001, 19 percent of the total economic resources destined for education in Buenos Aires City were directly transferred to the private sector without using any publicly transparent methods to decide which schools should benefit from the scheme.

Since the 1980s, strong criticisms have appeared in the press and in public opinion towards the increasing privatization of education and towards the deterioration of the public school system. It was quite clear that the State was experiencing serious difficulties in sustaining an efficient provision of educational services. The sense of educational crisis and a call for educational reform were rapidly increasing. However, it was not until the 1990s that educational problems were given a central position in the political agenda and systemic reform was initiated, as in most countries in Latin America.

THE REFORMS OF THE 1990s

The educational reform implemented in Argentina in the 1990s was an exhaustive reform, in the sense that it was aimed not only at changing some aspects of the educational system, but rather at transforming the whole logic of the Argentine system. The justification for such an important shift was found in "external pressures," mainly the need to adapt to globalization and the information age. Another characteristic of the Argentine reform is that, in a similar way to most of the Latin American reforms of the time, it has a strong influence from international agencies (Gvirtz and Beech 2007; Beech 2006). Argentine reform strongly promoted the defense of public education and the modernization of the administration at macro- and micro-policy levels. However, the tendency present since the 1960s—the movement of the most advantaged segments of society from the public to the private system—was not brought to an end.

The first steps in the transformation of the educational system were aimed at completing the process of decentralization of educational services that had started in 1978 with the military government forcing all responsibility for primary education into the provinces without their approval and without any technical, financial, or institutional resources (Rhoten 2000). In 1992, the Law of the Transfer of Educational Services extended the decentralization of Argentine education with the transfer of all secondary schools and non-university higher education to the provinces (Rhoten 2000, 603–5). This initial transformation was led by the Ministry of Economy, and was guided by an "economic efficiency" rationale: the National State was in charge of most of the educational system and this implied too many employees and too many costs that should be transferred to the provinces (Repetto 2001).

However, the transfer of educational services to the provinces was not enough for the transformation of an educational system that was perceived as being in crisis and frozen in the nineteenth century (Van Gelderen 1995). The "refoundation" of the Argentine educational system was launched by the *Ley Federal de Educación* (LFE) passed in 1993. For the first time in Argentine history, a law of education regulated all the levels and modalities of the educational system as an integrated unit. It is in this law that the final configuration of the relations among different levels of the state, educational institutions, and the community was established. The role that the LFE established for the National State was to design common national curricula for all levels, organize teacher training, and coordinate and implement research programs. The National Ministry of Education must also guarantee the functioning of the system by creating a national system of evaluation and developing federal programs for technical and financial cooperation aimed at attaining quality education in all of the national territory.

Meanwhile, Argentine provincial governments are in charge of planning, organizing, and administering their own educational systems. No responsibilities were assigned to the municipal level, leaving the administration of schools in charge of the provinces. Additionally, provincial governments would design their local curricula, following common national contents, and authorize and supervise private schools in their jurisdiction. In order to unify criteria and to obtain agreements between the national level and the different jurisdictions in the design of national policies, the LFE revitalized the roles of the Federal Council of Education. The National Minister of Education is the president of this council, and the provincial ministers of education are its other members.

In terms of financing, the LFE established that total public investment in education should be doubled in five years, at a minimum rate of 20 percent per year, starting in 1993. Through the 1990s, investments in education grew both at the basic and higher education levels (except for higher education in 1991). However, the percentage set in the law was not met.

One of the most significant changes introduced by the LFE was the design of a new structure for the Argentine educational system. The new structure extended compulsory education from seven to ten years. One year of preschool education had been made compulsory, and the seven years of primary education have been replaced by General Basic Education (EGB), which consists of nine years of compulsory instruction divided into three-year cycles. Finally, *Polimodal*, a post-compulsory level that lasts three years, has replaced a five-year secondary education.

These changes resulted in operational difficulties in public schools, since most of these institutions were either primary or secondary schools. Even in the case of schools which catered to both the primary and secondary levels, they were generally offered in separate buildings. Buildings needed to be refurbished and, in many cases, students had to attend lessons in parts of the buildings that were not adequately prepared to be used as classrooms. The extension of compulsory education implied an increase in enrollments and, thus, the need for larger facilities.

The new structure was implemented differently in each of the provinces. Therefore, various ways of organizing educational trajectories coexisted in the twenty-four Argentine provinces that used to have the same educational structure. First, some jurisdictions still maintained the traditional division into a seven-year primary school and a five- or six-year secondary school (Buenos Aires City). Others divided educational routes into two sets of two cycles each, annexing the third cycle of EGB to secondary education. Finally, a third model, in compliance with the LFE, established three cycles of EGB and a three-year *Polimodal* (Province of Buenos Aires).

Another central proposal in the educational reform of the 1990s was the strengthening of educational institutions. Until the 1990s, every strategy for educational change in Argentina had concentrated on changing the curricula and on reforming teacher education. The system was hierarchical, rigid, and organized in a clearly vertical structure. Supervisors received orders from the central organizations, which held the monopoly for decision-making. The supervisors then would transmit these orders to school principals, who would then instruct the teachers to execute the orders. The supervisor and principal of each school had to control the execution of these mandates. They observed lessons, they read students' notebooks, and inspected teachers' plans. They were the guarantors of compliance to orders by the central powers.

The 1990s reforms were aimed at changing this hierarchical and vertical structure of the educational system. These reforms proposed a certain degree of autonomy for schools, so that some decisions, like selecting some of the contents of instruction, could be made at the institutional level. In return, schools were required to present to the authorities their own "institutional project." Institutional projects were proposals for change designed in each school. Representatives of the whole school community (principals, parents, teachers, students) were required to participate in the design of the project. Consequently, the sequence and organization of curricular contents and the rhythm and method of teaching would vary from one school to another according to their institutional differences. In this sense, the existence of these projects implied a de-politicization of school practices: principals and teachers were no longer seen as members of the state apparatus, subject to political control. Instead, they were seen as professionals, subject to local and communitarian control.

However, the legal frame was not changed (for example, teachers were not chosen at the school level by the principal; they are appointed at the central level and imposed on the school). Supervisors and principals were not assigned new roles, and an information system that would allow schools that perform well to be distinguished from schools that do not perform so well was not established. Additionally, current literature has shown that even though the design of institutional projects has been made compulsory for schools, this has not been followed by processes that encouraged real autonomy in schools that were accustomed to a vertical structure (Andrada 2002). In this context, institutional projects became another bureaucratic document that the central administration required from schools. Far from fostering the participation of teachers and teamwork, projects were in most cases written by principals with the sole objective of presenting the documents to their superiors. Both the National State and the provinces invested great amounts of money in publishing a number of documents (some consisting of four volumes of more than 1,000 pages each) that were meant to teach the principals how to design an institutional project. However, since the overall legal frame was not altered, schools did not gain much real autonomy. The traditional model of administration overpowered the principle of school autonomy and with it, the institutional projects.

Additionally, Argentine educational policy in the 1990s included the implementation of a new curricular reform. This reform has its particularities when compared to past curricular changes. As mentioned above, until the 1990s programs and curricula for different educational levels were designed with great detail by the National State or provinces. Teachers had to restrict their lessons strictly to the contents included within these documents and they also had to follow the sequence that was established. Some curricular documents even defined the activities that the teacher should perform in the classroom in order to transmit the contents. The curricular design of Buenos Aires City in 1981 was one of the clearest cases of "curricular hyper-prescription" (De Titto 2002).

The curricular reform of the 1990s not only changed the contents that had to be taught, it was also aimed at redesigning the relationship among the National State, the provinces, teachers, and contents. The general proposal of the curricular reform, following the *provincialization* of educational services, was to leave in the hands of the provinces the responsibility for curricular design. However, in order to guarantee minimal common contents for all Argentine students, common basic contents (CBC) were designed to be used as guidelines for the design of provincial curricula. The National Ministry of Education produced these contents, which were then approved by the *Consejo Federal de Educación*. Common basic contents were designed for Initial Education, EGB, *Polimodal*, and for Teacher Education.

Even though these contents were supposed to serve as guidelines for the design of the actual curricula in the provinces and then in the institutions, in practice, they became the new curricular design used by schools. So many contents were considered to be "basic," that it became almost impossible for schools to teach anything other than the basic contents. Once the CBC were approved by the Federal Council, they were not sent to the provincial educational authorities. Instead, they were distributed directly to all schools in the country. When teachers received the CBC, they used the documents as if they were a traditional curriculum, and followed them in every single detail. At the same time, since publishing companies could not adapt to each of the provincial markets, they published the same textbooks—based on the CBC—for every province. Consequently, the CBC were not taken as "basic contents"—a guide that should be adapted to different local contexts—but rather as a prescriptive curriculum in the traditional sense in Argentina.

In-service training for teachers was another of the strategies used in the 1990s reforms for attaining real change in the educational system. New contents, a different structure, and new roles for the schools required teachers with new capacities. A massive scheme of in-service training was planned to include all of the 650,000 teachers in the system. The scheme was coordinated by the *Red Federal de Formación Docente Continua* (Federal Network for Continuous Teacher Training), which had been created by the National Ministry of Education.

The massive scheme was based on a credit system. The number of credits that each course would award participants depended on the length (in time) of the course, and not on what the teachers actually learned. In order for a course to be part of the credit system, it had to be authorized by the *Red*, but the authorization system was far from being clear and transparent. Consequently, the courses that were offered to teachers were not related to the needs of the reform. Instead, it was the lobbying capacity of the teachers who attended the courses, or of the institutions that offered them, that determined the inclusion of a given course within the scheme. Since the public schools never became the "agents of change," teachers attended courses to improve their individual careers, not considering the needs of the school in which they worked. It can be said that teacher training has been one of the weakest aspects of the reform.

One more principle that was central to the political agenda of the 1990s was the creation of an evaluation system. Before the reform—and for more than 100 years—the State had tried to guarantee the performance of the Argentine educational system by regulating teaching methods through a unified curriculum and through the daily control of principals and supervisors over teachers' work. After the reform, the State intended to guarantee the performance of the

Argentine educational system by evaluating what pupils had learned. Thus, the National System of Evaluation (SINEC) was created within the National Ministry of Education.

Consequently, evaluation programs are periodically conducted to assess the learning that takes place in schools, municipalities, or provinces. This, of course, allows for comparisons to be made. Different from what happens in other countries—such as Chile, for example—in Argentina, no school rankings are published. Thus, the evaluation system did not introduce a competitive element in the Argentine educational system. The culture of evaluation, which was initially resisted by teachers' unions, has been established in Argentine education; however, it has never been very clear, from the state policies, what kind of use should be made of the results of these evaluations. This has resulted in technical problems in the evaluation system.

However, the National Ministry of Education has retained responsibility for conducting evaluations. This implies that the usual defects of the state bureaucratic administration, such as lack of transparency and limited federal participation, have been transferred to the evaluation system (Llach 1999; Narodowski, Nores, and Andrada 2001).

Argentine educational reform in the 1990s was carried out by the political party that was in power at the national level, and which also controlled most of the provinces at that time: the Peronist Party. In 1999, the opposition (the Radical Party) rose to power while a profound economic crisis was emerging in Argentina. This, plus the problems and costs of implementation of the reform itself, implied an important shift in the course of educational policy.

In the following years, far from developing and improving the principles of the reform of the 1990s, educational policies aimed at restoring the educational system of the late nineteenth century with its 1960s reforms. Thus, some of the principles of the 1990s reforms were redefined by the traditional system. Other principles of this reform were gradually being abandoned and left outside the political agenda. What was made quite clear was that the continuity of the educational policy of the early twentieth century was resistant to the efforts to modernize or reform the educational system—revealing Argentina's institutional weakness in macro-political administration.

Centralized power, previously held by the National State, was left in hands of the provinces. Thus, the power to make decisions was not displaced from the central levels to the educators, families, or other social agents. Common basic contents were used as the new curricula, and the national evaluation system, instead of replacing the surveillance methods of the supervision, became an addition to traditional mechanisms of control. Consequently, the State not only was left to control the daily activities in schools through innumerable regulations, but also it ended up controlling through results. Thus, the efficacy of the educational policy of the early twentieth century proved to be the main obstacle in facing the challenges posed by the twenty-first century—mainly implementing criteria of educational justice.

FROM THE NINETIES TO THE PRESENT

Most of the principles that guided educational reform in the 1990s are currently being questioned both by civil society and by the actual government that ideologically positions itself as completely opposed to the "neo-liberal" policies of the 1990s. A new Law of Technical and Vocational Education was passed in 2005, aimed at revitalizing vocational education both in the secondary and tertiary level, after this type of education had been weakened by the policies of the 1990s. In a context in which the industrial sector has grown significantly in the last years (2002–6), the strengthening of work-oriented education in some sectors in which the demand for skilled workers has grown seems to be a coherent policy. Nevertheless, not much time has passed since the sanctioning of the law, and its practical effects cannot yet be assessed.

Also in 2005, a Law of Education Funding was passed. This law recovers the financial aims of the LFE which were not met by previous governments, but adds some interesting features, like the co-responsibility between the National State and provinces in increasing the funds for education to 6 percent of their gross domestic product, and the obligation to use the added funds in specific priorities, such as the inclusion of all children in preschool education, the guarantee of ten years of compulsory education, extended school days, and others. However, given previous experiences, it is clear that the fulfillment of these mandates will require the monitoring of civil society which, itself, requires more transparency in the way in which the national and (especially) the provincial budgets are defined and executed.

Finally, this new wave of reforms was completed in 2006 with a new Law of National Education. Previous to the writing of the law, the Ministry of Education opened a debate in which ample sectors of the educational community participated. The document that was put forward to initiate the debate took the criticism of the economic and educational reforms of the 1990s as a starting point. The law revises the role of the state, giving more participation to the National State in education policy, and making it the principal responsible for guaranteeing access and permanence of the educational system to all societal segments. The Law emphasizes the importance of "educational justice" and elimination of educational inequalities. The new Law also establishes that all of the provincial systems should tend to a single structure, gradually returning to the division between primary and secondary education.

In short, these laws provide some interesting proposals for change, but it should be kept in mind that laws in themselves do not necessarily change the real world, especially in Argentina, where we have a long history of regulations that are not always followed in practice. Meanwhile, the existence of different educational trajectories depending on socioeconomic positions, and the trend towards privatization are still worrying. Families with better socioeconomic conditions either in private or public schools access greater quality of education (Llach 2006) and, in this way, the educational system is still operating as a mechanism that collaborates with the widening of social differences. Also, some performance indicators of the educational system, such as repetition and drop-out rates, are still growing.

The challenge for Argentine education is to recover a high-quality educational system that allows for social mobility and gives similar opportunities to all children to progress on the basis of their merits, and not their place of birth. However, it is clear that such an educational system cannot be based on the nostalgic aim of restoring the system of the early twentieth century. The world has changed and Argentina needs to develop creative solutions both at the macro- and the micro-political levels in order to build the just, equitable, and democratic educational system that its people deserve.

A DAY IN THE LIFE

Diego goes to sleep complaining in a low voice about how early he has to wake up the next morning. His much older brothers graduated from school a few years ago. University timetables are far more flexible ... and pleasant. So, while everybody is wandering around the house, he's sent to brush his teeth, put on the braces, and go to bed.

Around 7:00 AM, Diego feels the usual footsteps entering the room. He acts as if he's completely asleep. Finally, the school uniform is on and extra help arrives to comb the rebellious curly hair. He takes a quick breakfast, descends the five-floor building and waits by the door for the school van to pick him up.

Other kids in the building are sitting there, too, waiting for some similar transport to arrive and take them to their private schools. If the van is running late (it often happens), he generally notices Ariel walking away dressed in a white *guardapolvo* carrying a small school bag. Ariel is a boy from the neighborhood that goes to the local state school. Actually, he's from the house next door. They don't talk to each other much. Diego believes he must be shy, but certainly very intelligent to go all the way to school and come back by himself.

At school, Diego says "good morning" to the English teacher. Activity begins. *Hands up* to tell the classroom "what the weekend was like" and/or "plans for the winter holidays." Then, "fill in the blanks" and, finally, a story read by the teacher. She reads lovely. Short break. Too short. Morning English lessons pass very quickly.

At 12:20 PM, Diego takes his lunch box to the school's dining room and opens it. It feels good to see the tasty menu Mom's prepared for him.

At 1:30 PM, he's back in the classroom. Afternoons at school always turn a bit tiresome. However, the switch to Spanish makes things easier. It's now the time for mathematics, sciences, and extracurricular activities. Mondays: Gym. A good way to start the week.

When Diego arrives home at 5:00 PM, he finds Ariel playing ball with a friend. It seems they've been doing this for a while. They're both sweating!

Diego thinks he'd like to play football in the afternoons. He wonders how a day in the life of Ariel might be.

In fact, Ariel spends half of Diego's time in school. Doors open from 7:50 AM to 12:00 PM. Before he enters the classroom, a warm cup of *mate cocido* and a slice of bread is served. Subjects are then all taught in Spanish, and there's a few "special subjects" organized throughout the week. The teacher is nice, at least to him—he's a good pupil. Ariel likes it when they allow him to use the library. At home, there are no books, and "books are a source of wisdom," he once heard from a stranger. He'd rather stay at school a bit longer—playing, working, keeping in touch with other kids and adults.

But he has to leave at 1:00 PM because other children arrive at his school for the afternoon schedule. He then picks up his stuff and heads back home. Hopefully, some kids from the neighborhood will join him to play. When Diego passes by, Ariel sees him staring at him. What does he wonder? Has he just arrived from school?

TIMELINE

1610	Jesuits create the *Colegio Maximo* (Córdoba).
1617	Jesuits create the *School of San Ignacio* (Buenos Aires).
1622	By initiative of the Bishop of Córdoba, fray Fernando de Trejo y Sanabria, Pope Gregorio XV grants the Colegio Máximo the University status, thus creating the University of Córdoba.
1680	Complication of the *Leyes de Indias,* a vast amount of laws and decrees that followed Queen Isabel's testament ordering the conversion of Indians to Catholicism.
1687	Jesuits create the *School of Monserrat* (Córdoba).
1727	Foundation of the school of *Niñas Huérfanas* (Buenos Aires), by initiative of the brother Franciso Avarez Campana.
1767	Jesuits are expelled.
1783	The *Real Colegio Convictorio of San Carlos* is created, on the basis of the *School of San Ignacio,* after the Jesuits are expelled.
1816	Independence from Spain.
1821	Foundation of the University of Buenos Aires.
1825	Creation of the Society of Beneficence (Buenos Aires).
1829	Rule of Juan Manuel de Rosas.
1852	Battle of Caseros that overthrows Rosas.
1853	Sanction of the National Constitution.
1856	Domingo F. Sarmiento is put in charge of the Education Department in the Province of Buenos Aires.
1863	Foundation of the *National School of Buenos Aires.*
1865	Creation of the Inspection of National Schools.
1870	Creation of the *Escuela Normal del Paraná* (School for Teacher Training).
1875	Law Number 888 of primary education in the province of Buenos Aires.
1881	International Pedagogic Congress in Buenos Aires.
1882	Creation of the Official Journal *El Monitor de la Educación Común.*
1883	First educational census.

1884   Law Number 1420 of Common Education.
        Creation of the National Education Council.
1885   Law Number 1597 of National Universities.
1889   Creation of the Provincial University of Santa Fe.
1890   Creation of the Provincial University of La Plata.
1905   Law Number 4874 of National Schools in the Provinces (*Ley Lainez*).
1916   The Radical Party, which represents the middle classes, rises to power for the first time.
1918   University reform.
1919   Nationalization of the Provincial University of Santa Fe.
1921   Nationalization of the Provincial University of Tucumán.
1923   Reform project to Law Number 1420 (Organic Education Law).
1932   Creation of the sub-inspection for private institutions.
1936   Creation of the Journal *La Obra*.
1946   First presidency of Perón.
        Law Number 12.921: childhood education and labor.
1947   Law Number 13.047: religious education.
1948   Law Number 13.339: the *Universidad Obrera Nacional*.
1958   Law Number 14.473: the teacher's statute.
1959   Law Number 14.557: private universities.
        Law Number 15.240: the National Council of Technical Education.
1960   Decree Number 12179, which enabled private schools to issue certificates that were recognized as valid by the State.
1961   First transfer of primary schools from the national level to the provinces.
1976   Military coup that started with the last and darkest military dictatorship in Argentina.
1978   Law Number 21.809: transferring primary schools dependent on the National Education Council to the provinces.
        Law Number 21.810: transferring primary schools dependent on the National Education Council to the Municipality of the City of Buenos Aires and the National Territory of Tierra del Fuego.
1983   Decree Number 1.853: intervention of national universities.
1984   Law Number 23.068: normalization of the national universities.
1988   National Pedagogic Congress.
1993   Law Number 24.125: federal education.
1995   Law Number 24.521: higher education.
2006   Law Number 26.075: educational funding.
        Law Number 26.210: national education.

NOTES

1. In 1895, out of 216,000 habitants in the City of Buenos Aires, only 42,000 were native Argentines. In 1924, only 1.4 percent of immigrants had obtained Argentine citizenship, which would grant them the right to vote. Eduardo Zimmermann, *Los Liberales Reformistas: la cuestion social en la Argentina 1890–1916* (Buenos Aires: Editorial Sudamericana, Universidad de San Andres, 1995).

2. *Desaparecidos* (the disappeared) was the term given to people who were kidnapped by security forces between 1976–83.

BIBLIOGRAPHY

Books

Alliaud, Andrea. 1993. *Estudios sobre la educación; Los maestros y su historia.* Buenos Aires: Centro Editor de América Latina.

Andrada, M. 2002. Autogestión y autonomía de la institución escolar moderna. *Finalidades, estrategias y regulaciones en el sistema educativo de la provincia de Buenos Aires (1993–2000).* MS Thesis. Buenos Aires: FLACSO.

Auza, Néstor Tomás. 1975. *Católicos y liberales en la generación del ochenta.* Buenos Aires: Culturales Argentinas. Balan, Jorge. 1993. "Politicas de financiamiento y gobierno de las universidades nacionales bajo un regimen democratico: Argentina 1983–92." In *Politicas comparadas de educacion superior en America Latina.* Edited by Hernan Courard, 131–84. Santiago: FLACSO.

Barrancos, Dora. 1990. *Anarquismo, educación y costumbres en la Argentina de principios de siglo.* Buenos Aires: Contrapunto.

Beech, Jason. 2006. "The Institutionalization of Education in Latin America: Loci of Attraction and Mechanisms of Diffusion." In *The Impact of Comparative Education Research on Institutional Theory.* Edited by David P. Baker and Alexander W. Wiseman. Oxford: Elsevier Science Ltd.

Bejarano, Manuel. 1969. "Imigracion y estructuras tradicionales en Buenos Aires (1854–1930)." In *Los Fragmentos del Poder: de la oligarquia a la poliarquia argentina.* Edited by Torcuato Di Tella and Tulio Halperin Donghi, 75–150. Buenos Aires: Editorial Jorge Alvarez S.A.

Bertoni, Lilia Ana. 2002. *Patriotas, cosmopolistas y nacionalistas. La construcción de la nacionalidad argentina a fines del siglo XIX.* Buenos Aires: Fondo de Cultura Económica.

Biagini, Hugo. 1985. *El movimiento positivista argentino.* Buenos Aires: Editorial Belgrano.

Botana, Natalio. 1996. *Domingo Faustino Sarmiento: una aventura republicana.* Buenos Aires: Fondo de Cultura Económica.

Braslavsky, C. 1980. *La educación argentina (1955–80).* Buenos Aires: CEAL.

Cano, Daniel. 1985. *La educacion superior en la Argentina.* 1st ed. Buenos Aires: FLACSO/Grupo Editor Latinoamericano.

Carli, Sandra. 2002. *Niñez, pedagogía y política: transformaciones de los discursos acerca de la infancia en la historia de la educación argentina entre 1880–1955.* Buenos Aires: Miño y Dávila.

Ciria, Alberto and Horacio Sanguinetti. 1983. *La reforma universitaria.* Buenos Aires: CEAL.

Debate parlamentario. 1984. Ley 1420. Buenos Aires: CEAL.

De Titto, R. (2002) *Políticas curriculares y prácticas docentes en la ciudad de Buenos Aires entre 1960–90.* Unpublished Masters Thesis. Universidad de San Andrés, School of Education.

De Vedia, M. 2005. *La educación aun espera.* Buenos Aires: EUDEBA.

Devoto, Fernando. 2002. *Nacionalismo, fascismo y tradicionalismo en la Argentina moderna.* Buenos Aires: Siglo Veintiuno.

Devoto, Fernando and Marta Madero, dir. 1999. *Historia de la vida privada en la Argentina.* 3 vols. Taurus.

Di Tella, Torcuato. 1969. "Los contendientes y sus batallas. Introducción." In *Los fragmentos del poder: de la oligarquia a la poliarquia Argentina*. Edited by Torcuato Di Tella and Tulio Halperin Donghi, 277–88. Buenos Aires: Editorial Jorge Alvarez S.A.

Di Tella, Torcuato. 1974. *Clases sociales y estructuras politicas*. Buenos Aires: Paidos.

Dussel, Inés. 1997. *Currículum, humanismo y democracia en la enseñanza media*. Buenos Aires: FLACSO.

Dussel, Inés. 2001. "School Uniforms and the Disciplining of Appearances: Towards a History of the Regulation of Bodies in Modern Educational Systems." In *Cultural History and Education: Critical Essays on Knowledge and Schooling*. Edited by Thomas S. Popkewitz, Barry M. Franklin, and Miguel A. Pereyra, 207–41. New York: Routledgefalmer.

Dussel, Inés-Carruso, Marcelo. 1999. *La invención del aula. Una genealogía de las formas de enseñar*. Buenos Aires: Santillana.

Escudé, Carlos. 1990. *El fracaso del proyecto escolar: educación e ideología*. Buenos Aires: Instituto Torcuato Di Tella.

Germani, Gino. 1955. *Estructura social de la Argentina*. Buenos Aires: Editorial Raigal.

Gvirtz, S. and C. Braslavsky. 2001. "Nuevos desafíos y dispositivos en la política educacional latinoamericana de fin de siglo." Chap. 2 in *Educación comparada. Política educativa en Ibero América*. Madrid, España: Organización de los Estados Iberoamericanos (OEI).

Gvirtz, S. and M. Narodowski. "Micro-politics of School Resistance. The Case of Argentine Teachers versus the Educational Policies of Perón and Evita Perón." *Discourse* 19, no. 2 (1998).

Gvirtz, Silvina. 1991. *Nuevas y viejas tendencias en la docencia 1945–55*. Buenos Aires: Centro Editor de América Latina.

Gvirtz, Silvina. 1999. *El discurso escolar a través de los cuadernos de clase: Argentina 1930–70*. Buenos Aires: Eudeba.

Gvirtz, Silvina, comp. 1996. *Escuela nueva en Argentina y Brasil: visiones comparadas*. Buenos Aires: Miño y Dávila.

Gvirtz, Silvina and Jason Beech. 2007. "The Internationalisation of Education Policy in Latin America." In M. Hayden, J. Levy, and J. Thompson, *Handbook of Research in International Education*. London: Sage.

Halperin Donghi, Tulio. 1969. "Las raices historicas. Introduccion." In *Los Fragmentos del Poder: de la oligarquia a la poliarquia argentina*. Edited by Torcuato Di Tella and Tulio Halperin Donghi, 15–21. Buenos Aires: Editorial Jorge Alvarez S.A.

Halperin Donghi, dir. *Colección biblioteca del pensamiento Argentino. Historia Argentina*. 7 vols. (1995–2004).

Kaufmann, C. 2000. *Paternalismos pedagógicos*. Rosario, Argentina: Laborde Editor.

Kaufmann, C. 2001. *Dictadura y educación*. Buenos Aires: Miño y Dávila.

Llach, Juan J. 2006. *El desafío de la equidad educativa. Diagnóstico y propuesta*. Buenos Aires: Granica.

Llach, J., S. Montoya, and F. Roldán. 1999. *Educación para todos*. Buenos Aires: IERA.

Mollis, Marcela. 1990. *Universidad y Estado Nacional: Argentina y Japon 1885–1930*. Buenos Aires: Biblos.

Morduchowicz, A., A. Marcón, G. Iglesias, M. Andrada, J. Pérez, A. Victoria, and L. Duro. 1999. *La educación privada en la Argentina: historia, regulaciones, y asignación de recursos públicos.* Serie Documentos de Trabajo, Doc. 38. Buenos Aires: Fundación Gobierno y Sociedad.

Morgade, Graciela, comp. 1997. *Mujeres en la educación: género y docencia en la Argentina 1870–1930.* Buenos Aires: Miño y Dávila.

Narodowski, M. and M. Andrada. "The Privatisation of Education in Argentina." *Journal of Education Policy* 16, no. 6 (2001): 585–95.

Narodowski, M. and L. Manolakis. "Defending the 'Argentine way of life.' The State and the School in Argentina (1884–1984)." *Paedagogica Historica. International Journal of History of Education* (2002).

Narodowski, M. and M. Nores. 2000. *¿Quiénes quedan y quienes salen? Características socioeconómicas en las escuelas públicas y privadas de la Argentina?* Buenos Aires: Fundación Gobierno y Sociedad.

Newland, Carlos. 1992. *Buenos Aires no es pampa: la educación elemental porteña 1820–60.* Buenos Aires: Grupo Editor Latinoamericano.

Pineau, Pablo. 1991. *Sindicatos, estado y educación técnica 1936–68.* Buenos Aires: Centro Editor de América Latina.

Pineau, Pablo. 1997. *La escolarización de la provincia de Buenos Aires 1875–1930, una versión posible.* Buenos Aires: FLACSO.

Plotkin, Mariano. 1994. *Mañana es San Perón: propaganda, rituales políticos y educación en el régimen peronista 1945–55.* Buenos Aires: Ariel.

Puiggrós, dir. *Historia de la Educación en Argentina.* 8 vols. Galerna.

Ramos, Juan Pedro. 1910. *Historia de la instrucción primaria en la República Argentina, 1810–1910.* Buenos Aires: Peuser.

Rein, M. E. 1998. *Politics and Education in Argentina, 1946–62.* New York: Armonk, M.E. Sharpe.

Repetto, Fabián. 2001. *Gestión pública y desarrollo social en los noventa: las trayectorias de Argentina y Chile.* Buenos Aires: Prometeo Libros.

Romero, Jose Luis. 1979. "University Reform." In *The Latin American University.* Edited by Joseph Maier and Richard Weatherhead, 135–47. Albuquerque: University of New Mexico Press.

Salonia, A. 1996. *Descentralización educativa, participación y democracia. Escuela autónoma y ciudadanía responsable.* Buenos Aires: Academia Nacional de Educación.

Salvadores, Antonino. 1941. *La instrucción primaria desde 1810 hasta la sanción de la ley 1420.* Buenos Aires: Consejo Nacional de Educación.

Schugurensky, Daniel. 1997. "University Restructuring in Argentina: The Political Debate." In *Latin American Education.* Edited by Carlos Alberto Torres and Adriana Puiggros, 237–88. Boulder, Colorado: Westview Press.

Suasnabar, C. 2004. *Universidad e intelectuales. Educación y política en la Argentina (1955–76).* Buenos Aires: Manantial.

Tedesco, Juan Carlos. 1993. *Educación y sociedad en la Argentina: 1880–1945.* Buenos Aires: Solar.

Tedesco, Juan Carlos. 2003. *Educación y sociedad en la Argentina: 1880–1945.* Buenos Aires: Ediciones Solar.

Tedesco, Juan Carlos and Cecilia Braslavsky. 1987. *El proyecto educativo autoritario 1976–82.* Buenos Aires: Miño y Dávila Editores.

Torre, Juan Carlos. 2002. *Los años peronistas: 1943–55.* Buenos Aires: Sudamericana.

Van Gelderen, Alfredo. 1995. *La ley federal de educación de la República Argentina.* Buenos Aires: Academia Nacional de Educación.

Wainerman, Catalina H. and Mariana Heredia. 1999. *¿Mamá amasa la masa? Cien años de libros de lectura de la escuela primaria.* Buenos Aires: Fundación Editorial de Belgrano.

Weinberg, Gregorio. 1987. *Modelos educativos en la historia de América Latina.* Buenos Aires: Kapelusz.

Zanotti, Luis Jorge. 1981. *Etapas históricas de la política argentina.* Buenos Aires: Eudeba.

Zimmermann, Eduardo. 1995. *Los liberales reformistas: la cuestion social en la Argentina 1890–1916.* Universidad de San Andres, Buenos Aires: Editorial Sudamericana.

Papers

Fischman and Gvirtz. "An Overview of Educational Policies in the Countries of Latin America during the 1990s." *Journal of Education Policy* 16, no. 6 (2001).

Gvirtz, S. "La politización de los contenidos escolares y la respuesta de los docentes primarios en los primeros gobiernos de Perón (Argentina: 1945–55)." *Estudios interdisciplinarios de América Latina y El Caribe* 10(1) (1999).

Narodowski, M. and M. Andrada. "The privatization of education in Argentina." *Journal of Education Policy* 16, no. 6 (2001).

Narodowski, M. and L. Manolakis. "Defending the 'Argentine Way of Life.' The State and the School in Argentina (1884–1984)." *Paedagogica Historica. International Journal of History of Education* (2002).

Newland, C. "Spanish American Elementary Education Before Independence. Continuity and Change in a Colonial Environment." *Itinerario* XV(2) (1991): 79–95.

Rhoten, Diana. "Education Decentralization in Argentina: 'A Global-Local Conditions of Possibility' Approach to State, Market and Society Change," *Journal of Education Policy* 15, no. 6 (2000).

Web Sites

Biblioteca Nacional del Maestro (BNM): http://www.bnm.me.gov.ar/.

CIPPEC (Centro de implementación de políticas públicas con Equidad y Calidad): http://www.cippec.org/nuevo/.

Escuela de Educación–Universidad de San Andrés: http://www.udesa.edu.ar/escedu.

Fundación Luminis: http://www.fundacionluminis.org.ar/.

IIPE/UNESCO Buenos Aires: http://www.iipe-buenosaires.org.ar/.

Ministerio de Educación Nacional; Dirección Nacional de Información y Evaluación de la Calidad Educativa: http://www.me.gov.ar/diniece/.

Portal de Historia de la Educación Argentina: http://www.bnm.me.gov.ar/s/proyectos/hea_sitio/home.htm.

Chapter 3

SCHOOLING IN BOLIVIA

Aurolyn Luykx and Luís Enrique López

INTRODUCTION

Bolivia (population: eight million) is the most "indigenous" country in South America. Though ethnic boundaries are increasingly blurry, census data from 2001 indicate that 50 percent of Bolivians self-identify as indigenous, mostly Quechua and Aymara, who mainly occupy the high *altiplano* and intermontaine valleys.[1] The eastern lowlands are home to some thirty smaller indigenous groups. The marginalization of indigenous people and the challenges they have raised against white and *mestizo* political elites have long been at the center of Bolivia's education debates. For most of the country's history, the education system's position with regard to indigenous groups was, at best, assimilationist and, at worst, exclusionary. In recent decades, changing social attitudes and shifts in political power have led to reforms that respond to many indigenous demands and explicitly address the country's linguistic and cultural diversity.

As is often the case in countries with high levels of poverty, ethno-linguistic diversity, and social inequality, mass education in Bolivia is a relatively recent phenomenon. Spanish has been the *de facto* official language since colonial times, and the exclusive language of public education since independence in 1825, although a majority of Bolivians did not speak it until the 1970s. Indigenous languages were granted official status in 2000, but Spanish still predominates in most urban and formal settings; outside the realm of elementary education, no real changes have been made to implement the 2000 presidential decree. Lack of fluency in Spanish constitutes a major disadvantage in interactions with governmental institutions, and discrimination against monolingual indigenous speakers is common. Literacy in indigenous languages, particularly Quechua and Aymara, is expanding but is by no means widespread. Although some private schools included either Aymara or Quechua in the curriculum, the languages most commonly taught in public schools (other than Spanish) were English and French until recently—usually with meager results.

Bolivia's history is complex, sometimes even chaotic. During the Spanish conquest and the subsequent colonial period, the indigenous population was decimated by disease, slavery, and appropriation of their lands. Indigenous communities were severely disrupted, but not destroyed; in fact, they remained strong enough to stage a series of rebellions that at times seriously threatened Spanish rule. These reached their peak between 1778–81 and, despite the massacre of 80,000 Indians in retaliation, continued sporadically for decades thereafter.

The 1825 revolution led by Simón Bolívar achieved independence from Spain, but did little to improve the lot of the indigenous masses. In fact, the most significant result of granting indigenous people (supposed) equality before the law was to facilitate the expropriation of the indigenous territories by *criollos*,[2] by prohibiting communal ownership of lands. From then on, political life was characterized by a series of coups in the capital and continuing Indian rebellions in the countryside. The economy depended on exports of metals, mainly silver and tin. By the early twentieth century, large landowners and the handful of families who dominated the mining industry dominated Bolivian political life as well. The majority endured conditions of serfdom until a popular revolution in 1952 abolished the literacy requirement for suffrage. This opened citizenship to the indigenous population and, practically overnight, increased the voting population from 200,000 to nearly 1,000,000. Other changes included the nationalization of Bolivia's mines, rural land reform, and the expansion of rural education.

The weakened revolutionary government was ousted by a military coup in 1964, giving way to a series of military dictatorships characterized by violent repression of dissent. From the 1982 elections until 2003, Bolivia enjoyed an unprecedented period of, if not true democracy in the full sense of the word, at least the orderly transfer of power. However, the new millennium dawned on an increasingly conflictive panorama, punctuated by sporadic violence and the ouster of two presidents. In 2006, Bolivia attracted international attention when union leader Evo Morales assumed the presidency—the first indigenous president in Latin America,[3] and the first Bolivian president in decades to be elected by an outright majority. Son of an Aymara father and a Quechua mother, Morales is fluent in neither language, but his years as the militant head of the *coca* growers' union cemented his reputation as a firm defender of indigenous rights.[4] Since his election, Morales has gradually assumed a more explicitly indigenous identity, including public use of the Aymara language.

A central problem throughout Bolivia's history has been the integration of the rural majority into the economic and cultural life of the urban minority. Rural dwellers' cultural and linguistic distinctiveness, and their reticence toward orienting their production towards urban priorities, have long been problematized as the primary obstacles to capitalist development. As in many third world countries, mass education first arose in order to bring indigenous people into the fold of the "national culture" and economy under the imported (and illusory) model of the uniform and homogeneous nation-state. Correspondingly, a central aim of schooling (rural schooling, in particular) has been to remake indigenous people as "Bolivian citizens." But, as we shall see below, the very definition of citizenship is changing, as the country comes to terms with the persistent cultural distinctiveness of its inhabitants.

THE COLONIAL PERIOD

While the region then known as *Alto Perú* was under Spanish rule, conflicting interests of church, crown, and colonial elites gave rise to two centuries of shifting and inconsistent educational policies. Originally, colonial administrators and clergy utilized the Quechua and Aymara languages to facilitate their control over the indigenous population. Convent-educated indigenous elites were crucial to the colonial administration, which led the Crown to take a liberal position toward indigenous languages. This policy had negative consequences for other powerful sectors, however, as bilingual clergy used their knowledge of indigenous languages to reinforce their own power. Furthermore, the Council of the Indies charged that many *criollos* who adopted the language of the Indians also adopted a far too liberal tolerance for their customs (Heath and Laprade 1982, 131).

Sectors threatened by this situation petitioned the Crown to implement the "*castellanización*" (forced adoption of Spanish) of all indigenous subjects, so that they might learn "good customs" and be more easily governed. Still, factional conflicts intervened between official policy and actual practice, as royal decrees to establish schools for indigenous children filtered through a state and religious bureaucracy that was unwilling to carry them out. Despite a general trend towards increased *castellanización*, the prospect of a subjugated but schooled Indian population was threatening to dominant elites. The ambivalent stance of colonial authorities is evidenced by a late-seventeenth-century decree making indigenous education compulsory until age ten, and forbidding it thereafter (Mannheim 1984, 298).

During this time, the education of the nonindigenous minority emphasized the appropriation of the skills and competencies necessary to rule the country. The first university in Alto Perú was Universidad de San Francisco Xavier, founded by the Jesuits in the city of Sucre in 1624. Its main areas of study were theology, scholastics, philosophy, Latin, and Aymara. Elite *criollo* graduates from San Francisco Xavier were among the main leaders of the 1809 revolution for independence against their Spanish forefathers, and also among those who organized the first Bolivian independent government.

THE REPUBLICAN PERIOD

Independence from Spain did little to improve the lot of the majority; rather, *criollos* exploited Indian labor with an even freer rein than before. There were scattered initiatives at founding rural schools in free communities, but education was denied to virtually all Indians living on *haciendas*.[5] Early curricula focused on hygiene, agriculture, and basic Spanish literacy; the use of indigenous languages in schools was unequivocally repressed. The rural rebellions that had reached their peak in the 1780s continued well into the nineteenth century, and embattled *criollo* landowners, drawing a (quite warranted) connection between indigenous literacy and threats to their own political power, organized against rural education. By the beginning of the twentieth century, indigenous people had begun to organize their own clandestine schools. These efforts, undertaken in the face of severe repression, predated by decades any serious government attempt at rural education.

From the beginning, the struggle for rural education was closely linked to the struggle for land. The legal assault on communal land ownership put intense pressure on the survival of indigenous communities; monolingual Aymaras and Quechuas had little recourse against land seizures carried out in Spanish, in writing, and in the distant capital of La Paz. The linked battles for land and literacy proceeded hand in hand, often directed by the same protagonists. The murder of indigenous teachers and the destruction of schools were often the catalyst to, or retribution for, peasant rebellions. The autonomous movement in support of indigenous education was thus a cultural as well as an economic struggle—for the material survival of indigenous communities, and also for the preservation of cultural and linguistic autonomy in the face of a rising nationalist ideology of homogenization.

Around this same time, liberal politicians began to look to schooling as a means of converting the indigenous masses into an effective labor force. This perspective, though thoroughly utilitarian and phrased in unabashedly racist terms, was strongly opposed by rural landowners. Education legislation was difficult to enforce where opposed by local authorities, and often provoked violent reprisals against indigenous educators. Conversely, indigenous leaders, in an effort to forge links with more powerful sectors, employed the discourses of liberalism and patriotism to present their educational demands as a step toward their conversion into dutiful state subjects.

Further impetus for the spread of indigenous literacy came, surprisingly, from the military. In 1907, obligatory military service was established for all able-bodied men, despite strenuous objections from rural landowners who argued that military training for Indians was a rash and dangerous policy, given the still-frequent rebellions in the countryside. Conscripts served for several years; the hardship that this entailed for rural families was officially justified by conscripts' being taught to read and write (Mamani 1992, 85). The army thus produced a steady stream of literate Quechuas and Aymaras, many of whom went on to serve as teachers in the clandestine educational networks that formed soon thereafter. Military instructors found their work easier if their charges could understand Spanish; thus the army had a stake in rural education, and even helped protect some rural schools from attack. In this way, military service furthered the spread of Spanish fluency and literacy among indigenous people, as well as their general integration into Bolivian national life—and continues to do so today.

Bolivia's most renowned educational experiment of this time was the *escuela-ayllu* of Warisata (1931–41), which combined socialist philosophy with Aymara cultural and organizational principles and inspired similar experiments throughout Latin America. Its founders, *mestizo* educator Elizardo Pérez and Aymara leader Avelino Siñani, symbolized the union of two important intellectual currents of the time. Decades ahead of its time, Warisata instituted coeducation, bilingual education, communal labor, community control over school decisions, and strategies akin to what is nowadays called intercultural education. It also eliminated grades, hourly schedules, and annual vacations. At the same time, Warisata also operated in cooperation with the Bolivian government, and thus entailed the extension of government control over otherwise free indigenous territories. Despite support from important governmental figures, Warisata's active role in indigenous struggles brought violent retaliation from the neighboring *mestizos*; participants and their supporters became targets for kidnap, torture, arson, murder, and accusations of treason. After ten years, the lifelines Warisata had drawn to a few powerful figures in Bolivian society could not save it, and the experiment came to an end. Nevertheless, its influence lasted for decades, reaching as far as Mexico. In later years, Pérez was named Minister of Education—though this was less a reflection of the government's acceptance of indigenous autonomy, than of its desire to appropriate Warisata as a national symbol of indigenous-*mestizo* cooperation.

By the 1940s, a rudimentary system of government-sponsored rural schools was in place, with a curriculum emphasizing agriculture, vocational skills, and hygiene. Schools were deficient in terms of infrastructure, salaries, and teaching quality, and only 11 percent of rural children attended. Instruction was completely in Spanish, though most students had little or no knowledge of the language. Literacy and math were secondary concerns, relative to the goals of "civilizing" the Indians and extending the reach of the state into indigenous communities.

THE POST-REVOLUTIONARY PERIOD

After the popular revolution in 1952, the number of students nationwide increased threefold, and the number of rural schools fivefold (Carter 1971, 144–45). This was largely due to the land reform, which broke the back of large landowners' resistance to rural education. The Educational Reform of 1953 and the subsequent *Código de la Educación Boliviana* remained the central documents of public education (though largely unfulfilled) for the next forty years. By the 1960s, education consumed one fourth of the national budget, and indigenous people had begun to enter the system as teachers themselves. However, with Spanish as the exclusive language of the classroom, dropout rates remained high; only half of urban students and 6.5 percent of rural student made it to the sixth grade (Carter 1971, 145). Female students were underrepresented both in terms of enrollment and in school curricula and materials. Indigenous students were often beaten for their inability to speak Spanish, or for speaking their own language in the classroom. Rural teachers were most often Spanish-speaking *mestizos* rather than members of the communities they served. Indigenous people had no voice in the planning of school curricula, and their knowledge, values, and history remained absent from the school curriculum. Lack of knowledge about indigenous languages and cultures contributed to student frustration and a humiliating classroom atmosphere.

The 1960s saw various attempts at bilingual education, beginning with the evangelical Summer Institute of Linguistics and continuing through the early 1980s under the auspices of USAID, the World Bank, and UNICEF. While some projects produced encouraging results, most suffered from deficiencies in community participation, linguistic training of personnel, program coordination, funding, long-term planning, and evaluation. Political instability made program continuity difficult, and laws containing basically the same objectives were passed by one administration after another. Despite some government coordination, there was no comprehensive bilingual education policy at the national level. In most cases, the aim was to move students into Spanish-medium classes as quickly as possible. Despite the proliferation of rural schools, the *quality* of education did not improve significantly. Needless to say, the emphasis of all these projects was more pedagogical than political, while for indigenous leaders the aim of bilingual education continued to be more political than pedagogical.

In the early 1980s, as Bolivia ended its long history of military dictatorships, a clearly defined new social actor emerged: the indigenous people, whose political participation was mobilized via new ethno-political organizations. In 1982–83, under a new nationalist and populist democratic government, a massive national plan was launched to promote literacy in rural communities. For almost ten years, the *Servicio Nacional de Alfabetización y Educación Popular* (National Popular Education and Literacy Agency, or SENALEP) directed and financed literacy campaigns in numerous rural communities, both indigenous and nonindigenous, targeting children and adults. The campaign developed and implemented literacy materials in Aymara, Quechua, two regional (nonstandard) varieties of Spanish, and recruited popular educators through locally-based NGOs. SENALEP's activities marked a turning point in Bolivia's educational history, significantly expanding the use of Aymara and Quechua as languages of education and mobilizing indigenous men and women around educational as well as wider social goals. This initiative later led to a successful governmental bilingual education project (*Proyecto de Educación Intercultural Bilingüe*, or PEIB) that promoted the maintenance and development of students' proficiencies in Aymara, Quechua, or Guaraní (depending on the region) in over 100 rural primary schools and communities. Under the PEIB, a new curriculum was designed, teachers were trained in new active methodologies, and indigenous language materials were produced and disseminated. Furthermore, the project stimulated the active involvement of indigenous parents, community leaders, and organizations.

Throughout this period, the divisions in Bolivian society were a reflection of the bifurcation of education into two parallel systems, rural and urban. The *escuelas normales* (teacher training institutes), both rural and urban, were often the only choices available to peasant or working-class youth with aspirations toward post-secondary education. The chasm between the *escuelas normales* and the universities reflected a system of higher education largely segregated by race and class.

Though most rural schools remained decidedly substandard, the national literacy rate rose from 31 percent to 67 percent between 1950–76 (Klein 1982, 264). In subsequent decades, classrooms became gentler, corporal punishment less frequent, and teachers more willing to use indigenous languages when necessary, rather than punish children for speaking them. These changes were partly due to the realization that the old methods were so oppressive as to drive children out of school altogether. Also, an increasing fraction of teachers were themselves Aymara or Quechua.

The latter half of the twentieth century saw the continued expansion of public education, both rural and urban, but acute disparities persisted. The 2001 census showed 85 percent of Bolivian children ages six to fourteen attending school, but enrollment remained lower in rural areas. Girls are also less likely to attend school than boys, especially in rural areas and particularly in the upper primary school grades.[6] While Bolivia's population is increasingly bilingual, many rural children still enter school with little or no knowledge of Spanish; until the implementation of a national policy of bilingual education in the mid-1990s, such children were often pushed out of school after only a couple of years. Gaining access to secondary education was a challenge for most rural students, and post-secondary education was out of reach for all but a few.

During most of the twentieth century, public schooling displayed strong continuities with the Bolivia's colonial past, in both its surface methodologies and underlying aims. Despite the phasing out of its more overtly cruel features, the underlying aims changed little. The curriculum remained centrally dictated, based on the values and practices of the *mestizo* middle and upper classes, with no input from teachers, students, or parents. Teaching remained an authoritarian, unidirectional process based on dictation, memorization, and copying. Classrooms continued to be organized around principles of regimentation and conformity. Even liberal intellectuals who supported indigenous education saw it primarily as a means to "civilize" a backwards race and transform it into a useful labor force. All in all, Bolivian schooling remained a far cry from the "democratic and liberating education" mandated by law.

PUBLIC ATTITUDES TOWARD EDUCATION

As might be expected, given the conflicts and contradictions that Bolivian education has traversed over the years, the popular ideology surrounding it is powerful and ambivalent. Many rural parents place an almost religious faith in education, viewing it as the salvation that will lift their children out of poverty and into the middle class. Contrasting with this belief in the value of schooling is a clear awareness of its shortcomings: the limited utility of much of what is taught, the neglect or active denigration of indigenous cultures and languages, the notorious inefficiency and corruption. A high school diploma and Spanish fluency undoubtedly broaden one's economic and social opportunities, but the costs have been high with regard to the devaluation of indigenous culture, changing relations within rural communities, and submission to the humiliating process of "*castellanización.*" While education often is revered in the abstract, the actual system and those it employs are subject to heavy criticism from parents, students, and educators themselves.

Schoolteachers occupy an ambiguous position in rural communities. Despite their "official" role as the hub of public life, most are occupational migrants without longstanding local ties. The idealized image of the rural schoolteacher as classroom instructor, town scribe, mediator, counselor, social worker, and community organizer is offset by popular images of teachers as agents of cultural imperialism, incompetent government hacks, and exploiters of rural communities. The perception that rural teachers are less competent than their urban counterparts stems from various sources: racism, linguistic prejudice, their relative isolation from urban intellectual currents, and rural schools' reputations as less rigorous. Rural teachers react indignantly to such notions, pointing out that not only do they work more closely with students and communities, but their job involves demands and challenges not required of urban teachers. As one rural teacher argued:

We have to do battle in the countryside, not just within the four walls [of the classroom], but organizing in the community.... The urban teacher simply shows up, signs his time card, goes into the class he's scheduled for ... they don't give their all like the rural teacher has to.... It's we who really bear the weight of this problem of education, educating the children of the peasantry. (Luykx 1999, 53)

Rural schools in remote communities often lack the most basic material resources. Many work in isolated conditions, teaching several grades at once—without any technical or professional orientation. (Noncredentialed "interim" teachers are more common in rural areas.) While lecturing, copying, and memorization have long been the predominant methods in urban schools as well, these tendencies are exacerbated in rural areas by scarcity of materials, inadequate training, and language barriers between teachers and students. In many rural schools, personnel shortages require teachers to teach outside their subject area, a shortcoming which is particularly acute in subjects like English and French.

Rural teachers often depend upon the community's generosity for part of their sustenance, and those who are perceived as competent and dedicated can count on such support. Not all teachers are equally well loved, however, and parents sometimes complain about teachers taking advantage of their position to demand favors from the community or extract gifts of food from students on holidays. Though parents often sympathize with teachers' efforts to obtain better wages, lengthy teacher strikes create hardships for parents, provoking a certain amount of ill will toward teachers. In communities where social diversions are few, drinking among male teachers is another common source of parental complaints.

Despite such tensions and limitations, it is worth noting that rural school-teachers are far more innovative than their urban peers. Most notable Bolivian educational innovations have originated in rural areas, as was the case with Warisata. Paradoxically, this likely stems from their very isolation, as well as the greater time they spend each day with their students. Single teachers in remote areas, faced with the need to "make do" with few supplies and little support, are under greater pressure (and fewer restrictions) to come up with creative solutions to pedagogical challenges. In fact, during the nationwide educational reform implemented at the end of the twentieth century (see below), many rural teachers adapted to the new pedagogy more easily than their urban counterparts, due to their prior experience with multigrade methodologies.

The 1980s and 1990s saw a proliferation of private schools (in urban areas) and mission schools (in urban and rural areas). Additionally, many public schools have begun charging parents a small monthly "quota," in return for which teachers continue to work even when called on by their union to strike. The generally low quality of public education, coupled with frequent and lengthy teacher strikes, leads most parents who can afford private school for their children to do so. However, only 11 percent to 13 percent of Bolivia's student enrollment corresponds to private education, and it is debatable whether many private schools actually offer a higher quality of instruction. In urban areas, a few elite private schools offer a curriculum oriented around U.S. content (for example, language, holidays, and monetary systems); one such school in Cochabamba participates in the International Baccalaureate program. These schools often include native English-speaking expatriates among the teaching staff, and are notably more successful than the public schools at developing students' English proficiency—an important marker of prestige among upper class families.

THE EDUCATION REFORM OF 1994

In 1992, as public perceptions of a "crisis" in education intensified, a nationwide education congress was held with participation from various social sectors. Out of this congress came a comprehensive reform plan put forth by the government, as well as parallel proposals from other groups.

At the same time, between 1990–94, a specific unit (*Equipo Técnico de Apoyo a la Reforma Educativa*, or ETARE) was created under the jurisdiction of the

Ministry of Planning and Development to devise a comprehensive national educational reform program. The government's plan addressed the entire system in its pedagogical, institutional, and administrative aspects, and gave central place to such progressive goals as gender equity, local control, and bilingual-intercultural education. In contrast to earlier policies of linguistic and cultural homogenization, the resulting 1994 Reform Law advocated the maintenance of indigenous languages and cultures and the incorporation of students' cultural knowledge into the curriculum. Nevertheless, many features of the reform law drew sharp criticism—none sharper than that from the teachers' unions.[7]

On the pedagogical front, teachers' criticisms focused mainly on the difficulties of adopting new methods and materials with insufficient retraining. The pedagogical *principles* underlying the reform did not encounter much public opposition, since they mirrored changes that teachers and others had been demanding for years, such as valorization of students' languages and cultures and less mechanical, more dialogic teaching methods. However, in private, many teachers (especially urban monolingual Spanish speakers) expressed misgivings about the wisdom of giving such prominent place to indigenous languages and cultures, and the implications of this new policy for their own professional status. But the most intense opposition was sparked by the proposed administrative changes, such as the decentralization of the educational system, which had been highly centralized in practically all aspects. Under the new law, financial, administrative, and operational responsibility for schools would shift from the national to the departmental and even the municipal level, with the justification that this would eliminate excessive bureaucracy, make school authorities more answerable to complaints, and permit curricula to be tailored to regional and local needs.

Critics, however, claimed that the government's real goal was not to increase local input in educational decisions, but to shift financial responsibility for schools to the local level. This would mean fewer resources for poorer regions, where many schools face a constant struggle simply to maintain operations. There were also fears that it could entail the eventual shift of the financial burden to parents (in the form of charges for school supplies, maintenance expenses, entrance fees for exams, etc.). Decentralization was thus assumed by many to be a first step towards the eventual privatization of education, and public suspicion to this effect (fueled by the teachers' unions) sparked harsh criticism and widespread outrage.[8] The government claimed that funds would be made available through the disbursement of federal monies to the departments, additional taxes at the departmental level, and "extra-budgetary funds," but remained vague on the details. Although large sums were injected into the system during the early years of the reform (to produce new materials, retrain personnel, stock school libraries, teach indigenous teachers to read and produce texts in their ancestral languages, etc.), much of this money was foreign aid specifically earmarked for the transition to the new system.

Teachers also complained that community oversight and involvement in schools opened the door to unwarranted "interference" from parents. Many parents, on the other hand, felt that such vigilance was entirely warranted, given the slip-shod manner in which some educators performed their duties and the cavalier attitude that many exhibited toward the peasant communities they served.

The reform was initiated in the earliest grades, advancing one grade per year; the same gradual strategy was applied in the teacher training institutions, with the result that the human resources necessary to carry out the reform were not in place during the early years of its implementation. Since it took three years for the first new generation of teachers to graduate, the reform's first phase depended on teachers who had been trained via the traditional, stultifying methods of copying and memorization. Although monetary funds were available, the human resources for training teachers and implementing the new pedagogical models were insufficient; furthermore, entrenched racism, sexism, and linguistic discrimination persisted at all levels of the system.

A national cadre of pedagogical specialists, hurriedly trained and pressed into service to aid the struggling teaching force, worked to ease the transition, but also provoked resentment among rank-and-file teachers (not least because of their high salaries, relative to those of classroom teachers). Similarly, the Ministry of Education itself changed its professional profile at the national level. In earlier decades, it had been exclusively in the hands of normal school graduates, but with the educational reform, liberal professionals (economists, linguists, pedagogues, psychologists, etc.) were incorporated into the system. This transformation facilitated the modernization of the system but also provoked resentment among teachers' unions as these gradually lost the control they had exercised since the National Revolution of 1952. The much-heralded emphasis on bilingual-intercultural education was encumbered by debates over standardization of native languages, resistance to their use in academic settings, and a deep legacy of racism, paternalism, and the hegemony of urban values.

Thus, the reform got off to a rocky start, punctuated by frequent teachers' strikes that sometimes erupted into violent street conflicts. Nevertheless, it moved forward despite widespread resistance, and was even advanced by several administrations in succession (a rarity in Bolivian political life). With time, additional human resources were trained, including indigenous professionals (mostly, former rural teachers) who came to occupy key positions within the national Ministry of Education as well as regional and local educational directorates. Organized resistance from the teachers' unions gradually deflated as the reform gathered more adherents among parents and teachers themselves. Additionally, administrative changes brought about by the reform significantly weakened the unions' political clout as union leaders themselves had foreseen.

In sum, the 1994 Educational Reform was the most comprehensive effort to date to break with the civilizatory project that made the destruction of indigenous identity one of the school's central objectives. Indeed, the reform incorporated two pressing demands that indigenous leaders and organizations had been struggling for since the beginning of the twentieth century: active community participation in the management of the educational system, and the incorporation of indigenous cultures and languages into the curriculum. Thereafter, the educational system officially recognized linguistic and cultural diversity as a resource to be fostered, rather than a problem to be eliminated. The reform also proposed, and attempted to implement, a constructivist, multicultural alternative to the ethnocentric, mechanical pedagogy of the past.

These efforts at change have faced formidable obstacles. While the progressive vision embodied in the reform raised hopes among many for a more democratic education (and, by implication, a more democratic society), the rigid, memorization models of the past remained deeply entrenched in teachers' classroom practice. Nevertheless, the proposed changes are making inroads even in urban areas, where an increasing number of public and private schools are becoming involved in bilingual education strategies. In the political arena, regional and local government institutions have adopted intercultural policies and opened spaces for the use of indigenous languages, while a prestigious NGO[9] periodically organizes intercultural campaigns in the nine most important cities of the country.

Universities have also been questioning their long-standing political and educational projects, and giving greater attention to access for indigenous students and the inclusion of indigenous perspectives. One important initiative at the university level was the *Proyecto de Formación en Educación Intercultural Bilingües para los Paises Andinos*, or PROEIB Andes. Established in the mid-1990s in one of Bolivia's foremost public universities (Universidad Mayor de San Simón in Cochabamba) and operating in cooperation with indigenous organizations, ministries of education, and universities from several countries, one of PROEIB Andes's principle aims was to provide graduate level training to indigenous educators (about half of whom were Bolivian). Aside from its endeavors in educational research and publishing, PROEIB Andes conferred master's degrees upon dozens of indigenous professionals, many of whom went on to occupy high-level positions in their respective countries' educational systems. In Bolivia and elsewhere, PROEIB Andes was a significant force in breaking through the "glass ceiling" that had long excluded indigenous people from higher education, and in addressing the scarcity of human resources needed to implement the reforms taking place around this time.

Although the transformation of the system remains uneven and incomplete, the face of Bolivian schooling, as well as the public discourse surrounding it, are much changed in comparison to earlier decades. "Unity in diversity" has become the ubiquitous motto; and while "unity" may still be a distant goal, official recognition of the country's diversity is certainly much more in evidence inside and outside of schools.

RADICALIZATION OF THE REFORM

Today, rural and urban schools in Bolivia face daunting, but different, challenges. Despite the large number of teachers nationwide—over 120,000—many rural schools have a single (often uncertified) teacher attending to 10–20 students of various ages and grades, due to low population density in much of the country and teachers' reluctance to work in remote rural communities. In contrast, urban schools tend to be overcrowded. Classrooms may contain up to fifty students, and a single structure often operates as two schools—one in the morning and one in the afternoon—each with a different name, teaching staff, and student body. Unlike many countries, Bolivia has the advantage of many teachers who are indigenous language speakers; but matching teachers' language proficiencies with those of the communities they are assigned to remains a challenge, and increasing rural-urban migration means that children whose dominant language is Quechua or Aymara are found in urban and peri-urban schools as well (Sichra 2006).

In many rural areas, schooling is still available only through the primary level, so that children either stop at the sixth grade or are sent to the provincial or departmental capital to continue studying. Rural families who aspire to continue their children's education must either move to the nearest town, send their children to live with urban-dwelling relatives, or have their children walk an hour or two to the nearest high school. While rural schools suffer from scarcity of materials, equipment, and basic services like water, plumbing, and electricity, urban schools must contend with inadequate recreational areas, competition with street noise (as diesel-powered buses pass within meters of classroom walls), and students who may work several hours a day as street vendors, shoeshine boys, or route-callers on buses.

When the present administration took office in January 2006, it brought substantial ideological opposition to the 1994–2004 reform. This opposition was based on the fact that the reform had originated during a period of neoliberal economic policy (in fact, it was part of a "package" of laws aimed at transforming and modernizing Bolivian society), and was substantially influenced by foreign NGOs and international lending institutions. After nationwide consultations in 2004–5 and an education congress in July 2006, opposition diminished significantly, and there is now a more mature attitude towards the positive aspects of the reform. New proposed changes deal mainly with aspects related to the role of religion and the Catholic Church in Bolivian education; a more integral view of the entire educational system, from preschool to the university (in contrast to the reform's initial emphasis on primary education); the radicalization of bilingual-intercultural education; technical and technology education; and the recuperation of the original political emphasis that indigenous leaders and organizations gave to education. Felix Patzi, a radical Aymara sociologist and university professor with ample experience in tertiary education (but little knowledge of primary and secondary education), became the first Minister of Education under Evo Morales's government. Like his neoliberal predecessors (whom he severely criticized), he also faced criticism from the Catholic Church and the teachers' unions—particularly urban teachers, who strongly opposed the indigenous orientation of the new regime.

When Patzi tried to undercut the importance of the policies he had inherited (including the emphasis on bilingual-intercultural education and the active involvement of parents and teachers in school management), the Indigenous Educational Councils organized under the 1994 Reform reacted; they approached the country's three key national indigenous organizations and organized a single united Indigenous Front (*Bloque Indígena*) as the maximum expression of popular participation in Bolivia. This Indigenous Front defended the gains in bilingual-intercultural education as well as community and grass-roots involvement in education, and presented to the National Education Congress a detailed proposal aimed at extending and radicalizing the mandates of the 1994 law. In this proposal, they noted that the so-called "neoliberal reform" had been forced to adopt proposals from indigenous leaders and organizations, which dated from before the introduction of neoliberal policies in Bolivia in 1985. They proposed extending bilingual-intercultural education to urban public and private schools. They also stressed the need to include indigenous knowledge and values in the curricula for all students, and implicitly stated the need to decolonize the Bolivian educational system and society. The resulting social pressure forced Education Minister Patzi to work with the Indigenous Front and to include indigenous representatives in the national commission for a new educational reform law. This new law was approved by the Human Development Commission of the House of Representatives in December 2006, but there has been no further progress to date (March 2007).

At the beginning of the second year of his mandate, President Morales made important changes in his cabinet in order to regain the confidence of the middle classes, who had expressed opposition to some of his policies. Hoping also to ensure the support of the urban teachers' union, in January 2007 he replaced Felix Patzi as Minister of Education with Victor Cáceres, a well-known urban teacher and union leader of Marxist orientation. It remains to be seen what will happen to the new educational proposals drawn up during the first year of the Morales government. Despite the persistence of racism and linguistic discrimination (as well as the rise of a racialized discourse among indigenous leaders and politicians), it cannot be denied that Bolivian society has changed radically, and that this change is reflected in a profoundly antiracist educational proposal. It also remains to be seen what Bolivia's new constitution (to be drawn up by a Constitutional Assembly, of which over 40 percent of representatives are indigenous) will have to say about the education system at a time when Bolivia's redefinition and a new indigenous hegemony are at stake.

CONCLUSION

One can identify two contrasting perspectives at work in Bolivia's educational history. The first views the dominant language (Spanish, spoken and written) as an avenue to political power; colonial and post-colonial elites thus tried to deny education to indigenous populations, who in turn strove for greater access to schooling. A contrasting perspective views the official language as a means to assimilate indigenous people into "national life"—that is, the capitalist market economy and urban cultural values. This perspective gave rise to policies of mandatory *castellanización* of the indigenous population, and also to indigenous demands for official recognition of their cultures and languages within the education system. Historically, national elites oscillated between these two perspectives in their search for the most efficient means of controlling the indigenous population, but events in the latter part of the twentieth century brought the second perspective to dominance in the opposed, but linked, discourses of capitalist modernization and indigenous rights.

Today, popular demands reflect both perspectives. Bolivian parents certainly want their children to have access to standard Spanish (as well as English), information technology, and the other hallmarks of a modern education. The utility of such knowledge as the keys to social and political efficacy is undisputed. However, as the country redefines itself within a more pluralistic framework, increasing numbers of Bolivians have also come to view the school as an arena for the resurgence of indigenous values, languages, and identities. The notion of an educated individual who speaks three languages,[10] is at ease with digital technology, and yet firmly embraces an indigenous identity is no longer an incongruous one; instead, it has become the archetype of Bolivia's educational goals. The growing number of indigenous professionals already manifests the viability of this goal; but whether the political will exists to expand their numbers, and how nonindigenous Bolivians will respond to being pushed off the center of the national stage, remains to be seen.

What evidently cannot be turned back is the collective questioning of the liberal concept of citizenship adopted at the birth of the Bolivian Republic, in imitation of the emerging European nation-states. The Bolivian understandings of citizenship is undergoing a rapid transformation, accompanied by evolving notions of an ethnically differentiated citizenry as well as the utopia of an intercultural citizenry that includes all Bolivians, indigenous and nonindigenous. To what degree can education meet the challenge of responding to the profound changes at work in Bolivian society? Will the country's schoolteachers be able to transcend the socialization that they themselves received under a radically different nationalist logic in favor of that taking shape within an emerging "plurinational Bolivia"?

A DAY IN THE LIFE

My name is Wara. I am seven years old and I live in the Bolivian altiplano. My community is called Yanapata; it is in the countryside and everyone here speaks Aymara, though some can speak Spanish, too. My day begins very early in the morning. I wake up at 5:00 AM and help my mother prepare the morning meal by going out to the well to collect fresh water.

We have our morning meal at about 6:30. Sometimes, it is just bread and tea, but if there is some soup left over from last night, I have that because

I have a long walk ahead. Then, I wash and get ready for school. I braid my hair with water and put on my *guardapolvo*, which is like a thin white coat, over my regular clothes. As I walk out, I look for two girlfriends of mine who live nearby, and we head to school together. We have to walk for about an hour; some of our classmates walk from even further away. We sing and play on the way. Sometimes we sing in Aymara but other times we sing in Spanish. We like singing very much.

We arrive at school about 8:15 and help those classmates who are in charge of keeping our classroom clean. By 8:30 our teacher arrives. She greets us in Spanish and in Aymara, and then asks us to line up in the schoolyard. A couple of our classmates raise the flag and we sing the national anthem. On Mondays, the teacher asks one or two of us to sing or to recite a poem. Sometimes we do it in Spanish and at other times in Aymara. I would rather do it in Aymara because I can speak that language better, but my parents have told me that I must not forget to practice my Spanish at school.

Today is Wednesday and the day begins with math class. Señorita Marta, my teacher, uses Spanish to teach math and only uses Aymara when one of us does not understand. Most of the time, she begins in Spanish and then switches to Aymara to make sure everyone in class understands what she says. I like math class because we work on our own, adding or subtracting either on the blackboard or at our tables. Señorita Marta walks through the classroom supervising our work, and we also move from one table to another to help our classmates or to look for help. We like helping each other!

After math class, we have Aymara class. We read and write in Aymara every day. In the Aymara classes, we work in groups with our Aymara textbooks. The teacher generally gives a task to solve in groups. I like Aymara class because we sing a lot in class and we also learn riddles and poems, and also because we get to work in groups. There are two boys and three girls in my group.

The bell rings at 10:30 and we rush to the schoolyard for our break. At break time, we line up outside and three mothers from the school parents' association serve us quinoa porridge. We stand in line with our bowls and spoons to receive our porridge. Sometimes we get milk and crackers, or maybe a banana. I eat with Eugenia and Maria, my best friends. When we finish eating we can play together before classes start again, but we must wash our bowls and spoons first.

By 11:00, we return to the classroom and have Spanish class. Spanish is harder because we're not so used to it, but I want to learn so I can understand the Spanish songs I hear on the radio. We try to pronounce the words just like Señorita Marta does. She writes the Spanish words for *mother, father, brother, sister, grandmother,* and *grandfather* on the board, and we copy the words in our notebooks. After Spanish, we have natural sciences. Today Señorita Marta takes us to the school orchard where we work pulling weeds and tending the young trees. Then she gives us homework; we have to draw a seedling and label the parts in Spanish and Aymara.

Around 1:30 PM our school day finishes and I walk back home with my friends. On the way back we play and tell each other funny stories. Walking back home can sometimes take us an hour and a half; we are tired from school and even though it was chilly this morning, the sun gets warm at this time of day.

When I arrive home, I help my mother cook and look after my younger brothers and sisters. In between, I try to do my homework. I show my mother my notebook so she knows I am working hard in school. My brother who is fifteen goes to school in another town, because Yanapata only has elementary school. He stays there with my aunt and uncle and comes home to us on the weekends.

My father and my oldest brother return from the field at about 4:30, and at about 5:30, we sit in the kitchen by the fire for our evening meal. I like this time of day very much because our grandparents talk to us in Aymara, telling us stories and giving us advice about how to live right. We enjoy listening to stories in Aymara and ask lots of questions that they always answer. We learn a lot from our grandparents and would like to listen to them for hours, but by about 7:00 it is getting darker and colder, and my mother reminds us that we must go to bed, since we must get up very early the next day.

TIMELINE

1624	Universidad de San Francisco Xavier founded by the Jesuits in the colonial city of Sucre (then part of Alto Perú).
1780	Rural indigenous rebellions reach their peak, provoking violent reprisals, and decline thereafter.
1825	Independence from Spain; the indigenous majority remains in conditions of servitude.
1907	Obligatory military service established, providing basic education and Spanish literacy for indigenous recruits, many of whom go on to work in clandestine educational networks in the countryside.
1931	Founding of Warisata, the *escuela-ayllu*, by Elizardo Pérez and Avelino Siñani.
1940s	Government establishes rudimentary system of rural schools.
1941	Warisata closes under political pressure from rural *mestizo* landowners.
1952	National revolution, enfranchisement of indigenous population. Expansion of rural education.
1960s	Various experiments with bilingual education in the countryside.
1971–82	Military governments, widespread corruption, and suppression of dissent. Universities are sporadically closed down during this period.
1982	Return to civilian rule.
1982–83	Nationwide literacy campaign (SENALEP) in Spanish, Quechua, and Aymara; many community educators trained by SENALEP later go on to work in other rural education initiatives.
1992	National Education Congress puts forth various proposals for nationwide reform.
1994	Bolivian Education Reform is signed into law, decentralizing school administration and giving prominent place to bilingual-intercultural education.

2000   Indigenous languages granted official status.
2005   Election of Evo Morales, Latin America's first indigenous president.
2006   Morales calls Nationwide Education Congress with participation from various
        social sectors.
2007   Morales signs New Law of Bolivian Education, superseding the 1994 Reform.

NOTES

1. http://www.ine.gov.bo/cgi-bin/piwdie1xx.exe/TIPO (accessed January 20, 2007). Throughout the Andean region, Quechua speakers outnumber Aymara speakers by approximately eight million to three million. However, since most Quechuas live in Peru, while Aymaras are concentrated in Bolivia, within Bolivia the two groups are more similar in size. Bolivia's capital, La Paz, is in the heart of the Aymara cultural area.

2. The term *criollo* refers to native-born Bolivians of Spanish (that is, nonindigenous) ancestry.

3. During the early 1990s, the vice-president (under President Gonzalo Sánchez de Lozada) was former university professor and Aymara intellectual Victor Hugo Cárdenas, heralded in the press as Bolivia's first indigenous vice-president. Though detractors often labeled him an ethnic token, Cárdenas's political rise was an important milestone in the breakdown of Bolivia's system of virtual ethnic apartheid, a process that would later culminate in the election of Morales to the presidency. Cárdenas was also a key figure in the Educational Reform of 1994.

4. The *coca* plant, which is the precursor for cocaine, is legal in Bolivia and has many non-narcotic uses. Used by indigenous people for millenia, the leaf when chewed is a mild stimulant that provides temporary relief from hunger, cold, and fatigue. It is an important element in many social and ritual gatherings, and is central to rural Andean social life and religious practice, as well as constituting a crucial (though illegal) support to the Bolivian economy. The coca industry employs tens of thousands of families, and its monetary value rivals that of all other exports combined. This has been a major bone of contention between Bolivia and the United States, which wields considerable economic and political pressure in efforts to force its eradication. This conflict, and more general perceptions of U.S. meddling in Bolivia's domestic policies, stoked much of the anti-U.S. sentiment that contributed to Morales's election.

5. Haciendas were a typical form of economic organization in the lands colonized by Spain. It consisted of a concession of a piece of land that included the right over the lives of all of the indigenous people who lived within its domains.

6. See note 1.

7. The urban teachers' union is dominated by the Trotskyite *Partido Obrero Revolucionario* (Revolutionary Workers' Party), whose explicit mission is to channel the tide of popular discontent toward the long-term goal of socialist revolution. This ideological stance leads them to reject "reformist" proposals in general.

8. The Reform Law did not mention privatization; public consternation arose partly from the fact that it guaranteed all Bolivian children access to *primary* education, without explicitly affirming government support for secondary education. The ambiguous wording was interpreted by many as evidence of the government's tacit withdrawal from secondary education. However, at the time, barely half of urban children and only 1 percent of rural children ever reached the secondary level; thus, ensuring universal

access even through the primary grades would have constituted a significant improvement.

9. Fundacion Unir, led by Ana María Campero, formerly Bolivia's first "*defensora del pueblo*" ("defender of the people," roughly akin to an ombudsman).

10. The new education law lists as an explicit goal that students should become fluent in Spanish, an indigenous language, and a foreign language.

BIBLIOGRAPHY

Arnold, Denise Y. and Juan de Dios Yapita. 2006. *The Metamorphosis of Heads: Textual Struggles, Education, and Land in the Andes*. Pittsburgh: University of Pittsburgh Press.

Biermayr-Jenzano, Patricia. 2001. *Intercultural Education for Quechua Women: A Participatory Study on Gender Relations, Cultural Preservation and Identity Formation in Rural Bolivia*. Doctoral dissertation. Cornell University.

Choque, Roberto, Vitaliano Soria, Humberto Mamani, Esteban Ticona, and Ramón Conde. 1992. *Educación indígena: ¿Ciudadanía o colonización?* La Paz: Taller de Historia Oral Andina/Ediciones Aruwiri.

Contreras, Manuel and María Luisa Talavera. 2003. *The Bolivian Education Reform 1992–2002: Case Studies in Large Scale Education Reforms*. Washington, D.C.: The World Bank.

CSUTCB (Confederación Sindical Única de Trabajadores Campesinos de Bolivia). 2001. *Voices and Processes Toward Pluralism: Indigenous Education in Bolivia*. New Education Division Documents No. 9. Stockholm: SIDA. (Originally published in Spanish under the title *Voces y procesos desde la pluralidad. La educación indígena en Bolivia*. La Paz, Bolivia: Plural Editores.)

Gustafson, Bret. 2002. *Native Languages and Hybrid States. A Political Ethnography of Guarani Engagement with Bilingual Education Reform in Bolivia, 1988–99*. Doctoral dissertation. Harvard University.

Heath, Shirley Brice and Richard Laprade. 1982. "Castilian Colonization and Indigenous Languages: The Cases of Aymara and Quechua." In *Language Spread: Studies in Diffusion and Social Change*. Edited by Robert L. Cooper, 118–47. Bloomington: Indiana University Press.

Hornberger, Nancy and Luís Enrique López. 1998. "Policy, Possibility, and Paradox: Indigenous Multilingualism and Education in Peru and Bolivia. In *Beyond Bilingualism: Multilingualism and Multiculturalism in Education*. Edited by J. Cenoz and F. Genesee, 206–42. London: Multilingual Matters.

Instituto Nacional de Estadística de Bolivia (INE). www.ine.gov.bo.

Klein, Herbert. 1982. *Bolivia: The Evolution of a Multi-Ethnic Society*. New York: Oxford University Press.

López, Luis Enrique. 2001. "Literacies and Intercultural Education in the Andes." In *Literacy and Social Development: The Making of Literate Societies*. Edited by D. Olson and N. Torrance, 201–24. Oxford: Blackwell.

López, Luis Enrique. "Top-down and bottom-up: Counterpoised visions of bilingual intercultural education in Latin America." In *Can Schools Revitalize Languages?* Edited by Nancy Hornberger. New York: Palgrave-Macmillan, forthcoming.

López, Luis Enrique and Pablo Regalsky, eds. 2005. *Movimientos indígenas y estado en Bolivia*. La Paz, Bolivia: PROEIB Andes/CENDA/Plural Editores.

Lora, Guillermo. 1977. *A History of the Bolivian Labour Movement, 1848–1971.* Edited and abridged by Laurence Whitehead. Translated by Christine Whitehead. New York: Cambridge University Press.

Luykx, Aurolyn. 1999. *The Citizen Factory: Schooling and Cultural Production in Bolivia.* Albany: State University of New York Press.

Luykx, Aurolyn, Nestor Hugo Quiroga, Ana María Gottret, Ivonne Velarde, and Victor Hugo Arrázola. 2001. "Education of Indigenous Adults in Bolivia: A National Study." In *Adult Education in Africa and Latin America: Intercultural Experience in a Multicultural Encounter.* Edited by Wolfgang Küper and Teresa Valiente-Catter, 347–90. Lima, Peru: GTZ.

Mannheim, Bruce. 1984. "Una nación acorralada: Southern Peruvian Quechua Language Planning and Politics in Historical Perspective." *Language in Society* 13: 291–309.

Patzi, Felix. 1999. *Etnofagia estatal: modernas formas de violencia simbólica (análisis de la reforma educativa en Bolivia).* La Paz: Alliance Français/Instituto Francés de Estudios Andinos.

Pérez, Elizardo. 1962. *Warisata: la escuela-ayllu.* La Paz: Burillo.

Talavera, María Luisa. 1999. *Otras Voces, otros maestros: aproximación a los procesos de innovación y resistencia en tres escuelas del programa de reforma educativa, Ciudad de La Paz, 1997–98.* La Paz: Fundación PIEB.

Taylor, Solange. 2004. *Intercultural and Bilingual Education in Bolivia: The Challenge of Ethnic Diversity and National Identity* (Instituto de Investigaciones Socio Económicas Working Paper No. 01/04). La Paz: Universidad Católica Boliviana.

Von Gleich, Utta. 2004. "New Quechua Literacies in Bolivia." *International Journal of the Sociology of Language* 167: 111–46.

Yapu, Mario and Cassandra Torrico. 2003. *Escuelas primarias y formación docente en tiempos de reforma educativa: enseñanza de lectoescritura y socialización.* La Paz: Fundación PIEB.

Web Sites

Ministerio de Educación y Culturas: www.minedu.gov.bo.

Proyecto de Formación en Educación Intercultural Bilingües para los Paises Andinos (PROEIB Andes): www.proeibandes.org.

UNICEF-Bolivia: www.unicef.org/bolivia/spanish/education.html.

The World Bank, Bolivia: http://go.worldbank.org/RH4SUVWPZ0.

Chapter 4

SCHOOLING IN BRAZIL

Diana Gonçalves Vidal and
Luciano Mendes de Faria Filho

The formal schooling process in the region that would become the Brazilian territory started in 1549 with the arrival of Jesuit priests, nearly fifty years after the *discovery* of the land by the Portuguese in 1500. It was the beginning of what was known in the history of Brazil as the colonial period, which would last until 1822 when Brazilian independence from the Portuguese Crown was proclaimed.

Founded in 1534 as one of the central strategies of the Catholic anti-reform movement, the Society of Jesus intended to come to Brazil to save the souls for the Church and increase the domains of the Portuguese kingdom. As a missionary and evangelizing order, the Society of Jesus focused, at least in the beginning, its attention on the indoctrination and *conversion* of the Indians, which at times, included teaching reading and writing. From the Jesuits' European perspective, as well as all the colonizers, the inhabitants of the newly-discovered land, who at times were compared to animals, were no more than blank sheets of paper where the character of civilization ought to be printed. The priest Manoel da Nóbrega, who led the first group of Ignatians bound for Brazil, once declared that "the Indians are like dogs as they eat and kill themselves and like pigs in their vices and in the way they treated each other" (Nobrega 1954, 54). As they did not acknowledge any values in the indigenous culture, the colonizers believed that the only thing left for the Indians was to submit themselves to the social and cultural rules announced by the civilized *invaders*.

The *discovery* of the indigenous childhood as the most appropriate moment for the Jesuits, through their educational action, to instill the so-called *true* values of the Christian civilization—those of the Catholic Church and Portuguese kingdom—was one of the most important aspects of contact between the two civilizations. However, it did not take long for the Jesuits to realize that the indigenous children did not accept the imposition of the new culture so easily.

This awareness by the members of the Society of Jesus, as well as other demands made by colonization growth, changed their focus towards schooling of the *landowners' children*—justifying the shift of a good part of their educational efforts to the white colonizing elite. This meant that, as from the last quarter of the sixteenth century on, the Jesuits focused their educational efforts mainly on children of the Portuguese colonizers.

However, this shift should not make us think that from this point on the indigenous people did not matter to the Jesuits. On the contrary, during the whole colonial period, the indigenous question was fundamental in the internal debates of the Society of Jesus and among the Jesuit priests, white elite, and Portuguese government. In these debates, the issue of the need of indigenous enslavement and under which circumstances this would be considered legitimate was discussed, among other subjects.

There was still a more diffuse action of the practice and propagation of the Catholic doctrine, the catechesis, which also contributed to the dissemination of the written culture in Brazil. Having the holy book—the Bible—as its reference, the catechesis disseminated among all the peoples the written text and its meaning. Within an eminently oral culture of indigenous people and the majority of Africans that were later brought as slaves, the development of social, economic, political, and cultural activities that had the written text as support asserted the importance of reading in the context of colonization.

The most significant educational feat of the Society of Jesus during the colonial period was represented by the secondary schools. By accurately following the teaching method and program determined by *Ratio Studiorum* (the plan established in its last version in 1599), a model Jesuit school should offer Latin grammar lessons, rhetoric, humanities, and philosophy in a progressive way so that at the end of eight or nine years, the student would graduate if the program had been fully accomplished. However, we are aware that the accomplishment of this program relied on aspects such as the existence of master priests and students in the school as well as on the fact that the students could read Latin. Until 1727, when it was banished, the spoken language in Brazil was Tupi, and many children could not speak Portuguese. For this reason, it was not unusual that the schools kept a reading, writing, and speaking class in Portuguese. While the secondary schools were focused on the education of the colonial ruling elite, they also served as a necessary preparation for those who wanted and could continue their studies in overseas universities, especially at the University of Coimbra in Portugal.

Throughout the sixteenth and seventeenth century until the middle of the eighteenth century, the growth of Jesuit education in Brazil was remarkable. Subsidized by the Portuguese Crown, the schools built in the most diverse places such as Salvador (BA), São Luiz (MA), São Tiago (ES), Rio de Janeiro (RJ), and São Paulo (SP) comprised a total of seventeen teaching institutions in 1759 when the Jesuits were expelled from Portugal and all its colonies, including Brazil, by Sebastião Carvalho e Melo, the Marquee of Pombal. After the expulsion, which was largely justified by positions the Jesuits assumed defending the Indians, the financial difficulties faced by the Portuguese Empire, and the Society's alleged responsibility for Portuguese cultural backwardness; schooling became the direct responsibility of the State for the first time.

ADVENT OF OFFICIAL EDUCATION: CLASSES IN PARTICULAR AREAS (TUTORIALS)

The educational reforms imposed by the Marquee of Pombal in Portugal and in the colonies separated schooling into major and minor studies. Major studies contemplated education at the universities. Minor studies, the only ones which were implemented in Brazil, were composed by the secondary *royal classes* of Latin, Greek, and Hebrew grammar; rhetoric; philosophy; and by *royal classes* of basic education where students learned the basis of reading, writing (spelling and grammar), mathematics (arithmetic applied to the study of currencies, weights, and fractions), Christian doctrine, and the history of the native land in addition to civility norms.

The royal classes were authorized by the Portuguese State and, in general, took place at the house of the teachers, selected through public examination. They were aimed at boys only. In the legislation of that period, the only mention of girls' schools was public schools of elementary education in Indian villages. In those schools, which aimed at teaching civility and fighting the use of Tupi as a language, the girls were taught the Christian doctrine, reading, writing, spinning, lace-making, sewing, and all the other activities considered appropriate for women. The law even allowed girls of age ten or less to attend classes for boys in the Indian villages where it was not possible to have two schools.

Unlike the Jesuit schools, which offered a set of subjects in the same institution, the secondary *royal classes* occurred separately, quite often in different towns or villages, and were under the responsibility of different teachers. Thus, the pupil did not do a structured and articulated course, but had to assemble his own course. In 1772, there were forty-four *royal classes* in Brazil: seventeen for elementary education, fifteen for Latin grammar, six for rhetoric, three for Greek grammar, and three for philosophy.

This organization of classes in particular areas lasted well into the nineteenth century, despite the functioning of a few secondary schools belonging to other religious orders such as the Olinda Seminar, founded in 1798 by the Franciscan Order; private schools; and even some public schools like Colégio Pedro II, founded in 1837. As far as primary education was concerned, the *one-teacher schools* lasted throughout the nineteenth century, and it was necessary to wait until 1893 for the creation of graded schools—the *collective institutes*—to experience a new teaching organization system.

Not even the transfer of the Portuguese court to Brazil in 1808 changed this scenario, despite the heavy impact on all aspects of Brazilian life, which meant relocation of the whole structure of the Portuguese State to Brazil, with the empire being ruled from the city of Rio de Janeiro. No sooner had the Portuguese King Dom João VI arrived in Brazil when he took a series of measures aimed at developing conditions for exercising the government under Portuguese rule. He created the Royal Press, the National Library, and the Botanical Gardens, in addition to the Royal School of Sciences, Arts and Crafts (founded in 1816 as the Fine Arts School), and various classes in particular areas (tutorials) for secondary and higher levels aimed at organizing elite political officers and the Court administration. Among the higher level tutorials, the ones that stood out were the classes for surgery and anatomy introduced in 1808 in the states of Bahia and Rio de Janeiro, which were the start of medical schools in Brazil. The measures contributed not only to the formation of a political and cultural elite in tune with the national interests, which in 1822 performed an important role in the independence process, but also to the organization of the newly-born Brazilian culture.

ATTEMPTS AT ORGANIZING THE EDUCATIONAL SYSTEM

At the heart of their discussions, inspired by the enlightenment ideals, Brazilian intellectuals and politicians, especially during the years immediately preceding and following independence, defended the need to elaborate and conduct a large *civilizing* project of the Brazilian population at large, mainly the poorer people and those who did not possess the so-called civilized attributes of the dominant elite.

Schooling, which was to be *poured* like rain falling on dry land, occupied a privileged position. After Independence in 1822, schools were supposed to carry to the most remote places of the new fatherland the messages of *good news*, that is, of the new empire that was being inaugurated. At the same time, the need to create leading groups, who identified themselves with the new national ideals, was brought to light. Two measures were taken in 1827. On August 11, the São Paulo and Olinda Schools of Law were founded—the cradle for new Brazilian law school graduates who were going to occupy prestigious political posts during the whole period of the empire and even after the instauration of the republic in 1889. This measure intended to educate the political elite in the Brazilian territory rather than in the Portuguese universities. In order to be admitted to the law courses in 1827, candidates were required to present "approval certificates" in Latin, French, rhetoric, philosophy, and geometry, which were checked by government-authorized teachers who taught public or private classes in particular areas. The second measure was taken on October 15, 1827, when the only general law concerning primary education in imperial Brazil was passed. In its first article, it stated that "there will be as many primary schools as necessary in all the towns, villages and highly populated areas."

In these schools, the teachers were supposed to teach reading, writing, the four basic arithmetic operations, fractions, the decimal system and proportions, general notions of practical geometry, grammar, Christian morals, and Catholic doctrine. The great innovation was the inclusion of girls, who were going to have the same education except for geometry, which was to be substituted by "home economics." The legislation revealed a clear separation of genders: for boys, the cultivation of abstract thought; for girls, the menial work of domestic chores. The law also stated that men and women would be hired as teachers. The proposal intended to create the first normal schools for teacher training in 1835, which initially were for men only, but during the next few decades were open to women.

These laws were contemporary to the slow but steady, strengthening process of a political-cultural perspective for the formation of the Brazilian nation and the national state, which considered education one of the main strategies for civilizing and governing the Brazilian people. Instructing the *lower classes* and educating the *higher classes* was a fundamental task of the State and at the same time the very condition for the existence of the State and the Nation, according to the imperial elites.

Education would enable the organization of the Brazilian people to create an independent country and conditions for controlled participation in defining the future of the nation. In this scenario, education, used as a governmental tool, would not only indicate the best paths to be taken by free people, but also help them to avoid from going astray. In 1825, the paper *O Universal* stated, "The population needs to be free to make a choice, and it needs to be educated to make the best choice."

Over the next two decades, after attaining independence, most discussions about the importance of education would be associated with the need to establish laws in the Brazilian Empire. On the one hand, this would mean establishing the judicial-institutional framework of legal sustainability of the Imperial State with its most diverse manifestations and tasks (which was certainly aided by the foundation of the law schools). While on the other hand, it would make the most diverse social classes living in the land or even those working for the government obey legal requirements.

Following the 1827 laws, the 1834 Additional Act was another important landmark in the schooling process in Brazil. This act was a set of legal rules that modified the 1824 Constitution. As far as education was concerned, the Additional Act established that the Provincial Assemblies would be able to influence and establish laws on primary and secondary education, and that the Imperial State would be responsible for higher education throughout the national territory and the other levels of education only in the municipality of the Court.

The problem concerning the Additional Act was that, in general, the provinces had little financial resources to invest and solve their various needs. As a consequence, primary education did not receive enough investment for its growth, whereas one could observe a greater concern by the Empire in educating the elite in the secondary schools and higher education courses, especially medicine and law—which became evident mainly with the foundation of the *Imperial Colégio Pedro II* in Rio de Janeiro in 1837.

As a model institution, the *Colégio Pedro II* awarded a bachelor's degree to its graduates and enabled them to enroll in any school of the Empire without having to go through the preparatory exams of higher education institutions. The college provided a six-year course for young men only. The curriculum included national grammar, Latin, Greek, French, English, fundamentals of geography, history, zoology, mineralogy, botany, physics, chemistry, astronomy, philosophy, rhetoric and poetics, arithmetic, algebra, geometry, drawing, and singing. The importance of this institution in the formation of the imperial political elite is demonstrated by the fact that the teaching staff was hired and controlled directly by the second Brazilian emperor, D. Pedro II, who had the institution named after him, attended it himself, and took classes there as well.

Another consequence of the Additional Act was the nonexistence of a single teaching system in the country. Instead, there was a set of provincial systems that were very different and unequal among the provinces, since each one could organize primary education as it pleased.

However, one must take into account the fact that the Brazilian Imperial State and, especially from the 1834 Additional Act on, the provinces of the Empire were prolific in establishing laws concerning public instruction. As far as the Imperial State was concerned, many laws were passed after the 1827 laws, aimed at regulating instructional activities in the municipality of the Court. Such laws, within certain limits, were eventually used as guidelines for the provinces. As far as the latter were concerned, from 1835 on, throughout the Empire, the Provincial Assemblies and Presidents of the Provinces had a significant number of legal texts published—suggesting that legal regulations was one of the major means of State intervention in the education sector.

Another characteristic, which would leave its mark in the history of education in Brazil throughout the nineteenth century, was its elitist and exclusive character. It was elitist because it was focused on the education of a few and exclusive because it excluded slaves, most poor people (black or white), and women. Black people, either slaves or free men, were rarely seen in private or public schools of the time even though there were very few private schools during the first decades of the nineteenth century, associated to black catholic fraternities or not, that during the eighteenth century were already concerned with instruction in specific areas (maneira pontual). The municipal or provincial government would sometimes offer school supplies and sometimes pay a fee to private teachers so that they could take these students in. In spite of having the right to go to primary school since 1827, women had the first secondary school for girls founded only in 1858, and would only have access to the school of law in 1881. Their presence in normal schools' teaching courses only grew during the 1870s when they rapidly occupied most of the vacancies.

Notwithstanding an exclusive and elitist character, education did receive attention. Intellectuals, politicians, scholars, doctors, and many other educated segments of society passionately defended education as the only way to transform the country into a prosperous and civilized nation. The illuminist ideals set its roots here as well.

Nevertheless, different from European countries, the illuminist ideals had to exist in a society based on slavery, where most of its population, slave and/ or poor, was previously excluded from the right to citizenship. It is important to remember that throughout the Imperial period, the election of the legislative body for the House of Representatives and Senate was done through "*censitário*" vote; that is, it was necessary that the voter and candidate were free and had a certain annual income (that varied according to the office being pleaded) to be able to vote and be elected.

Concerning schooling, strictly speaking, scholars and politicians assumed that Brazilians, especially the poorest, lacked traces of civility. Thus, in the same fashion as the indigenous people and the Africans, the poor, even the white, ought to go through schooling to acquire the rudiments of western culture and civilization.

Civilizing was, therefore, a word of command in the nineteenth century. This word was related to the practices that would make known to the uneducated people the habits, customs, practices, sensitivities, and beliefs of the white elite under a markedly European influence. The ideal of a civilized man was an educated white male of European origin who lived in the urban area. As one can see, such a definition alone, excluded from the bosom of the civilized world the great majority of the population, which was comprised of blacks, poor people, the uneducated, residents of the rural areas, and women.

It was after 1870, thus, at the end of the nineteenth century—a time of propagation and expansion of republican ideals—that new ideas concerning education emerged. Even considering that most of the republicans defended a simple change of governmental regime more than an effective change in the extremely unequal social-economic relations present in the Brazilian society, one must understand that they fiercely defended the need to educate the people because they believed that without education, there could be neither *order* nor *progress*. When order and progress were associated with the education of the population, the republicans promised that, with the Republic, schools would reach the most secluded places of the nation. However, that was not exactly what happened. Once the Republic was proclaimed, in 1889, a good part of the ruling body devised ways for the new regime to live peacefully with a population composed of more than 90 percent of illiterates, many of whom came from slavery, which had been abolished in 1888, a year before the change in the political regime.

Thus, the Republic was born and developed, as far as schooling goes, with problems which were very similar to those of the imperial period. On the one hand, school was still an institution for a few privileged people: if the republicans were not able to build enough schools to cater even for the children, what could be said for the millions of illiterate adults? The poor people from the rural areas and the cities, and the free or newly freed, still had to face great difficulties to attend school, either because of the lack of these institutions or because of their exhausting work routine, which was necessary to make a living. On the other hand, the policies which had been inaugurated by the 1834 Additional Act were still in force: the central government of the Republic was still in charge of the elites' higher education, leaving primary, secondary, and professional education in the hands of each state of the country. The result was still the lack of a national educational system and the existence of several different and unequal state systems that relied on the public funds of each state.

Such facts, however, cannot make us think that nothing new happened in that period. On the contrary, major innovations were introduced in schooling during the last years of the nineteenth century and in the beginning of the twentieth century. From a methodological point of view, for example, we saw the expansion of groundbreaking practices concerning the so-called intuitive method, according to which, sight is the most important human sense involved in learning. The intuitive method stated that it was necessary to see to learn, that knowledge should be taught from the concrete to the abstract, from the nearest to the farthest, and condemned memorization methods used until then. Another important innovation was related to the construction of suitable buildings for the functioning of schools and the introduction of a grading system in primary education.

THE FIRST REPUBLICAN DECADES AND CREATION OF THE MINISTRY OF HEALTH AND EDUCATION

The first Republican Constitution (1891) put an end to the "censitário" vote, a trademark of the Empire, sanctioning the right to vote and be elected to all males, of a certain age who could read and write, except members of religious orders and low rank military people. It established a connection between citizenship and literacy that would be disrupted in Brazil in 1988, practically a hundred years later. In practice, it established a restriction mechanism to the number of people entitled to vote. In 1920, for example, only 20 percent of the population could read and write, but not everyone within this contingent could vote. It is necessary to remember that women's vote was only allowed in 1932.

Increasing the number of voters, and consequently the number of people who could read and write was, nevertheless, the way that certain political and intellectual groups proposed to fight against the power of the old, rural oligarchies. They were the big landowners who had held an important role in the development of the Brazilian economy, but who little-by-little were losing their power and prestige with the growth of the urban population and the industrial production.

In order for that to happen, a vital stimulus was given to primary education. The first "Grupos Escolares" (primary schools)—the name given to the first graded schools in Brazil—were created in 1893. Their curriculum was expanded and incorporated subjects of scientific character aimed at the physical, intellectual, and moral education of the pupil. In spite of keeping home economics for girls, it ensured girls' access to the other subjects in the curriculum, breaking off with the inequality of the Empire. As we have already mentioned, investments were finally made in the construction of school buildings.

All this enthusiasm, nonetheless, wore out gradually. In the 1920s, there was intense criticism over the small political, social, and economic improvements brought by the Republic to the vast majority of the population. Therefore, the discourse which stated that only education would enable the country to move towards development and greater social equality, and was the solution of all social-political problems, reappeared with great strength. It coincided with the growth of the propaganda of a worldwide movement which was proposing educational reformation: the *escolanovista* movement.

The *Escola Nova* proposed to reinvent school and its inner relations, as well as its relations with other social institutions, based on scientific knowledge being produced by sociology, psychology, biology, and statistics from other sciences combined with a social critique. It was believed, within the school, that the student should be the center of attention, and that if one wanted to teach well, it was necessary, first of all, to get to know the learner. This perspective, present in the pedagogical ideas since at least the end of the nineteenth century, would be resumed by the *escolanovista* movement, emphasizing that the student was the most important element at school.

However, in order to have this change of focus, it was also necessary to change the teaching methods, making them more participative; change the teachers, bringing them closer to scientific innovations in the field of education and culture; and, finally, it was still necessary to restructure the school programs and curriculums so that the information would be closer to children's interests and student's reality.

From the point of view of the relationship between school and society in general, the *escolanovistas* defended the idea that the school should be more aware of the needs of its time and converse with contemporary culture. If the Brazilian society was modernizing and urbanizing itself, it was necessary that schools followed its steps. If society demanded the active participation of all citizens in the definition of its destiny, it was also necessary for schools to do the same. It was necessary, then, that schools open up to the world, to the reality of its students, and talk actively with the families and other social institutions.

Another point that was fiercely defended by these intellectuals and politicians was the need to create a national educational system with national guidelines. As well as being the articulator of the different educational state systems, such a system would organize the integration between the various levels of education (primary, secondary, and higher).

Bearing these ideals in mind, many educational reforms in different Brazilian states were made: in São Paulo (1920, 1930, and 1933); in Minas Gerais

(1927); in Rio de Janeiro (1927 and 1931); in Pernambuco (1928); and in Ceará (1922). Based on *escolanovista* principles, these reforms, each one in its own different way, introduced changes in the curriculums of the primary and normal schools, and changed the teaching methodologies incorporating project methods and interest centers, among others.

At that time, the fight for democratization of schools was a subject that interested many sectors of society, including the Catholic Church. In spite of also defending the innovations in the teaching methods, certain Catholic groups associated with education did not always agree with some of the reforms proposed. For example, the idea of a free, nonreligious, public school where boys and girls studied together (coeducational) was not well accepted. These groups defended the idea that the state should keep free public schools for the population. But they also felt that Catholic Christian beliefs should be taught because most of the population was Catholic. Also, they defended the idea that a family had the right to choose where their children would be educated: either in public or in private schools. In case a family chose the latter, the tuition would be the responsibility of the State. Finally, Catholic sectors alleged that coeducation was an affront to good customs—a moral and good upbringing—and it would be responsible for the perversion of children. In spite of these differences, the various groups came together with each other in defense of a change in the Brazilian educational scenario. Many Catholics, for example, were interested in promoting certain *escolanovistas* precepts, which, according to them, did not jeopardize fundamental beliefs of the Catholic faith and education.

However, from 1930 onwards, with the creation of the Ministry of Health and Education, and above all, with the upcoming elections for the Constituent Assembly in 1934, the mood darkened and divergences became more and more demarcated. Such divergences separated on one side the group led by the Catholics, with nearly all of its members supporting private education and, on the other, the group led by self-proclaimed pioneers of the new education that was formed by a group of intellectuals with different educational backgrounds and occupations, who nearly all defended public and nonreligious schools.

During the following years, with the country either under the *lawful government* or under the *aegis* of the *Estado Novo*—authoritarian regime (1937–45)—these groups would try to win the leadership of education offices at the federal, state, and municipal levels. The 1934 and 1937 Constitutions show the imprint of these disputes, such as the introduction of elective religious studies in primary schools, which had been abolished since 1891.

Although it can be stated that the *escolanovista's* proposals had an impact on primary education, the same cannot be said for secondary education. Even though secondary education incorporated some aspects of the new ideals—for example, the introduction of modern mathematics—it was far from incorporating any significant changes according to the *escolanovista* movement. The principles of an encyclopedic education that focused on the education of the elite and with a propaedeutic character; that is, aimed at attending higher education were kept.

Immediately after the creation of the Ministry of Health and Education, the reform introduced in 1931 broke away with the practice of preparatory exams conducted by the universities in the selection process of its candidates and promoted changes in the organization of secondary education, although it did not upset the priorities of the encyclopedic and propaedeutic teaching.

Secondary education would now last seven years, divided in two cycles: basic (five years) and complementary (two years). The complementary cycle was subdivided into three groups of courses focused on preparation for university entrance (engineering, medicine, and law). It was the start of a separation that ten years later would organize secondary teaching in two levels: the *ginasial* (middle school); and the *clássico* (classic) and *científico* (secondary school). The first cycle aimed at broadening primary education studies. It acquired its own meaning which favored the adoption of new teaching methods and allowed the experimentation of some *escolanovista's* ideas as we have seen. However, it kept a clearly encyclopedic-designed curriculum. The second cycle still aimed at access to higher education, preserving its propaedeutic role.

In spite of the separation in cycles, secondary education remained without any technical courses. During the whole period of the Empire and the first decades of the Republic, technical courses, even those taken after the conclusion of primary education, did not provide entry to the university, as they did not correspond to secondary education. Access to the university was only allowed to students who had finished their secondary education and/or had passed the preparatory exams. Therefore, the technical course was seen as a final stage that emphasized the concept of the Brazilian State divided between the education of the worker, and the lawyer (bachelor), politician, or intellectual. The division between labor and intellect, cemented by three hundred years of slavery, was revealed in the organization of the educational system.

The second change in 1931 was intended for higher education with the creation of the Estatuto das Universidades (Universities Act). Until then, Brazilian universities were characterized by the juxtaposition of institutions that already existed. That is what happened to the University of Rio de Janeiro, created in 1920, from the assemblage of the Schools of Engineering, Medicine, and Law; and to the University of Minas Gerais in 1927, which assembled not only those three fields, but also the Schools of Odontology and Pharmacy. The universities from the 1930s would, differently, have their teaching, sciences, and languages courses, recently created, as the core for preparation of secondary education teachers. If it was certain that concern with the development of teachers dates from the nineteenth century with the creation of the first normal schools in 1835, it is necessary to stress that such institutions focused only on the training of primary school teachers. There were no specific university courses for the training of secondary school teachers at that time. The universities of São Paulo (1934) and of the Distrito Federal (1935) were created bearing this in mind.

For this reason, the Institutes of Education of São Paulo and the Distrito Federal were founded within these universities.

Although the Ministry of Health and Education was created in 1930, Brazil had to wait until 1961 to have a general law that governed education on all levels. The effects of the 1834 Act lasted for over 100 years. The lack of sole legislation and the distinct investments made by each Brazilian state explain the disparities that persist in public education until today.

THE FIRST LAW OF PRINCIPLES AND BASIS FOR THE NATIONAL EDUCATION (LEI DE DIRETRIZES E BASES DA EDUCAÇÃO NACIONAL)

Between 1937 and 1945 the country lived under the authoritarian government of Getúlio Vargas. The new regime, which had irrefutable empathy with the European fascist states, considered that education played a fundamental role in the education of society and the spread of nationalist values and practices. The persecution and closing of foreign schools; ban on foreign language teaching; and control and censorship of didactic books (through the creation of the National Institute of the Book in 1938), cinema, and educational radio stations (through the creation of the National Institute of Educational Cinema and of the Service of the Educational Radio Broadcasting in the same year) were some of the measures taken during that period. Other schemes interfered directly with school practices that involved teachers and students and school field trips. Civic celebrations gathered thousands of children in choir presentations which took place in football stadiums. Uniformed students who were members of movements such as the Juventude Brasileira (Brazilian Youth) paraded on the streets displaying the national symbols.

During the restructuring process of the education system, despite the intention to redefine the organization of Brazilian education, create a national plan to guide all education activities in the country, and overcome the dispersion sanctioned by the 1834 Act, the legal distinction between educational levels was kept, determining the Organic Laws for Secondary Education (1942), Professionalizing Technical Education (1942–46), Primary School (1946), and Teaching Courses (1946).

The proposal for the elaboration of a National Educational Plan, however, would be resumed with the reestablishment of the *lawful government* in 1945. That is what was determined by the new Constitution, proclaimed in 1946. For that reason, the project of the *Lei de Diretrizes e Bases* of National Education was submitted to House of Representatives in 1948. The legal proceedings for this project in the National Congress was, nevertheless, very turbulent. The Committee that was tasked to study the project recommended a replacement that was lost in the drawers of Congress until 1956. Once resumed, it was again replaced by another one written by Carlos Lacerda who was a well-known supporter of private schools. After being discussed in Congress and in society, the project, rewritten, and voted on by Congress in 1961, became the first

Lei de Diretrizes e Bases of national education, more popularly known as Law 4024/61.

The lengthy time that it took for the project to be voted in Congress showed how important the subject was as well as the great range of interests mobilized by it. As we have already seen, since the beginning of the 1930s, different groups tried to win political control of Brazilian education. The same dispute was updated and amplified in the 1950s and 1960s. Once more, what was at stake was the establishment, or not, of a nonreligious, free, and compulsory public system for the poorest segment of the Brazilian population. For this reason, basically the same opponents and its respective allies in the parliament, in the press, and society as a whole returned to the scene: on one side, the supporters of public school and, on the other, the supporters of private school.

As in other moments of the Brazilian history, the law, passed and enforced as the first law of *Diretrizes de Bases da Educação Nacional-LDB* (Principles and Basis of National Education) (LBBEN 4024/61), was a clear victory for the sectors defending private interests. It assured free schooling only for primary education, though it was not compulsory, and it also did not guarantee the organization of a more democratic and egalitarian teaching system. It kept the traditional structure of teaching and renamed the levels: primary education, which lasted four years, secondary education, which was subdivided in two cycles (middle school: four years; high school: three years); and higher education.

With reference to nonreligious public education, even though religious studies had officially been warranted in the 1946 Constitution, Law 4024 minimized its importance. It kept open the possibility of having the discipline offered to students as long as "it did not incur in any expenses to the treasury," which made it virtually impracticable. The great novelty of the law, however, was that it put technical education (industrial, agricultural, commercial technician, and teacher training) on the same level as secondary education, allowing the former to have access to higher education. It also responded to social pressures concerning the expansion of the teaching system that began in the 1950s due to Brazilian economic growth after World War II.

It must be stressed that the 1950s were not only marked by the LDB discussions. Besides the intense campaigns in defense of public school, campaigns and projects to teach adults to read and write were also launched, having as a key element the need to educate the population so that they could participate in Brazilian political and social life. The National Literacy Campaigns left their mark during that period. They involved a considerable number of people throughout the country, teachers and students, motivated by the possibility of learning how to read, write, calculate, as well as learn other basic subjects. It was also during this period that Paulo Freire, who would become the most famous Brazilian educator, started (in 1958) his adults' literacy project. This project, reformulated and amplified during the following years, would become known nationally and internationally as the Paulo Freire method for adults' literacy.

The start of the 1960s was marked by great mobilizations and discussions in the field of education and culture. Brazil was going through an intense moment of mobilizations in defense of free public education, agrarian reform, and a more significant participation by the population in the nation's destiny. All this was happening in a country that was in the midst of urbanization and industrialization, which deteriorated the already unstable situation of the big Brazilian cities, and stressed debates over the economic development model to be adopted in Brazil. Two projects were then being discussed: one liberal and another nationalist. The main point of contention was the proposal to accept foreign capital in the Brazilian economy, which was defended by the first group (that, as a matter of fact, prevailed with the military coup of 1964) but rejected by the second.

If the prospect of a political participation of the literates encouraged the most diverse sectors towards the organization of education and literacy campaigns, and courses for adults, the schooling of children and teenagers was still a matter of concern for the same sectors and for a variety of other actors and social movements. The idea of education as a right for all and as a basic component of citizenship or, still, the need for better technical and professional training to face the competitive urban, industrialized job market involved thousands of teachers and families in the fight for the construction of new schools.

Despite the opposition of various state governments, from the 1950s onwards, more and more people from the lower classes succeeded in their fights for more schools for their children. Therefore, it was due to the struggles and initiatives of the popular sectors, which quite frequently donated or built areas for the functioning of schools and also contributed furniture, that thousands of poor children managed to go to public school in all Brazilian states.

THE TECHNICAL TURN IN EDUCATION DURING
THE MILITARY DICTATORSHIP

The movements in support of public schools and expansion of educational opportunities, as well as the other social movements (for example, the fight for land and the political mobilization of broad social sectors), were, however, severely affected in 1964. At that time, the military, which was supported by large sectors of the middle classes and by Brazilian entrepreneurs associated with international corporations, assumed political command of the Nation and, in an act of authoritarianism and arbitrary resolution, fought and destroyed any and all organized democratic movements.

After the military coup, there was an attempt towards an education policy that aimed to produce the human resources necessary for economic development, submitting, as never seen before, education to economic decisions. The alignment of education with the economic policy, which served the interests of big capitalists, gave education a strictly economic focus. Also, North American influence on Brazilian education, which was felt since the beginning of the post-war period, and especially from the end of the 1950s, increased considerably in the late 1960s.

Therefore, on the one hand, the Brazilian State fought the organized movements which strived to expand educational opportunities on various levels. There was not only popular pressure for the extension of primary schooling, but also demands involving social sectors for the increase in the number of secondary and higher education schools, showing that although insufficient to provide for the entire population, the primary school served a growing section of the society. On the other hand, the Brazilian State joined the national and international antidemocratic sectors, seeking to conduct educational reforms that served the interests of the business classes. Consequently, important social movements, such as the *Movimento de Educação de Base-MEB* (Basic Education Movement) and others, which dealt with adult education in various parts of Brazil, as well as the Students Movement, which fought for more openings in higher education, were dismembered or had to change their action principles to satisfy themselves to what was determined by the authoritarian policies of the military governments.

The military government also had some proposals for action. Campaigns were created such as the one developed by *Movimento Brasileiro de Alfabetização—MOBRAL* (Brazilian Movement for Literacy), which sought to move the political focus away from the battle for literacy and, at the same time, gather popular support for military policies.

The military government, by Law 5692 of 1971, carried out an important reform of the primary and secondary school. Concerning this reform, it is important to emphasize three aspects: the first was related to increasing compulsory education to eight years; second, introducing vocational education in secondary schools as the central aim of this level; and third, the limitation of access to higher education.

Concerning the first aspect, the law organized the educational system in three successive stages. Elementary school (the former primary and middle schools were combined into eight years of schooling) was made compulsory. As a result of this policy, the admission exams, which were introduced in 1925 and hindered school progress, were suspended. This law aimed at stopping the movements that pleaded for more openings for secondary schools. The implementation of the law, however, was slow, because public investments in education were not correspondingly augmented and there were difficulties in finding available locations for the new schools. For example, in São Paulo until 1978, the operation of the new structure was very difficult since there were not enough school buildings or human resources; that is, the increase in school time resulted in the need for a greater number of teachers, but also in a proportional decrease in their salaries.

Secondary school (second grade) corresponded to what was named in the previous legislation collegial or technical, maintaining the equivalency between the two teaching sections. Higher education was named *third grade*.

Concerning professional development, as we have seen, the military government and their allies defined that education policy should be part of the economic development policy. History and geography were replaced in the curriculum by social studies, and moral and civic education, which mostly used textbooks written by military officers and promoted values of respect towards the established social order. On the other hand, education was seen as a means for preparing human resources, that is, workers for a job market organized under the capitalist logic and patronage of large, international capitalists. Therefore, the proposal was not to form working citizens conscious of their rights and duties, but workers who submitted themselves to the conditions imposed by their bosses. If we bear in mind that during this period free political expression was forbidden and unions were deeply controlled by the State, we will see how vicious the adopted policy was for the workers.

Related to this aspect was the intention of limiting access to higher education. The government, its technocrats and consultants, believed that if students received schooling which enabled them to have a job, they would not develop or would give up their educational ambitions, that is, their search for higher studies. The solution created and stated in Law 5692/71 was that all secondary school courses, without exception, should have a technical approach preparing students for a specific job. Thus, besides staffing the industry and service sectors, they intended to reduce the demand for the expansion of the higher education system, which had been growing since the mid-1960s. This compulsory technical educational policy for secondary schools was unsuccessful and abolished in 1982 by Law 7044.

The intention of subsidizing industrial development was also felt in the remodeling of higher education proposed by the 1968 University Reform. The modernization of Brazilian universities aimed not only at restraining students' demands who, since the 1964 coup, held public demonstrations against the imposed regime and claimed more openings in higher education, but also at increasing the control over academic life and scientific research in the country. As a result, many students and professors opposing the regime were persecuted, the university structure and its research capacity were dismantled, and the opening of private universities, unconcerned for knowledge production, but rather aimed at preparing professionals for the job market was encouraged.

Despite the military regime's strength and its strong opposition to the social movements, the latter were not completely dismantled, and whether organized or not, they represented a resistance against the full establishment of the authoritarian policy of the militaries and their allies. Therefore, in the late 1970s, when the regime underwent a crisis, a large number of social movements emerged—trade unions, struggles for amnesty, women's rights, and educational demands, among others—that, for a long time, had slowly been organized. Such movements, in general, proposed to reinvent democracy in all sectors of public life and education was not left out.

In the late 1970s and early 1980s, there was a demand for the construction of new schools and more opportunities for working class children, as well as for the improvement in the quality of education, respect for the teaching profession, and for actual democratization of education. The motto, at that time, was that citizenship should be understood as a right, a duty, a practice, and a value to be taught and nurtured at school. For the most diverse social and popular movements, it was not enough to ensure schooling for all. It was also necessary to guarantee the quality of education, which should be socially defined. In this perspective, it was believed, as it is still believed today, that school alone does not create a democratic society. However, it is difficult to create a democratic and egalitarian society with an authoritarian school that perpetuates inequality. Once more, it could be understood that the reform of society had to be linked to school reform and vice versa.

In the 1980s, reforming schools meant to create a more participatory school that would not discriminate against blacks, women, and the poor; teach social practices and matters of interest to the majority; and respect teachers and other education workers. Finally, it can be said that the 1980s recovered from history those ideas and practices that aimed to make schooling an institution aligned with the interests of most people.

PRESENT CHALLENGES

In 1988, a new Constitution was voted on and, based on it, a process of construction of a new *Lei de Diretrizes e Bases da Educação* (Law of Principles and Basis of Education), promulgated in 1996, known as Law 9394/96 began. This is the law that currently governs the education system in Brazil. Besides renaming education levels, this law asserted, among others measures, the importance of preschool education; it instituted a system of three-year cycles, replacing the grading system to allow for a better adaptation of the school to the individual learning processes; it envisioned the implementation of full-time schools; and it instituted the decade of education, establishing that all teachers' education should take place at the higher education level.

However, there are still many challenges to overcome in the construction of this school envisioned by the social and popular movements. Some data is important to outline the scenario of these challenges. According to the census of the *Instituto Brasileiro de Geografia e Estatística* (Brazilian Institute of Geography and Statistics) conducted in 2003, the Brazilian average schooling rate was about 6.4 school years, and illiteracy for those over fifteen years of age reaches 11.6 percent. Illiterates are mainly people over forty who live in the rural areas. In the same way that there is an unequal schooling distribution between the urban and rural zones and among children and adults, there is a difference in school attendance for men and women and for blacks and whites. Besides remaining longer in school, girls, seven to fourteen years old, tend to present a more regular school development than boys, with a less intense grade-age discrepancy, in both the racial segments and in the various income bands. In 1999, for example, among twenty male students, one attended higher education. Among women, one in each sixteen was in college. Among blacks, school attendance was lower and had illiteracy rates higher than whites. In 1999, while 8 percent of young blacks, between fifteen and twenty-five years old were illiterates, the rate was 3 percent for whites; and 5 percent of black children between seven and thirteen years old did not attend school that year compared to only 2 percent of whites. In general, in Brazil, whites remain two years longer at school than blacks.

Ten years after the 9394 Law was passed, we are still fighting to implement a quality public school that could respond to the demands of the various social sectors and to offer equal opportunities of access and permanence. The current discussion of quotas for blacks and/or poor people in Brazilian public universities is only a sign that the goals were not achieved and that we still have a lot to do concerning the implementation of a democratic and egalitarian school in Brazil.

A DAY IN THE LIFE

Francisco de Assis Vieira Bueno turned 14 years old in 1830. He lived in the *Seminário dos Educandos* (Seminary of Students), which was located about five kilometers away from the city of São Paulo. The *Seminário* lodged poor and abandoned children. Besides him, another twenty-three children were under its care. Its facilities were not the best. The roof was full of leaks and some parts of the classroom did not even have a roof. It had been destroyed by lightning six months ago.

When he woke up, at 6:00 AM, Francisco put his pants and shirt on. He left his only pair of shoes. They were only used on special occasions. He drank a mug of cold water with maize flour prepared by one of the house slaves who was responsible for the domestic work. He still had to wait a long time for lunch (only served at 9:00 AM) when he would be given a mixture of beans and flour. If they were lucky, they would also receive some pork sausage with the meal. The *Seminário* could not always offer them that privilege. The best meal, however, was supper, at 3:00 PM. Sometimes roasted meat with vegetables and some rice were offered at the table. That was Francisco's dream since he started his daily activities, helping with the household chores.

At 10:00 AM, after lunch, the teacher, João Francisco dos Santos, was waiting for them to start class. He practiced the *Lancasterian* method. The children were divided into groups according to their level and the tasks were supervised by the teacher or by a monitor-student. The classroom furniture consisted of only four benches, a table, and a chair for the teacher.

Francisco was an advanced student and he could even help the rest. He wrote with a fountain pen and ink on a sheet of paper. The days when he used chalk and slate were far away. After the writing exercises, he turned to reading. Given the lack of specific material, the students read a little of everything—printed and manuscript—always aloud. The teacher never got tired of requesting books from the public authorities. The *Seminário* did not even have the *Gramática da Língua Nacional* (the basic book of grammar in the national language).

That was why reading and religion were combined in the classrooms. In general, they read a book of prayers. That was the one that Francisco took, despite the fact that he always got frightened by the terrifying paintings of Hell that it contained, and he started reading (or repeating) the text which he knew by heart. He did not know anything about the other obligatory contents that had been established in the First Law of Public Instruction of the Empire, such as decimals and proportions, notions of practical geometry, and grammar in the national language. The teacher did not have time to approach these subjects.

At 3:00 PM, classes finished and the children had supper. Until nightfall, Francisco walked through the building, playing with the other kids, and doing some small errands, such as the confection of tallow candles, which were lighted at night and filled the air with a disgusting smell while dinner was served. That day, the meal was not special at all. Some cabbage and some soup (also made from cabbage) covered with maize flour were the only things they had to eat. After supper, Francisco had nothing else to do but wash his feet (completely dirty after a whole day barefoot) and go to bed.

TIMELINE

1500	Discovery of Brazil.
1549	Arrival of the Society of Jesus.
1599	Consolidation of the *Ratio Studiorum* of the Jesuits.
1727	Banning of the Tupi language.
1757	Beginning of the Pombalina reforms.
1759	Expelling of the Jesuits.
	Instruction for teachers of secondary classes (Pombalina reforms).
1772	Pombalina reforms for primary schools.
1798	Foundation of the Olinda Seminar (Franciscan Order).
1808	Creation of surgery and anatomy classes in Bahia and Rio de Janeiro; creation of medical schools.
1822	Proclamation of independence.
1824	First Constitution of independent Brazil.
1827	First general law of public instruction at elementary level.
	Creation of the Olinda and São Paulo schools of law.
1831	Abdication of Dom Pedro I, Triple Provisional and Triple Permanent Regency.
1834	Additional Act of the 1824 Constitution, which transfers the responsibility of elementary and technical education to the provinces.
1835	Creation of the first teacher training college for elementary school teachers in Rio de Janeiro.
1837	Creation of Pedro II School.
1841	Dom Pedro II is crowned emperor at the age of 15.
1850	Law Eusébio de Queirós forbids slave trade.

1854   Minister Couto Ferraz teaching reform.
1858   Creation of the first secondary school for girls.
1864–70 Paraguay war.
1871   Publication of the "Lei do Ventre Livre" (law of the free womb).
1872   Foundation of the Republican Party.
1879   Minister Leôncio de Carvalho teaching reform.
         Primary education made compulsory.
1881   The first woman enters law school.
1888   Liberation of the slaves.
1889   Proclamation of the Republic.
1890   Minister Benjamim Constant teaching reform.
1891   First Republican Constitution.
1893   Creation of graded schools.
1896   Creation of the first public nursery school in São Paulo.
1898   Minister Amaro Cavalcanti teaching reform.
1901   Minister Epitácio Pessoa teaching reform.
1911   Minister Rivadávia Correa teaching reform
1915   Minister Carlos Maximiliano teaching reform.
1920–35 Primary teaching reform based on the ideals of the New School, in the states of
         São Paulo, Ceará, Rio de Janeiro, Minas Gerais, and Pernambuco.
1920   Creation of the University of Rio de Janeiro.
1925   Teaching reform Rocha Vaz of the Minister João Luís Alves.
1927   Creation of the University of Minas Gerais.
1930   Creation of the Ministry of Health and Education.
1931   Francisco Campos secondary and higher education teaching reform.
1932   Protests of the Pioneers of the New Education in Defense of public schooling.
         Voting for women authorized.
1934   Second Republican Constitution.
         Creation of the University of São Paulo.
1935   Creation of the University of Brazil.
1937   Third Republican Constitution.
1937–45 Authoritarian Regime called "Estado Novo" or Getúlio Vargas dictatorship.
1942–46 Organic laws Gustavo Capanema for primary, technical, and teaching education.
1946   Fourth Republican Constitution.
1958   Beginning of the Paulo Freire project to teach adults how to read and write.
1961   First Normative Law of the National Education: Law Number 4024.
1964–84 Authoritarian regime, military dictatorship.
1967   Fifth Republican Constitution.
1968   University reform.
1971   General Law for National Education: Law Number 5692.
1988   Last Brazilian Constitution.
1996   Second Normative Law of the National Education: Law Number 9394.

BIBLIOGRAPHY

Azevedo, Fernando. 1976. *A transmissão da cultura*. São Paulo: Melhoramentos.
Bastos, Maria Helena Câmara and Luciano Mendes de Faria Filho, orgs. 1999. *A escola
     elementar no século XIX: o método monitorial/mútuo*. Passo Fundo: EdUPF.

Cunha, Luiz Antonio. 1980. *A universidade temporã. O ensino superior da Colônia à Era Vargas.* Rio de Janeiro: Civilização Brasileira.

Faria Filho, L.M. and D.G. Vidal. 2005. *As lentes da história.* Campinas: Autores Associados.

Faria Filho, L.M. and D.G. Vidal. "History of Brazilian Urban Education: Space and Time in Primary Schools." In W. Pink and G. Noblit, orgs. *The International Handbook on Urban Education.* Dordrecht: Springer, forthcoming.

França, Jean M. Carvalho. July 1998. "Aspectos civilizatórios da passagem de D. João VI pelo Rio de Janeiro." *Belo Horizonte: Educação em Revista* 27, 17–28.

Hansen, João A. 1999. "Padre Antônio Vieira—Sermões." In *Introdução ao Brasil: um banquete no trópico.* Organized by Lourenço D. Mota, 23–54. São Paulo: Editora SENAC.

Hilsdorf, Maria Lúcia. 2003. *História da Educação Brasileira: leituras.* São Paulo: Thomson.

Mello e Souza, Laura de. 1987. *O diabo e a terra de Santa Cruz.* São Paulo: Cia. Das letras.

Vilela, Heloisa. 2000. "O mestre-escola e a professora." In *500 anos de educação no Brasil.* By Eliane M. T. Lopes, Luciano M. de Faria Filho, and Cynthia Greive Veiga, orgs., 95–134. Belo Horizonte: Autêntica Editora.

Chapter 5

SCHOOLING IN CHILE

Rolando Poblete Melis

INTRODUCTION: BETWEEN QUANTITY AND QUALITY

This article revises in a summarized manner the main historical landmarks of the development of education in Chile. The phrase between quantity and quality illustrates the character of education evolution and discussions. In fact, the first efforts were centered on increasing the number of boys and girls that went to school, both in colonial times and afterwards, when the independent national state was formed. Then, especially at the end of the twentieth century and even to this day, the main preoccupation has been to give an education of better quality to all citizens and to guarantee the access to knowledge in the same conditions. Equity seems to be the central issue of our times.

The text is organized on the basis of three large historical periods. The first addresses the evolution of education during colonial times—comprising a summary of three centuries. The second, centered on the nineteenth century, describes the development of education within the frame of Chile's constitution as an independent nation-state. The third part, centered on the twentieth century and part of the present day, points out the way in which education in Chile evolved until today's development.

COLONIAL TIMES

The arrival of the religious orders in Chile that accompanied the Spanish conquerors in their expeditions constitutes one of the most important factors in the development of education during the colonial epoch. Though the main mission of these priests was to evangelize the "savages" of the territory, many of them also embarked on educational missions for the benefit of the European colonizers and, later, their descendants.

In general, the people that came to Chile possessed no academic skills what-soever: many of them could not read, far less write, and their only motivation to come to this end of the world was to make a fortune and then to return to Spain with their riches. The labor of the priests was considered to be funda-mental, because it was seen as contributing to the "humanization" of the con-quest. In the entourage of Pedro de Valdivia (known as the conqueror of Chile, who took possession of the territory in the name of his majesty Carlos V at the end of 1541), there was a priest who dedicated part of his time to teach-ing the alphabet to the only woman present in the expedition, Doña Inés de Suárez. This priest was called Rodrigo González, and as told by the chroniclers, he used a new and playful method to teach the basic elements of the alphabet: "It was necessary to draw the letters (on the floor or in the air) with a stick (as a pencil) or with the index finger. The next step was to put them together, pro-nouncing until words were formed" (Rojas 1997, 16).

According to Amanda Labarca (1939), one of the main historians on educa-tion in Chile, the process to educate began officially in 1548. Father González's efforts were copied by other priests, among them Pedro Hernández de Paterna, Alonso de Escudero, Juan de Herrera, and Gonzalo Segovia, who taught the alphabet to the first inhabitants of Chile.

However, among historians there is no agreement on the foundation date of the first school. Some say it was in 1550 when a school opened its doors in the city of Santiago, in Plaza de Armas. This project did not pass the test of time and was closed a little while later. On the other hand, Eyzaguirre (1973) states that the "Seminario de La Imperial must be considered as the first school founded in the country, towards 1558" (Eyzaguirre 1973, 129). Other authors point out that there were some attempts in 1578 with the Escuela de Gramá-tica under Fray Juan Blas's control, and also in 1580, when Gabriel Moya founded a school in Santiago with support from the municipal council (Cabildo).

All these initiatives had one thing in common: they were at all occasions related to the religious orders of the country, or to individual priests who had the support of some of the authorities of that time. This is explained by the Spanish Crown's concept of education as an act of charity that had to be met precisely by the priests. They had the legal right to teach. There were countless restrictions to teach for laymen; among others, they needed a license from the municipal council and, more importantly, to be "purebreds," that is to say, not born out of wedlock; they could not have legal trials pending with the civil justice or tribunal of the Holy Office (Inquisition); and they previously could not have been exerting services commonly done by Indians, negroes, mulattos, or *zambos* (persons of half American-Indian and half-African mixture).

These restrictions, and the lack of sufficient priests, meant that there were not enough people with the skills to teach. However, the families installed in the territory that demanded this service were not many, so the spreading of education initiatives was a slow and difficult process. Besides, the population lived in a permanent state of war because of conflicts with the Araucanos, an indigenous ethnic group that the Spaniards never managed to conquer. Repeated uprisings, the destruction of cities, and lootings were common at that time.

At the end of the sixteenth century, two relevant events occurred. In 1595, the Dominicans founded the Colegio de Santo Domingo, where they taught theology, philosophy, and arts, while the Jesuits founded the Colegio de San Miguel and a primary school. The priests formed in those congregations were the teachers of those schools (Rojas 1997), and their students were largely the children of Spaniards. As time went by, these schools obtained the rank of Pontifical Universities and began to hand out degrees of baccalaureate, licentiate, master, and doctor. However, the Jesuits were the ones to achieve the highest levels of development and they even founded schools in other parts of the empire far from Santiago, like Bucalemu, La Serena, Quillota, Mendoza, Rere, Chillán, Concepción, and Castro. According to Rojas (1997), during this period, one can clearly distinguish the three classic levels of education: primary (elementary school of first letters); secondary (schools of grammar and Latin); university or higher (with pontifical rank that gave academic degrees).

The schools of first letters taught reading, writing, the four arithmetic operations, some Latin grammar, and especially catechism. According to Villalobos (1989), these establishments did not reach an ideal level of functioning; on the contrary, their organization and the content of its studies were precarious. The secondary schools, of which the most famous was the Convictorio de San Francisco Javier run by the Jesuits, received the sons of Santiago's aristocracy and provided a high quality education (Villalobos 1989). Higher education was offered by pontifical universities, which functioned inside some convents and possessed a mainly academic and religious character. There was also an intermediate level between secondary and higher education—the seminaries of Santiago and Concepción—for the training of priests.

During the seventeenth century, the municipal council took on an active role in the process of schooling. However, the costs of this education had to be paid by parents. That is why this type of school did not have a large number of students. According to Izquierdo (1990), there were approximately 187 pupils in the schools run by the municipal councils in Santiago, while the Jesuits had more than 400 in their schools. There were no important differences between the two types of schools; the religious character was primordial in both, and the main objective was to form habits in the students like piousness, reverence, humility, and faith (Labarca 1993). Some of the core activities of the education process were praying and learning Christian doctrine and catechism, which at the same time constituted the main curriculum.

The entire schooling process was done with strict discipline and the teacher was allowed to punish students physically. According to texts of that time, "The preceptors could give bodily punishments, like whippings, slaps in the face and locking up, either publicly or in private, all under the consent of their superiors and parents" (Rojas 1997, 22). Students who misbehaved were taken to special places where they were whipped on the back. It was also common to submit them to public humiliations when they did not know their lessons. These punishments were used for a long time, and they were even commonplace until the beginning of the twentieth century.

Teaching methods were based on memorization. Through repetitions, the students had to learn their catechism, grammar, and Christian doctrine. Their mastery of lessons was evaluated in competitions, in which a subject was proposed and the students were divided in two teams, called "Romans" and "Cartagens." The teams posed questions to each other and the one that made a mistake was punished. The team that answered more questions won. Often these competitions took place in public places, like the cathedral or Plaza de Armas. Some of the materials used were alphabet texts published in Lima. There were also reading books with sentences, parables, and examples related to daily life. The students took notes on washable boards (Rojas 1997).

During the seventeenth century, education was thinly spread, and only available to the sons of Spanish families with power or an administrative role in the colony. The rest of the population had no access to this benefit. The native population (which consisted mainly of the Mapuche peoples) was excluded from these sorts of initiatives. The perpetual state of war made it hard for them to participate in institutions belonging to the "white enemies."

The development of education in Chile was influenced by some relevant events in the eighteenth century: first, the foundation of the Real Universidad de San Felipe; then, the expulsion of the Jesuits; and lastly the foundation of the Academia de San Luis (Rojas 1997). The Real Universidad de San Felipe was an initiative by a group of citizens and the mayor of Santiago, don Francisco Ruiz de Berecedo. Together they asked King Felipe V for a state university that would receive more students at lower prices and also offer more attractive studies. In 1738, the King signed the related decree, and the university would open its doors for the first time in 1758.

Initially there were lectures on rhetoric, Latin, mathematics, philosophy, theology, law, cannons, and medicine. The university was organized into four schools: theology, jurisprudence, medicine, and mathematics. Students from other regions and even other countries enrolled. The university also managed to attract students from pontifical universities, which brought about difficulties and rivalries between institutions. The number of graduates totaled more than 200, and included historical figures of the struggle for independence, like Manuel Rodríguez. According to Villalobos (1989), theology and law were the most popular courses because of their enormous social prestige.

The expulsion of the Jesuits marked a change of epoch. The Jesuit's contribution to the social, political, and cultural development of the country was meaningful. They expanded humanistic ideas at a time of profound obscurantism, and fought for the respect of indigenous peoples' rights. In the field of education, their achievements were significant. In the middle of the eighteenth century, the Jesuits controlled almost all schools in Chile. They had schools in almost every city of the country; they built libraries and facilitated the development of the communities. They produced abundant scientific research about the territory's flora, fauna, geography, language, and history.

The founding of the Academia de San Luis in 1797 was fundamental for the country's development of education. This academy imparted the technical knowledge for different professions related to production and economical development. That it constituted a change from traditional teaching methods was more meaningful; new educational tendencies that combined theory and practice were adopted (Villalobos 1989). The curriculum included subjects like arithmetic, reading and writing, grammar, geometry, drawing, physics and natural sciences, chemistry, and mineralogy.

Education remained a privilege of the enlightened elites of the country, the groups in power, and the merchants. Indigenous people (called "Indians") had no access to the schools; neither did the mixed races and the lower class. A large part of the population could not read or write and lacked the minimum abilities to develop their intellect. While education conditions had improved at the end of the century, the benefits of this progress were not distributed equally in the entire population. As Egaña (2000) says, in the colonial epoch, it was not possible to conceive of the Spanish State as being responsible for education, far less for the benefit of the poor and marginalized areas of society, which included women. However, in the illustrated mindset at the end of the eighteenth century and beginning of the nineteenth, a preoccupation to educate the colonies' poor began to occur.

EDUCATION AND THE NATIONAL STATE

In 1803, the governor don Luis Muñoz de Guzmán commissioned a census to begin to understand the functioning of the education system. After visiting the schools in Santiago (six in total), the inspector endowed with this task made a report that said: "There is a lack of comfort for the youngsters, an extraordinary shabbiness, so much that some establishments seemed to be stables instead of schools; and in one of them there was a negro amongst the students" (Labarca 1939, 59).

As a consequence of this report, there were rules established for the functioning of the schools: a calendar for classes, schedules, and basic improvements in infrastructure. The school year lasted from March to December and for some weeks in January and February. Classes started at 7 AM; there was a break at 12:00; and at 2:30 PM, the students returned for afternoon classes.

The crisis of the Spanish monarchy, caused by Napoleon's imprisonment of King Fernando VII, and the growing discontent of the local population motivated the establishment of the *Junta de Gobierno* (Board of Government), which took charge of the colony in the absence of the king. On September 18, 1810, the junta took control of the reign of Chile. The municipal council of

Santiago gave the government of the whole country to don Mateo de Toro y Zambrano. This is the first event in the process of independence that would culminate with the constitution of Chile as a sovereign national state. The junta's first initiatives were aimed at increasing the number of schools in the country to cover a wider scope of the population. As sustained by Egaña (2000b), there was an explicit interest in "moralizing and civilizing" the most poor, so as to integrate them to a new social order.

In 1811, José Miguel Carrera ordered the convents and municipal councils to found schools of first letters for boys; then in 1812, this disposition was extended to the nunneries: the new schools had to include women, too. In 1813, the government dictated a new disposition to regulate primary education and established the importance of the state in education matters. That same year, the *Instituto Nacional* was founded with the fusion of different schools and universities, such as the Seminario Conciliar, Academia de San Luis, Colegio Carolino, and Real Universidad de San Felipe. This was and still is one of the most important institutions of the country. This school taught the three educational levels: primary, secondary, and university. However, as stated by Rojas (1997), during the process of reconquering the territory by the Spanish Crown, its doors remained closed until definitive independence was attained. In 1819, the *Instituto Nacional* began functioning again with the policy of educating greater parts of the population. There was even a school for women. They were taught orthography and grammar, sewing, embroidery, English, French, and singing. The president of the republic himself sent his daughters to school so as to set a precedent about the importance of educating women (Rojas 1997). The first institutional ordaining and political constitutions guaranteed the right to education for all social classes. The illustrated ideas of the new men in power included the view that the population should be educated in political matters to attain their definitive emancipation (Egaña 2000a).

However, it is significant that the new State maintained the exclusion of the indigenous people. The segregation that existed during colonial times intensified once independence was attained because "the liberal state was born as an imitation of its European namesake and faced with the dilemma of civilization or barbarism, it preferred the marginalization and exclusion of other ethnic groups, so it gave up the integration it initially aimed for" (Barnach-Calvo 1997, 13–33). The liberal tradition that served as basis for the new national state led to denial of the native peoples' political rights. The members of the new government believed the indigenous cultures to be inferior. In the new policies of development, the Indians (as they were called) were seen as one of the main obstacles to progress.

In South America, modern nations used education as a tool for change, to construct a feeling of unity, and to advance towards progress. However, the processes of teaching and learning often employed coercive and violent methods: teachers would only speak Spanish or Portuguese in front of Indian students; children that went to school were forced to change clothes; they lost all possibilities to use their own resources and had to adapt themselves to characteristics of the official national culture. In Chile, this situation lasted throughout all of the nineteenth century and a large part of the twentieth century, and would only be modified with the beginning of democracy in 1990. It was only in 1992 that the promulgation of the *Ley Indigena* (Indian Law) allowed for the use of native languages and cultures in those schools with assistance of Indian children.

In 1822, D. Thompson came to Chile, and divulged the teaching method developed by Joseph Lancaster in England that facilitated the expansion of primary education in the country. The method consisted of identifying the best students who would become monitors. Once they had developed the necessary skills, they had to transmit their knowledge to their peers. There were close to 200 student-teachers under this modality. After some difficulties caused by the political situation of the country, in 1828 a normal school was founded that used this method. This school occupied some of the facilities at the *Instituto Nacional.*

At the end of the 1830s, there were eleven secondary schools in Santiago and twenty-six schools of first letters. Only four of them were public and the rest were private. The main subjects taught were first letters, Latin, French, philosophy, mathematics, geography, and law. In 1832, the first serious effort to organize a curriculum was made. An official decree established a basic program of reading, writing, arithmetic, morality, urbanity, and Christian doctrine. Though there were many norms, the role of the state wasn't completely defined because of the lack of resources in the country.

This was modified in 1833 with a new constitution that would be in use until 1925. One of its principles was that public education was defined as a service of the State, and it must protect access of all social groups to education and the functioning of the educational system. This initiative was protected by Congress. Parliament wrote a general plan for national education that included the creation of a superintendent of education. This institution had to inspect and direct education nationwide. Finally, the Constitution of 1833 also guaranteed the freedom of teaching and established three levels of administration and educational management: municipal schools, schools sustained by the public treasury, and convent schools (Rojas 1997).

The nineteenth century was marked by the effort of different governments to increase education quantitatively and to create public institutions. The State took on larger responsibilities in the development of schooling for all citizens. As sustained by Egaña (2000a), the progressive development of a popular primary education system was a product of the preoccupation of politicians and statesmen who took on these illustrated ideas. The schools of the poor had a local character up until the 1850s. Their teachers belonged to the same communities as the students and taught those abilities that the parents considered necessary for the development of their children. However, from then onwards, the State tried to give these schools an increasingly institutional character (Egaña 2000b).

One of the most unfavorable applications of this new process can be seen in a number of norms that regulated the functions of the State in education and the work of education institutions. Many of those regulations referred to "the use of space and time by teachers and students ... different and more formal ways of expressions were adopted, working hours regulated by a schedule, the location and movements of students was organized according to certain rules, their bodily postures had to be related to the tasks they had to perform. The classroom became a formal area of disciplining, different from that of family and neighborhood" (Egaña 2000b, 2).

In 1860, the *Ley de Instrucción Primaria* (Law of Primary Education) was passed. It established a structure of functioning for the system that classified schools into "normal," "superior," or "elemental," and it also established that there should be a school for men and women for every 2,000 inhabitants. However, many of these measures would not be applied until 1863 with the creation of the *Reglamento General de Instrucción Primaria* (General Ordinance of Primary Education) that regulated the entire national education system. Among other things, it regulated the activities inside normal schools, the work and wages of teachers, the provision of schools, materials, and books, and the administration of funds provided by municipal treasuries (Egaña 2000a). One of the consequences of the State's increased involvement in educational matters was an increase in the quantity of students and the progressive closing of municipal schools. The municipalities understood that the National State was responsible for the administration of education and step by step, they surrendered maintenance of the schools. In this way, the National State became the main sustainer, as shown in table 5.1.

The data illustrates a tendency for growth of student enrollment, especially in the national schools from 1852–60. On the other hand, municipal schools decreased in number of establishments and also in students. Finally, private education was also growing, although the growth is not as significant when compared with the expansion of national schools and students.

One of the other relevant events in the country's development of education is the foundation in 1842 of the Universidad de Chile, the first

Table 5.1
National, Municipal, and Private Schools: 1852–60

	Schools		Students	
Type of Administration	1852	1860	1852	1860
National	186	486	8,982	23,882
Municipal	92	80	5,433	4,246
Private	273	394	8,708	11,529

Source: Egaña 2000a.

public institution of higher education. One of its functions was the tuition of the national education system. By 1864, 13.8 percent of boys attended public schools, compared to 7.3 percent of girls. In 1880, 12 percent of boys and 12.2 percent of girls went to public schools (Egaña 2000a). Other authors, such as Rojas (1997), point out that the period between 1880–90 was particularly productive because many schools were built and the number of students attending them increased. However, education was not yet widespread and, according to the census of 1895, 72.1 percent of the population was illiterate.

There were two tendencies that influenced the construction of the national education system in the nineteenth century: French tradition and German orientations. Conejeros (1999) suggests that French tradition is more clearly visible between 1840–80, while Nuñez (1997) states there is a strong German influence since 1880. The ideas of the French Illustration influenced thinkers and politicians who considered education to be an effective means to spread the new national values. This new vision included an interest in scientific discoveries and the promotion of an active role of the State in education matters. In this way, "Instructing the population became an unavoidable imperative for the ruling class" (Conejeros 1999, 12). Conejeros also mentions other principles as part of the strong French influence. For example, he points out the laic orientation of education and the importance of moral and civic instruction of the people; the fact that the school was free of charge for students; the national sense of education (with uniform characteristics) and, lastly, the role of the State in centralizing control over teacher education.

However, German influence was to be seen in the schooling of teachers who were trained in theoretical and methodological principles of the German educational current. One of the most influential educators of that time was José Abelardo Nuñez, who traveled through Europe inviting different educators to Chile. He also introduced subjects like drawing, gymnastics, and manual chores in the curriculum. Physical punishments ended and psycho-pedagogical sanctions were incorporated, such as students rankings, grades, etc. The teachers formed in Germany influenced two areas: first, the reform of primary education with its expansion; and second, the foundation and direction of the normal schools for teachers. German professors founded the *Instituto Pedagógico* in 1889. This institution was in charge of training secondary school teachers, as they were so scarce. With the passing of time, the *Instituto Pedagógico* became part of the Universidad de Chile, and the basis for the School of Philosophy and Letters. The reform also involved the construction of large and comfortable schools that would allow for better development of teaching and learning processes (Nuñez 1999).

The end of the nineteenth century brought important advances in terms of quality of education, but there was still a large part of the population that did not go to school. The popular classes only reached primary education *(when they did so)*; the middle class attended through to secondary school; and only the rich went to the universities (Rojas 1997). This stratification continued for many years, including a large part of the twentieth century.

THE TWENTIETH CENTURY: SEARCH FOR QUALITY

The first years of the twentieth century did not change the development of the education process substantially. In fact, the basic functioning structure of the system remained more or less stable during the first two decades of the new century. However, indications like quantity, percentage of attendance, and other data indicate that "the poorest did not go to school. Their extreme poverty: the need to have children working, the lack of clothing, the disinterest of the parents who were also illiterate, kept the poorest children from going to school" (Egaña 2000c, 15). In 1910, the mayor of Santiago entrusted the police commissaries with the drawing of a school census to determine the number of children older than eight that did not go to school and the reasons why they did not: the main reason was the extreme poverty they lived in (MINEDUC, 2004). Women of well-established families were motivated by this reality to perform acts of charity. However, the State developed a series of actions to help the poorest groups and thus generated a system of assistance that in its beginnings suffered from serious problems and was not successful in attracting most of the poor to school (Illanes 1991).

The absence of children of the working class in schools generated an ample national debate on how to include this group in education. The conservatives pointed to the importance of promoting subsidies for private schools, while the liberals assumed the State should guarantee access to education for all children of the country through an increase in resources invested in education. This debate reached parliament, where diverse political groups proposed a number of legal initiatives about the obligatory character of primary education and the need of State assistance, especially for the poorer students. In 1900, the first legal initiative was presented in the Senate. Its author was Senator Pedro Bannen. This was the first landmark in a long process that culminated in the promulgation of the *Ley de Instrucción Primaria Obligatoria* (Law of Obligatory Primary Education) that, among other things, established that basic education was obligatory for all children of the country.

After a series of difficulties, debates, formulations, and reformulations, on August 26, 1920, a definitive project was promulgated (Egaña 2000c); that is, twenty years passed since the first legal initiative was presented before Chile could have a law about education.

The Law of Obligatory Primary Education consisted of 108 articles and nine titles. The Law obliged parents to send their children to school (children between seven and thirteen years of age of both sexes). The parents and guardians were responsible for the fulfillment of this law. Children could no longer be employed for work, and those who did employ them had to pay high fines. The Law had a quick effect on enrollments: in 1920, 335,047 children were enrolled in schools while in 1930, there were 439,937. Illiteracy diminished from 49 percent in 1920 to 43 percent in 1930 (Rojas 1997).

The 1920s were important not only for education matters but also because of the State's preoccupation with "social issues" and the new Constitution of 1925. One of the core principles of this legal body was the separation of church and state for the first time. However, the principle of freedom of education was maintained, which allowed religious organization and other private institutions to continue teaching. Education was declared a "preferential service of the State" (Nuñez 1997).

The pedagogical tendencies of the 1920s promoted an active pedagogy centered on the pupil, especially in primary education, and the creation of the Ministry of Education. Nuñez (1997) suggests that this was a time of experimentation in the public education system, and curricular reforms influenced the public schools and the construction of "experimental schools" in which teachers tried to do their work more efficiently through the use of new methods. This change, which also reached secondary education, was aimed at having an education that was more appropriate to the economic and industrial development of Chile, and to end the encyclopedic character of the nineteenth century. The new times called for prepared human resources that could contribute to the development of the country.

Elementary or basic schools could be national, private, or municipal. In all cases, the State supervised them. There were three kinds of national schools: the first ones taught levels up to sixth grade; the second ones, up to fourth grade; and the last kind only included first and second grades. In this time, there were also "home schools," for children with economical instability, who were given a place to sleep, education, food, clothes, etc.

Between 1925 and 1932, the global economic crisis and the government's difficulty regulating it made it difficult to implement the Law of Primary Education. At the end of that decade, even though poor children had more access to education, the higher educational levels (secondary school and universities) were still reserved for a few. Class stratification had its correspondence with different educational levels: poor children only reached primary education; the middle classes managed to study in secondary school and even some universities; while the upper classes were present in all levels. One of the important landmarks of this period is the constitution of the *Sociedad Constructora de Establecimientos Educacionales* (Building Society of Educational Establishments) in 1936 that built high-quality schools in the whole country with public and private funds. By 1938, Chile had 420 complete or advanced schools (that taught a professional career); 539 elementary schools (from first to sixth grades); and 2,640 schools of tertiary class (that only taught first and second grades)—here, the children with malnutrition from the poorest families received educations (Rojas 1997).

That same year, the lawyer and educator don Pedro Aguirre Cerda from the radical party became president. His government's motto was "educating is governing." Several authors agree that during his government and the later ones, education was given a bigger force in comparison with previous years. The governments after Cerda's, which were also radical, promoted a series of reforms and above all managed to increase the reaches of education in Chile. In fact, the last radical government diminished illiteracy substantially, increased the number of primary schools, home schools, technical and industrial schools, and created the Universidad Técnica del Estado in 1947.

By 1950, access to education had reached a sustained development with close to 27 percent of the population between zero and twenty-four years of age enrolled in the system. However, the period between 1950–64 had moderate growth and that number reached 35.8 percent. The State made a high investment in building schools, education materials, and training and specialization of teachers, in addition to the support of programs of education assistance. As for the curriculum, basic education contents were included that served the processes of political and social democratization related with industrialization and the development of the national market. In secondary education, the experimental public schools with a more flexible curriculum were not able to modify the encyclopedic character of education, so there was mainly a traditional approach based on memorization (Nuñez 1997). Basic education kept its traditional six-year structure and secondary education was organized from five to seven years.

In 1964, Eduardo Frei Montalva became president and one year later he signed three decrees that introduced structural modifications to the education system. One of them was the automatic promotion from first grade (nobody could repeat that grade). Basic education was increased to eight years and secondary education reduced to four. Basic education also reached rural and poor urban areas. This reform was inspired by the humane principles and ideas put forward by the Economic Commission for Latin America and the Caribbean (a research center from the United Nations) and the Alliance for Progress. In that sense, the reform had to consider a quantitative expansion of the system, an administrative diversification and reorganization, and finally, a qualitative improvement to modernize education. Some data of that time indicate that school enrollments increased from 1,725,302 in 1964 to 2,477,254 in 1970 (Rojas 1997). A new technology curriculum was designed, there were evaluations of education performance, and new education texts and teaching materials.[1]

In 1970, Salvador Allende was elected president. His government implemented a series of reforms with socialist inspiration. Besides substantial betterments in the system, quantitative increment, and guaranteeing social rights to the most poor, in education matters there was a reform entitled *Escuela Nacional Unificada* (Unified National School). As Nuñez (1997) explains, this reform recovered the issues of the previous period, especially in basic education. In secondary education, the notion of "general polytechnic education" was introduced together with some ideological contents that were rejected by the opposition.

After the military coup of 1973, the dictatorship of General Pinochet extensively revised the system. First, it promoted changes in the management of education, giving this responsibility to the municipalities and private investors interested in this area. In the 1980s, this measure was put into practice to decentralize the system. This new system consisted of the transfer of funds to each school depending on the number of students that regularly attended it. With the modification of the financing method, the State began to give a monetary subvention directly to the schools through private owners or municipalities when they were public schools. In this way, the funds given to schools depended on their capacity to recruit and retain students. One of the direct consequences of this measure was that private investors became increasingly involved in education to the detriment of municipalities.

Between 1981–86, enrollments in private subsidized institutions doubled as private basic and secondary schools totaled 36 percent of the students. Presently, this number is an estimated 42 percent, and together with the private schools that have no support from the State (8 percent), there is 50 percent of student enrollment concentrated in private institutions (MINEDUC 2006). Clearly, the reform initiated in the 1980s restructured the education system, decentralized it, and made it dependent on consumer's choices. The administration was given to municipalities as well as private institutions, and consequently, three types of functioning schools were established: municipal schools that are only financed by the State; private schools with subventions, financed by the treasury and the families; and private schools that depend exclusively on the families' investments.

The process of decentralization was firmly established with the promulgation of the *Ley Orgánica Constitucional de Educación* (Organic Constitutional Law of Education) Number 18,962, passed in 1990. This document established the "freedom of teaching," which in Chile meant that private institutions or individuals could participate in education matters without much control by the State. There was also a process of decentralization of the curriculum, while the Ministry of Education had to define a framework of *Objetivos Fundamentales and Contenidos Mínimos Obligatorios* (Fundamental Objectives and Minimum Obligatory Contents, OF-CMO) that had to be met by all schools. However, once the OF-CMO were assumed as the minimum prerequisites by the Ministry, schools had the possibility and freedom of formulating their own study plans and programs. Those that could not had to use the plans designed by the Ministry of Education.

The consequences of transferring education to the municipalities clearly revealed the profound inequity in the distribution of education among the different socioeconomic groups—a salient characteristic of the Chilean educational system. This problem has multiple manifestations; however, it is most patent with regard to the achievements of the students that go to different types of schools. Results from national evaluation tests (SIMCE)[2] reveal these inequalities. The three different school types (administered by municipalities, private with State subvention, and private) are directly related to socioeconomic groups: overall, the largest part of the poor children are enrolled in the municipal schools, the richest in the private schools, and the middle classes in the private schools with state subsidies. Educational achievements show a deep inequity with regard to access to knowledge by boys and girls: the pupils of private, paid-for schools have the best results, while those of municipal schools perform worst. First, this situation shows the profound division of the national educational system, which is determined by the economic means of the students, and second, the poor quality of learning obtained by those who go to the poor schools of the country.

In 1996, with democracy restored, a new process of reform was initiated to intervene in the education system in a global manner, affecting areas like teaching methods, contents of education, organization of institutions of education, education materials and infrastructure, financing, and the improvement of working conditions for teachers. All of this was going to be achieved—in principle—by giving more autonomy to the schools so they could construct programs that were more adequate to the reality of their students and the students' backgrounds. Formally, the educational reform was structured on the basis of four large areas: pedagogical innovation; reform of the curriculum; professional development of the teachers; and an extended school day for the students.

The basic curricular model originates from the Organic Constitutional Law of Education inherited from the dictatorship, and presents the fundamental objectives and minimum obligatory contents (OF-CMO) that the students must fulfill to graduate from basic and secondary school. The OF-CMO have a national character and its application is obligatory in all schools in the country. The basic curricular model is organized around eight areas of learning that encompass the types of knowledge and experiences students have to cultivate to attain the objectives and requisites of graduation: language and communication; mathematics; science; technology; arts; physical education; orientation; religion.

The reform also implemented an extended school day. Until 1996, boys and girls went to school for half a day, during the morning or afternoon. Although in previous years the schedule was being increased gradually—for example, from thirty-seven to forty weeks of classes per year—a significant increase was needed so that students would have more hours of classes to learn more and better. This was applied in basic and secondary schools so there would be more time for implementing changes in curriculum and pedagogy. The extended school day increased the weekly school hours from thirty to thirty-eight in basic education and thirty to forty-two in secondary education.

The main objective of the reform implemented since 1996 was to improve the quality of education. According to data by the Ministry of Education in Chile, by 2000 the enrollment in basic education was 98.8 percent, while in secondary education it was 90 percent. That is why, once the objective of having the children inside the classroom is reached, the aim is to improve the quality of school activities and learning, and that is the most important preoccupation nowadays.

EPILOGUE

2006

"Students call for national strike on May 10th"
"More than a thousand detainees in national students' protest"
"Students take over fiscal schools all over the country"
"Government calls all students to dialogue"
"Impressive offer from Bachelet to students"[3]

These are some of the headlines that were on the front pages of national newspapers for more than a month. Between May and June 2006, secondary school students headed one of the most important protests in memory, and managed to paralyze the functioning of the education system. State schools were occupied by the students, who said that they would not return to class until the Organic Constitutional Law of Education left by the dictatorship was revoked, the duration of the school day was diminished, and there were improvements in the quality of public education.

The conflict that lasted a month cost the Minister of Education his position. The government answered with a series of measures that are being implemented and that only in the next few years will allow for a better quality of education in public schools—at least for now, in Chile this remains an assignment that is pending.

A DAY IN THE LIFE

The alarm clock rings, it's 6:30 AM. I put on my uniform[4] while my mother prepares breakfast. My sister takes her time in the bathroom and my father tells her to hurry up. Once we're all dressed, we sit at the table for breakfast. I like to have bread with avocado and nice warm milk with coffee. My mother puts some sandwiches and fruits in my backpack and gives me a kiss goodbye. It is still dark outside, and cold.

At 7:15 AM, I'm waiting at the bus stop. The bus is always crowded, so I have to stand next to other boys on their way to school and workers that go to their offices. At 7:50, I've stepped off the bus. I have to walk two blocks to school. I meet my friends at the entrance and we talk a while before going inside. The doorman tells us it is already time to go in. It is Monday and a long week stretches out before us. I'm in eighth grade, the last year of basic education.

The bell rings at 8:00. All boys and girls have to line up on the school grounds and listen to the director encouraging us to start the week's work. Afterwards, we go to our classroom with the teacher. First, she takes attendance and writes down the names of those who are late or absent. The first class is math, which I like, but as we have two school hours (of forty-five minutes each) in a row, it is a bit long. The teacher tells us we have a final test next week, which counts for two grades. Every time we finish a unit, they make us take this kind of test, so you have to study. You could fail the trimester if you don't get a good grade. This time, the test is about equations, one of the most difficult subjects, but I'll do alright because I have done the exercises in class and my homework.

At 9:30, the bell rings and we can go outside for a break. I eat one of the sandwiches my mother made me. Luckily, it has avocado. My classmates have their snacks, too, and sometimes we share them. We also play football; we divide the group in two teams and the first one that makes five goals wins the game.

The break lasts ten minutes. We go back to our classroom for language. The teacher has made us read Chilean literature and today we are going to talk about "Gracia and the Stranger." It is a love story with an unhappy ending because her father is against the relationship. I only hope something like that won't happen to me once I have a girlfriend. Some of my classmates already have girlfriends; it also seems that González makes out with Graciela during the breaks, but they have to do it in secret because if the inspector sees them he will report it to their parents. We aren't allowed to kiss and hold hands in school. At the end of the class, the languages teacher tells us there will be a test, too. At the end of the trimester, all teachers plan final tests.

During the fourth hour, we have "understanding of society." We are reviewing the world wars. I like this subject, but you have to learn many names and dates by heart and I will surely forget all of them just before the exam. In any case, we have a good teacher who always helps us learn the subject.

The second break also lasts ten minutes. The girls get together to talk and we resume our football game. I eat the rest of the snack my mother made me. I always save the fruits for the second break. Back in the classroom we have another period of two hours, this time "Understanding of natural surroundings." The teacher tells us of the states of matter which I think is very boring. And it is also a bit difficult because you have to learn some chemical formulae by heart.

It is 12:50 PM and time for lunch. Those who live nearby go home and the rest of us stay over for lunch in the school's casino.[5] The good thing is we have a lot of time to rest and play. Some of my classmates go to the library to study or do research for projects. At 2:50 PM, we have to go back to class. This is the hardest period because at this time we are all very tired. In the next two school hours, they teach us English. The teacher tells us how important it is to learn this language, and that it will help us in the future in the university or to find a good job.

We go outside for the last break of the day. But at this time (4:20 PM), almost no one wants to play so we just talk with each other. We are all tired because the extended school day is so long. The last class is art.

It is 5:15 PM and I go out to wait for the bus that will take me home. Once I get there, it is dark. I sit at the dining room table and complete my homework. Today, I have to do math and understanding of natural surroundings. Sometimes when I feel like it, I go out to the playground to play with my friends in the neighborhood, but at 8:00 I go back because my mother serves supper.

Afterwards I watch the news with my parents for a while; we talk about what is going on in Chile and the rest of the world. I'm in bed before ten. I fall asleep almost at once; tomorrow, there's another long school day waiting for me.

This account of an eighth grader is characteristic of a large part of urban children that attend schools with an extended school day. They have to study diverse subjects that are part of the core curriculum. Long centuries of educational development would have to pass before this could happen. The history of this process is told in this chapter.

TIMELINE

1535   Diego de Almagro discovers Chile.

1541   Pedro de Valdivia takes possession of the Chilean territory in the name of his majesty Carlos V.

1548   Missionaries formally initiate the process of education in Chile.

1550   The first Chilean school is founded in Santiago.

1595   Dominicans found the Santo Domingo School (*Colegio de Santo Domingo*).

1600   From the seventeen century, religious orders start an educational expansion throughout the country.

1758   The Royal University of San Felipe (*Real Universidad de San Felipe*) opens its doors.

1797   San Luis Academy is founded (*Academia de San Luis*).

1810   The first Junta Government takes control of the kingdom of Chile.

1813   The National Institute (*Instituto Nacional*) is founded.

1818   Chile declares independence from the Kingdom of Spain.

1833   The first Chilean political constitution is proclaimed.

1842   The University of Chile (*Universidad de Chile*) is founded.

1860   The Law of Primary Instruction (*Ley de Instrucción Primaria*), which organizes the education system, is proclaimed.

1889   The Pedagogical Institute of Chile (*Instituto Pedagógico de Chile*) is founded.

1900   The Senate is presented with the first drawing of the Law of Obligatory Primary Instruction (*Ley de Instrucción Primaria Obligatoria*).

1920   The definitive project that establishes mandatory primary education is proclaimed.

1925   The Second Political Constitution establishes the separation of church and state.

1936   The "Society of Educational Establishments Construction" is created.

1938   Pedro Aguirre Cerda comes to power and pursues the development of Chilean education.

1947   Technical State University (*Universidad Técnica del Estado*) is founded.

1965   During the government of Eduardo Frei Montalva, education reform is initiated, establishing eight years of primary education and four of secondary education.

1970   Salvador Allende is elected president.
1973   A military coup ousts the government and the worst dictatorship in the history of Chile begins.
1980   The military in power proclaims a new political constitution. A series of educational reforms is implemented, one of them initiates municipal control of schools.
1990   Before leaving the government, the military proclaims the Organic Constitutional Law of Education. After seventeen years of dictatorship, democratically-elected Patricio Aylwin Azocar comes to power.
1996   New educational reform is initiated.
2006   Secondary students across the country protest for more than two months against the Organic Constitutional Law of Education, demanding a better quality public education.
2007   President Michelle Bachelet's government sends a project to congress to modify the Organic Constitutional Law inherited from the military.

NOTES

The author thanks Cristina Labarca for the corrections done on the document and for making it presentable in English.

1. Economic Commission for Latin America and the Caribbean. This is a United Nations research center.

2. System to measure the quality of education. It is applied every year in all schools of the country.

3. Headlines of the online version of national newspapers "La Nación" (http://www.lanacion.cl) and "La Tercera" (http://www.tercera.cl) during May 2006.

4. In Chile, all basic and secondary school students wear the same clothing to attend classes: black shoes, gray pants, white or light blue shirt, tie, and a blue blazer. Girls commonly wear a white shirt and blue jumper, tie, black shoes, and blue socks.

5. The State finances free lunches in some schools, depending on the parents' socioeconomic condition.

BIBLIOGRAPHY

Books

Egaña, M. 2000a. *La educación primaria popular en el siglo XIX en Chile: una práctica de política estatal.* Santiago: LOM.
Egaña, M. 2000b. *La educación primaria popular en el siglo XIX en Chile. Reconstrucción del espacio escolar.* Santiago: PIIE.
Illanes, M. 1991. *Ausente, señorita. El niño chileno, la escuela para pobres y el auxilio. Chile, 1890–1990.* Santiago: JUNAEB.
Labarca, A. 1939. *Historia de la enseñanza en Chile.* Santiago: Universitaria.
Ministerio de Educación de Chile. 2006. *Hacia un sistema escolar descentralizado, sólido y fuerte. El diseño y las capacidades hacen la diferencia.* Santiago: MINEDUC.
Nuñez, I. 1997. *Historia reciente de la educación en Chile.* N.p.
Rojas, L. 1997. *Historia y crisis de la educación en Chile.* Santiago: Cantaclaro.

Books on Chilean History

Eyzaguirre, J. 1973. *Historia de Chile.* vol. 1. Santiago: Zigzag.
Izquierdo, G. 1990. *Historia de Chile.* Santiago: Andrés Bello.
Villalobos, et al. 1989. *Historia de Chile.* Santiago: Universitaria.

Articles

Barnach-Calvo, E. "La nueva educación indígena en Iberoamérica." *Revista Iberoamericana de educación* 13 (1997): 13–33.
Conejeros, J.P. "La influencia cultural francesa en la educación chilena, 1840–80." *Serie de investigación* 17 (1999).
Egaña, M. "Ley de instrucción primaria obligatoria: un debate político." *Revista de educación* 315 (2000c): 14–29.
Larrañaga, O. "Descentralización de la educación en Chile: una evaluación económica." *Revista del centro de estudio públicos* 60 (1995): 243–86.
MINEDUC. "Asistencialidad: pan y luz." *Revista de educación* 315 (2004): 78–82.
Toro, P. "Nuevos recuerdos de las viejas escuelas: notas sobre la historia de la educación escolar en Chile y algunos de sus temas emergentes." *Revista persona y sociedad* 5, no. 16 (2002).

Web Sites

Centro de Investigación para el desarrollo de la educación: http://www.cide.cl/.
Chilean Ministry of Education: http://www.mineduc.cl.
Chilean Ministry of Education electronic review: http://www.mineduc.cl/index.php?id_portal=1&id_seccion=790&id_contenido=3671.
PRELAC: http://www.unesco.cl/revistaprelac/esp/.
Programa Interdisciplinario de Investigaciones en Educación: http://www.piie.cl/.
United Nations Educational, Cultural, and Scientific Organization (UNESCO): http://www.unesco.cl/esp/.

Chapter 6

SCHOOLING IN COLOMBIA[*]

Javier Sáenz Obregón and
Oscar Saldarriaga Vélez

INTRODUCTION

In Colombia, one of the countries born out of the Spanish colonization of
America, there have been three historical periods—the colonial period (sixteenth to eighteenth centuries), the period of formation of the national State
(nineteenth century), and the democratic period (twentieth century)—that correspond to three ways in which schools were related to the different social
classes, ethnicities, and gender. Between the sixteenth and eighteenth centuries,
the system of schooling was part of a colonial and stratified society; in the nineteenth century, it was an instrument for the construction of a republican but
exclusive society; and in the twentieth century, it sought to create an open
democratic society.

SCHOOLING IN THE COLONIAL PERIOD

The "Doctrines for Indians"

In Latin America, schooling was installed after the arrival of the *conquista-
dores* and Spanish missionaries; for the native Indians of the "New World" had
no *alphabetic* writing.

Around 1550, after the initial plundering by the *conquistadores,* colonial
order began to be consolidated through a network of urban centers, which
extracted Indian labor, taxes, and gold. But the discipline of reading and writing would only be introduced to the native population two centuries later by
ordering the distribution of Indians to *encomiendas*,[1] so that a priest could

---

[*]This chapter is based mostly on the results of the research project *Bases para una historia
comparada de la educación en Iberoamérica-BADHICEI*.

teach the Christian doctrine (Jaramillo 1978, 207). All Indians from the time they could speak to the moment they were married were to be assembled every morning and evening to pray aloud and to learn Christian doctrine by memory. Those who did not attend these meetings were punished (López, 2001, 99).

In 1555, new dispositions required that the Indian population be congregated, not only to learn the Christian doctrine, but also to "read our language" (Romero 1988, 13–14). The first catechism for the Colombian territory (1574) used a teaching method that was clearly based on memorization. Archbishop of Santafé de Bogotá[2] took another step in the progressive schooling for native Indians in 1576 when he ordered the "separation of up to twenty of the sons of the chiefs and most important Indians, in order to teach them to read and write and other saintly political and Christian customs" (Zapata de Cárdenas 1576, 38). These Indians were interned, and became inscribed in the usual method of Spanish domination: co-optation of the Indian elite as a means of transmission of colonial power.

Schools for Piety and Schools for First Letters

The use of native languages had dramatically decreased, when, throughout the sixteenth century, the *Indian towns* and the *towns for whites* that had been separated by colonial power were fused in *parishes* where the majority of the population was already racially mixed. From 1687, this new social context made the foundation of "schools for piety" possible in the five cities where the Jesuits already had their own schools (Martínez et al. 1999, 42, 57). Until then, white children and youth had been educated by private tutors in their own homes, by priests, and monks who taught children to read and write Latin in their houses and convents, as well as in some schools supported by private donations.

After the first expulsion of the Jesuits in 1767, these *schools for piety* became the first five "public schools of first letters" (Martínez 1984, 111) that had their own place for education, a pedagogical method, and a proper schoolteacher. Between 1767–1800, the specific role of a schoolteacher appeared, and the wandering scholars who taught reading and writing independently, became gradually normalized by the State and circumscribed to exercise their craft in schools (Martínez 1984, 4).

Between 1785–1809, a series of plans and decrees for the schools of first letters signaled the appearance of a school that was to be "public, free and under government inspection" as well as "open to children of all classes" (Martínez 1984, 69). The State also promoted the establishment of schools in those regions where the local authorities could finance them. Public instruction was now seen as indispensable, not only to form good citizens and good Christians. Despite these lofty purposes, these public schools did not accept those who had "blood of the land" but only white males; and although they were open to both rich and poor, once in school, these groups were strictly separated. In addition to reading and writing, they also taught arithmetic, catechism, and "civility." By the end of Spanish domination (1819) "only a few towns and cities could support schools financially ... Santafé, a city of 30,000, had only one public school of first letters" (Jaramillo 1978, 254).

General Studies

Although formally the function of colonial higher education was the preparation of the different sectors of the intellectual group that would later evangelize the population, in practice, its role was larger. It constituted a corporation with the mission of safeguarding philosophical, religious, and juridical principles. It was open to no more than 200 students, most of them male clergy, required the use of Latin, demanded "purity of blood," and was concentrated in the major cities (Silva 1992, 80).

In the *Nuevo Reino de Granada*,[3] there were no public universities such as those in México and Lima, which followed the model of the Spanish university in Salamanca, but only *Colegios Mayores* governed by the clergy—San Bartolomé directed by the Jesuits and the *Colegio Mayor de Nuestra Señora del Rosario*, under secular clergy (Silva 1992, 31). Studies in these *Colegios* included the three cycles introduced in the low medieval period: the *Studium Generale*, with three years of arts: the *Trivium*—grammar, logic, and rhetoric, and the *Quadrivium*—metaphysics, mathematics, music, and physics. These were followed by four years in one of the schools of jurisprudence, canon law, or theology. Middle and higher education was not differentiated. If a *Colegio Mayor* had a school of first letters, the child of ten to twelve years who entered was considered a university student. Despite successive reforms, this organization was maintained until the end of the nineteen century. Studies in the *Colegios* were conducted in Latin and used scholastic authors and methods: the form of conveying knowledge was syllogistic, through the classical procedures of *lectio, dictatio*, and *disputatio*.[4]

THE NINETEENTH CENTURY

Results of the Century

Although the ideologues of independence (1810) declared the need to forget most of what had been learned with the Spanish, the educational policy of the republican elite throughout the century constituted a reactivation of *enlightened* policy. Its primary aim was the development of a professional and technical elite, and the generalization of the ideals of citizenship and civilization (Safford 1989). This meant confronting the resistances of an illiterate and rural society under the control of Catholic clergy, while at the same time guaranteeing the political control of the capital and the avoidance of social and racial unrest.

Towards the end of the nineteenth century, after a series of educational reforms, the results were mixed: a modern educational system had been organized—gradated in three levels (primary, secondary, and university), funded by the State, and open to all of the population—but under the moral and intellectual control of the Catholic Church, and with a university level fragmented into different faculties. On the other hand, the ideal of peace, order, and progress was in conflict with a bipartisan political system that generated permanent conflict between the Liberal and Conservative parties and transformed social and regional tensions into chronic civil wars.[5] The most devastating civil war of the century that took place between 1898–1902—*La guerra de los mil días*—almost completely destroyed the education infrastructure of the country.

The increase in schooling coverage was also mixed: primary schooling multiplied by five between 1836–97, and girls comprised 45 percent of the schooled population in 1881. However, the literacy rate was low: in 1912, it was 17 percent for the 4,130,000 Colombians older than eight years old. The schooling rate was 30 percent for children between the ages of seven and fourteen. The situation was even worse for secondary education: at the start of the twentieth century, there were no more than 30,000 students in public secondary schools; that is, less than 7 percent of the total primary school population.[6] After presenting an overview of the results of the century, the next sections will analyze in more detail the educational events of the period in Colombia.

The Plan of Studies of 1826

In the midst of the destruction left by the war of independence, the group of intellectuals and liberal clergy close to the leaders of the liberation struggle established the legal and ideological foundations of the system of public instruction between 1821–26 in the *Republic of Gran Colombia*.[7] The system offered "liberation through enlightenment" but it had scant economic and political resources to counter the forces of resistance by the Church and local powers. The universal right to primary instruction was declared for all classes, races, and for both girls and boys, a series of *Political-constitutional catechisms* was distributed, and literacy was established as the condition to exercise the rights of citizenship.

From 1821, the system of *mutual teaching* for primary schools designed by the Englishmen Bell and Lancaster was introduced. The system offered to alphabetize up to one thousand children with only one teacher, by the use of more advanced students as monitors, and through a mechanical system of orders, repetitions, prizes, and punishments. The teaching method was based on repetition, imitation, and correction; on the separation of students in different classes according to their capacity; and on a strict system of order and discipline.

These schools served as the basis for the first normal schools for training of teachers. By 1827, in all of Gran Colombia, there were "52 Lancastrian schools, 434 of the old type, with a total of 20,000 students, in a country with a population of 2 or 3 million" (Bushnell 1966, 129). The educational system also included women, but their education was circumscribed to religious convents and private institutions.

The 1826 study plan ordered the establishment of schools of first letters both in towns for whites as in Indian towns, but these were financed by the local population, so that the system was limited both in terms of funding and by the weight of the traditionalism of local customs.

On the other hand, the possibility of opening educational institutions was dependent on the size of the locality: public schools could be opened in villages and cities of more than one hundred neighbors, secondary schools in the capitals of the different states, and universities in the major cities—Bogotá, Cartagena, and Popayán. In practice, the *Universidad Central de Bogotá*—a fusion of the *colegios* de *San Bartolomé* and that of *del Rosario*—continued to monopolize the granting of university titles. This generated permanent pressure on the part of regional elites to obtain the right to grant university titles, and those who were interested in locally acquiring those academic titles that had become the new symbol of social progress, especially in law, which was the primary avenue to public posts and political advantages needed for business enterprises. During the entire century, very few studied natural sciences or engineering (Safford 1989).

With regard to the Catholic Church in education, the situation was ambivalent. The State took advantage of the local clergy for the promotion of local educational boards and kept religion and Catholic morality as primary school subjects, but also used liberal strategies in order to strengthen the public sphere, such as the expropriation of ecclesiastical buildings to be used for public education, and the deincentivation of the use of Latin in universities. The government also propagated the utilitarian ethic of the Englishman Jeremy Bentham, the sensualist philosophy of the Frenchman Destutt de Tracy, and the political economy of J. B. Say. All this generated a violent intellectual and political battle with the Church that would last up to 1880.

The Ospina Plan, 1842–1847

The next education reform was devised by a group that represented an enlightened and progressive but pro-Church wing of the Conservative Party. The 1842 plan intensified a strategy to centralize university studies by increasing the academic requirements for their creation. It also strengthened the centralized model of university schools and faculties and created a new School of Physical Sciences and Mathematics. Schools, seminaries, and even religious convents were to establish faculties of literature and philosophy in order to guarantee access to professional educational, especially in the "useful sciences."

On the other hand, the State decided to support the Church as an instrument of education, and welcomed the Jesuits back and charged them with the direction of schools and universities. It also banned the teaching of utilitarian and sensualist doctrines which were replaced by Catholic authors. Primary schooling remained unchanged, while schools for adults and for girls were created. By 1844, only 1,397 girls were in schools, while boys numbered 17,964. The *Plan Ospina* designed detailed legal reforms for normal schools, elevating the sophistication of the pedagogical knowledge imparted to teachers vis-à-vis the mechanical routine of the Lancastrian method, but this was only accomplished in one normal school in the capital city and only for a few years.

Freedom of Teaching, 1848–1868

A radical political turn made possible one of the most controversial educational reforms of the country, that of "freedom of teaching," which was part of the liberal reforms sought to put a definitive end to colonial institutions. These reforms included the expulsion, once more, of the Jesuits; separation of church and state; abolition of mandatory financing of the Church by the population; political federalism; economic *laissez faire*; and the abolition of educational monopolies. The 1848 law declared that "teaching, in all of its modalities is free," and this put an end to the university monopoly for granting educational diplomas. In 1850, universities were converted into national schools, and the exercise of any profession or craft, with the exception of pharmacy, was allowed without a university title. This measure meant devolution of power to the regions and blurred the distinction between secondary and university education. As a result of the reform, the number of private schools increased, many of them under the control of religious congregations. Another civil war, in 1860, made matters worse (Zuluaga, Saldarriaga, et al. 2004). This was the price liberals had to pay for amplifying the traditional frontier of the literate society in order to eliminate the cultural monopoly of clergy and lawyers.

Instructional Reform, 1868–1886

After eighteen years of "freedom of teaching," there was another liberal reaction in the opposite direction. In 1870, the first great national and centralized effort to universalize primary, obligatory, free, lay, and popular instruction was launched. The aim was to school all children from the ages of five to fifteen through the creation of a fully funded education system free from politics and religion. The public National University was created, a Pedagogical Mission of twelve German teachers was brought to the country, a normal school was opened in each of the states, and the new teaching method "objective pedagogy" or "the Pestalozzian method" was introduced.

The organizers of this reform declared that public education constituted the "social mission" of the State. But the fragmentation of the radical liberal group in power meant that it was not able to defeat the Catholic conservative opposition. In 1876, this group lost its hegemony in the "schools war" and this signified the end of its project to create an education system free from religion and politics. The war pitted the pro-church and anti-clerical factions of the country over the issue of radical instructional reform, especially regarding whether to teach Catholic religion in schools. Furthermore, the consolidation of schooling among the population was not achieved—more than 65 percent of school-aged children did not attend school.

The Regeneration and the Plan Zerda, 1886–1902

Unlike most Latin American countries, towards the end of the nineteenth century, Colombia witnessed the triumph of a coalition of Spencerian liberals and Catholic traditionalists that promulgated a new centralist, authoritarian, and confessional Constitution in 1886. A treaty was signed with the Vatican that once more put public instruction in the hands of the Catholic Church. At the primary level, Pestalozzian teaching methods were maintained, but all references to religious tolerance and to a lay ethic were eliminated. In secondary schools, a modern system was finally organized, based on the experiences and resources of the different religious orders. The paradox at the end of century in Colombia was that the Catholic Church used neo-scholastic philosophy to make instruction compatible with modern experimental science, but it established a hierarchical and pastoral educational system under the intellectual and moral direction of a Catholic institution, the *Colegio Mayor del Rosario.*

THE TWENTIETH CENTURY

Education for Peace, Morality, and Progress: 1903–1946

In the first half of the twentieth century, the state and the elite viewed schooling as the key to the attainment of the desired moral, political, and economic ends of the country. Following the political violence of the *Thousand Day War* and until the mid-1930s, national governments tried to create a national consensus regarding educational policy, whose primary aim was still seen as that of civilizing the poor population that was considered to be a "degenerate race," as a consequence of both the mix between Indians, Africans, and Europeans and the effects of the "inhospitable" climates of the country. With the arrival to power in 1934 of a sectarian and decidedly secular and progressive liberal government, the tacit agreement between the political parties and between State and Church to keep conflict out of educational issues was broken, and educational policy, schools, teacher-training institutions, and universities were turned into fields of battle over the souls of teachers and students. From 1934 to 1946, under successive liberal governments, educational programs and policies sought to democratize, secularize, and modernize national culture. This often meant an explicit critique to Catholic dogma and the openly racist and anti-Semitic views of conservative leaders and educators.

The Church and the Conservative Party, in turn, mounted a fierce opposition to liberal education reform, attacking it as atheistic, materialistic, communist, and pragmatist.[8] Opposition tactics included the deployment of priests to state schools in order to convince parents to move their children to Catholic private schools, and the excommunication in some regions of those who continued to send their children to state schools.

State policy during the first half of the century and up to the 1960s focused on the increase in coverage of primary education, attended primarily by the poor population, leaving secondary education for the upper classes and some members of the middle classes mostly in the hands of private institutions, generally run by Catholic orders and concentrated in urban areas. The dominance of the private sector in secondary education was such that by 1923 more than two-thirds of students attended private institutions, a proportion that would remain almost unchanged until the end of the 1950s. However, in primary education during the same period, only around 7 percent of students attended private institutions that were run mostly by Catholic orders. Enrollment rates during the first half of the twentieth century reveal great regional and class inequalities. While only some 30 percent of the school-age population attended schools, less than 7 percent went on to secondary institutions (concentrated in five states). While the capital Bogotá and the state of Atlántico had enrollment rates of more than 18 percent, five predominantly rural states had enrollment rates of less then 4 percent and the more peripheral *national territories*, predominantly inhabited by Indian groups and Afro-descendants, were virtually unschooled at the secondary level.[9] The proportion of boys who attended primary schools was relatively higher (53 percent) than that of girls (47 percent), and a similar ratio existed in secondary schools.

The State funded nine different Catholic orders so that they would Christianize and "civilize" Indian groups in the national territories. These orders had total freedom to impart an education that was characterized by its brutality and its attack on Indian cultures as "savage" and "heathen." This situation remained unchanged until the 1970s. Most of the missionaries of these churches were foreign; the dominant group was the Capuchin order organized in Indian regions, mostly by Spanish priests. This order used a series of coercive methods in order to fulfill their mission. They set up so-called "orphanages" in which they interned children from the age of five, separating them by force from their families. In these prison-schools, they forbade children from speaking their mother tongue, took away their traditional clothing, prevented their families from visiting, and in some regions gave money and land to those who married outside their group. In the words of an Arhuaco (*Iku*) leader of the *Sierra Nevada de Santa Marta* who was interned in 1916 in one of these Capuchin "orphanages":

They forbade all our customs and laws ... cut the hair of children and changed their clothes in order to convert them to the life of civilization ... because they wanted to control us in every sense, so that we would not continue to be what we had been in accordance to our needs and interests.... That is why they moved the children far away from their fathers and mothers ... till the Arhuaco children became older and could then leave once they had married ladies form the civilization, so that they would forget to live according to Indian customs. (Torres Márquez 1978, 100–101)

The Uribe Law of 1903

In 1903, the conservative government passed one of the most comprehensive educational reform laws in the history of Colombia, known as the *Uribe* law, named for the Minister of Education of the time. The law introduced a series of concepts, purposes, and practices, most of which would dominate institutional educational reform at all levels—from primary schools to universities—for the next five decades. The reform promoted a practical education geared towards economic progress, the development of individuals that would be of "social utility," rejection of what was seen as the excessive oral and memorization teaching methods, and introduction of teaching practices based on the individual needs and characteristics of students. The law aimed at a far-reaching educational reform for the development of productive individuals that would be hard-working, practical, healthy, and motivated. The ideal image of the individuals to be developed was that of the German and Anglo-Saxon people, considered to be the most "civilized" races. Side by side with this agenda for the modernization and civilization of the country, the law explicitly promoted the moral ends and practices of the Catholic Church and gave a central place to the dogmatic teaching of Catholic religion in study plans (Uribe, 1927).

The educational programs established by the law had different intensity in urban and rural areas: rural schools had only three years of study while urban schools, with a six-year plan, prepared for entrance to secondary schools. The Vatican's opposition to coeducation was respected, and schools were separated along gender lines, a situation that would remain virtually unchanged until the 1960s in primary schools. The education of girls was to be exclusively in the hands of female teachers while women could teach in boys' schools but only up to the age of twelve. The study plan for rural schools centered on religion, reading, writing, and arithmetic, while that of urban schools also included grammar, geography, history, physics, drawing, singing, manual work, gymnastics, and "objective lessons" based on the methods devised by the Swiss pedagogue Johann Heinrich Pestalozzi. These objective lessons that, as we have seen, had been introduced to the country in the nineteenth century, were based on the presentation of different objects in classrooms, mostly drawn from nature (for example, corn or a sheaf of wheat) that children were to observe intently and describe, while the teacher verbally associated the object to more general and abstract ideas in different fields of study. The presentation of a sheaf of wheat could thus lead, through successive associations, to a lesson on morality based on its appearance in a biblical passage.

Secondary education was divided into three modalities: normal schools for the training of teachers, technical schools, and classical schools. Given the shortage of trained teachers, emphasis was placed on the strengthening and creation of normal schools for both girls and boys. The image of the teacher to be formed was that of a teacher-apostle: a teacher obedient to the dogmas and precepts of the Catholic Church and a model of Christian virtues. In addition to the subjects to be taught in primary schools, the study plan included religion and morals to be taught by a priest, and theoretical and practical pedagogy, methodology, and hygiene. The normal schools for boys taught manual work while those for girls taught needlework and clothes-making. In technical institutions, emphasis was placed on translations from English and French, on algebra, trigonometry, logic, and drawing. In classical schools, the following subjects were taught: Spanish, Latin, French, English, arithmetic, accounting, algebra, geometry, geography, elementary cosmography, ancient and modern history, experimental physics, rhetoric, religion, and philosophy.

The Catholic Church's institutional and symbolic domination over education during the first four decades of the twentieth century can be seen in the enormous influence of the order of the Christian Brothers in primary education, secondary education for the elite, and in normal schools for teachers. Together with the institutions of other Catholic orders, they trained most of the teachers of the country in this period at the *Escuela Normal Central de Institutores*—the only national normal school in the country, which they ran until 1935 when it was closed by the liberal government. It was the Christian Brothers' detailed pedagogical system based on *La Conduite*, one of the earliest pedagogical treatises for the modern school written by their French founder St. Jean Baptiste de La Salle in 1680, that dominated the daily life of schools in the country in this period. The system was based on a strict discipline of teachers' constant surveillance of students, the imitation of the moral virtues of the teacher, and on competitive practices between students intensified through a permanent system of punishments and rewards.[10]

The New School Reforms: 1930–1946

Mostly through the appropriation of concepts and practices of the international *New School* or *Active School* movement from 1930 to 1946 by the State, the country underwent one of the most intense periods of educational and pedagogical reform of its history. But given the weak controls of the central State over the educational system, partial reforms had been underway since the turn of the century in private institutions and in some regions—mostly through the introduction of Ovide Decroly's global method for teaching of reading and his system of *Interest Centers*, and some of the practices of the experimental pedagogy of Edouard Claparéde and Ernest Meumann.

The *Gimnasio Moderno,* a private lay school for the elite founded in 1914, became the first educational institution to implement an integral pedagogical system founded on the precepts of the *New School* movement. Under Agustín Nieto Caballero's leadership—who introduced the school's pedagogical system to public education in the 1930s—the school designed disciplinary practices based on the "trust in students" and teaching methods for the development of democratic citizens through a novel combination of a study plan structure based on Decroly's *Interest Centers*, and an emphasis on social issues, practices of cooperation among students, and social goals, inspired by John Dewey's pedagogical ideas.

In the early 1920s, medical examination practices and the *New School* movement teaching methods were introduced to some private and public schools for "abnormal" and "delinquent" children. These schools became institutions for the detection and correction of physical and psychological abnormalities and of the "degeneration" of students, through a set of practices of observation, measurement, physical and mental testing, and classification of students. These institutions were also pioneers in a movement to reduce the class time of overcharged school programs considered to lead to intellectual fatigue, and oppose the harsh disciplinary systems prevalent in schools, which were considered contrary to the healthy development of character.

Another case of pedagogical experimentation in the 1920s took place in the state of Boyacá under Rafael Bernal Jiménez's leadership. He was the director of Boyacá's public education and implemented a policy for the creation of *Defensive Schools*: through school restaurants, intensification of hygienic practices in schools, teaching methods reform, and the involvement of teachers in students' family lives, sought to "defend" the poor population against its progressive "moral and physical degeneration." The significance of the Boyacá experiment was that it was the first example of state schools to break their isolation from the local community and of a state institution intervening directly in family life, that had been viewed, until then, as the exclusive sphere of the Catholic Church.

The profound educational reforms between 1930 and 1946 under liberal governments were the result of a particular combination of factors. First, in a decisive political movement that freed the educational system from the institutional and symbolic control of the Church (with the exception of their work in Indian communities), Catholic orders lost their educational privileges in the state system. The Constitutional Reform of 1936 introduced the principle of freedom of teaching and conscience, which prohibited barring children from schools for religious, racial, or class reasons. Second, appropriation by the State of new concepts on the value and worth of the culture of the poor population (including native Indian groups) and its open critique to elitist and racist images of the poor as a degenerate population. Third, introduction of liberal and progressive social and political goals for the development of democratic citizens and the democratization of social relations that replaced the previous hegemony of Catholic moral purposes centered on obedience and individual virtue. Fourth, modernization of practices in administration and knowledge in educational institutions through the appropriation of *New School* movement concepts and practices.

The most important legal and institutional reforms took place between 1934–38 under Alfonso López Pumarejo's government. The study plans for primary and secondary schools were reformed in 1935 (Ministerio de Educación Nacional 1935). The reform of primary education followed *Gimnasio Moderno* practices and established one program for all schools, divided into a first section of four years based on the *Interest Centers* system and the last two years of a *Complementary School* centered on practical activities relevant to the community, such as carpentry, mechanics, agriculture, and handicrafts. The program emphasized social and political problems and was organized in *Interest Centers* with the following themes for each year: life at home and school, life in the community, the municipality and the local state, and the Nation. These organizing themes integrated the different subjects, while emphasizing games, physical education, and field trips. In terms of the teaching method, Pestalozzian *objective lessons* were replaced by the direct observation of natural and social phenomena.

The impetus of pedagogical reform was not as evident in the new secondary school program which continued to be organized on the basis of isolated subjects. The main changes were a reduction of hours for the study of religion, an increase in time dedicated to the social sciences, and in the status of Latin, which became optional. More profound changes were made in teacher-training institutions, such as their pedagogical reorientation in the light of the *New School* practices, the liberalization of their disciplinary regimes, their secularization, and their articulation to local community life, especially in rural areas. The ideal of the Catholic teacher-apostle was replaced by that of a healthy, modern, and progressive individual with strong training in social sciences that would enable her to contribute to the resolution of the social problems of the poor population. Important changes also took place in higher education. First, the creation in 1936 of the *Escuela Normal Superior* for training secondary school teachers, directors of normal schools, and school inspectors. The *Escuela Normal Superior* hired republican Spanish exiles as well as German intellectuals fleeing form Nazism, who together with some of the foremost national intellectuals, introduced some of the latest advances in western knowledge in the fields of ethnology, Marxist thought, Deweyan pedagogy, and psychoanalysis. Second, academic freedom was established for universities that were opened to women for the first time.

Conservative Counter-reform and Internationalization of Education: 1946–1957

With the arrival of the Conservative Party's power in 1946, a period of counter-reform began and the initiation of a new bloody period of political violence between the two main political parties. Public education was refounded on an authoritarian pedagogy based on Catholic dogma that sought to return the nation to its "traditional and Catholic" roots through the formation of a ruling minority that would expel the "corrupting materialism" of liberal reforms. The main practical effects of this counter-reform were the elimination of *New School* methods; intensification of teaching national history based on the formation of virtues of obedience and respect for the authoritarian tradition of the country; the return to strict disciplinary practices of surveillance and control based on distrust towards students; reintroduction of the requirement that teachers be good Catholics; and intensification of teaching Catholic religion, viewed by the government as the main concern of the State.

With this militant return to the past that included the massive firing of liberal teachers, in this period there was another major transformation that pointed to the future: the institutionalization of *planning* in the State that was accompanied by an intense process of *internationalization* of educational policy that, to the present day, would increasingly remove educational decisions from the national sphere. The country gradually adopted UNESCO's education recommendations as well as the recommendations of the International Bank for Reconstruction and Development (which would become the World Bank). These multilateral organizations directed state policy towards the quantitative dimension of education—such as the levels of attendance, dropout, and repetition—that would eventually dominate State policy, overriding the pedagogical and political concerns that had characterized Colombian education in the previous decades. This process was accelerated between 1953 and 1957 under General Rojas Pinilla's government. Pinilla had seized power with the support of the two traditional parties in hopes that he would put an end to partisan violence. Under Pinilla, the process of re-Catholization of public education continued, and he sought the support of foreign missions in the design of educational policy. The main recommendations of these missions that would define State policy in the following decades focused on the relationships between education and economic development, and included proposals for the universalization of primary and secondary education and strengthening of technical and professional education.

Planning, Education Technology, and the Pedagogical Movement

Primary and secondary educational policy since the 1960s can be characterized in very general terms in two major periods. Until the early 1990s, there was a movement towards strengthening the logic of planning and directing control of study plans and teaching practices by the national State. This was followed by a period in which local governments, teachers, and educational institutions gained substantial levels of pedagogical autonomy, while the central State, especially in the past eight years, sought to regulate pedagogical practices through indirect means. Also, since the 1970s, child-centered teaching methods once more began to dominate State educational policy, shifting attention from the knowledge and authority of the teacher to the learning process of the child, through the re-introduction of methods akin to those of the *New School* movement, especially those derived from constructivist theories of knowledge. Between 1968–84, a series of reforms took place that sought to directly control teaching and learning practices in schools.[11] In 1968, a German *Pedagogical Mission* was brought to the country in order to assist in the implementation of education reform at the primary level. The reform included the design and use of new teaching guides and education materials, as well as an intensive teacher-training program for their use. The idea of the reform was that specific directions for classroom practice were the perfect antidote to a teaching body viewed as ineffectual and badly prepared. The teachers' guides introduced a *teaching planning* methodology with certain general and specific teaching objectives, defined the education resources to be used as well as the activities to be undertaken by teachers and students, and promoted practices of permanent evaluation. The ends of education were conceived for the first time in the country in terms of the changes in the students' conduct, such as the development of skills and specific knowledge.

This move towards the technification in education was intensified through the *Program for the Improvement of the Quality of Education* initiated in 1975, which had as one of its central purposes that it would be at the forefront of the State's vision of education policy until the present, and in which economic and administrative concerns would be paramount: "to obtain optimum returns, both qualitative and quantitative in the operation of the whole system, rationalizing resources and reducing costs" (República de Colombia, Ministerio de Educación Nacional 1975). In the context of this program, *instructional technology* was introduced to schools through a process of "curricular renovation," which was organized around short- and long-term learning objectives defined in terms of observable conduct and detailed methodological orientations for the teacher. These reforms were implemented in various regions of the country and were adamantly opposed by the teachers' union and by a significant number of teachers, who viewed them as a behaviorist strategy that drastically reduced their autonomy and initiative and that sought to create a "teacher-proof" curriculum. In 1984, when the central government decided to apply the reform in the entire country, the resistance by teachers and academics was formalized in the *Pedagogical Movement*—a movement that promoted the autonomous pedagogical experimentation of groups of teachers, sought to convert the teacher into an intellectual of pedagogical knowledge, and emphasized the political and cultural dimension of school practices.[12] The effectiveness of the political and intellectual resistance of the movement led to the withdrawal of the State's reform. The *Pedagogical Movement* was one of the most important cultural movements in the history of the country: it sought to strengthen the role of teachers as autonomous intellectuals, emphasized pedagogical pluralism, and resisted State efforts to homogenize teaching practices. As the most significant institutional force behind the movement, the national teachers' union emerged as one of the main political actors in the debate over educational policy in opposition to State policy, which continued to be highly influenced by multilateral agencies, such as the World Bank and the Inter-American Development Bank.

The New Constitution of 1991 and Education Reforms

The new Constitution of 1991 was the culmination of a process of peace and conciliation between the State and several guerrilla groups. The Constitution emphasized citizens' rights, including those of minority ethnic groups. It established education as a basic right of the individual, compulsory schooling for nine years, the right to free development of the individual, and freedom of teaching and research. It also decentralized educational provision and granted control to local governments.

The General Education Law of 1993, based on the new constitutional principles, was the result of a negotiation process between the State and the teachers' union. It had two major impacts on schooling at the primary and secondary levels: it granted a significant degree of autonomy to schools to organize their practices through *Institutional Educational Projects*, and emphasized the democratic means and ends of schooling by establishing school administrations with the participation of teachers, pupils, and the local community. In the last six years, the central State has sought to regain some of the pedagogical control over schools and teachers that it relinquished in the law through indirect strategies, such as the establishment of national standards, permanent evaluation of students' academic results, strengthening the managerial role of school principals, and stricter norms for entrance to the teaching profession and for promotion in the teaching hierarchy. One of the major changes in the teaching profession is that it was opened to undergraduates of any discipline, where in the past it had been restricted to those who were trained in teacher-training institutions and programs. In all these measures, emphasis has been placed on a series of student "competences" that emphasized the application, rather than the accumulation, of knowledge in the following fields: language, mathematics, social and natural sciences, and civics. Similar reforms have been undertaken in higher education through the introduction of national graduation examinations for most disciplines and professions, and the creation of a system of financial incentives for university professors that is based on academic productivity.

Indian and Rural Education

The trajectory of Indian and rural education since the 1970s has had its own specificity. Rural educational reform has been centered on the *Escuela Nueva* program, designed by Colombian pedagogues and inspired by UNESCO's education policies. The program, directed to primary schools, was introduced in 1973 and is being implemented in most rural schools and some urban ones.

It is based on a methodology of student-centered learning and makes it possible for one teacher to oversee the activities of groups of different levels. It is founded on active pedagogy and seeks to develop attitudes of participation and democracy among students, establish close relations with the local community, and adapt study plans to the local culture. It views the teacher as a learning "facilitator" and community leader.[13]

Until the end of the 1960s, public education in Indian communities was still in the hands of Catholic orders. As a result of the struggles of these communities for political and cultural autonomy, some of them began to implement bilingual-intercultural programs of their own, based on their own worldview and practices. Their political pressure led to the State's issuance of a decree in 1978 that recognized their cultural specificity for the first time. This recognition led to the hiring and training of Indian teachers by the State, which granted these groups some degree of autonomy in the development of their own educational programs. This process was strengthened by the new 1991 Constitution that recognized Colombia is a multiethnic and multicultural nation.

THE PRESENT: CRISIS OF MODERNITY AND LIMITS OF MODERNIZATION

The central contemporary debate in national schooling, and one which will mark future developments, is that around the crisis of modernity and its limits. It is a debate over whether the development of common values, practices, and institutional arrangements of modernity needs to be intensified in schools, or whether schools have to become more sensitive to new discourses and practices that are critical of modernity, such as those which question the modern concept of the truth, morality and the individual, and the practices of the emerging urban youth cultures that are contrary and in open opposition to the authority of the teacher and the hegemony of rational and abstract "truths." It is also a debate over the ways schools are to be governed, which confronts the economic emphasis on efficiency, central regulations, and the economic returns of schooling, with more cultural visions that emphasize subjective and cultural differences and the pedagogical and cultural autonomy of teachers and students. In political terms, this debate can be represented by the conflict between national education policies and those of the capital city of Bogotá that, in some aspects, can be viewed as a continuation of the *Pedagogical Movement.*

While the educational policy of the national government is focused on increased coverage at all levels of the system, there is widespread criticism that this increase in coverage sacrifices the quality of education. On one hand, it has been achieved without an increase in funding, which has meant that teacher-pupil ratios in primary and secondary education are around one teacher for every forty children in urban areas. On the other hand, the government does not have a clear vision regarding the nature of qualitative problems in education, such as the need for on-the-job training for teachers, the significance in

education that Colombia is a multicultural and multiethnic society, the importance of opening schools to their social milieu, and the need for schools to
rethink their formative—and not simply instructive—role that, to our minds,
should include courses in schools that are not viewed as contributing to economic growth, such as art and literature, life skills, the ability to "read" the
messages in mass media, and the relationship between everyday life and politics.
Furthermore, given the close relationship—as we have seen—between religion
and violence in the country, public education needs to become more radically
secular. Against the tenets of religious freedom in the 1991 Constitution, it is
not rare for public schools to enshrine Catholic images and to pay Catholic
priests as teachers with public funds, who do not only teach "ethics" but who
also act as school priests.

It can be said that in the world stage, Colombia's pedagogical culture is quite
sophisticated: the country introduced the pedagogical system of the *New School
Movement* forty years before France; it prohibited physical punishments in
schools nearly fifty years before the United Kingdom; contrary to many other
countries, there are presently more women than men in higher education; and
the *Pedagogical Movement* is considered in Latin America as a political and
cultural experience from which much can be learned. Nevertheless, there are
great challenges for schools: the situation of widespread violence and corruption fueled by drug trafficking and political violence; the still weak recognition
in schools of popular cultures and cultural, ethnic, and gender diversity; and
the "pending lessons" of modernity: secularization, equity, and democracy as a
way of life.

A DAY IN THE LIFE[14]

In 1928 in Pasto, a midsize city in the southern province of Nariño in
Colombia, Aureliano a fourteen-year-old boy from a lower middle class family
that has made great efforts to put him through primary school begins his first
day in the *Escuela Normal de Varones de Pasto*—a lay, boarding institution for
the preparation of male teachers. With the rest of the new boys, he wakes up at
the sound of the bell at 4 AM. The ice-cold water of the showers does not dispel
his nervousness as he is faced with the enormous responsibility of being the first
in his family to have entered secondary education, and with the fear produced
by the solemn warnings of the head teacher that the school expects newcomers
to maintain the strict disciplinary rules of the institution, to behave as virtuous
Catholics, and to restrain from "idle play" and concentrate on their studies.

One hour later, he is reprimanded by a senior monitor who inspects the
group for his untidy uniform and, from 5:00–6:00 AM, he attends mass with
the whole school. From 6:00–7:00 AM, his group of thirty pupils do gymnastics
under the direction of a former military officer who emphasizes their importance in order to strengthen pupils' character. After a frugal breakfast, he
attends class on religion and scriptures given by a priest, who underlines that

the most important feature of a teacher is his obedience to the Catholic Church. With a half-hour break at 10:00 AM, the rest of the morning is spent in classes of reading and writing, grammar, and arithmetic, in which he dutifully copies the exercises presented by the teacher on the blackboard. At noon, he has lunch and writes a letter to his parents whom he is beginning to miss. The afternoon, until 5:30, with a short break at 4:00 PM, is occupied with classes of theoretical pedagogy, geography of Colombia, and drawing. Of these, which require listening attentively to the teachers' words, while remaining in total silence unless asked a question, he finds the pedagogy class to be the more interesting: the teacher has taught them about the Catholic moral foundation of education and the importance of "objective" lessons based on the methodological precepts of the Swiss pedagogue, Johann Heinrich Pestalozzi.

After classes, he goes for prayers at the school's church, followed by dinner and supervised individual study from 7:30–9:00 PM, after which he goes to bed exhausted and looking forward to the only leave of the week on Sunday afternoon, when he plans to explore the city of Pasto with some of his fellow pupils. While lying in bed, he wonders whether his academic homework for the next day's classes is correct: whether he has adequately memorized the grammar and arithmetic exercises, whether he has correctly understood the cardinal virtues of a Catholic, whether he has correctly copied the map of the province of Nariño, and whether he can improve his physical stamina in order to avoid the stern looks of the gymnastics teacher.

There were classes from Monday to Saturday based on this timetable, except for Thursdays when there was a group walk for some two hours. On Sunday morning, there was mass and individual supervised study, and after lunch they were allowed to leave the institution.

TIMELINE

1555	Dispositions for the teaching of Christian doctrine and reading and writing to the Indian population.
1687	Foundation of *Schools for Piety*.
1767	Transformation of *Schools for Piety* into public schools of *first letters*.
1767–1800	Appearance of the school teacher.
1774	University reform *Plan de Estudios de Moreno y Escandón*: rejection of syllogistic method and introduction of "useful science."
1819	Independence from Spain.
1819–41	Creation of a national system of *Public Instruction*. Distribution by the State of Jeremy Bentham's utilitarian ethic, Destutt de Tracy's sensualist philosophy, and J.B. Say's political economy.
1821	Introduction of Bell and Lancaster's *mutual system* of pedagogy.
1826	Establishment of *schools for first letters* both in *towns for whites* and *Indian towns*.
1842–46	*Ospina Plan*: university studies are centralized and the School of Physical Sciences and Mathematics created. Teaching utilitarian and sensualist doctrines is banned.

1848–68   *Freedom of teaching reform*: descentralization and end of universities' monopoly for granting education diplomas.

1868–86   *Instructional reform*: the National University of Colombia is founded; German Pedagogical Mission; introduction of Pestalozzian method.

1876   *Schools War* over the role of the Catholic Church in education.

1886   Promulgation of a centralist, authoritarian, and confessional Constitution.

1898–1902 *Thousand Days War* between the Liberals and the Conservatives; destruction of education infrastructure.

1900–30   Partial institutional and regional reforms based on *New School* methods; introduction of Decroly's methods and emphasis on the concept of the poor population as a "degenerate" race.

1903   *Uribe* Law: emphasis on practical education and the "regeneration" of the national race, different programs for rural and urban schools, difusion of the Pestalozzian teaching method.

1903–28   Teacher-training dominated by Catholic orders, especially the *Christian Brothers*.

1934–46   Liberal reforms: democratization, secularization, and modernization of schooling accompanied by Conservative opposition; introduction of *New School* methods and coeducation to all levels of the educational system; introduction of John Dewey's pedagogy and defense of the cultural values of the Colombian culture.

1946–57   Conservative counter-reform: re-Catholization of education, adoption of reforms promulgated by multilateral agencies.

1968   German Pedagogical Mission: introduction of teaching planning.

1973   Introduction of the *Escuela Nueva* program for primary rural education.

1975   *Program for the improvement of the quality of education*: introduction of instructional technology and emphasis on the efficiency of the educational system.

1978   Introduction of bilingual-intercultural education with the participation of Indian communities; end of Catholic control over education in Indian communities.

1984   *Pedagogical Movement* is formalized.

1991   New Constitution: descentralization, education is made a fundamental right; recognition that Colombia is a multiethnic and multicultural nation.

1993   General Education Law: pedagogical autonomy for schools and school administration.

2000–2006 Re-regulation of schools: educational standards, evaluation of students' competences, and greater control over teachers.

NOTES

1. The *encomienda* was an institution that assigned a Spanish colonial a group of Indians so that he would profit from their work and taxes.

2. *Santa Fé de Bogotá* became the capital city of the Republic of Colombia.

3. The *Nuevo Reino de Granada* included the present republics of Colombia and Panama and parts of Venezuela and Brazil.

4. That is, reading, dictation, and public and competitive argumentation.

5. Palacios, 1995. Nine national civil wars (1816–19, 1839–41, 1851, 1854, 1859–62, 1876–77, 1885–86, 1895, 1898–1902), more than forty local uprisings, and two border wars took place in the nineteenth century in Colombia.

6. All satistics are from Helg, 1984.

7. *La República de la Gran Colombia*, which existed until 1830, included the present republics of Colombia, Venezuela and Ecuador.

8. The attack on Pragmatism was related to the influence of John Dewey's education ideas on the Liberal governments of this period.

9. For a careful statistical analysis of this period see Helg.

10. See Hermanos de las Escuelas Cristianas, *Guía de las Escuelas Cristianas* (Bogotá: Libreria Stella, 1903).

11. The main source for the analysis of this period is Alberto Boom Martínez, Carlos E. Noguera, and Joge O. Castro, *Currículo y modernización: Cuatro décadas de educación en Colombia* (Bogotá: Foro Nacional por Colombia, Tercer Milenio, 1994).

12. For an in-depth analysis of the *Pedagogical Movement*, see Suárez, 2002.

13. For a description of the *Escuela Nueva* program, see V. Colbert, C. Chiappe, and J. Arboleda, "The New School Program: Moral and Better Primary Education for Children in Rural Areas in Colombia," in *Effective Schools in Developing Countries*, ed. Henry Levin et al. N.p., n.d.

14. Based on Buendía Jorge, *La escuela normal de varones de Pasto* (Pasto: Imprenta Departamental, 1969; República de Colombia, 1893); "Reglamento para las escuelas normales," *El monitor. Revista de instrucción pública del departamento* 3, Nos. 136–37 (1969).

BIBLIOGRAPHY

Books

Applebaum, N.P. 2003. *Muddied Waters: Race, Region and Local History in Colombia; 1846–1948*. Durham: Duke University Press.

Benoit, A. 1974. *Changing the Educational System: A Colombian Case-study*. Munchen.

Bushnell, D. 1969. "Education in Colombia." In *History of Latin American Civilization* 2: 26–63. Edited by Lewis Hanke. London.

Bushnell, David. 1966. *El régimen de Santander en la Gran Colombia*. Bogotá: Tercer Mundo, Universidad Nacional.

Dewey, J. 1897. "My Pedagogical Creed." In *The Philosophy of John Dewey*. Edited by J.J. McDermontt, 442–54. Chicago: University of Chicago Press.

Dewey, J. 1916. *Democracy and Education; An Introduction to the Philosophy of Education*. New York: The Free Press, 1997.

Dueñas, G. 1995. *Gender, Race and Class: Illegitimacy and Family Life in Santa Fe*. Nuevo Reino de Granada, University of Texas.

Gale, L. 1969. *Education and Development in Latin America with Special Reference to Colombia and Some Comparison with Guayane, South America*. London: Routledge and Kegan Paul.

Hanson, M. 1986. *Educational Reform and Administrative Development: The Cases of Colombia and Venezuela*. Hoover Institutional Press.

Helg, A. 2004. *Liberty and Equality in Caribbean Colombia 1770–1833*. The University of North Carolina Press.

Helg, Aline. 1984. *Civiliser le peuple et former les élites; L'education en Colombie 1918–57.* Paris: L'Harmattan.

Jaramillo Uribe, Jaime. 1980. "El proceso de la educación del virreinato a la época contemporánea." In *Manual de historia de Colombia* 3: 247–339. Bogotá: Colcultura.

López Rodríguez, Mercedes. 2001. *Tiempos para rezar y tiempos para trabajar: La cristianización de las comunidades muiscas coloniales durante el siglo XVI (1550–1600).* Bogotá: ICANH.

Martínez Boom, Alberto, Carlos E. Noguera, and Joge O. Castro. 1994. *Currículo y modernización. Cuatro décadas de educación en Colombia.* Bogotá: Foro Nacional por Colombia, Tercer Milenio.

Martínez Boom, Alberto and Renán Silva. 1984. *Dos estudios sobre educación en la colonia.* Bogotá: UPN-CIUP.

McFarlane, A. 1993. *Colombia before Independence: Economy, Society and Politics under Bourbon Rule.* Cambridge: Cambridge University Press.

Ministerio de Educación Nacional. 1935. *Resolución 179 de 1935* and *El texto de los programas de la primera y segunda enseñanza.*

Pestalozzi, J.H. 1801. "How Gertrude Teaches Her Children." In *How Gertrude Teaches Her Children. An attempt to Help Mothers to Teach Their Own Children and an Account of the Method.* Edited by E. Cooke, 1–197. London: Swan Sonnenschein, 1907.

Quiceno Humberto, Javier Sáenz Obregón, and Luis A. Vahos. 2004. "La instrucción y la educación pública en Colombia: 1903–97." In *Modernización de los sistemas educativos Iberoamericanos siglo xx.* Edited by Olga Lucía Zuluaga and Gabriela Ossenbach, 105–70. Bogotá: Colciencias, Universidad de Antioquia, Universidad de los Andes, Universidad Pedagógica, Grupo Historia de la Práctica Pedagógica, Editorial Magisterio.

Rappaport, J. 2005. *Intercultural Utopias: Cultural Experimentation and Ethnic Dialogue in Colombia.* Durham: Duke University Press, 2005.

Rausch, Jane M. 1993. *La reforma escolar durante el federalismo. La reforma escolar de 1870.* Bogotá: Universidad Pedagógica Nacional/Instituto Caro y Cuervo.

República de Colombia, Ministerio de Educación Nacional, 1975. *Programa de mejoramiento cualitativo de la educación,* 1975.

Sáenz Obregón, Javier. 2005. "The Appropriation of Dewey's Pedagogy in Colombia as a Cultural Event." In *Inventing the Modern Self and John Dewey: Modernities and the Traveling of Pragmatism in Education.* Edited by Thomas, 231–54. Popkewitz. London: Palgrave.

Sáenz Obregón Javier, Oscar Saldarriaga, and Armando Ospina. 1997. *Mirar la infancia; Pedagogía, moral y modernidad en Colombia 1903–46.* Vols. 1, 2. Medellín: Ediciones de la Universidad de Antioquia, Ediciones Uniandes y Ediciones Foro Nacional por Colombia, Medellín

Safford, Frank. 1969. *The Ideal of the Practical; Colombia's Struggle to Form a Technical Elite.* Austin and London: University of Texas Press.

Safford, Frank and Marco Palacios. 2000. *Colombia: Fragmented Land, Divided Society.* New York: Oxford University Press.

Sarmiento, Alfredo. 2001. "Equity and Education in Colombia." In *Unequal Schools, Unequal Chances; The Challenges to Equal Opportunity in the Americas.* Edited by Fernando Reimers, 203–44. Boston: Harvard University.

Silva, Renán. 1992. *Universidad y sociedad en el nuevo reino de Granada*. Bogotá, Banco de la República.

Silva, Renán. 1996. "La vida cotidiana universitaria en el nuevo reino de Granada." In *Historia de la vida cotidiana en Colombia*. Edited by Beatriz Castro Carvajal, 391–420. Bogotá: Editorial Norma.

Silva, Renán. 2002. *Los ilustrados de Nueva Granada 1760–1808; Genealogía de una comunidad de interpretación*. Medellín: EAFIT

Suárez, Hernán, ed. 2002. *Veinte años del movimiento pedagógico 1982–2002; Entre mitos y realidades*. Bogotá: Cooperativa Editorial Magisterio, Corporación Tercer Milenio.

Torres Márquez, Vicencio. 1978. *Los indígenas Arhuacos y "la vida de la civilización."* Bogotá: Liberría y Editorial América Latina.

Uribe, Antonio José, 1927. *Instrucción pública, disposiciones vigentes, exposición de motivos*. Bogotá: Imprenta Nacional. (The study plans were established in 1904, República de Colombia. Ministerio de Instrucción Pública. 1904. *Decreto 491 de 1904*.)

Vives, J.L. 1913. *On Education*. Translation of "De tradendis disiplinis," 1531b. Introduction by F. Watson. Cambridge: University Press.

Young, John Lane. 1994. *La reforma universitaria de la Nueva Granada (1820–50)*. Bogotá: Universidad Pedagógica Nacional/Instituto Caro y Cuervo.

Zapata de Cárdenas, Luis. 1576. *Primer catecismo en Santafé de Bogotá. Manual de pastoral diocesana del siglo XVI*. Presentación y trancripción de Mons. Fray Alberto Lee López. Bogotá: CELAM, 1988.

Zuluaga, Olga Lucía, Oscar Saldarriaga, Diego Osorio, Alberto Echeverri, and Vladimir Zapata. 2004. "La instrucción pública en Colombia, 1809–1902: surgimiento y desarrollo del sistema educativo." In *Génesis y desarrollo de los Sistemas Educativos Iberoamericanos Siglo XIX*. Compiled by Olga Lucía Zuluaga and Gabriela Ossenbach, 203–87. Bogotá: U. del Valle/U. de los Andes/U. Pedagógica Nacional/U. de Antioquia/Colciencias.

Web Sites

Minsterio de Educación Nacional. República de Colombia. http://www.mineducacion.gov.co.

Universidad pedagógica nacional. http://atra.pedagogica.edu.co.

Chapter 7

SCHOOLING IN COSTA RICA

Alejandrina Mata Segreda

INTRODUCTION

Costa Rica is located in the Central American region with a surface area of 51,100 square kilometers. In the twentieth century, Costa Rica went from an agricultural economy base or economic model to one whose major income came from services, especially tourism. A fundamental characteristic which differentiates it from other Latin American countries is the absence of an army and the permanent declaration of peace and neutrality. This country has a rich biodiversity, and both characteristics, its peace and exuberant natural beauty, are the main attraction for international tourism.

During the first half of the twentieth century, Costa Rican society was mainly comprised of a middle class with a low school attendance (but attendance was continually rising). Nevertheless, the country suffered a severe depression between the 1960s and 1980s, which produced unequal development and a decrease of the middle class. Consequently, there was a growth in the gap between the rich and poor. The efforts made by the Costa Rican state resulted in an improvement of the social situation during the last years.

- Free and compulsory preschool education takes two years. The starting age is four years and six months, and five years and six months, respectively. More than 90 percent of children in the population attend at this level of education.
- Free and compulsory general education takes nine years: the first six in elementary school, and three in middle school. The attendance rate in elementary is 100 percent and in middle school is 70 percent.
- High school education, which is free but not compulsory, consists of two years in the academic module and three years in the technical module. Coverage decreases to 60 percent of the population, and only one-third of those students that enter the education system are able to graduate with the high school degree.

- Other education modalites are offered to adult students or those with specific circumstances, like adolescent mothers and young people who dropped out of school—coverage is 6 percent of the population.
- For students with special education needs, the national policy has been to include them in regular education. Every day, there are less of these students that remain in special schools.
- There are other education modalites that seek to develop students with diverse talents such as scientific, humanities, artistic, ecological, and bilingual schools. The latest module is technology—schools that depend on computer and scientific laboratories, and other similar resources as a methodological strategy to stimulate student learning.
- The subjects that address the basic national curriculum for elementary school are mathematics, social studies, science, and English. Furthermore, other subjects are included, such as arts, music, physical education, home education, IT or information technologies, industrial arts, and religion. However, coverage of these latter subjects is not complete.
- The subjects that structure basic secondary education are mathematics, social studies, civics, science, English, and French (provided until the ninth year and optional in high school education). Also, students are offered arts, music, physical education, home education, industrial arts, agronomy, IT or information technologies, religion, and technology.
- Technical education prepares students for work in agriculture, in industries, and in the service sector. About forty different types of specialties exist, mostly in the service industry since it is the one area that has given the best promise in the last years, and that has created a lot of specialties related to tourism. With this type of diploma, students can immediately join the working force.
- It is important to point out the support that students receive from counseling services; the emphasis is educational, psychosocial, and vocational intervention. In schools whose students come from families at risk, interdisciplinary teams are formed to provide attention from counselors, psychologists, and social workers.
- Informatics education is an important component in the education system. It seeks to enforce cognitive and social capacities in students, and to prepare the country to face scientific and technological challenges. This program is included in preschool, elementary, and middle school.[1]

Education in Costa Rica before the Arrival of the First Spaniards

According to anthropological studies regarding the Americas, between the years 300 BC–1500 AD, Costa Rica formed part of the Intermediate Archeological Area, which comprised the modern-day southern countries of Central America (Nicaragua, Costa Rica, and Panama), as well as the northern part of South America (Colombia and Ecuador). This region, which has also been called Mesoamerica, was characterized by a transformation in the social organization, which evolved from a tribal system to one of political leadership. This change has been highlighted as a milestone that had a great impact on the history of Mesoamerica's indigenous population, and by extension, on the indigenous population that lived in what we know today as Costa Rica. This transition took place between 300 BC–800 AD, and it derives its importance from the fact that the social structure evolved from one that was based on family relationships (tribes) to an organization signaled by the presence of a community leader (*cacique*), intermediary leaders, specialized artisans, familial lineages, and hereditary power. This new structure represented a more complex and sophisticated organization that paralleled its production methods. Beginning in 800 AD until the arrival of the Spaniards in the sixteenth century, there was an increase in the size and complexity of the villages where three different things were happening: the production of sumptuous goods, an important development in goldsmith work, and the establishment of regional interchanges which led to inevitable conflicts between caciques and their villages over territory and resources.[2]

The new forms of social organization had an effect on the type of education that was practiced. In Costa Rica, the native populations did not build big cities or centers of civilization, as was the case with the Mayas, Aztecs, and Incas. Instead, they built agricultural villages. They reached significant advances in regards to their social and production organization, as well as in their artistic achievements—indicative of their esthetic development. In terms of their cultural characteristics, it is important to highlight a type of *cacical* social organization, as detailed above; a social specialization of work that included warriors, shamans, farmers, artisans, goldsmiths, among others; mythical-religious and idolatry beliefs; production systems based on grain and tubers and commerce; circular living quarters; and elaboration of instruments and other ornamental elements, among other things. The forms of education arose from within the social group's own culture. This meant that the inferences that have been made based on archeological finds indicate that initially, the indigenous villages partook in a spontaneous education practiced in the community by the younger members, who were in direct contact with the adults and with the environment. The primary objective of this type of education was the integration of individuals to the group's way of life, taking as their context the culture acquired by the adult generation. This type of education is labeled informal or socialization. However, there is also evidence that the villagers also partook in intentional education, since archeologists have found leather books that illustrated very clear goals, such as indications on how and where to farm. In conclusion, the education of the Mesoamerican villages had two types of parallel developments: spontaneous education experienced in everyday life, and intentional education, received, in some cases, by everyone on a permanent basis, and in others, in a specialized form and perhaps institutionalized.[3]

EDUCATION DURING THE CONQUEST PERIOD

In 1492, Christopher Columbus, in search of a new route to India, and whose voyage was being financed by the Spanish crown, arrived in what is now called America. With the arrival of the Spaniards in the sixteenth century, the existing societal structure of the indigenous population was destroyed and sub-ordinated to European interests. The Spanish conquest of America came as a result of Spain's struggle to vanquish the Muslims from the Iberian Peninsula and to consolidate their sovereignty over lands that existed far from this penin-sula. It was also the result of Portuguese maritime expansion, which arose from their need to import wheat from Morocco, develop their fishing industry, and in general from the European economic expansion towards other lands. These reasons justified (to the Europeans) not only the discovery of America, but its conquest as well.[4]

During this period (seventeenth and eighteenth centuries mostly), education played an important role with regards to the interests of the Spanish *conquista-dores*. Its influence was felt in two different ways: the conquest and subjugation of the indigenous people by the Spaniards, and the pacific education carried out mostly by the missionaries. The missionaries acted as agents for two of the most powerful cultural transmitters: Christianization or evangelization, and the transmission of the Castilian language, which is now known as Spanish. The missionaries felt that baptism was not sufficient, and that the indigenous population needed to be indoctrinated with the Christian faith. As a result, the native population was taught Spanish. It is important to note that the educa-tional interaction was not unilateral, since the missionaries also learned about the power of the shamans, the medicinal practices, and even the indigenous languages. Nevertheless, as a characteristic of this period, one finds that once the missionaries finished their labor, the Native Americans would return to using their own language and religious practices.[5]

An important fact that should be noted is the Spanish government's wish to establish higher education institutions in America. In 1551, King Charles V, issued a law, later passed again by Philip II in 1562, that declared that the vas-sals, subjects, and American natives needed to be educated with the objective of eradicating ignorance. As a result, the University of San Carlos in Guatemala and the University of Leon in Nicaragua (*College de San Ramon de Leon*) were founded in 1680. The former institution began instructing its students in theology, philosophy, medicine, as well as in Pipil, the principal language of the Guatemalan natives. Those in charge of the departments were professors that came mostly from the University of Salamanca in Spain. Because of the great distance between Guatemala and Costa Rica, the Costa Rican population lent this university very little support. The impact of the University of Leon in Nicaragua was much stronger. This was the real cultural center where most of Costa Rica's students gathered.[6] With the establishment of these universities, the colonial period began.

EDUCATION DURING THE COLONIAL ERA

In order to govern from Spain, the Spanish Crown established an adminis-trative organization for the Central American region called the District of

Guatemala, or the Reign of Guatemala. The government's chair was located in the city of Santiago of Guatemala, and the district consisted of the present day state of Chiapas in Mexico, Guatemala, El Salvador, Honduras, Nicaragua, and Costa Rica. At the time, because Belize was an unexplored region populated by the Mayans, it was not part of this organization and went mostly unnoticed during this period. The colonial period spans from 1575 to 1821. In 1821, Central America, including Costa Rica, was granted independence.[7]

The University of San Carlos in Guatemala and the University of Leon in Nicaragua continued to grow during the colonial period. It is important to note the Spanish University's hegemony over the Central American provinces, a fact made possible because of the governing structure that favored colonial interests. In all of Hispanic America, the Spanish crown was concerned with ruling and exploiting the new territories and their habitants, aided by the religious and cultural control they already wielded, with the sole purpose of facilitating Spain's transformation into an economic power among the European states.

Because of Costa Rica's great distance from Guatemala, its poverty, its smaller indigenous population, and the dispersion of the colonizers due to their agricultural activities, the situation in this province developed in a very different manner from the rest of the Central American countries, a fact that led to a slower urban concentration. Two limiting elements had a strong impact on the quality of the cultural development of the province: the clerical dominion and their religious intolerance, and the impoverishing of the indigenous culture. Thus, cultural life was very limited; elementary schools for the colonizers' children were rare, the terms were very short, and the instruction was rudimentary— limited to the Christian doctrine as its main subject matter, with very elemental instruction in reading, writing, and math. Nevertheless, two events which occurred close to the end of the colonial period made a difference in the province of Costa Rica. The first was the adoption by Costa Rica in 1812 of a Spanish normative instrument, the Constitution of Cadiz,[8] which, among other things, promulgated the obligation to establish primary schools for all children and the creation of higher learning institutions. The second event was a byproduct of the first one: the founding of the School of Learning of Santo Tomas (*Casa de Enseñanza de Santo Tomás*), an institution seen as a hybrid, since it consisted of a primary school as well as classes in higher learning subjects. Nevertheless, this institution became an important steppingstone with regards to the rudimentary state of education in the province, and it energized the stagnant cultural environment of the period.[9]

The School of Learning of Santo Tomas started as a place for grammar, philosophy, and sacred canon classes. It was in this institution where solid instruction was imparted for the first time, instruction that went beyond simple reading, writing, and arithmetic, and which touched on issues concerning morality, urbanity, and doctrine. The teaching method utilized at this primary school was a mutual system that consisted in teaching a great number of students with the help of the students that were already at a higher education level. In terms of the higher education, this school of learning was ruled by the orientation established by the University of Leon in Nicaragua.[10]

The Constitution of Cadiz was suspended between 1814 and 1820 due to the absolutist reign of Ferdinand VII of Spain, but it was put into effect once more in 1820. This constitution created the Provincial Delegations, a form of local governments that granted certain autonomy and strength to the provinces, a situation that led to the independence of Mexico and Central America from Spanish Rule in 1821, and which gave way to a new era in the region.[11]

EDUCATION IN COSTA RICA DURING THE PERIOD FOLLOWING INDEPENDENCE

During the early nineteenth century, Costa Rica played an important role within the sociopolitical situation of the American region. Due to that fact that the region shared a common ideology that generated geographical and social unity, three important events signaled the importance of the century regarding the genesis of modernism. These events are: the independence of Central America from Spain (a subject that will be addressed in this section); the union movements in Latin America; and the liberal reforms that occurred in most of the countries at the end of the nineteenth century—the latter two subjects will be addressed further on. The most important characteristic lay in the belief that the mental emancipation of Latin American could only be achieved by means of education, and that decrees and war would never result in progress or in the creation of a true democratic spirit. The triumph of law and order could only be reached by means of education, and only through education would people learn to reason.[12]

In 1821, the independence of the Central American provinces (among them Costa Rica) from Spain was declared. Chiapas, a part of present-day Mexico, was also declared independent. Costa Rica and Nicaragua formed part of the Mexican Empire until 1823, when they opted to become part of the federation of states that was called the United Provinces of Central America, formed by the Federal Constitution of 1824 and the Founding Law of Costa Rica of 1825. Both laws complemented each other, one with regards to federal aspects and the other with state aspects. It is interesting to note that the Constitution of Cadiz remained active in some of its articles during the years that followed independence. Later on, it also served as the basis for the creation of the state constitutions.[13]

During this period, many texts dealing with the European ideals of liberty, equality, justice, and their influence in the history of Hispanic America abounded. The circulation of the constitutional texts written during the French Revolution gave rise to the creation of nation states, which were nevertheless formed in a manner different from the European nations, since the State assumed a protagonist role not only in the economic but in the political and social fields as well. If European liberalism proclaimed that the state should abstain from intervention in society, then the state became an essential part in achieving national unity and a homogenous economy in Latin America. From the beginning of the independence period, the nations faced great socioeconomic differences among their citizens. As a result, in addition to territorial and administrative unity, the states had to assure economic unity, political representation, and an ideological consensus that would bring the nation together. Despite all efforts, not all of the social sectors benefited. For example, the rural sector was marginalized while the cities became the basis of the nation state, which later consolidated the oligarchy; in other words, the dominant classes held the political and economic power of the country.[14]

Within this context, Costa Rica faced a somewhat different situation. Although the ideas of the French Revolution were important, the country did not completely sever ties with the ideas of the colonial period, due in part to the prolonged influence of the Constitution of Cadiz. This meant that the search for a new national identity was always rooted in the past. The historical period from 1812–42 is characterized by a desire to strengthen the education system, which stressed the need to make citizens aware of their civil obligation. The government of this era tried to encourage a sense of citizenship and a consciousness of the rights and obligations that come with it in regards to the State. When the School of Learning of Santo Tomas became a university in 1843, the constitutional decree stated that citizens can only learn about their rights and obligations through education and that education will help them control and direct their passions. For these reasons, education is an indestructible bulwark that defends the liberty of the nations, and it is the government's duty to promote public education. These statements summarize the education ideals of the era.[15]

It is important to note that with Costa Rica's independence, an education ideal based on Illustration (Spanish Tradition) and on the ideas defined by the French Revolution reaches its apogee. The state took on a prevailing role in regards to the political and social development of the nation. It promoted education as a tool to achieve unity, as well as the formation of a solid education system that eventually led to stability in Costa Rica long before other Latin American countries reached it. In spite of the fact that the oligarchy sectors assumed economic and social control that excluded the rural population, education was the principal means for reaching a consensus and a national unity that was lacking in the rest of Central America, regardless of the existing exclusions.

EDUCATION DURING THE POLITICAL MOVEMENTS FOR INTEGRATION

The independence of the Central American colonies in 1821 gave rise to the debate centering on the idea of creating separate nations or a united Latin America. It is likely that the success of the United States of America at maintaining its unity permeated Latin American thinking.[16] At the very beginning of this century, the federal ideal gained importance in diverse territories, being asserted by the likes of Bolívar, O'Higgins, San Martín in the south, and Francisco Morazán in Central America.

In South America, Simón Bolívar strongly believed in a natural alliance among the countries that had been Spanish colonies, with obligations and rights created by their common histories, and with a deep contempt for Spain. Indigenous movements began that aimed to define the identity of those born in America as completely distinct from the Europeans.[17] Bolívar envisioned the transforming function of education, without which liberty and independence had no lasting basis. He believed that education was a function of the State that aimed at making the law a means for progress. His principal influence came from Rousseau's philosophy, which declared that public education was linked to a society of free men. For Bolívar, liberty was attained through education. Ignorance, tyranny, and vice, situations that plagued the American people, could only be overcome by means of an education that generated knowledge, power, and virtue. Bolívar's thoughts centered around four fundamental characteristics: the belief in education as a transforming force; faith in a future in which education would be the center; belief in the actual possibility of transforming a person by means of education; and a creative capacity that would put material and spiritual resources at the service of education.[18]

Francisco Morazán also shared these ideals for Central America. Morazán has always been controversial. His fight for an integration of the region spanned twenty years, with actions that ranged from voluntary alliances to acts of blatant imposition and coercion on his part. He was the Chief of the Provisory State in Costa Rica, and among the actions that led to the coup d'etat that overthrew him was his intention to create a Central American Union by force and, consequently, the declaration of war against Costa Rica by the rest of the Central American countries. The unequal economic development among the nations, especially the establishment of independent markets between the American countries and Europe, made the Latin American Confederation dream impossible.[19]

It must be noted that Morazán fought for a political and social consolidation of the region that lay in sharp contrast to the conservative interests that impeded the development of the growing nations. As a representative of an ideology that was shared by many during the nineteenth century, Morazán believed in the value of education and in the learned man as the most solid guarantee for the survival of the free nations. He believed in public education provided by the state, centered on reading, writing, arithmetic, ethics, and politics, as well as crafts and trades.[20]

By 1870, the idea of an integrated Latin American region had bowed to the reality of the creation of the different nations. Nevertheless, in Costa Rica, the integrationist movements had left their mark on the education system and in society, which then regarded the consolidation of a national identity as the most permanent option for continued freedom and autonomy from Spain. The leaders of these movements viewed education as the tool for forming citizens which would defend their nation.

LIBERAL REFORMS AT THE END OF THE CENTURY

By the end of the nineteenth century, Costa Rica had consolidated a republican government. By this time, the possibility of a federal government that would unite all of the different Central American regions had lost its momentum. The republican government was based on the principle that it would be its citizens' prerogative to establish their own laws, within the framework previously established by fundamental laws [the constitution], and that these laws would be enforced by the representatives elected by society. This idea, originating from the principles of the French Revolution, promoted the formation of a citizen with rights and duties in regard to the State who could elect others or be elected for public office. Nevertheless, the reality was that the governing authority was held by a dominant class that continued to wield power after independence. This oligarchy originated from a few families with substantial power dating back to the colonial period, which had acquired their hegemony from their control of vast commercial capital, fertile lands, and the commercialization of products for exportation, especially coffee. As a reaction to the dominant Spanish colonial actions at the end of the nineteenth century, many liberal movements led by the oligarchy arose and finally attained power. The establishment of a new political project for society also launched a new cultural project that incorporated an important number of liberal, positivist, and rationalist thinkers.[21]

The main goal of Latin American liberalism was the creation of a representative, democratic, and republican government whose representatives were to be appointed by popular suffrage. A laical and sovereign state was established, free from ecclesiastical control, in which public education played a vital role. In order to foment the intellectual and scientific development of the population, the new government aimed to minimize the obstacles that jeopardized public education. Many of the government officials became aware of the twofold role that education played; as a mechanism for material growth and as a means to form citizens. Despite these general characteristics, there were certain differences in the way liberalism progressed within the Central American countries as a result of their separate histories. Costa Rica and Guatemala serve as examples. During the nineteenth century, Guatemala, the richest country of the region, wielded most of the political and military power. Internally, Guatemala consisted of a sharply divided society in which the Church and the dominant groups employed repressive mechanisms to strengthen these conditions. In contrast, Costa Rica, being the poorest and least culturally developed country of the region, and its Catholic Church, counting on limited economic resources, conformed to a more flexible society that was less differentiated. These variations between both countries resulted in a very different adoption and assimilation of the liberal project within each. For example, although the liberal reforms called for uniformity, compulsoriness, government funding, and the laical character of education, as well as a citizenry and republican formation of the population, the Guatemalan education project was subject to a utilitarian, martial ideology, while in Costa Rica, the consensual triumphed over the repressive.[22]

During this period, the dominant political groups in Costa Rica consolidated a capitalist, market society that afforded everyone the possibility to develop their abilities; in other words, a society that respected equal rights for everyone. The liberal politicians understood the importance of social participation, attainable only by education, as a means to maintain legitimate power.[23]

The Krausist, liberal thinking supported by Dr. Fernández Ferraz predominated during this period, as well as the positivist movement promoted within the fields of politics and education by don Mauro Fernández. Krausism was a German movement that incorporated the ideas of Kantian rationalism and German Neo-Kantianism, a synthesis, which at the time was termed Harmonic Rationalism. This movement was born as a counter reaction to the encyclopedism that had dominated education in Europe. The founder of Spanish Krausism was Professor Julián Sanz del Río. One of his disciples, don Valeriano Fernández Ferraz, became the movement's promoter as well as the founder of secondary education in Costa Rica. The Constitution of 1869 incorporated the education ideal that endorsed a scientific and liberal education that would provide the necessary tools to face the constant struggle against the powerful nature that surrounds the human being. This focus on education was to accompany the more practical and immediate education, already being provided, that could be used to address more immediate needs. Don Mauro Fernández, as the principle defender of the positivist movement, supported a general scientific and technical formation in high school, which would leave more specialized education for the university level.[24]

Mauro Fernández issued the legal dispositions that consolidated the Liberal Reform within the education field that came to be known as the General Law for Public Instruction in 1885 and the General Law of Common Education in 1886. During his period as Minister of Public Instruction, he accomplished many things, including the creation of an integrated education system that spanned from a kindergarten to university level. He aimed to restructure the education project from its very basis and in accordance to a scientific plan. The direction and inspection of elementary education was awarded to the executive power, which delegated it to the minister. In addition, several supervisor posts were created. There was a sizable increase in the number of primary schools, and four new high schools were inaugurated. A plan to organize, rationalize, and professionalize the education project resulted in a qualitative improvement as well. By separating the Church from public education, it was possible to change the content of the instruction. Consequently, more programs dealing with the economic and social organization of the country were introduced, such as science and technology, physical education, ethics and esthetics. There were important changes in the methods of teaching, such as placing greater importance on the intuitive, experimental method and in the applied sciences. When laical education was decreed, new texts were made available and new horizons appeared.[25]

Mauro Fernández surrounded himself with the country's intellectuals, some of which accompanied him during his administration while others dedicated themselves to write textbooks to be used for teaching and learning. The fundamental ideas of the General Law of Common Education included the centralization of the educative function of the State, the establishment of graduate schools, the decree that education should be integral, free, and compulsory, a ban on corporeal punishments, and the creation of syllabi, among other elements that can still be recognized as part of an education system. The reform of primary education was inspired by the thinking of Domingo Faustino Sarmiento, the supporter of popular education in Argentina. Although Costa Rica had already delved into the matter of high school education, it was up to Mauro Fernández to create a system that would be the responsibility of the State in all of its aspects. A very important element that needs to be pointed out is the adoption of a system for the professionalizing of teachers.[26]

In summary, it is useful to state the elements that characterized liberal education reforms in Costa Rica: democratization of education resulting from becoming common, free, and obligatory; centralization of education by the State, which made it possible to create a uniform system; separation of the Church, which opened up new paths for the students; and the stipulation that teachers should be trained professionally, which would lead to an improvement in the quality of education. Of course, these ideals needed more than a few decades to become a reality, but the basis was stated, and from then on, any achievement was the result of visionary minds that enacted one of the biggest education reforms in the history of Costa Rica.

THE DECLINE OF THE OLIGARCHIC STATE AND THE CONSOLIDATION OF THE WELFARE STATE

Education reforms at the end of the nineteenth century were based more on a vision of the future than on the needs to solve the social problems of the time. This was due to the fact that the dominant mode of production in Costa Rica's case, one revolving around the growth and exportation of coffee, did not require any type of qualified labor. Nevertheless, the liberal reforms held as one of their premises that citizenry could only be attained by means of education, which is why this right was awarded to the whole population. This led to an increase in the middle class, who, having acquired an education, were able to vie for political power. This condition can be evinced in Latin American societies at the beginning of the twentieth century, especially in Costa Rica, where two populations coexisted: the dominant, oligarchy class, which had held economic and social power since the independence, and a large middle class that for the first time faced the real possibility of wielding political power. The changing social strata profoundly affected the hegemonic power of the oligarchy, and very soon popular movements arose, reaching their peak during the 1920s and 1930s. The creation of education institutions with a liberal ideology was highly convenient for the interests of the new social classes, which is why these groups applied a great pressure to increase the reach of said programs. In this way, the existing social scenario strengthened the liberal orientation of the education of the era.[27]

The emerging struggle among social classes developed in a very different way in Costa Rica from the rest of the Central American countries. In these countries, the rise of the new social classes and the accompanying farmers' uprisings and strikes demanding a minimum salary became a threat to the oligarchy. Such upheavals were eventually brought to an end by the rise of dictatorships. Examples of these are Ubico's reign in Guatemala (1931–44), Hernandez Martínez's reign in El Salvador (1935–44), Carías Andino in Honduras (1921–49), and Somoza in Nicaragua beginning in 1929 and later disguised as a presidency until 1956. These dictators spent most of their nation's budget on the consolidation of military power, ignoring many social needs, especially education, since maintaining an uneducated population favored their agendas. In contrast to these countries, Costa Rica's labor movement brought about creation of a minimum salary for agricultural workers, foundation of the Institute for the Defense of Coffee (meant to regulate the relationships between small and large coffee growers), and banana plantation strikes, which resulted in the implementation of constructive solutions with a tinge of "communism a la Tica."[28] It is important to point out that the principal intellectual leaders of these sociopolitical movements were the same intellectuals that had been until then concerned with the education project of the country.

Another phenomenon that occurred during this period pertains to the influence of the United States of America over Central American countries. Although the efforts to integrate the Latin American countries into one union had ceased with the consolidation of the independent republics by 1870, a new movement for integration arose during this period. However, this movement fit into the United States' policy of imperialism, which began in 1898, and the "Hispanic War" event, which led the United States of America to become the most powerful economic and military power in the Americas. The Caribbean countries, as well as Nicaragua and Panama, virtually became territories of the United States, whose goal was to wield political power over the entire region. This control also influenced the education systems, which served as effective interventionist mechanisms aimed at exalting the "American Dream" and undermining the local cultures. As argued earlier, the situation in Costa Rica was very uncharacteristic—although it was to a certain extent an accomplice to the advances made by the United States, its position was not entirely that of an ally. The nation's efforts to distance itself from any Central American integrationist movements, as well as its new educational aspirations, were more important than the regional agenda.[29]

During the first half of the twentieth century, Costa Rica was characterized by a progressive democratization of education services, evolving from education of the privileged classes to education for the masses, and by a growing interest for the education of women, which resulted in an important increase in the number of citizens that were able to claim their right to education. Some of the qualitative advances during this period included the pedagogical techniques applied to the educational processes, resulting from professional training of educators, and a reformist vocation that was made apparent in the curricula at all education levels. There was an increase in the quality of pedagogical practices, enriched by the contributions made by professionals educated abroad, as well as by those educated at the *Escuela Normal de Costa Rica*, an institution that brought together the most prominent intellectuals of the country. These academics contributed to the education system by focusing on training of educators. They also actively participated in elaboration of the curriculum and textbooks, introduction of new teaching methods, and application of new pedagogical experiments, such as the creation of the Maternal Montessorian Kinder, the first preschool institution with a scientific, pedagogical basis.[30]

The influence of the liberal period at the end of the nineteenth century was felt until 1940, when a group of representatives with a political ideology that differed from liberalism came to power in Costa Rica. The Social Christian movement reflected a new mentality with regards to the State and the function of education. Without losing its laical character, education was once again influenced by the Church, which had changed its position with regards to society by the end of the nineteenth century, evolving from a supporter of the dominant classes to a defender of the rights of all citizens. With the rise of the Social Christian movement, the State assumed the role of welfare provider. In other words, it aimed to provide all its citizens with the services that would guarantee their survival, not only in biological terms, but in social terms as well.[31] This is the period of the Social Reforms in Costa Rica. As a product of the oligarchic organization, the development of the country had centered on coffee and bananas until then—the latter crop being cultivated by transnational companies. The new model for economic development was aimed at the principles of product diversification and economic rationality, which made it imperative that education be a mechanism for reform and a channel for social mobility. A strengthening process of the education system was begun. It was characterized by the consolidation of primary education, whose reach became almost universal, and a rapid expansion of secondary education. Great strides against illiteracy were made, and there was an increase in the level of enrollments of the population as well. By the 1970s, the education program included technical instruction, university and college level education, all of which were aimed at preparing the labor force needed for the industrial development of the country.[32]

In this way, the country underwent a political and social transition that was reflected in the education system. As stated previously, liberal ideals were prominent until the 1940s, and paradoxically defended by the middle class, which had forged a path for the social integration of said ideas by means of education, as well as by the dominion of the oligarchy class. It is during this decade that a new model for the State was put into practice: the Benefactor State, which increased the coverage of the education system and assumed a more decisive role in the efforts made to improve citizens' quality of life, placing special emphasis on public health services, the rights of workers, the right to an education, and social guarantees.

THE NATION'S EDUCATION SYSTEM PUT TO THE TEST: UNESCO

During the mid-twentieth century, the country's education authorities acknowledged the importance of analyzing the quality of the education that the Costa Rican population was being offered. In 1951, Costa Rica joined the United Nations Education Science and Culture Organization (UNESCO). That same year, the first technical team for this entity visited the country in order to scientifically study the Costa Rican education system. As a result, education policy was modified to stress the need to genuinely incorporate into the programs and methods of Costa Rican education the ideals regarding a democratic way of life. With the support of this committee, model projects were established for primary and secondary education, technical education, and educator training. Among the most important results was the creation of technical programs as an additional option for those high school students who wanted to receive the training necessary to qualify for new jobs that were being created as the modes of production of the developing country. Furthermore, special programs for teachers lacking a professional degree were created. A second UNESCO team, made up principally of Chilean educators, visited the country in 1958 and helped to create proposals aimed at modernizing high school education programs, especially within the areas of science and mathematics.[33]

Driven by a demographic explosion, the Costa Rican education system greatly expanded from 1950–60 and 1970–80. Beginning in 1970, the growth also included higher education. UNESCO collaborated with the Ministry of Education in the proposal of special projects within the field of teacher training and in the creation of laboratories for the teaching of science in education institutions. UNESCO also provided technical assistance from 1970 to 1974 during the creation of the National Plan for Educational Development, whose purpose was to introduce important changes throughout that decade, if not longer. This plan was a clear response to the education movements of that period, one of which was the concept of permanent education, spread internationally by UNESCO.[34]

From the time that Costa Rica joined UNESCO until the present day, Costa Rican education has been framed within the general policies decreed by this international organization, since the country has invariably subscribed itself to its declarations and has developed, with varying states of commitment and success, the established courses of action. The Ministry of Education's proposal to develop the main programs concerning national education between 2003 and 2015[35] serves as an example of a proposal developed within the framework of Education for Everyone, a declaration by UNESCO made in 1990. This subject will be expounded on further ahead.

THE SOCIOPOLITICAL SITUATION AT THE END OF THE TWENTIETH CENTURY

In order to better understand the Costa Rican situation at the end of the twentieth century and at the beginning of the twenty-first century, it is necessary to examine certain sociopolitical conditions in Latin American societies and the rest of the world, mainly the rise of globalization and the global trend for economic policies of a neo-liberal nature. During the last forty years, the areas of local education institutions as well as construction of new schools visibly increased in all of Latin America, especially in Costa Rica. The rates of illiteracy dramatically decreased and the rates of enrollment grew steadily until the 1990s. The funds allotted to education by the government also increased during this period. For example, in 1970, the gross rate of enrollment in Central America and the Hispanic Caribbean was 37.7 percent. By 1980, it was 46.8 percent. Nevertheless, during the 1980s, these countries suffered severe economic crises that affected the image and effectiveness of the Welfare State. By 1990, the enrollment rate had decreased to 44.6 percent. Paradoxically, there was a notable increase in the percentage of GDP allotted to the funding of education programs; in 1970, the percentage was 2.9 percent for Latin America, but by 1993, it was 4.1 percent.[36] Regrettably, the advances made at the core of education systems have been disparate, due to inequalities caused by regional and urban-rural differences as well as social, ethnic, and gender characteristics. These are aspects that must not be forgotten no matter how promising some of the indicators are. It was during this period that globalization and the neo-liberal policies arose.

In Latin American countries, as a result of globalization, the Welfare State went into a crisis, since the pressure exerted by international competition forced nations to look for methods to alleviate any "dead weight" in their economies. Industrialized countries, such as the United States and Great Britain, arrived at alternatives grounded in the neo-liberal policies that advocated for ambitious programs of privatization and deregulation, which were aimed at strengthening economic competitiveness at an international level. Nevertheless, a paradox arises: even though the level of education of a country's citizens strongly determines its competitiveness within a world market, the financing of this activity by the State is one of its most costly responsibilities. The solution consisted of keeping the education systems under the care of the State and, consequently, under political power, but in establishing alliances with community entities and other social organizations that would assume part of the economic burden, thus reducing the cost that education represented for the State.

The State is assigned a new role with a simple central idea; it is no longer its responsibility to directly administrate or provide education services, but it is its duty to guarantee that the services meet the quality and range demanded by the times. The State's responsibilities include the definition of sector priorities, the evaluation of results, and the special protection or compensation for groups that are vulnerable to inequalities.[37]

This solution, adopted by many industrialized countries, has also been applied in Latin America and the Caribbean, with certain unique characteristics, such as an emphasis on the need to compensate or protect the less fortunate. However, by trying to implement the neo-liberal policies in a relatively short period of time, great social resistances to change have arisen in the countries, causing serious political crisis. The principal argument used by social movements that oppose implementation of this type of policy is the fact that the accelerated impulse towards State reform does not necessarily take into consideration the particular conditions of Latin American countries. For this reason, the Latin American region shows particular characteristics in regards to the way neoliberal policies have been implemented. The socioeconomic situation has clearly influenced changes within the field of education. The policies implemented at the end of the 1980s were characterized by four principle objectives: improving the efficiency of the complete system and all of its parts, adapting the curriculum to the demands of globalization, making parents and communities responsible for the administration of the education system, and directing subsidies towards the populations with the greater needs.[38]

The situation in Costa Rica was strongly characterized by these elements, but the characteristics were quite peculiar. During the 1980s, many programs aimed at transforming the structure and function of the State were implemented, based on policies that lessened its responsibilities within the social field—responsibilities that were transferred to the citizens. These programs, called "Programs for Structural Change," did not effectively influence the development of the education system, due mostly to opposition by concerned social groups. Unlike other Central American countries, the Costa Rican nation passed an amendment to their constitution in 1997 which extended the coverage of the education system to preschool levels and determined that at least 6 percent of the GDP would be invested in education. The struggle to implement neo-liberal policies meant to lessen the State's expense regarding the provision of social services was more successful in areas concerning the production of goods and services than in the educational realm.

THE COSTA RICAN EDUCATION SYSTEM AT THE BEGINNING OF THE TWENTY-FIRST CENTURY: A MATTER OF QUALITY

The previous sections have detailed how the education authorities initially focused on increasing the coverage of the education system, in accordance with the ideals and policies that arose in this field as a consequence of the social and cultural developments in the nation. To a lesser extent, these authorities were always concerned with the quality of education, but this preoccupation became extremely relevant to education policies with the rise of globalization, in view of the fact that the country needed to effectively compete against worldwide demands. Beginning in 1986, new decisions meant to increase the quality of education were taken. By 1987, the National Tests, a set of comprehensive exams that all students needed to pass, had been instituted in an effort to ensure that all school programs meet the same standards for quantity and quality.[39] For many years, the curriculum for each school subject had not been standardized. Instead, education practices focused on describing appropriate pedagogical methods, defining what kinds of skills students should develop, and defining desirable conducts, to the detriment of the definition of cognitive objectives for each of the different subjects.

At the beginning of the 1990s, with the purpose of implementing a decentralized education policy within the different regions of the country, the school programs were once again focused on a basic education profile meant to develop certain conducts in students. The move was meant to facilitate the implementation of regionalized curricula that would better address the social and cultural conditions of the school zone.[40] Decentralization was the predominant school of thought in Latin America. In fact, several successful experiments that upheld the political ideal of maintaining the State's hegemony in education matters with a conscious and committed participation of the communities and families had been carried out. In other words, even though the State's role in the financing of education was not minimized, there was a move towards the lessening of the State's role within this area. Nevertheless, this initiative was not successful, and by 1997 a new education policy based on four pillars had been passed:

- A Basic National curriculum meant to establish a standard study plan for all of the country, with the ability to broaden it in accordance to the particular needs of each region.
- The dissemination of the plans and study programs that correspond to this curriculum, meant to guarantee its execution around the whole country.
- The elaboration of didactical resources for all of the schools, including a series of books titled *Towards the XXI Century*, published by the University of Costa Rica for all of subjects and school levels.
- The implementation of evaluative procedures to diagnose the needs of the education system and to measure results.[41]

This policy, which is still in place at the present time (2006), has been enriched in subsequent years by advanced initiatives, such as: broadening of information technology education, which now begins during preschool (a project that had its beginnings at the end of the 1980s); teaching of a second language (English or French) at all school levels; creation of new high school programs that provide adequate access to students with particular conditions (teenage mothers, young workers, students from remote areas, among others); new laws meant to provide equal access to education for people with disabilities; and creation of technical education programs geared towards the country's new production models, such as tourism and the technological industry. One of the subjects that had the greatest impact on national education at the beginning of the twenty-first century was the idea of the creation of values within the classrooms, which suggested that the great and enormous purpose of education would become obsolete if it was not accompanied by coordinated and coherent efforts to retake and strengthen the formation of values within society. This perspective became the central element in the education process, not as a separate subject, but as a way of life, as a common-day occurrence in the classroom meant to extend itself into the nation's society.[42] The emphasis on values within the Costa Rican curriculum covered four fundamental subjects: an environmentally-friendly culture for sustainable development; human sexuality as an integral part of education; health education; and the values of democracy and peace. These subjects were incorporated into the programs of all levels and modes of education in such a way that educators gained a clearer understanding of their responsibility regarding the integral development of their students, going beyond the specific subject matter that they had to teach.

The country remains committed to the principles set forth by UNESCO, and is focused on its recent education efforts to implement the Plan for Action for Education for Everyone, which proposes special attention to education at an early age, improvement of basic general education, attention to teenagers and young adults in accordance to their specific conditions, the fomenting of learning in students that will help them be better prepared for the future and simultaneously educate them for life.[43]

Paradoxically, even though this scenario is as a positive example in Latin America, Costa Rican education has suffered great problems that have put the current and future well being of the students in jeopardy. Some of these problems are detailed below:

- Lack of funding by the government for secondary education. Only 60 percent of children between the ages of thirteen to eighteen are covered, and only one-third of these students are able to successfully graduate from high school. Even though the State has made great efforts to open high schools in all areas of the country during the last few years, many students drop out before finishing. This situation can be attributed to three factors: the need of many families to have their children work in order to help their financial situations, the little interest that many students have for school and its study plans, and difficulties that many students face when trying to attain academic success, especially in subjects like math and foreign languages.
- Low number of students that pass from one grade to the next. This is a problem that might not always cause students to drop out but that does create a problem regarding efficiency and efficacy in regards to the education goals of the country. Both drop out and repetition are highest between sixth and seventh grade (the period between elementary and high school) and between ninth and tenth grade.

- Low scores in the National Tests: a situation that makes it impossible for many of the students to get their diploma at the end of high school—a requirement for higher-paying jobs. Low scores are mostly due to problems with the quality of education provided.
- Low standards in teacher training and practice—one of the principal factors that threaten the quality of education around the country and that results in the afore-mentioned problems. The country has undergone a drop in the quality of teaching practice in the newer generation of education professionals, in part due to the poor training that they receive in private universities, and in part due to a vicious circle that has been transforming the professional culture—there is an increasing number of people that have received a substandard education, then enter the universities, follow a major in education, and later take jobs in schools in the country.[44]

Many alternatives have been proposed and implemented to address these education problems and to improve the quality of the system. The first initiative is the plan to invest 8 percent of the GDP in education funding—a resolution that is set to be incorporated into the Costa Rican constitution. Furthermore, it is necessary to consolidate a system for the global administration of education, creating a pertinent and advantageous centralization of the areas that should be standardized when it comes to services that are provided, and decentralizing those that require a focus more in tune with the specific needs of each education region. The specific attention required by young people that remain unable to graduate from high school should not be forgotten. Special attention should be given to professional improvement of teachers of subjects that are most difficult for students and to the special classes that will enable these students to overcome these obstacles. Even though the country's competitiveness is currently dependent on the ability of the workers to speak English, their ability to use information technologies, and the development of entrepreneurial attitudes and abilities (conditions that the education system tries to promote in its students), one cannot forget the need to strengthen the students' ethical and esthetic attitudes as well as their ability to learn to live and cope in their natural and social surroundings. This great challenge for the education system is undergoing a process of strengthening and transformation in such a way that it will stop being seen as an addition to students' development and become the real basis. In this manner, the country seeks to increase the social and cultural capital of the student populations, preparing them for the world that they will have to face during the twenty-first century.[45]

A DAY IN THE LIFE

My name is Claudia. I am nine years old and in third grade at *Joaquín García Monge School* in Desamparados, San José, Costa Rica. This is the biggest public school in my community, and because there are many children, I go to school from 7:00 AM to noon three times a week and from noon to 5:40 PM on the other two days.

In the mornings, I wake up at 5:00 AM and get ready for school. I prepare my own breakfast because my mother and father are getting ready for work, and my grandfather is involved in his own activities. After I brush my teeth, the school bus comes to pick me up, and before 7:00 AM I arrive at school with my classmates. Before the bell rings, I have a good time with my best friend, Carol, talking about what we watched on television or about what happened the day before.

To begin classes, with my teacher, *niña Vanessa,* we say a small prayer and afterwards sing the National Anthem. There are thirty-three children in my class, half of them are girls and half are boys, but I almost never talk to boys because they are a little rough and I do not like the way they play. To study math, language, science, and social studies, my teacher asks us to read from our books. Sometimes, she writes on the blackboard information that we copy in our notebooks, or she explains things that we have to understand to do our work. Very often, she reads stories and poetry to us because, in my country, all elementary teachers have an obligation to read out loud to their students. We have a library at school and my teacher sent us to pick out books to use in class. Even though I have the best grades of my class, some things are hard to understand, and that is why I always pay attention to what is happening in class. My mother says that I have been very lucky because my teachers have been very good. I agree with my mother.

I have other teachers, too. My music teacher likes to sing very strange songs with a very strange voice to us. He plays a guitar and a flute. We sing, too, copy the lyrics of the songs, and learn a little bit about musical notes. My English teacher is not a very good teacher. She hardly speaks English to us and we almost never speak in English. It is a shame because last year my English teacher was very good and I was learning a lot. When we go to physical education, we spend time playing soccer, throwing the ball through the basketball ring, jumping rope, and running. At the computer lab, things get complicated sometimes because a lot of computers do not work and six children have to sit in front of one computer. It is hard to look for images and to make the little turtle walk when there are so many people in front of a single computer. Even though we have religion classes, my family is not Catholic, so I do not receive this class. Meanwhile, I spend my time reading, drawing, and doing my homework. One thing I do not like about my school is that we do not have an art class. I love to paint and make funny things with art materials, and I would like to learn more about art.

At recess, I prefer to walk and talk with the girls in my class, and have the snack I brought from home. Some of the children receive their snacks from school because their families do not have a lot of money to buy them. At the end of the school day, the bus takes me back home if my mother is there. If not, I go to the house of a lady who has been taking care of me since I was born. I do my homework, watch some television, and go to bed.

TIMELINE

1492	First arrival of Spaniards in America.
1500	Evangelization and Castilian language. Primary schools and the *Casa de Enseñanza de Santo Tomás* were founded.
1575–1821	Colonial period.
1812	Costa Rica adopts a Spanish normative instrument, the Constitution of Cadiz, which promulgated the obligation to establish primary schools for all children and the creation of higher learning institutions.
1812–42	Period characterized by a desire to strengthen the education system, which stressed the need to make citizens aware of their civil obligation.
Between 1814–20	The Constitution of Cadiz was suspended due to the absolutist reign of Ferdinand VII of Spain, but it was put into effect once more in 1820.
1821	Costa Rican independence from Spain.
1823	Costa Rica and Nicaragua stopped being part of the Mexican Empire, and opted to become part of the federation of states that was called the United Provinces of Central America.
1824	Federal Constitution.
1825	Founding Law of Costa Rica.
1843	The School of Learning of Santo Tomas became a university.
1869	Constitution that endorsed a scientific and liberal education.
1870s	Although the efforts to integrate the Latin American countries into one union had ceased with the consolidation of the independent republics, a new movement for integration arose during this period.
1885	Mauro Fernández (Minister of Public Instruction) issued the legal dispositions that consolidated the Liberal Reform within the education field that came to be known as the General Law for Public Instruction.
1886	The General Law for Common Education was passed.
1940	The Social Christian movement, a group of representatives with a political ideology that differed from liberalism, came to power in Costa Rica interrupting the influence of the liberal period. Social reforms, Welfare State.
1950–60 and 1970–80	The Costa Rican education system was greatly expanded, driven by a demographic explosion.
1951	Costa Rica joined the United Nations Education Science and Culture Organization (UNESCO). The first technical team for this entity visited the country in order to study the Costa Rican education system.
1958	A second UNESCO team visited the country and helped create proposals meant to modernize high school education programs.
1970–74	National Plan for Educational Development, receiving technical assistance from UNESCO.

1980s	Advances in the field of Information Technology began.
1987	The National Tests, a set of comprehensive exams that all students needed to pass, were instituted in an effort to ensure that all school programs met the same standards for quantity and quality.
1990s	Until this period, rates of illiteracy dramatically decreased and the rates of enrollment steadily increased. Funds allotted to education by the government also increased during this period.
1997	The Costa Rican nation passed an amendment to their constitution in which they extended the coverage of the education system to preschool levels and determined that at least 6 percent of the GDP would be invested in education.

NOTES

1. Fundación Omar Dengo, *Marco General de Implantación del PRONIE IIIC* (San José, Costa Rica: FOD, 2004).

2. Francisco Corrales, "Más de diez mil años de historia precolombina," in *Costa Rica: Desde las sociedades autóctonas hasta 1914*, ed. A.M. Botey (San José, Costa Rica: Editorial de la Universidad de Costa Rica, 1999), 25–65.

3. Maria Eugenia Dengo, *Educación costarricense* (San José, Costa Rica: EUNED, 1998).

4. Juan Carlos Solórzano, "Descubrimiento y conquista de Costa Rica, 1502–75," in *Costa Rica. Desde las sociedades autóctonas hasta 1914*, ed. A.M. Botey (San José, Costa Rica: Editorial de la Universidad de Costa Rica, 1999), 113–61.

5. Maria Eugenia Dengo, *Educación costarricense* (San José, Costa Rica: EUNED, 1998).

6. Femando González, *Educación Costarricense* (San José, Costa Rica: EUNED, 1984).

7. Juan Carlos Solórzano, "La sociedad colonial 1575–1821," in *Costa Rica. Desde las sociedades autóctonas hasta 1914*, ed. A.M. Botey (San José, Costa Rica: Editorial de la Universidad de Costa Rica, 1999), 67–111, 161.

8. In 1810, a Parliament (*Corte*) emerged in Cadiz to represent both Spain and Spanish America. Two years later, it produced a new, liberal constitution that proclaimed Spain's American possessions to be full members of the kingdom and not mere colonies. Yet, the Creoles who participated in the new *Cortes* were denied equal representation.

9. Maria Eugenia Dengo, *Educación costarricense* (San José, Costa Rica: EUNED, 1998).

10. Femando González, *Educación Costarricense* (San José, Costa Rica: EUNED, 1984).

11. Clotilde Obregón, *Nuestros gobernantes* (San José, Costa Rica: Editorial de la Universidad de Costa Rica, 1999).

12. Lisandro Chávez, "Limen," in Alejandro Serrano Caldera, *El doble rostro de la postmodernidad* (San José, Costa Rica: CSUCA, 1994), 7–8.

13. Clotilde Obregón, *Nuestros gobernantes* (San José, Costa Rica: Editorial de la Universidad de Costa Rica, 1999).

14. Gabriela Ossenbach, "Las transformaciones del Estado y de la educación pública en América Latina en los siglos XIX y XX," in *Escuela, historia y poder; Miradas desde*

América Latina, comp. A. Martínez Boom, and M. Naradowski (Buenos Aires: Ediciones Novedades Educativas, 1996).

15. Maria Eugenia Dengo, *Educación costarricense* (San José, Costa Rica: EUNED, 1998).

16. Ruy Mauro Marini, "La idea de la integración en América Latina," in Gioconda Belli et al., *1492–1992 La interminable conquista* (San José, Costa Rica: Dei, 1991), 239–56.

17. Miguel Rojas Mx, *Los cien nombres de América; Eso que descubrió Colón* (San José, Costa Rica: Editorial de la Universidad de Costa Rica, 1997).

18. Luis B. Prieto Figueroa, *El magisterio americano de Bolívar* (Caracas, Venezuela: Arte, 1978).

19. Clotilde Obregón, *Nuestros gobernantes* (San José, Costa Rica: Editorial de la Universidad de Costa Rica, 1999).

20. Néstor Enrique Alvarado, *Morazán, político y maestro* (Tegucigalpa, Honduras: Imprenta Bulnes, n.d).

21. Gerardo Morales, Cultura oligárquica y nueva intelectualidad en Costa Rica: 1880–1914 (Heredia, Costa Rica: EUNA, 1995).

22. Astrid Fischel, *Consenso y represión, una interpretación socio-política de la educación costarricense* (San José, Costa Rica: Editorial de la Universidad de Costa Rica, 1990).

23. Orlando Salazar, *El apogeo de la república liberal en Costa Rica, 1870–1914* (San José, Costa Rica: Editorial de la Universidad de Costa Rica, 1998).

24. José Alberto Soto and Amalia Bernardini, *Historia de las ideas pedagógicas en Costa Rica* (San José, Costa Rica: Vicerrectoría de Investigación, UCR, 1986).

25. Orlando Salazar, *El apogeo de la república liberal en Costa Rica, 1870–1914* (San José, Costa Rica: Editorial de la Universidad de Costa Rica, 1998).

26. Maria Eugenia Dengo, *Educación costarricense* (San José, Costa Rica: EUNED, 1998).

27. Gabriela Ossenbach, "Las transformaciones del Estado y de la educación pública en América Latina en los siglos XIX y XX," in *Escuela, historia y poder; Miradas desde América Latina*, comp. A. Martínez Boom, and M. Naradowski (Buenos Aires: Ediciones Novedades Educativas, 1996).

28. Juan Rafael Quesada, "Evolución a la tica," in *Costa Rica contemporánea; Raíces del estado de la nación*, ed. Juan Rafael Quesada (San José, Costa Rica: Editorial de la Universidad de Costa Rica, 1999), 17–42.

29. Jorge Rhenán Segura, "Costa Rica y su contexto internacional," in *Costa Rica contemporánea; Raíces del estado de la nación*, ed. Juan Rafael Quesada (San José, Costa Rica: Editorial de la Universidad de Costa Rica, 1999), 309–50.

30. Maria Eugenia Dengo, *Educación costarricense* (San José, Costa Rica: EUNED, 1998).

31. Antonio Petrus, *Pedagogía social* (Barcelona: Ariel Educación, 1997).

32. Manuel Barahona, "El desarrollo social," in *Costa Rica contemporánea; Raíces del estado de la nación*, ed. Juan Rafael Quesada (San José, Costa Rica: Editorial de la Universidad de Costa Rica, 1999), 151–94.

33. Maria Eugenia Dengo, *Educación costarricense* (San José, Costa Rica: EUNED, 1998).

34. Ibid.

35. Gobierno de Costa Rica. *Principales programas para el desarrollo educativo nacional, 2003–15* (San José, Costa Rica: Ministerio de Educación Pública, 2003).

36. Hernando Gómez Buendía, ed. *Educación; La agenda del siglo XXI* (Colombia: PNUD-Tercer Mundo Editores, 1998).

37. Ibid.

38. Ibid.

39. Francisco Antonio Pacheco, "Evaluación y pruebas nacionales," in *Política social y educación en Costa Rica* (San José, Costa Rica: UNICEF, 1999), 257–78.

40. Marvin Herrera, *Educación, prioridad de gobierno* (San José, Costa Rica: Edición Propia, 2000).

41. Eduardo Doryan and Eleonora Badilla, "El cambio histórico y las implicaciones para la educación," in *Política social y educación en Costa Rica* (San José, Costa Rica: UNICEF, 1999), 111–43.

42. Ministerio de Educación Pública, *Memoria 1999* (San José, Costa Rica: Edición Propia, 1999).

43. Ministerio de Educación Pública, *Principales programas para el desarrollo educativo nacional 2003–15* (San José, Costa Rica: MEP, 2003).

44. Programa Estado de la Nación. *Educación y conocimiento en Costa Rica: Desafíos para avanzar hacia una política de Estado* (2004).

45. Propuesta de trabajo del Ministerio de Educación Pública para el período 2006–10.

Chapter 8

SCHOOLING IN CUBA

Yamilet Hernández-Galano and Lyding R. Rodríguez Fuentes

THE FIRST CENTURIES OF THE COLONIAL PERIOD

Types of Education System: Tutorial, Private, State

Initially, education was in the hands of families, private tutors, and governesses. During these first three centuries, wealthy families preferred tutorial education, although a few did send their children to private schools. Colonial government contribution to the field of education was very poor in general. In the seventeenth century, state education was sustained by a small number of reading teachers receiving low wages from the government, and by *escuelitas de amigas* or "schools run by friends."[1] Only in some of the convents did the work of priests supplement these deficiencies.

Education and Social Classes

During this century in Cuba, the organization of society was strongly influenced by social changes associated with new economic development and the growth of the port of Havana. Society was structured into social classes imposed by the plantation system, which had introduced slavery to the island and caused racial discrimination towards blacks, who were considered mere instruments of labor.[2]

Black slaves, free *mestizos* (of Indian and Spanish mixture), and poor whites had no access to education whatsoever. Only a few were able to send their children to small, free, district schools. Children belonging to larger, wealthier families went to convent schools or other more prestigious institutions.

Gender and Education

Boys tended to receive a more privileged education, teaching centers for boys were established from early on; for example, the Santo Domingo Convent admitted secular boys from all around the island. On the other hand, female religious orders were in charge of the education of young girls of different social classes, including the orders of Saint Clare, Saint Catherine of Siena, and Saint Teresa of Avila, among others. In 1688, the Saint Francis de Sales school for girls was created. The first schools for the working poor—*escuelitas de amiga* ("schools run by friends" hereafter)—were also established for boys and girls lacking basic resources.[3]

Education for boys was very good in general, covering a wide range of subjects, whereas girls were only taught domestic duties or how to further enhance their feminine qualities as members of the "fairer sex."

Levels of Education

Primary

At some point between the sixteenth and eighteenth century, demands for child education begin to be made by the general population in larger towns. However, initial establishments only covered elementary education and the teaching of arts and crafts. During this period, no real distinction between primary and secondary education existed.

According to the *Patronato Real* (Royal Patronage) awarded to the kings of Spain for control of the Church in America, education was in the hands of the religious authorities. Thus, the first elementary schools were established in convents. Until the eighteenth century, religious orders present on the island were the Franciscans, the Dominicans, the Augustines, the Bethlemites, and the Jesuits, and among the orders for women were those belonging to Saint Claire, Saint Catherine, and Saint Teresa.

For example, Franciscan convents provided free early education to many children from very poor families of different villages, and in exchange for a low stipend also taught children from wealthier families. Lay clergy also played an active role in education. In 1683, Bishop Diego Evelino de Compostela (1635–1704) created the first primary schools by convincing the king of the alarming lack of education in the colonies.

Secondary Level

Methods used at the time made distinguishing between secondary and post-secondary education difficult. Some orders such as the Bethlemites and the Franciscans were in charge of secondary education. For example, in 1606, subjects such as grammar and philosophy were already being taught at the *Purísima Concepción* Convent for the Young in Havana.

Bishop Diego Evelino de Compostela created the Saint Ambrosius Seminary (1689) and the School of Saint Francis de Sales (1688–89) in Havana. The Saint Basilius the Great Seminary (1722) and the Saint Agnes School were founded in Santiago and Puerto Príncipe, respectively, by the Bishop Francisco Gerónimo Valdés (1646–1729). These institutions provided secondary level education and they were created specifically to instruct the young boys of upper class families who aspired to become priests.[4]

Postsecondary Education

This level of education did not exist before the eighteenth century and very few were able to obtain a university degree. Wealthy students would usually attend universities abroad.[5]

The first steps towards the creation of a university in Cuba are linked to the prestigious Santo Domingo Convent. Due to intense confrontation existing between the bishop and this order for control over education, teaching imparted by the Dominicans only reached a *stadium generale* level, although comparable to a university degree. However, it was not until 1670 that the members of the order in Havana requested university diploma recognition for their pupils from the king, which was finally granted on January 5, 1728, giving rise to the creation in Havana of the Royal and Pontifical University of Saint Jerome, the eighth education center of its kind in America.[6] A School of Medicine was introduced as well as schools for other professions. The first universities taught theology, canonic law, civil law, medicine, and the arts (philosophy).

Students

The Franciscan and Bethlemite orders also provided free early education to poor children at all of their convents on the island. The Jesuits taught children from wealthier families. Initially, Saint Francis de Sales was only for poor girls over the age of seven years and until they married. Twelve full grants were offered to poor children, however others who could afford to pay a fee were also later admitted. The Saint Carlos and Saint Basilius Seminaries, as well as the University of Saint Jerome had similar regulations. Admission criteria were very strict, selection demanded "clean blood," namely no relatives punished by the Holy Office, as well as being "longstanding" Christians. Students were admitted to these seminars at eight to fourteen years of age and to university at the age of twelve.

Blacks, mulattos, and mestizos were not admitted. Scholarships were given to poor white children only and did not exceed twenty-four in number.

Teachers

By 1544, there is evidence that the village of Santiago already had its first teacher.[7] School teachers and instructors for subjects such as Latin grammar and Christian doctrine were both appointed and paid for by local Havana government, in response to demands made by upper social classes. In 1606, the town hall signed a petition asking the king for a special grammar teacher for the city.[8] Wages were very low in general, and teachers lacked personal development; many were almost illiterate, particularly those belonging to the school of friends (see above).[9]

In 1639, an examiners post was created in order to guarantee the skills and knowledge of those who were to be in charge of teaching subjects such as reading, writing, mathematics, religion, and good habits. In Sales, the teaching staff was made up exclusively by pious, single or widowed women. University statutes established that the Dominicans held maximum authority over the teaching staff within the university campus. Members of the order were the only ones to access the posts of principal, vice principal, secretaries, or counselors. The university had a total of twenty department chairs, occupied exclusively by men having extensive encyclopedic knowledge. Tenure could last for six years or could be granted for life if so expressed by the monarch.[10] However, lay university professors who received no payment for their services were often forced to seek employment elsewhere.

Curricula

Subjects such as reading, writing, and Christian doctrine were taught at primary schools. Exceptionally, private instructors introduced the teaching of subjects like math and languages. By the second half of the seventeenth century, the Dominicans were teaching grammar, art, and theology, reaching a level equivalent to *general studies* by 1667.[11]

The Saint Carlos and Saint Basilius seminaries had severe regulations and strict schedules both for work and for the practice of physical and mental exercises. Subjects taught reached secondary education level and included the following topics: religious history, religion, morality, music, singing, world history, Latin, French, rhetoric, natural theology, literature, physics, Spanish, and Latin.[12] The Jesuits included mathematics, philosophy, Latin studies, arts, and theology in the curriculum. Salesian education programs for girls prioritized housework activities and did not include teaching to read or physical exercise.

Teaching Methods

Throughout this period, teachers used memorization techniques and teaching methods that did not require rational thinking. Subject contents were mostly obsolete, and restricted to reading, writing, Christian doctrine, and more rarely, learning how to perform basic mathematical calculations. Higher ecclesiastic authorities controlled initial education in all schools, whereas each religious order held control over middle and superior education. Middle education was imparted in Latin, and never included methods such as induction, experimentation, or empiric or rational based research. In Saint Francis de Sales, pedagogical methods were outdated, with young girls being taught manual tasks and prayer only, while keeping intellectual activities to a minimum.[13]

The Dominicans based teaching on Thomistic Scholasticism as opposed to illustrated innovation. In the eighteenth century, a university was very far from being the scientific center of education it is today—even mathematics was read aloud at the time.

NINETEENTH CENTURY

Type of Education Systems: Tutorial, Private, State

During this century, the metropolitan government established a series of special laws for the regulation of education for its territories overseas. Among the most relevant were those passed in the years 1843, 1863, and 1880. These laws established division of the education system into separate levels—namely, primary, secondary, and superior; private education was separated into three separate levels as well.

The School Law of 1863 instituted government supervision over private education and oversight of all public education. It established every child's right to a primary education either at school or at home. Public schools would receive public funding or donations, and private ones were to be subsidized by individuals, corporations, or private entities. However, in practice, this was seldom the case, and education in general would depend mostly on the private schools given the limited available government resources.[14]

Both before and after the war of independence, education conditions in rural areas were very unstable compared to those existing in urban ones. Very few families could afford to pay for teachers for their children to acquire basic learning. When available, these were often elderly individuals or amateurs completely lacking in teaching skills.

At the end of the Ten-Year War (1868–78), peace was reached but misery and illnesses continued to prevail in the region, thus favoring an increase in the number of regional mutual-help societies which founded and subsidized many schools. Blacks and mestizos were concerned over their situation, particularly after the abolition of slavery in 1886. Black illiteracy rates reached 87.7 percent at the time.

By 1895, there were 904 municipal schools in Cuba with 36,308 children; and 740 private schools, both secular and religious, with 25,384 students. The number of schools doubled in twelve years as a result of the 1880 Government Plan. Nevertheless, by the end of the war in 1898, only 15.7 percent of children between the ages of five and seventeen attended school.[15]

Social Class and Education

Poor and middle class children attended small, free district schools, convent schools, or "schools of friends." In order to be admitted to a non-fee paying school in the local neighborhood, a child had to provide a certificate of poverty issued by the local parish priest. This certificate validated conditions of extreme poverty, thus assigning an individual "solemn poor" status. However, black and mestizo children did not share the same possibilities. Because of prevalent racism, they could only rarely attend public schools together with white children, and were otherwise segregated in centers limited to those of the same racial group. One of the worst consequences of living in slavery was the rampant illiteracy among slaves after gaining their freedom. The scarce attention they did receive was due to work carried out by the SEAP (*Sociedad Económica de Amigos del País*).[16] As was already the prevailing tradition, the benefits of a good education at one of the best schools, both in Cuba and abroad, were privy to descendants of the enslaving, merchant bourgeoisie.

Race and Education

The plantation system left profound racial scars vis-à-vis the black population in general, regardless of whether these were free individuals, freed slaves, blacks, or mestizos. In 1809, the Economic Society had established the government's Regulation for Teachers that abolished the local custom of white and non-white students sharing the same classroom. Nonetheless, this practice persisted in the more modest "schools of friends." Private schools continued to be exclusively for white children, as were the schools for the poor funded by the Economic Society.[17] The Plan passed in 1843 dictated that every village should have a school for freed black children where they were taught the basic principles of religion and morality, reading, writing, and arithmetic. For slaves, the plan considered the slave-master responsible for providing religious and moral education.

By 1887, there were 139 different societies providing education and recreation for blacks and mestizos in the most important cities, significantly improving conditions for these social classes.[18] Education promoted better jobs and economic status, giving rise to greater social flexibility. Among these societies were included: The Horse Carriage Driver's, The Cooks, the Belle Union of Havana, The Divine Charity Society, *La Igualdad* (Equality), and others.[19]

Despite the existence of a school law passed in 1883 regulating the mixed race nature of schools, racial segregation persisted. On the rest of the island, the situation was even worse; hence, the concern of the local societies for creating their own schools to educate their children.[20] In 1883, Havana had twenty-four municipal schools for boys: eighteen for whites, and six for blacks and mestizos in the city; and twenty schools for girls: fifteen for whites and five for blacks. The consequences of slavery and racism were reflected in low levels of literacy: by 1898, only 50.8 percent of the white population and barely 28 percent of blacks were able to read and write.[21]

Gender and Education

In the second half of the nineteenth century, the school to population ratio was 1,517:1. Thirty-eight percent of women had received education, whereas 42 percent of men were literate, showing clear gender discrimination in the field.[22] Under Spanish Colonial Rule, subjects taught were designed to favor those responding to the ideal for women at the time: namely to become select housewives or "queens of the household," as women were bittersweetly referred to in private. School instruction was tailored to learning useful household activities, namely sewing, cooking, first aid, and Christian doctrine, which was compulsory at all schools. These activities were known as "women's work" and clearly indicated they were not meant for men. Women were also banned from the study of certain subjects such as science, history, and politics since they were considered to be of no benefit to them. By tradition, women could only become mothers, wives, or remain spinsters.[23] Boys on the other hand, were educated with a broader, more pragmatic view of their circumstances. They were taught mathematics, accounting, history, and natural sciences, responding to the concept of men as providers imposed by family tradition and by society.

The 1846 census reports a clear lack of teachers for women, only nineteen were available at the time, for a total population of 114,573 white and freed-women slaves; in other words, one teacher for every 6,030 students. The Havana City School District had nine white women teachers and one black woman teacher, and there were nine white teachers in Puerto Príncipe. There were 298 white teachers for 120,726 male students, which meant there was one teacher for every 405 children. These figures reflect the critical education situation existing for both genders.

Young girls were excluded from secondary education until 1879, when the first secondary school for girls called "*Isabel La Católica*" was created. In that same year, the first course for women was launched at the San Alejandro School of Art, with 50 percent registrants being women. The first Cuban woman to enter a university was Mercedes Riba Pinós in 1883; she enrolled in Arts and Literature.[24] Other centers that oriented towards preparing women to join the workforce were also created, such as The Havana Typographers and Bookbinders Academy and the School of Arts and Crafts for women (1883).

Primary Education Level

With the creation of the Economic Society's Educational Section in 1816, all primary schools in the capital were run from this office. The Royal Society favored the creation of primary schools in the capital city promoted by private individuals assisted by tutors, who had access to the government's regulation for teachers between 1809–12.[25] Despite the Society's dedication to primary education, this activity had not progressed much by 1817. Most of the new schools created in the first decades of the nineteenth century were small with few students, although many grew at a later date.

Some of the private schools exclusively for white children were extremely poor, students and teachers were virtually indigent; examples include the *Rafael Bolaños* or the *Tomás Violá* schools.[26] These establishments coexisted with the "schools for friends," which although rejected by the Economic Society, were tolerated due to the prevailing local custom of sending white boys and girls and children freed slaves to school together.[27]

There were four free secular schools: two *Regla Lancastrians* and two belonging to the *Casa de Beneficencia (The Poorhouse)*, situated beyond city limits. Of the 1,211 students who received free tuition, 215 were sponsored by the Society in five private schools outside the city.[28]

The national war of independence began on October 10, 1868, to free the island from Spanish control. The country was at war for ten years. Consequently in 1869, the Captain General decided to close down sixty-four of the 712 public schools. By 1872, the education situation had not improved although some centers had been restored and four new schools had been built for black children.

By 1883, the island had 535 public schools, sixty-seven vacant schools, and 184 private ones—fifty-six more schools than thirty years earlier, many of which were run from the teachers' own homes because of a lack of facilities.[29] Private schools charged a fee for the education of white children, values of which varied depending on school curriculum, location, and teacher reputation.[30] Some schools had boarders, half-boarders, and day students; these schools were generally expensive, with fees including boarding costs and so called "filler" courses.[31]

On becoming a member of The Havana Friends Society, the Bishop of Espada improved teaching methods and school discipline, granting licenses and donations for the foundation of new primary schools. Among these were the Parish Primary and Sunday School for boys in *Regla* near Havana and a girls school. His main contribution, however, was with respect to middle and higher level education.[32]

In the 1830s, the rest of the country, and rural areas in particular, had virtually no public education available at all—only a few private institutions and some non-fee paying schools founded with generous contributions from local townships. These were mostly in the Havana district, small and only for whites, with meager budgets they seldom survived very long.[33]

Wealthy families living in main cities would pay to educate their children at private schools, although some preferred private tutoring at home. Many of these high-end schools accepted boarders, half-boarders, and day students but were small, although some were slightly larger in size, and lagged behind with regards to progress in teaching methods.

Secondary Level

The Education Section of the Economic Society also sponsored secondary and higher education, particularly during its golden years between 1816–24, at which time it received state subsidy.[34]

The Economic Society promoted the foundation of private elementary schools and large schools for boys during the 1820s. These schools began to include courses and topics which later were considered to be high school level subjects.[35] Secondary education was only officially introduced in Cuba on July 15, 1863, by Royal Decree. Before this, most students who aspired to a university degree started out with elementary level studies only, with very few having had access to the better private schools. The Plan for Schools implemented at the time prioritized literary studies over science.[36]

In 1880, a plan was approved which required the creation of a Center for Secondary Education in each provincial capital. Also, the Saint Alexander Academy of Drawing, Painting, and Sculpture was created in 1817. Some of the better-known private schools in the capital city were Belén, directed by Jesuit priests, the Pious Schools in Guanabacoa, Saint Francis of Paola, Saint Rafael, Saint Luis, The Great Antilles, Queen Isabel the Catholic (*Isabel la Católica*), El Salvador, Saint Anacletus, among others; in Cienfuegos, The Evangelic School for young ladies, Our Lady of Montserrat, Saint Carlos, El Siglo, Junco Academy, and Jesus Humanities College and Saint Christopher's; in Matanzas, the school called *La Empresa*, etc.; in Puerto Príncipe, most notably the Pious Schools; and in Santiago de Cuba, the Catholic Institute. However, the Training School for Teachers (1880) which offered free tuition and helped improve teaching skills was affected during the war in 1895.

Towards the end of the century many new institutes had sprung up offering specialized, work-oriented training such as the Dental School in Havana, and the Preparatory School of Arts and Crafts. The latter opened its doors to women in 1883 with the introduction of sewing, flower-arranging, typing, and bookkeeping courses.[37]

Higher Level Education

The University of Havana was the only center for higher studies in the country, it had five Schools: Philosophy and Literature; Physics-Mathematics; Chemistry-Natural Sciences; Pharmacy; and Medicine and Law. In 1883, the Administrative Law, Philosophy and Literature, and Sciences Schools began to award doctoral and masters' degrees; Medicine and Pharmacy started to do so as well in 1887.

The nineteenth century started out with a university which remained scholastic, but still firmly seeking to overcome its limitations. Meanwhile, opportunities for a more thorough study of the sciences lay outside the scope of the university campus or at least of its curriculum, and fell to the Economic Society or other private initiatives.[38] The creation of a special school for the study of anatomy for example, was created in 1817 as a prelude to the study of surgery.[39]

A turning point in the history of the University was the announcement made by the Royal Order in 1888 that all university books had to have been written or translated by university professors.[40] In 1892, doctorates were eliminated from all schools belonging to Havana University, leaving a large number of university professors and assistants unemployed, a measure fortunately revoked after only eight months due to strong opposition from the teaching staff.

Students

Children could begin secondary education at the age of ten years as established in 1863. Teaching schools were attended by boys at fourteen and by girls at thirteen years of age although separately. As in earlier days, only the children of influential families were allowed to enter University, and although there were no laws forbidding it, prevailing moral customs did not allow women access to higher education. Nonetheless, as from the 1880s, women started going to university and many obtained medical and teaching degrees. During the ensuing decade, high fees precluded many students from entering university.

The Arts and Crafts School was created for poor, orphan children of both genders, free of charge. In 1898 the school for orphan girls had 350 students, with ages ranging from four years on. These were children whose parents had died in war or because of epidemics or famine. This school is considered the first step towards the introduction of preschool education in Cuba.

Teachers

At the "school of friends," classes were given by unlicensed black women. Lessons were free, with only the better off families contributing small fees, with teachers occasionally receiving gifts or tokens from their pupils. Teacher numbers increased between 1830–37, with almost twice as many white men being granted teaching licenses compared to the numbers of white women. Conversely, the great majority of teaching licences approved for freed black slave teachers were awarded to women.[41] Teaching conditions in rural areas on the island were deplorable, with extremely low wages, which meant that these positions were generally taken by very humble individuals with no other work options.

The Plan passed in 1843 established that elementary school teachers had to be older than twenty, have passed an examination in order to obtain their teachers title, and had to present a health certificate with a blood test. The School Law of 1880 gave priority to teach in private institutions to Spanish citizens, and to parish priests best suited to teach Christian moral doctrine. All teachers in general received very meager wages. Annual salaries varied between six hundred pesos and one-thousand pesos cash, half the nominal value compared to stronger currencies. For this reason many teachers would request leave of absence in order to work at better paid jobs. Although most teachers were inefficient, there were many others who loved their work.[42]

Teachers at the *Saint Alexander* Academy were mostly foreigners.[43] Teacher training was hugely inefficient, and in 1878 the SEAP, concerned over the effects this might cause to education, founded the Preparatory School for Teachers. In 1880, Teacher Schools were created, initial programs however were insular, applying outdated methods and study programs.

Curricula

At the beginning of the nineteenth century, primary education was encouraged on the rest of the island and teaching curricula improved, both in Society subsidized schools and in private schools. Spanish grammar was taught in almost all of these and in a few, other subjects such as geometry, geography, French, and bookkeeping were also introduced. Both private and public basic secondary education included the following subjects: Spanish grammar, arithmetic, algebra, geometry, gym, etc., and lasted four years. On the other hand higher secondary education prepared students for university as determined by the Plan approved in 1843, and therefore included subjects like mathematics, physics, chemistry, history, philosophy, dialectics, and metaphysics. In 1852, the Saint Alexander School expanded its curriculum, the three main subjects were painting, sculpture and linear drawing, but geometry, mythology, history, costumes, and color, were included as well.[44]

The Bishop of Espada[45] introduced new subjects to the San Carlos seminary, namely chemistry, experimental physics, political economics, and promoted the creation of a Chair on Constitutional Studies in 1820, headed by a young clergyman named Félix Varela.

According to the Plan approved in 1880, primary education was mandatory, and was divided into elementary and upper level education. Initial levels included reading, writing, and basic grammar, whereas the higher level was extended to geometry, lineal drawing, surveying, basic principles of physics, natural history, and an introduction to commerce, agriculture, and industry.[46]

Teaching Methods

At the beginning of the century fundamental teaching principles barely existed in Cuba and teaching at the primary level was based mostly on memorizing and mnemonic techniques and verbal cues. Discipline was often imposed through physical or mental punishment. School lessons were held in two daily sessions, from 8:00–11:00 AM and from 12:00–4:00 PM.[47]

In Spain, the Pestalozzi method was well known and held in high esteem, and efforts were made to introduce it in Cuba, however the failure of the Pestalozzi Institute in Madrid eventually caused these plans to be dropped. The Bell and Lancaster teaching method was implemented in 1817 with the help of a teacher called Esteban de Navea.[48] Lancastrian schools were founded in *Regla*, the *Casa de Beneficencia,* the town of Guanabacoa, and in the rest of the country, however the flaws of the method soon became evident.[49]

One of the schools to radically change its teaching methods was the famous El Salvador School, which abandoned corporal and otherwise humiliating punishments and promoted reason-based study methods and hard work ethics.

Secondary schools were grouped into separate subject areas: sciences, philosophy, and history. The teaching of classical and modern languages was also relevant, as well as physical education (gym, swimming, horse riding) and self-defense (fencing).[50]

Major Reforms

January 23, 1809	Regulations for Teacher Governance were approved by the Economic Society, to direct and supervise primary school teachers in Havana.
July 13, 1812	The Court of Cadiz passes a Constitutional Law approving the creation of a General Study Department under government authority.
August 26, 1816	The Education Department of the Economic Society is established.
1863	Secondary Education is introduced.
1879	Women and young girls are allowed to study at secondary schools.
1880	Royal Decree establishing the creation of one secondary school for each province and in consequence abolishing secondary degrees granted by universities.
1884	First Pedagogic Congress in the Matanzas province. The congress advocated the use of better texts, programs, and methods, as well as recommending the creation of modern Teaching Schools applying European methods.[51]
1887	Law passed in favor of Free Education.
1895	Greek is eliminated from the curriculum, and physics and chemistry are merged into one course.

TWENTIETH CENTURY: THE REPUBLIC (1902–58)

Type of Education System: Tutorial, Private, State

On January 1, 1899, North American forces formally occupied Cuban territory. Cuba had reached the turn of the century without ever achieving independence. In an attempt to promote education the occupation government appointed Alexis Frye, a North American pedagogue, as Commissioner of Public Schools, who developed teacher training colleges and summer schools for teachers. A large group of Cuban teachers even attended summer school at Harvard University. Many Cuban intellectuals participated in the project, such as Enrique José Varona for example, who worked in the reorganization of higher education under a plan that bore his name. They also participated in the writing of new textbooks for elementary education, which would be seminal in generating civic awareness and fostering a sense of history amongst Cuban nationals.

Proclamation of the Republican State on May 20, 1902, brought institutional education under the direction of the Education Secretariat. At the primary level, public education was both free and compulsory, secondary education was geared towards vocational training, and higher education was further amplified with the creation of new public and private institutes.

Successive republican governments however, showed little interest in education institutions. More often than not, education budgets were mismanaged, which caused public schools to suffer abandonment.[52]

Moreover, governments failed to solve the crucial issue of social, racial, and gender-related injustice.

Education and Social Class

Repeated economic crises affecting the country left many families poverty-stricken and excluded from society. Low income and unemployment rendered access to education difficult, whereas members of the middle class could continue sending their children to Catholic or secular schools for boys or for girls, like Belén, La Salle or The Marist School. Members of small-town bourgeois sectors were able to do so, thanks to the benefit of free registration offered to these particular groups.[53]

Both primary and secondary public schools were in pitiful condition. Pupil absenteeism increased because students were often forced to work in order to contribute to household income.[54] The situation was similar in higher level education, where expensive registration fees often precluded access to the majority of students.

Race and Education

Blacks had restricted access to education because of racial discrimination and low income. During Frye's superintendence, 3,000 public schools were created without the racial segregation established by the United States.[55] Nevertheless, in 1907, of the total number of children registered in schools 82,164 were white and 40,050 were blacks.[56] Teachers also suffered this exclusion. During the trip to Harvard University, black women were housed in respectable family homes in Boston, however black men did not receive similar hospitality.[57]

The Constitution of 1940 established racial equality, but segregation persisted in protestant and catholic schools, privileging white children.[58]

Regarding higher education, no restrictions existed for black students to access university, yet racist customs and work demands made the presence of black students uncommon.

Gender and Education

Opportunities for women to acquire an education improved in comparison to colonial times. Maternity-related professions were encouraged and in 1918 the Domestic School (*Escuela del Hogar*) was created by presidential decree.[59] In 1902, shorthand academies and teacher training or normal schools were opened where 88 percent of students were women.[60] *Saint Alexander* academy remained an excellent option for further improvement, and university careers for nurses, teachers, and midwives were created. However, men were the ones who actually obtained higher education, since most women married after finishing high school and were forced to abandon their studies.[61] In summary, women had fewer opportunities than men to further themselves.

Levels of Education

Primary

During the early years of the century, public primary education was emphasized. Between 1902 and 1958, many different types of primary schools were created: urban (111), rural (28), elementary urban (1824), and rural (4754), as well as kindergartens for preschoolers (1,610). These schools consisted of the kindergarten followed by six grades. Nevertheless, the number of children attending schools still remained very low: 172,273 in 1902; 234,038 in 1919; only 234,038 in 1931; increasing to 520,000 in 1947; and to 736,606 children in 1958.[62] One of the major problems confronted by primary schools was absenteeism, which significantly affected promotion to higher grades, generating huge discrepancies between numbers of pupils registering in lower grades and those actually completing the sixth grade.[63]

Secondary or Middle Level Education

Some of the six secondary education institutes were refurbished and equipped with modern labs. These were non-fee paying institutions where most of the students belonged to middle class families. The Havana Institute was expanded to include a nautical school; a school of commerce and stenography; a botanical garden; and for those schools located in the provinces, surveying schools were also incorporated.[64]

Special middle education was in the hands of schools recently reopened such as the prestigious private school *Saint Alexander* and public Teacher Training schools (*Escuelas Normales*). Training to become a primary school teacher lasted four years, before entering the University School of Pedagogy. Other middle education institutes were created such as professional schools for: journalism, technical careers, The National Institute for Physical Education, advertising, agriculture, arts, commerce, arts and crafts, and civil-military institutes. Studies lasted three years with the objective of qualifying students for university entry.

Higher Education

With the turn of the century, the university underwent substantial improvement, new careers were added, methods improved and the campus was transferred to a new site on the outskirts of the city.[65] The Varona Plan[66] divided studies available at this level into three separate schools: law, medicine and languages, and sciences. As a result of scientific and technological development, science-related careers flourished under capitalist growth, and new university buildings were equipped with libraries, museums, a stadium, and an archive. This Plan was defended by university students during the 1923 Reform, opposed to obsolete teaching methods and to government control.[67]

In 1937, the number of university schools had increased to thirteen with the addition of education, astronomical engineering, a sugar research institute, social science, public law, commercial science, and dentistry.[68] In spite of these measures, the number of students entering university remained low, with only 6.4 percent of young people between the ages of fifteen and nineteen actually joining.

During the 1940s, more than twenty new private universities were created, among the most famous, the Catholic University of Saint Tomas at Villanueva, and the La Salle University.[69] Most of the old academies became university centers. Havana University remained nonetheless the best in Cuba, the bastion of local culture and tradition.[70] Other officially approved universities with state backing were opened such as Santiago de Cuba (1947) and *Marta Abreu* in Las Villas (1952).

Students

At the start of the century only 36 percent of school-aged children were registered in schools: 66,322 boys and 55,892 girls.[71] Secondary education imparted proficiency for working in varied professional fields. Baccalaureate or *bachillerato* students usually came from middle class families, courses lasted four years and were geared towards the study of sciences; the degree rendered was a baccalaureate in languages or sciences depending on the choice of subjects.[72] Specialized middle schools were mostly fee-free and coeducational, although the majority of students were men; for example, the industrial technology schools, arts and crafts, and trade schools. However, *Saint Alexander* was mainly for young girls, and trained artists and art teachers.[73]

To enter a university, students had to be eighteen years old, and annual fees were eighty pesos, whereas in private institutes they paid twenty-five pesos for each course as well as application fees.[74]

Teachers

Different censuses obtained at the beginning of the century revealed deficiencies in the number of school teachers in Cuba. In 1899, young men and women prepared to help further education were called on.[75] This first group of teachers was quite heterogeneous. For this reason, educational boards[76] were created to oversee teaching quality and contracts were extended for only one year. A teacher handbook for primary education was prepared and distributed, and summer schools were also organized. In 1900, North American authorities in Cuba sent 1,256 teachers to Harvard University to teacher training courses.[77] Middle school teachers had different categories, tutors, auxiliaries, and extra-helpers, the latter category was eliminated in 1900. Posts for lab and library assistants and for music teachers were created at a later date. Trainers of school teachers had to meet more stringent criteria and were required to have doctorate degrees in their field of expertise. University professors were selected on the basis of academic and professional standing. Chair professors received an annual stipend of two-thousand pesos and assistants were paid 720 pesos. Primary teachers received a monthly salary of fifty to seventy-five pesos, depending on where they worked.[78]

Curricula

Cuban history and moral and civic instruction became leading subjects in the new education programs replacing Christian doctrine. New textbooks had to be written by Cuban teachers or intellectuals. Notable examples include *Principles of Moral and Civil Instruction* (1902) by Rafael Montoro, and *Notions of Cuban History* (1904) by Vidal Morales y Morales. A new curriculum for primary schools was also published, including a History of the United States of America by *Sloyd*[79] and English language.[80]

The Varona Plan introduced new careers at Havana University, such as pedagogy for example with subjects such as teacher psychology, methodology, and history of teaching. Technical careers, namely civil engineering, electrical engineering, architecture, and veterinary medicine acquired relevance later on, following growing capitalist development in the country.[81] Although existing regulations required uniformity between teaching plans and programs, individual institutions usually applied their own, prior to approval by the local education inspector.[82] Study programs at the time attempted to reach a balance between science and the humanities, namely history, geography, literature, civic and constitutional studies, and all teachers of these subjects had to be Cuban nationals.

Teaching Methods

Educational reform was introduced in order to change old-fashioned teaching methods and to shape the behavior of the citizens of the new Republic. In this context, the Varona Plan favored objective and rational education and promoted the teaching of national history, based on the lives of national heroes and military campaigns.[83] History lessons were aided with maps, books, guided visits to museums and historical sites; however, methods promoting productive potential were not entirely abandoned.[84] With the reform introduced in 1914, classes became more interactive, exercises in critical reading were permitted, and student elaborated questionnaires were generated. Reading and writing classes were of vital importance because of their direct correlation with civic responsibilities like a citizen's right to vote.[85] University classes were open to the public, divided in theory and experimental practice, for which professors adopted personal scientific methods.

Major Reforms

1899   Colonial legislation was replaced, and the secular, state, Cuban school was created. Military Decree 226.

1900   Varona Plan (Military Decree 266). Schools belonging to the University of Havana were reduced to three: sciences and languages, medicine and pharmacy, and law. Textbooks had to be written by Cuban teachers (Military Decree 454).

1915   School Reform. Rigid civic–moral doctrine was maintained. Cuban history taught twice a week from third grade on. Schools for teachers were created.

1917   Creation of the Cuban Society for Pedagogical Studies.

1923   University Reform. Demanded university autonomy and renovation of study programs and methods.

1940   The Republic was established; official or private universities were authorized.

CUBAN REVOLUTION (1959–2007)

Type of Education System (State Run)

On January 1, 1959, the victory of the Cuban Revolution marked the beginning of a new era.[86] The old dictatorship was abolished and a new society created. From the outset, the revolutionary government established effective policies of justice and social equality. Military headquarters formerly used as torture centers were turned into schools, an Integral Educational Reform was introduced, private education was nationalized, and a successful reading campaign was implemented. The Cuban education transformation process had two important turning points: first, 1961 was named the "Year of Education" after the relevant social changes occurring in the country after 1956; and second, the constitution of the National Education System in 1975.[87]

The education institutionalization process began with the Constitution of the Republic of Cuba in 1976, and continues to supervise the workings of today's education system.[88] Education is free, and all levels have been improved to provide these new citizens with professional skills. Opportunities are open to people of all ages, from preschool, through primary, secondary, special education, classes for adults, and on to higher and specialized training. One of the achievements of the new regime has been to offer all Cuban citizens access to learning, free of any racial or gender discrimination.[89]

Social Classes and Education

The right to education is guaranteed through ample access to free schooling, full and half-day boarding schools and grants, as well as free study materials. This has helped each child or youngster to complete their studies according to their individual capacity, as well as on varying social demands and economic development needs.[90] Social welfare has been another tool applied by the revolution in an attempt to close the social and economic gap. Social security provides school meals (breakfast and lunch) and bussing services. Children and adolescents benefit from equal education with no differences between social classes.[91]

Race and Education

Racial discrimination, or discrimination of any other order is condemned by law. State institutions educate all citizens from early childhood under the principle of equal rights for everyone.[92] The revolution also took interest in special education needs for children with physical or mental disabilities or behavioral problems to prevent social exclusion.[93]

Gender and Education

Both boys and girls are thus assured free education under equal conditions and with extra support from programs for the teaching of adults, technical and professional training in state companies or organizations, and higher education for working class individuals.[94]

Women in particular have been granted a leading role in different revolution initiatives, the *Ana Betancourt* studies plan created in 1961 for young women from rural areas, the reading program for women from all social sectors.[95] In elementary and middle school institutions, women are often elected as leaders of study unions.[96] And women's involvement in university studies has also increased substantially.[97] During the 1990s, an increasing number of women completed agricultural studies at technical and professional schools, where they currently represent 43 percent of the student body at the national level, a number reaching 50 percent in other areas of production and services.

Levels of Education

Primary

Preschool and primary education were the areas that received most attention compared to previous administrations. Schooling became mandatory up to sixth grade.[98] Primary education represents the basis for general education. This stage was structured in order to emphasize solid civic knowledge, improvement in the use of language, environmental awareness, among others. It was also conceived to be the key stage for physical and psychological learning and development in children. This period of early learning includes three main areas: circle time, preschool grades, and informal approaches.[99]

Between 1959 and 1975, numbers of students receiving primary education increased 2.7 percent. Schooling rates for children between six and twelve years of age reached 100 percent. The number of children graduating from sixth grade increased from under 30,000 in 1958 to 190,000 in 1975, and by 1985 the rate of five-year-olds attending school rose from 80 percent to 100 percent.[100]

Middle Education

Middle school comprises grades seven to nine, thus completing basic middle level education in Urban (*Escuelas Secundarias Urbanas ESBU*) and in Rural Secondary Schools (*Escuelas Secundarias en le Campo ESBEC*).[101] The objectives of the level are to impart general knowledge, vocational guidance, and work commitment.[102] At the same time, many new cultural centers sprang up, like the National Art School (ENA) and ballet schools. Other new schools include those for crafts, agriculture and industrial technology, and primary teacher schools.[103] Upper-middle studies (baccalaureate) can be completed at pre-university institutes, both urban (IPU) and rural (IPUEC), similar to basic rural secondary schools. This stage lasts three years and corresponds to grades ten, eleven, and twelve.[104]

Other specialized pre-university institutes with particular objectives or special characteristics, and applying strict selection criteria include: the Preuniversity Vocational Institute in Exact Sciences (IPVCE), the Preuniversity Vocational Institute in Pedagogical Sciences (IPVCP), the Preuniversity Vocational Military Institute (IPVM), schools for School Sports Training (EIDE), and Vocational Art School (EVA).[105]

Higher Education

After the victory of the revolution, Havana, Las Villas, and Oriente Universities, where teaching had been interrupted for two years, reopened. The University Reform Bill, passed on January 10, 1962, created new careers, generated new grants, and instituted free education, measures which helped to increase university student body numbers between 1962 and 1975.[106]

Cuban universities are under autonomous jurisdiction, although they have links to state educational organizations under the direction of the Ministry of Higher Education. Academic courses are classified as regular day courses, day courses for workers, and remote learning courses.[107] Aside from existing universities, new specialized education institutes were created: the Higher Polytechnic Institute, Medical Sciences, Pedagogy, Physical Education and Military Sciences, and the Latin American School of Medicine.

From the academic year 2000–2001 onward, twelfth-grade graduates could receive training to become social workers. These students have priority entry to higher education at schools teaching social sciences and humanities combining work with remote learning, with teacher support.[108] Postgraduate studies (doctorates and masters degrees) comprise the highest level of the national education system, and are aimed at furthering university graduate academic training as far as possible. These programs, which include degrees in many different fields, last two years and conclude with the presentation of original research work.[109] Titles issued are "Doctor in Sciences" or PhD, or doctoral titles for a specific branch of science (for example, Doctor in Agricultural Sciences).[110]

Students

Access to education follows democratic steps, given the fact that it is free with equal opportunities for all citizens. Anyone who is interested may apply to any of the levels available. A national grants system is available throughout the country, guaranteeing student access to education centers, regardless of origin or financial possibilities.[111] Circle time sessions are attended by boys and girls between six months to five years of age,[112] and primary school by children between six and eleven years of age. Whereas middle and higher education level is for twelve- to seventeen-year-old students.

Entry to higher education is based on a tier ranking system rated on the basis of strict examination results. Students who complete the military service can also apply, on the basis of results obtained after a course designed specifically to this end, as well as the winners of general knowledge competitions, and students graduating with honors from technical or profession-oriented schools.[113]

Total numbers of higher education students registered for the academic year 2000–2001 reached 129,000, of which 35,500 students were admitted and 17,000 professionals graduated, the vast majority in Medical Sciences and Teaching careers.[114]

Teachers

In August 1959, the revolutionary government had intended to open 10,000 new classrooms, but had only enough of a budget for half the number of teachers needed to fill them. However, in response to the appeal made by the government, teachers agreed to work for half their wages during one whole school term.[115]

By 1960–61, sufficient teachers were available for the growing number of students. The National Institute of Agricultural Reform (INRA) undertook reading campaigns together with teachers, reading instructors, the rebel army, and more than 100,000 illiterate individuals were taught to read and write.[116] Later, primary teachers were selected on the basis of their credentials, and life-long tenure eliminated.[117] Different categories corresponding to higher educa-tion teachers were established in 1975, and included principal, complementary, and special categories.[118]

More than 90 percent of higher level teachers are full-time staff, and their numbers had risen to 22,000 by the year 2002. Twenty-four percent of these teachers work in fields related to teaching, and 40 percent in medicine. More than 50 percent are women, and the majority are graduates from teaching, nat-ural science, and social science and humanities schools, with a mean age of forty-five years, or older for medicine and social sciences.[119]

During the revolution, higher education was at a critical stage regarding teacher numbers, but by the 1990s the situation had improved substantially, and in the year 2000 the number of university professors had risen to 20,753.

Curricula

The Plan for the Improvement of Education introduced in 1975, as well as adjustments implemented in 1988 and during the 1990s, are all part of a continuous process aimed at improving the quality of education. Teachers from all around the country have helped to establish changes that needed to be made in contents, methods, and textbooks.[120] Primary education was divided into two stages, the first stage from first to fourth grade of propaedeutic value, including basic concepts in language and math, favoring the development of skills for better learning. The second stage from fifth to sixth grade, is defined as a transition period to middle school with the acquisition of more complex intellectual abilities.

During the 1990–91 school year, primary school curricula were improved emphasizing oral and written language, mathematical calculations, and guide-lines for acceptable behavior. Use of games in teaching was increased, as well as field trips and outings. Basic elementary instruction was completed for language and mathematics, and geography and history of Cuba were incorpo-rated as new subjects, as well as natural sciences and civic studies.[121] Middle level education emphasizes vocational guidance counseling to help graduating students better select a career and continue their training at the higher educa-tion level. Science contents were updated during the 1999–2000 school year in order to define responsibilities in patriotic, judicial, labor, environmental, and aesthetics related topics, as well as health and sex education.[122] During the last decade, preuniversity education also underwent reform, with a new study plan introduced during the 1991–92 school year. The curricular subjects include natural sciences, mathematics, Spanish language and literature, history, English language, geography, and physical education. New subjects have also been introduced, namely social sciences, basic military training, and computer sciences.[123]

University careers have maintained high standards of training, with state-of-the-art education programs developed encouraging occupational skills and acquisition of professional capabilities, while also providing sound theoretical instruction imparted through updated technical and scientific information, and the link of both teachers and students to production-related activities.[124]

Teaching Methods

In order to eradicate illiteracy, language used in rural areas was taken into account from the outset in the design of reading cards, because mass distribution of the printed material required everyone to be able to understand the contents.[125] Later, teaching at the primary level sought to emphasize the national identity, helping children understand the history of the Cuban nation and of its international relations with other countries.[126] Middle level education seeks to promote a high standard of moral and civic awareness away from oral learning, while favoring critical thinking and reasoning.[127] Programs promote use of calculus, reasoning and research opportunities, links to art-related activities, observing and understanding of one's geographic environment, study of the country's resources, and economic development potential. Oral and written communication skills are developed, as well personal initiative, building a "culture of effort," and encouraging good work habits.[128] The new millennium brought modern teaching methods, with generalized use of computers, and televised class transmission available at all education centers in the country.

Major Reforms

January 1959	Law 11. Annulled all degrees issued during time in which the university remained closed.
January 14, 1959	Decree formulated by the revolutionary government's board of ministers, annulling all academic titles from private universities issued after November 30, 1956, and the closing down of official universities with the exception of *Oriente*, *Havana*, and *Las Villas* universities.
February 1959	The Reform of the National Education System begins with decentralization of the Ministry of Education (MINED).
March 1959	The MINED organizes the National Reading and Basic Education Commission.
December 26, 1959	The Complete Teaching Reform is approved.
June 6, 1961	The Law for General Nationalization of Education is passed, ensuring free education.

January 10, 1962	Proclamation of University Reform.
July 31, 1976	The Ministry of Higher Education is created (Law 1306).
June 7 and	Ministry resolutions Number 216 and 403, redefining study
July 22, 1989	program contents for compulsory education (general, technology, and work-related), as well as content evaluation methods respectively.
September 9, 2002	Training courses for comprehensive general professors are started.

A DAY IN THE LIFE

Nicolás Martínez was a nine-year-old white boy living in what was then called the walled city of Old Havana. He and his mother lived on a narrow street known as *Poor Peña*, in a very humble home, which managed to remain standing solely through divine intervention. At 6:00 AM, Nicolás would be woken by his mother who brought him a cup of coffee with milk. He could hear the church bells ringing at the Church of the Angel through his window. He needed to get up very early in order to help his mother deliver clean laundry to the *Ursuline* nuns, whom she worked for once a week. Because Nicolas' father passed away in 1833 during the cholera epidemic, the year in which this disease had ravaged Havana, meant that he was an orphan and had to help his mother.

By 8:00 AM, the boy was off to the small makeshift school humbly run from the home of a mestizo woman by the name of María Merced Pérez. The school had close to twenty-five pupils between the ages of six and fourteen years, all from the poorer sectors, just like Nicolás. That morning the parish priest stopped by to visit, just as he did every month, and to cast a disapproving eye on anything not to his liking, such as children of different genders or races sitting together on the same wooden benches. Morning lessons were taken up going over previous ones from memory, repeating out loud things learned the day before. Several got into trouble that day for not remembering them.

At around 10:00 AM, the children were allowed a short break, limited to going out into the courtyard, drinking water, and using the toilet. Nicolás would use this opportunity to scrutinize an old map of the Iberian Peninsula looking for the place where his grandfather had come from many years ago when he had joined the army and set sail for the New World. Then came time for arithmetic class, with knowledge on sizes, quantities, and magnitudes— subjects Nicolás failed to understand because his teacher used abstract language. Once again, everyone made fun of him when he was picked to go up to the blackboard, but was unable to solve the exercise assigned him.

Lunch break comes at 11:00 AM. On that day, Nicolas was only able to eat a small loaf of bread. At noon, classes began once more. It was time to practice handwriting. Spelling and calligraphy were practiced in a copybook with yellow-lined pages.

When the bells rang at 4:00 PM, the children stampeded out. Nicolás liked to take a detour to *Cortina de Valdés* to catch a glimpse of the sea and of the new brigs sailing in and out of the bay. Back at home, his mother would be waiting for him to run errands, maybe to go down to the Campeche district to buy chocolate, sugar, and salted fish. Back at home, he would enjoy a well-earned bath and dinner, and would fall asleep watching his mother knit white lace *mantillas*. By 9:00 PM, the sound of the canon would tell him the city gates were closing. The city sleeps.

TIMELINE

January 5, 1728	San Geronimo University is founded at the Dominican Convent of San Juan de Letran in Havana.
January 9, 1793	The Economic Society of Friends (*Sociedad Económica de Amigos del País*) (SEAP) is founded.
August 26, 1816	The Education Section of the Economic Society is founded.
1863	Secondary Education is officially approved in Cuba.
October 10, 1868–78	The Ten-Year War is waged, also known as the Big War for national independence from Spanish Rule, which ends unsuccessfully.
1880	By Royal Decree, a center for secondary teaching is approved for every province, and the baccalaureate university title is abolished.
1883	Cuban women begin attending university classes.
February 24, 1895–98	Second War of Independence.
January 1, 1899	Spanish domination over Cuba ends and the first U.S. government occupation is established. The title of Royal and Literary University is lost, and simply becomes *The University of Havana*.
1899	Colonial rule gone, the first public Cuban lay school was created.
1900	The Varona Plan (Military Decree 266). Reducing the University of Havana to three Schools: Letters and Sciences, Medicine and Pharmacy, and Law.
May 29, 1902	Military occupation ends and the republican state is established under the presidency of Tomas Estrada Palma.
1915	Schools for teachers are created.
1923	University Reform. Demands for an independent university are made, as well as for renewal of program contents and study methods.
1940	Republic constituted, giving rise to the possibility of establishing state or private universities.
March 10, 1952	Military coup that gave rise to Fulgencio Batista y Zaldívar's dictatorship.
January 1, 1959	Political government control taken over by rebel forces under Fidel Castro Ruz's leadership.
January 14, 1959	Revolutionary government Ministers Council annuls by decree all academic titles awarded after November 30, 1956, by private universities, and "official" universities are closed down, with the exception of *Oriente*, *Havana*, and *Las Villas*.

January 1, 1961	National reading campaign is launched.
June 6, 1961	All private schools disappear after the Law for the General Nationalization of Teaching is passed.
January 10, 1962	University Reform Bill proclamation.
July 31, 1976	Higher Education Ministry established.
June 7, 1989 and July 22, 1989	Ministry resolutions are signed defining study plan contents for compulsory education programs (general, technology, and work-related), as well as evaluation procedures for this education level, respectively.
September 2000	The first school for Emerging Learning for Primary Teachers for the city of Havana and for Matanzas is opened.
2000–2001	Twelfth-grade graduates begin training as social workers.

NOTES

1. Translator's note: In Cuban history, these were schools not just for the poor but also run by the poor, without real teachers, where adults or children could learn from one another, in particular different types of trade.

2. Higher echelons dominating society included tradesmen, government officials, and landowners, all having greater educational privileges. Middle class groups were comprised of craftsmen, farmers, or foremen, and the lower end of society comprised slaves, rank soldiers, some Indians working the land, small landowners, and former slaves carrying out an assortment of different jobs. Societal classes were made up by "whites," as opposed to "blacks," "colored people," or "non-whites," which implied dark-skinned individuals (mulattos) or blacks. Closely linked to the concept of society constituted by a series of different levels, was the distribution of social classes into castes, groups, or sectors following a pyramidal structure, where rigid norms were imposed regarding social decorum. See Cuban History Institute, *La Colonia; Desde los orígenes hasta 1867 [The Colony; From Origins to 1867]* (Havana, Política Publishers, 1995).

3. Lyding Rodríguez Fuentes, *Santa Clara de Asís: un convento de las élites habaneras (1644–1850) [Saint Claire Assisi: a convent for the elite in Havana (1644–1850)]* (Havana: unpublished, 2003), 5.

4. Antonio Bachiller y Morales, *Apuntes para la historia de las letras y la instrucción pública en la Isla de Cuba [Notes on the History of Literature and Public Teaching in Cuba]* (Havana: Literature and Linguistic Institute, 1965), book 1, p. 296.

5. Some of these centers were *Saint Tomas University, Santiago de la Paz* or *Gorjón School at La Española; Comendadores School San Ramón Nonato; Saint Mary of All Saints; Saint Peter, Saint Paul and Saint Idelphonsus* in Nueva España. (See Enrique Sosa Rodríguez and Alejandrina Penabad Félix, *Historia de la educación en Cuba [History of Education in Cuba]* (Havana: Boloña Publishing, 2003), book 4, p. 16).

6. Antonio Bachiller y Morales, *Apuntes para la historia de las letras y la instrucción pública en la Isla de Cuba [Notes on the History of Literature and Public Teaching in Cuba]* (Havana: Literature and Linguistic Institute, 1965), book 1, p. 244.

7. His name was Miguel Velásquez, from the town of Santiago de Cuba, born to an Indian mother and Spanish father. He had also studied in Seville and in Alcalá de Henares, and some of the lessons he taught were singing, grammar, and organ playing.

8. See Cuban History Institute, *La Colonia; Desde los orígenes hasta 1867 [The Colony; From Origins to 1867]* (Havana, Política Publishers, 1990), 173–214.

9. Enrique Sosa Rodríguez and Alejandrina Penabad Félix, *Historia de la educación en Cuba [History of Education in Cuba]* (Havana: Boloña Publishing, 2005), book 5, p. 122.

10. Antonio Bachiller y Morales, *Apuntes para la historia de las letras y la instrucción pública en la Isla de Cuba* [*Notes on the History of Literature and Public Teaching in Cuba*] (Havana: Literature and Linguistic Institute, 1965), book 1, p. 244.

11. One of the differences, among others, between general and university studies was that the former were aimed at the training of members of religious orders. In Havana, just like the rest of America, lay students were also permitted, and young people came from all around the island.

12. Antonio Bachiller y Morales, *Apuntes para la historia de las letras y la instrucción pública en la Isla de Cuba [Notes on the History of Literature and Public Teaching in Cuba]* (Havana: Literature and Linguistic Institute, 1965), book 1.

13. Enrique Sosa Rodríguez and Alejandrina Penabad Félix, *Historia de la educación en Cuba [History of Education in Cuba]* (Havana: Boloña Publishing, 2005), book 3, p. 71.

14. Official policy was aimed at minimizing patriotic education in schools, and attempted through implementation of outdated study programs to counter the separatist ideas of Cubans. Some North American schools began to attract the more influential families, who would send their children to study abroad, and to the United States, in particular. With respect to private schools, the only ones authorized to open were those conducted by individuals with clear integrationist inclinations, or by women mistakenly considered harmless by the government. María del Carmen Barcia Zequeira, in *Cuban History Institute: Las luchas por la independencia nacional y las transformaciones estructurales 1868–98 [Battles over National Independence and Structural Transformations 1868–98]* (Havana; Política Publishers, 1995), 306.

15. María del Carmen Barcia Zequeira, in *Cuban History Institute: Las luchas por la independencia nacional y las transformaciones estructurales 1868–98 [Battles over National Independence and Structural Transformations 1868–98]* (Havana; Política Publishers, 1995).

16. Translator's note: A library founded in Cuba in 1793 and through "negro societies" which fostered education for this population group.

17. Enrique Sosa Rodríguez and Alejandrina Penabad Félix, *Historia de la educación en Cuba [History of Education in Cuba]* (Havana: Boloña Publishing, 2003), book 5, p. 71.

18. María del Carmen Barcia Zequeira, *Capas populares y modernidad 1880–1930 [Layers of Society and Modern Times]* (Havana: Fernando Ortiz Foundation, 2005), 142.

19. Ibid., 148.

20. Ibid., 282.

21. By the end of the century, 70 percent of the population on the island knew how to read, 34 percent could read and write, but only 1.2 percent had higher studies, and in total 34 percent of all readers lived in the capital, Havana. See María del Carmen Barcia Zequeira, in *Cuban History Institute: Las luchas por la independencia nacional y las transformaciones estructurales 1868–98 [Battles over National Independence and Structural Transformations 1868–98]* (Havana; Política Publishers, 1995), 309.

22. *Cuban Census Report, 1899* (Washington, D.C.: Government Printing Office, 1900), 373.

23. Yamilet Hernández Galano, *El diseño de nuevos arquetipo de las mujeres cubana por la educación y los empleos 1899–1902 [The Design of New Archetypes for Cuban*

Women through Education and Employment] (Havana: Diploma Thesis, Havana University, 2003).

24. Three years later, Dolores Figueroa from Cienfuegos obtained her doctor's degree in pharmacy from the University of Philadelphia. Later, Laura Martínez y Carvajal was the first woman in Cuba to graduate in ophthalmology. See Yamilet Hernández Galano, *El diseño de nuevos arquetipo de las mujeres cubana por la educación y los empleos 1899–1902* [*The Design of New Archetypes for Cuban Women through Education and Employment*] (Havana: Diploma Thesis, Havana University, 2003).

25. Enrique Sosa Rodríguez and Alejandrina Penabad Félix, *Historia de la educación en Cuba [History of Education in Cuba]* (Havana: Boloña Publishing, 2005), book 5, p. 56.

26. Ibid., 71.

27. Ibid., 69.

28. Ibid., 123–24.

29. Barcia Zequeira, in *Cuban History Institute*, 306–08.

30. Enrique Sosa Rodríguez and Alejandrina Penabad Félix, *Historia de la educación en Cuba [History of Education in Cuba]* (Havana: Boloña Publishing, 2003), book 5, p. 71.

31. Ibid., 71.

32. Nevertheless, teaching activities carried out by regular clergy continued to take place in convents such as *Santo Domingo, Saint Francis, Saint Catherine*'s, *Saint Claire*'s, and *Santa Teresa*'s. However, halfway into this century, clear decline of the religious communities was evident, therefore affecting the quality of the education they could provide. See Enrique Sosa Rodríguez and Alejandrina Penabad Félix, *Historia de la educación en Cuba [History of Education in Cuba]* (Havana: Boloña Publishing, 2005), book 5, p. 110.

33. Enrique Sosa Rodríguez and Alejandrina Penabad Félix, *Historia de la educación en Cuba [History of Education in Cuba]* (Havana: Boloña Publishing, 2005), book 5, p. 177.

34. Ibid., 43.

35. Enrique Sosa Rodríguez and Alejandrina Penabad Félix, *Historia de la educación en Cuba [History of Education in Cuba]* (Havana: Boloña Publishing, 2003), book 6, p. 12.

36. Secondary Teaching Institute, *Academic Yearbook for 1863 (Memoria anual correspondiente al curso académico de 1863)* (Havana: El Avisador Comercial [The Commercial Advertiser], 1863).

37. Raquel Vinat de la Mata, *Female Education in Cuba 1648–1898 [Educación femenina en Cuba]* (Havana: Política Publishers, 2005), 63.

38. Enrique Sosa Rodríguez and Alejandrina Penabad Félix, *Historia de la educación en Cuba [History of Education in Cuba]* (Havana: Boloña Publishing, 2003), book 4, p. 94.

39. Antonio Bachiller y Morales, *Apuntes para la historia de las letras y la instrucción pública en la Isla de Cuba [Notes on the History of Literature and Public Teaching in Cuba]* (Havana: Literature and Linguistic Institute, 1965), book 1, p. 170.

40. Barcia Zequeira, in *Cuban History Institute*, 311.

41. Enrique Sosa Rodríguez and Alejandrina Penabad Félix, *Historia de la educación en Cuba* [*History of Education in Cuba*] (Havana: Boloña Publishing, 2005), book 5, p. 127.

42. There were several excellent black primary school teachers like Matías and Eugenio Velasco, former slaves who knew Latin and had been given an education by their masters. They had schools in the *Jesús María* and *los Sitios* neighborhoods. Other well-known teachers were José Calzada, Pilar Borrego, León Monzón, and Juana Pastor, the last being the head at a mixed-race co-ed school in *Jesús María*, which was shut down by the authorities because of not adhering to approved study programs. Ibid., p. 309.

43. Antonio Bachiller y Morales, *Apuntes para la historia de las letras y la instrucción pública en la Isla de Cuba [Notes on the History of Literature and Public Teaching in Cuba]* (Havana: Literature and Linguistic Institute, 1965), book 1, p. 173.

44. Ibid., p. 229–244.

45. Thanks to negotiations conducted by this bishop, expensive equipment was purchased in Europe for subjects such as hydrostatics, magnetism, electricity, galvanism, and astronomy. See Enrique Sosa Rodríguez and Alejandrina Penabad Félix, *Historia de la educación en Cuba [History of Education in Cuba]* (Havana: Boloña Publishing, 2005), book 5, p. 120.

46. Ibid., p. 307.

47. José Francisco Martínez y Díaz, *Historia de la educación pública en Cuba, desde el descubrimiento hasta nuestros días y causas de su fracaso [History of Public Education in Cuba from the Discovery of the New World to the Present and its Demise]* (Havana: La Casa Villalba, 1943).

48. Enrique Sosa Rodríguez and Alejandrina Penabad Félix, *Historia de la educación en Cuba [History of Education in Cuba]* (Havana: Boloña Publishing, 2005), book 5, p. 53.

49. Ibid., pp. 93–100.

50. Enrique Sosa Rodríguez and Alejandrina Penabad Félix, *Historia de la educación en Cuba [History of Education in Cuba]* (Havana: Boloña Publishing, 2003), book 6, p. 29.

51. Barcia Zequeira, in Cuban History Institute, 310–11.

52. María del Pilar Díaz Castañón, "La forja del hombre nuevo: las paradojas de la ilustración subversiva," in *Perfiles de la Nación II* (Havana: Ciencias Sociales Publishers, 2006), 170.

53. Carlos del Toro, *La alta burguesía cubana; 1902–58 [Cuban Upper Bourgoisie; 1902–58]* (Havana: Ciencias Sociales Publishers, 2003), 26.

54. Pablo A. Riaño San Marful, "Asociaciones cívicas en Cuba en la antesala de la revolución" ["Civil Associations in Cuba prior to the Revolution"], in *Perfiles de la Nación II [National Profiles II]* (Havana: Ciencias Sociales Publishers, 2006), 144.

55. Enrique Sosa Rodríguez, "Fracaso de la descentralización y americanización de la instrucción pública de primaria en Cuba (1899–1902)," *Debates Americanos* (2001): 21.

56. *Cuban Census 1907* (Washington, D.C.; U.S. Census Office, 1908), 148, 149–150.

57. Enrique Sosa Rodríguez, "Fracaso de la descentralización y americanización de la instrucción pública de primaria en Cuba (1899–1902)," *Debates Americanos* (2001): 24.

58. Oscar Zanetti Lecuona, *La República: notas sobre economía y sociedad* (Havana: Ciencias Sociales Publishers, 2006), 157.

59. Its full name was "School for the Home, Economics, Arts, Domestic Science and Industry for Women." Its objectives were to train women in domestic science,

clothes-making, and industry. This type of school was modeled after French schools preparing housewives to become efficient managers of their home. In 1927, it also began training teachers and received state funding. Studies lasted three years and students consisted of women from middle and lower income sectors.

60. Zanetti Lecuona, *La República*, 157.

61. In 1919 there were 234,038 students of which 116,602 were men and 117,436 women. Absenteeism however was higher for girls. See *Cuban Republic Census* (Havana: Maza Press, Arroyo y Caso, S. in C., 1919), 239.

62. *La enciclopedia de Cuba* (Madrid: Playor S.A. Editors, 1974), book 6, p. 539.

63. Between 1931 and 1953, registered students represented 35 percent to 45 percent of school-aged children, most of whom dropped out. Thus, of the 614,924 students in primary school in 1952–53, only 85,000 were in higher grades (fifth to eighth grades) with over 50 percent in the early years. See Zanetti Lecuona, *La República*, 160.

64. *La enciclopedia de Cuba* (Madrid: Playor S.A. Editors, 1974), book 6, p. 539.

65. In 1902, U.S. occupation forces moved the university building to an old military arsenal, on the top of a hill in the *Vedado* neighborhood, where it currently resides. See Joaquín Llerena, *La instrucción superior en Cuba en el primer cuarto de siglo de vida republicana* (Havana: n.p., 1927), 86.

66. The Varona Plan was designed by a teacher, Enrique José Varona, on June 30, 1900, and passed by Military Decree 266, with the aim to reform higher education on the island.

67. As a consequence of this reform, in November 1923, the Popular University *José Martí* was founded and run by university and labor avant-garde leaders, Julio Antonia Mella and Rubén Martínez Villena. It operated on the Havana University campus in the evenings, especially for workers. See Jorge Ibarra Cuesta, "La sociedad cubana en las tres primeras décadas del siglo XX," in *La Neocolonia; Organización y crisis* (Cuban History Institute, Havana; Política Publishers, 1998), 177.

68. *La enciclopedia de Cuba* (Madrid: Playor S.A. Editors, 1974), book 6, p. 548–49.

69. In 1950, President Carlos Prío passed the Private Universities and Higher Study Centers Law, governing the functioning of these institutions and affording them legal status. See *La enciclopedia de Cuba* (Madrid: Playor S.A. Editors, 1974), book 6, p. 551.

70. María del Pilar Díaz Castañón, "La forja del hombre nuevo: las paradojas de la ilustración subversiva," in *Perfiles de la Nación II* (Havana: Ciencias Sociales Publishers, 2006), 172–73.

71. *Cuban Census 1907* (Washington, D.C.; U.S. Census Office, 1908), 148.

72. Díaz Castañón, "La forja," 184.

73. *La enciclopedia de Cuba* (Madrid: Playor S.A. Editors, 1974), book 6, p. 544.

74. Joaquín Llerena, *La instrucción superior en Cuba en el primer cuarto de siglo de vida republicana* (Havana: n.p., 1927), 44.

75. By 1919, the number of registered teachers was 4,560 women (83.3 percent) and 913 men (16.7 percent). Of these, blacks were a minority, only 775 (14.2 percent), whereas whites reached 4,698 (85.8 percent). See *Cuban Republic Census* (Havana: Maza Press, Arroyo y Caso, S. in C., 1919), 239.

76. Education Boards were created from the outset of the republic, which established an exam system for teachers. Their duties included application of new teaching methods and selection of appropriate text material.

77. Enrique Sosa Rodríguez, "Fracaso de la descentralización y americanización de la instrucción pública de primaria en Cuba (1899–1902)," *Debates Americanos* (2001): 25.

78. Joaquín Llerena, *La instrucción superior en Cuba en el primer cuarto de siglo de vida republicana* (Havana: n.p., 1927), 239.

79. Subject introduced in Cuba 1901 by Aaron Heindengren. These classes taught children wood and paper crafts among other manual skills.

80. Enrique Sosa Rodríguez, "Fracaso de la descentralización y americanización de la instrucción pública de primaria en Cuba (1899–1902)," *Debates Americanos* (2001): 26–27.

81. *La enciclopedia de Cuba* (Madrid: Playor S.A. Editors, 1974), book 6, p. 548.

82. María del Pilar Díaz Castañón, "La forja del hombre nuevo: las paradojas de la ilustración subversiva," in *Perfiles de la Nación II* (Havana: Ciencias Sociales Publishers, 2006), 172.

83. Yoel Cordoví Núñez, "Las enseñazas de la historia nacional y local en las escuelas públicas de Cuba (1899–1930)," In *Perfiles de la Nación II* (Havana: Editorial Ciencias Sociales), 41.

84. Ibid., 42.

85. Ricardo Quiza Moreno, *El cuento al revés: historia, nacionalismo y poder en Cuba (190–30)* (Havana: Unicornio Publishers, 2003), 49.

86. The Revolution succeeds in 1959, putting an end to the dictatorial regime imposed until March 10, 1952, by Fulgencio Batista Zaldívar, who fled the country on the dawn of January 1, 1952. The new leading forces were under the command of Fidel Castro Ruz and a large group of young men and women opposing tyranny. Revolutionary forces had operated in cities and in the mountains until they had managed to destabilize Batista's army and take power.

87. Report to UNESCO from the International Education Office: Cuban Republic Ministry of Education, *El desarrollo de la educación; Informe Nacional* (April 2001); http://www.mes.edu.cu/index.php?option=com_content&task=view&id=5&Itemid=6 (Web site visited January 12, 2007).

88. The Constitution in its chapter on "Education and Culture," holds the Cuban state responsible for the direction, fostering, and promotion of education, culture, and the sciences. It emphasizes that education is a function of the state and should be free of charge, with an extensive scholarship program and providing multiple facilities for all workers to study, so that they may achieve the highest level of scientific and technical training. Furthermore, it promotes patriotic education, giving freedom to scientific creativity and research, prioritizing activities which are of interest to the public at large and contribute to its welfare. See Elvira Martín Sabina, *Informe nacional sobre educación superior en Cuba* IES/2003/ED/PI/75, 2003 (2003); http://www.iesalc.unesco.orq .ve/ (Web site visited on January 12, 2007).

89. Ministry of Education policy enforced article 26 of the Universal Declaration of Human Rights which states that everyone has the right to education; education shall be free, at least in the elementary and preparatory stages; elementary education shall be compulsory; technical and professional education shall be made generally available and higher education shall be equally accessible to all on the basis of merit. See Armando Hart Dávalos, *Mensaje educacional al pueblo de Cuba* (Havana: Cultural Publishers, 1960), 54–55.

90. Elvira Martín Sabina, *Informe nacional sobre educación superior en Cuba* IES/ 2003/ED/PI/75, 2003 (2003); http://www.iesalc.unesco.orq.ve/ (Web site visited on January 12, 2007).

91. Hart Dávalos, *Mensaje*, 100.

92. Elvira Martín Sabina, *Informe nacional sobre educación superior en Cuba* IES/ 2003/ED/PI/75, 2003 (2003); http://www.iesalc.unesco.orq.ve/ (Web site visited on January 12, 2007).

93. Report to UNESCO from the International Education Office: Cuban Republic Ministry of Education, *El desarrollo de la educación; Informe Nacional* (April 2001); http://www.mes.edu.cu/index.php?option=com_content&task=view&id=5&Itemid=6 (Web site visited January 12, 2007).

94. Elvira Martín Sabina, *Informe nacional sobre educación superior en Cuba* IES/ 2003/ED/PI/75, 2003 (2003); http://www.iesalc.unesco.orq.ve/ (Web site visited on January 12, 2007).

95. Olga Moltalván Lamas, "Un trascendente hecho de cultura: la Campaña de Alfabetización," in *American Debates* 11 (2001): 50–51.

96. According to the Latin American Laboratory for the Assessment of Quality in Education, girls obtained better grades than boys in evaluations at primary school level. "Laboratorio Latinoamericano de Evaluación—LLECE, UNESCO; http://llece.unesco. cl/esp (web site visited on January 12, 2007).

97. The number of women went up to 57 percent during the 1990–91 school year, and up to 61 percent in 2000–01. University careers with predominant numbers of women included humanities, teaching, and economics. See Elvira Martín Sabina, *Informe nacional sobre educación superior en Cuba* IES/2003/ED/PI/75, 2003 (2003); http://www.iesalc.unesco.orq.ve/ (Web site visited on January 12, 2007).

98. Díaz Castañón, "La forja," 193.

99. Preschool will admit children from three to five years of age and is organized under natural, clean conditions guaranteeing normal growth and development during this stage. See Hart Dávalos, *Mensaje*, 63–64.

100. Arnaldo Silva León, *Breve historia de la revolución cubana 1959–2000* (Havana: Ciencias Sociales Publishers, 2003), 80.

101. Rural schools are part of important national development programs. Created in 1972, they represent one of the main achievements of Cuban education because they allow for the balanced combination between work and study. All pupils who finish primary school have access to this level of education. See Report to UNESCO from the International Education Office: Cuban Republic Ministry of Education, *El desarrollo de la educación; Informe Nacional* (April 2001), p. 11; http://www.mes.edu.cu/index. php?option=com_content&task=view&id=5&Itemid=6 (Web site visited January 12, 2007).

102. Middle education grew 6.1 times; schooling levels reached 87 percent for those between thirteen and sixteen years of age, figures above those for 1958; 600,000 students had scholarships, including borders and half-boarders. Arnaldo Silva León, *Breve historia de la revolución cubana 1959–2000* (Havana: Ciencias Sociales Publishers, 2003), 45.

103. Díaz Castañón, "La forja," 190.

104. Report to UNESCO from the International Education Office: Cuban Republic Ministry of Education, *El desarrollo de la educación; Informe Nacional* (April 2001), p. 12; http://www.mes.edu.cu/index.php?option=com_content&task=view&id=5&Ite mid=6 (Web site visited January 12, 2007).

105. Ibid.

106. Numbers of students at this level were 15,000 in 1958 whereas in 1975 this number reached 83,000. See Luis González Pérez, Marisel Sansó, and Nelsa Coronado,

"La reforma universitaria y su proyección en la Universidad de Oriente," *American Debates* (2001): 113.

107. Remote learning at the higher level is one of the ways to access the university. It is available for five careers very much in demand, namely: law, history, economics, accounting, library studies, and information technology. Study plans are flexible, there are no limits to the numbers who can register, no age restrictions or prior work requirements. Any interested citizen has access if they have a certificate showing they have completed middle school. See Elvira Martín Sabina, *Informe nacional sobre educación superior en Cuba* IES/2003/ED/PI/75, 2003 (2003); http://www.iesalc.unesco.o rq.ve/ (Web site visited on January 12, 2007).

108. These courses for social workers have been expanded to solve demands in areas such as nursing, and for more primary teachers, middle school, and art teachers. See Elvira Martín Sabina, *Informe nacional sobre educación superior en Cuba* IES/2003/ED/PI/75, 2003 (2003); http://www.iesalc.unesco.orq.ve/ (Web site visited on January 12, 2007).

109. For example, in the year 2002, there were 363 masters programs. Seventy of these were in technology, 72 in teaching, 47 in social sciences and the humanities, 33 in agricultural sciences, 51 in biomedical sciences, 46 in natural science, and 44 in economics. See Elvira Martín Sabina, *Informe nacional sobre educación superior en Cuba* IES/2003/ED/PI/75, 2003 (2003); http://www.iesalc.unesco. orq.ve/ (Web site visited on January 12, 2007).

110. The number of PhDs grew from 200 in 1976, to 1,815 in 1985; 4,000 physical education professors graduating at higher education level and 12,000 at middle level. See Arnaldo Silva León, *Breve historia de la revolución cubana 1959–2000* (Havana: Ciencias Sociales Publishers, 2003), 81–82.

111. Elvira Martín Sabina, *Informe nacional sobre educación superior en Cuba* IES/2003/ED/PI/75, 2003 (2003); http://www.iesalc.unesco.orq.ve/ (Web site visited on January 12, 2007).

112. Report to UNESCO from the International Education Office: Cuban Republic Ministry of Education, *El desarrollo de la educación; Informe Nacional* (April 2001), p. 6; http://www.mes.edu.cu/index.php?option=com_content&task=view&id=5&Ite mid=6 (Web site visited January 12, 2007).

113. Elvira Martín Sabina, *Informe nacional sobre educación superior en Cuba* IES/2003/ED/PI/75, 2003 (2003); http://www.iesalc.unesco.orq.ve/ (Web site visited on January 12, 2007).

114. Ibid.

115. María del Pilar Díaz Castañón, "La forja del hombre nuevo: las paradojas de la ilustración subversiva," in *Perfiles de la Nación II* (Havana: Ciencias Sociales Publishers, 2006), 187.

116. Olga Moltalván Lamas, "Un trascendente hecho de cultura: la Campaña de Alfabetización," in *American Debates* 11 (2001): 50.

117. Armando Hart Dávalos, *Mensaje educacional al pueblo de Cuba* (Havana: Cultural Publishers, 1960), 104.

118. Elvira Martín Sabina, *Informe nacional sobre educación superior en Cuba* IES/2003/ED/PI/75, 2003 (2003); http://www.iesalc.unesco.orq.ve/ (Web site visited on January 12, 2007).

119. Ibid.

120. Ministry resolutions numbers 216 and 403 dated June 7, 1989, and July 22, 1989, respectively, defined and evaluated study plans for compulsory education (general, technology, and labor). See Report to UNESCO from the International Education Office: Cuban Republic Ministry of Education, *El desarrollo de la educación; Informe Nacional* (April 2001), p. 4.

121. Ibid., 9.

122. Ibid., 11.

123. Ibid., 13.

124. Higher Education Ministry, *Historia Universitaria* (August 2004). Web site: http://www.mes.edu.cu/index.php?option=com_content&task=view&id=5&Itemid=6 (Web site visited March 16, 2007).

125. Olga Moltalván Lamas, "Un trascendente hecho de cultura: la Campaña de Alfabetización," in *American Debates* 11 (2001): 56.

126. María del Pilar Díaz Castañón, "La forja del hombre nuevo: las paradojas de la ilustración subversiva," in *Perfiles de la Nación II* (Havana: Ciencias Sociales Publishers, 2006), 189.

127. Ibid., 191.

128. Ibid., 61–66.

BIBLIOGRAPHY

Books

Bachiller y Morales, Antonio. 1965. *Apuntes para la historia de las letras y la instrucción pública en la Isla de Cuba*. La Habana: Instituto de Literatura y Lingüística, T1.

Barcia Zequeira, María del Carmen. 2005. *Capas populares y modernidad (1880–1930)*. La Habana: Fundación Fernando Ortiz.

Censo de la República de Cuba 1907. 1908. Washington, D.C.: Oficina del Censo de los Estados Unidos.

Censo de la República de Cuba. 1919. La Habana: Imprenta Maza, Arroyo y Caso.

Cordoví Núñez, Yoel. 2006. "Las enseñazas de la historia nacional y local en las escuelas públicas de Cuba (1899–1930)." In *Perfiles de la nación II*. La Habana: Editorial Ciencias Sociales.

Cuba en la mano; Enciclopedia Popular Ilustrada. 1940. La Habana: Imprenta Ucar García y Cía.

Díaz Castañón, María del Pilar. 2006. "La forja del hombre nuevo: las paradojas de la ilustración subversive." In *Perfiles de la nación II*. La Habana: Editorial Ciencias Sociales.

La Enciclopedia de Cuba. 1974. Madrid: Ed. Playor S.A., T.6.

Hart Dávalos, Armando. 1960. *Mensaje educacional al pueblo de Cuba*. La Habana: Editorial Cultural S.A.

Hernández Galano, Yamilet. 2003. *El diseño de nuevos arquetipo de las mujeres cubana por la educación y los empleos (1899–1902)*. La Habana: Tesis de Grado, Universidad de La Habana.

Ibarra Cuesta, Jorge. 1998. "La sociedad cubana en las tres primeras décadas del siglo XX." In *Instituto de Historia de Cuba; La Neocolonia; Organización y crisis*. La Habana: Editora Política.

Informe del Censo de Cuba, 1899. 1900. Washington, D.C.: Government Printing Office.

Instituto de Historia de Cuba. 1995. *La Colonia; Desde los orígenes hasta 1867.* Havana: Editora Política.
Instituto de Historia de Cuba. 1996. *Las Luchas por la independencia nacional y las transformaciones estructurales (1868–98).* La Habana: Editora Política.
Instituto de Segunda Enseñanza. 1863. *Memoria anual correspondiente al curso académico de 1863.* La Habana: Imp. El Avisador Comercial.
Llerena, Joaquín. 1927. *La Instrucción superior en Cuba en el primer cuarto de siglo de vida republicana.* La Habana: n.p.
Martínez y Díaz, José Francisco.1943. *Historia de la educación pública en Cuba, desde el descubrimiento hasta nuestros días y causas de su fracaso.* La Habana: La Casa Villalba.
Quiza Moreno, Ricardo. 2003. *El cuento al revés: historia, nacionalismo y poder en Cuba (1902–30).* La Habana: Editorial Unicornio.
Riaño San Marful, Pablo A. 2006. "Asociaciones cívicas en Cuba en la antesala de la Revolución." In *Perfiles de la Nación II.* La Habana: Editorial Ciencias Sociales.
Rodríguez Fuentes, Lyding. 2003. *Santa Clara de Asís: un convento de las elites habaneras (1644–1850).* La Habana: Tesis de Grado, Universidad de La Habana.
Silva León, Arnaldo. 2003. *Breve historia de la revolución Cubana; 1959–2000.* La Habana: Editorial de Ciencias Sociales.
Sosa Rodríguez, Enrique and Alejandrina Penabad Félix. 2003. *Historia de la educación en Cuba.* La Habana: Ediciones Boloña, T.4.
Toro, Carlos del. 2003. *La alta burguesía cubana; 1902–58.* La Habana: Editorial Ciencias Sociales.
Vinat de la Mata, Raquel. 2005. *Educación femenina en Cuba 1648–1898.* La Habana: Editora Política.
Zanetti Lecuona, Oscar. 2006. *La República: notas sobre economía y sociedad.* La Habana: Editorial Ciencias Sociales.

Articles

González Pérez, Luis, Marisel Sansó, and Nelsa Coronado. "La reforma universitaria y su proyección en la universidad de oriente." *Debates Americanos* no. 11 (2001): 107–13. La Habana: Editorial Imagen Contemporánea.
Moltalván Lamas, Olga. "Un trascendente hecho de cultura: la campaña de alfabetización." *Debates Americanos* no. 11 (2001): 47–64. La Habana: Editorial Imagen Contemporánea.
Sosa Rodríguez, Enrique. "Fracaso de la descentralización y americanización de la instrucción pública de primaria en Cuba (1899–1902). *Debates Americanos* no. 11 (2001): 16–30. La Habana: Editorial Imagen Contemporánea.

Reports

Informe a la UNESCO de la Oficina Internacional de Educación. April 2001. *El desarrollo de la educación; Informe Nacional.* Ministerio de Educación, República de Cuba.

Newspaper Sources

INRA.1961. Havana, año II, no 1.
INRA.1961. Havana, año II, no 4.
INRA. 1961. Havana, año III, no 1.

Web Sites

Historia Universitaria. Agosto 2004. M.E.S. http://www.mes.edu.cu/index.php?option=
   com_content&task=view&id=5&Itemid=6 (visited March 16, 2007).
Martín Sabina, Elvira. 2003. *Informe Nacional sobre educación superior en Cuba*. IES/
   2003/ED/PI/75, 2003: http://www.iesalc.unesco.orq.ve/ (visited January 12,
   2007).
Ministerio de Educación. April 2001. *El desarrollo de la educación; Informe Nacional*.
   República de Cuba. abril 2001. http://www.mes.edu.cu/index.php?option=com_
   content&task=view&id=5&Itemid=6 (visited January 12, 2007).

Chapter 9

SCHOOLING IN EL SALVADOR

Héctor Lindo-Fuentes

Well into the twentieth century, in El Salvador the world of childhood was not necessarily the world of schooling. The percentage of school-age children who attended primary school did not reach 50 percent until the 1950s and 100 percent until 2000. Despite frequent pronouncements regarding the importance of education, the Salvadoran state's attention to the school system was intermittent and half-hearted for most of the country's history. Even taking into account the small size of the country (roughly the size of Massachusetts) and its limited resources, the development of the educational system in El Salvador was slow and uneven. The scant attention by the colonial Spanish authorities toward education, political instability, and the role given to education by elite-controlled authoritarian governments played a role in producing a school system of limited coverage and questionable quality.

NINETEENTH CENTURY

El Salvador obtained its independence from Spain in 1821. The main characteristics of the educational system were honed at the end of the colonial period. The Spanish colonial authorities established a system funded at the local level, thus putting it at the mercy of local conditions. In 1778 the *Audiencia* (the main judicial body) decreed that teachers' salaries had to be paid by each Indian community out of their communal funds. Few studies exist of the state of education during this period, but available evidence indicates that very few children had access to formal education. An official report of 1807 summarized the state of education as "extremely backward." At that time the *Intendencia de San Salvador*, the territory that we know today as El Salvador, had only eighty-eight teachers, one for every 1,878 inhabitants. Later improvements introduced by the colonial authorities were modest at best. Young men from the Intendancy who wanted to receive higher education had to travel to Guatemala to attend the University of San Carlos. Women had even less access to education. Although the 1807 report indicated that some attended primary school, by and large their education took place at home, and even elite women, such as some of the wives of the leaders of the independence movement, were illiterate.

After independence from Spain, the funding and administration of schools continued to be a local responsibility. The five Central American countries formed a confederation between 1821 and 1839 and then parted ways. The period of the confederation was marked by political instability and frequent armed confrontations that impeded the consolidation of all governmental institutions, including an educational system. Moreover, the process of independence and the turbulent years of the federation strengthened the role of municipalities at the expense of any form of central government. Municipal boards of education opened and closed schools, appointed and supervised teachers, presided over public exams, and weighed in on the curriculum. As a result of this highly decentralized structure, the school system grew slowly and unevenly depending on local conditions. Given the frequency of armed conflict, it was not unusual for schools to close to protect students against the dangers of war time or because the only teacher was recruited for armed service. School funds were often diverted to finance militias.

Religion and the education for citizenship were considered the main objectives of education. In 1802, a decree of the King of Spain stressed the importance of education to form good Christians and citizens for the benefit of the kingdom. The authors of the first Spanish Constitution (1812) initiated the practice of issuing "political catechisms" to teach basic constitutional principles to the pupils. This practice was followed until the end of the nineteenth century. The goal of public education was, then, to establish the foundation of social and political institutions. The primary school curriculum extending into the entire nineteenth century was limited to reading, writing, arithmetic, religion, and civic education.

As in many other countries in Latin America, shortly after independence the authorities experimented with the Lancasterian method. In a country where the scarcity of teachers was most acute, the reliance on older children to teach younger ones was seen as the most attractive feature of this method, more so than the system of incentives and the stress in efficiency Joseph Lancaster had advocated. An expert in the method, Antonio José Coehlo, arrived at San Salvador in 1833 and established a school named *La Aurora de El Salvador* that trained individuals who later gained prominence as politicians and professionals. The Lancasterian method was a prominent feature of primary education until the end of the nineteenth century.

Children attended school from January to October and had a long vacation from late October to January. The timing of these vacations had to do with the season to harvest coffee when children helped their families pick coffee on the plantations. Students attended poorly equipped schools led by teachers who, by and large, had no professional training and were paid poorly and irregularly. A teacher in 1859 complained that the children in his school had no place to sit and nothing to write on. His complaint was a description of a reality that prevailed in many schools. The government did not invest consistently in the construction of adequate school buildings until the 1920s. Classes were taught in poorly lit structures built originally for private housing or for the municipality. More often than not they had dirt floors, mud walls, and leaky thatched or tile roofs. Girls and boys attended separate schools. By the 1840s, girls' schools were mentioned more frequently in the official reports. The limited statistics available for the early part of the nineteenth century suggest that twice as many boys as girls attended schools. Occasionally the lack of teachers made it necessary to mix boys and girls in the same school. Twenty-three mixed schools operated in 1875, out of a total of 333 schools. Only under extraordinary circumstances did the local authorities provide textbooks and notebooks to poor students. Few poor students had access to school materials since their families were rarely capable of providing more than subsistence needs.

School absenteeism was a chronic problem, particularly in rural areas. Children often missed classes because their families used their labor in the fields. Absenteeism was more frequent during the corn harvest or periods of locust plagues. The teachers' tendency to resort to corporal punishment to keep class discipline was another reason to avoid school.

Once a year, primary school students had to prepare for a public exam in front of local authorities including the leaders of the municipality and the parish. Teachers often resisted this obligation, either because it was an unwelcome intrusion of outsiders or because they had something to hide. Witnesses of the examinations complained about the lack of progress of the pupils.

Schools in indigenous communities shared the same problems but they also had to deal with the patronizing attitude of teachers coming from the outside who had little respect for their culture and even less trust in the innate ability of children. Contemporary accounts indicate that teachers approached Indian communities as "civilizers" who desired to force their charges to learn Spanish. These attitudes towards Indian children are expressed in a teacher's report of 1853: "[Indian children] by their habits, language, and other circumstances are naturally rough, and as a result they cannot learn what they are taught as easily and quickly as non-Indian children" (Archivo Municipal de Sonsonate 1853). As a result, Indian parents had a difficult relationship with teachers and often resisted sending their children to school. Thus, Indian communities faced a double handicap in their access of education, one for being located mostly in rural areas where few schools were available, and second for the "civilizing" agenda of the teachers sent to staff their schools. Although no accurate statistics are available, scattered data suggests that by the 1880s Indians may have accounted for up to 50 percent of the total population in the western part of the country.

The idea that education was a tool to form citizens explains the lack of enthusiasm to make school available to women and Indians. The definition of citizenship in the nation's constitution excluded women, domestic servants who "were dominated by their masters," criminals or men with notorious vices, failed men, beggars, and idle men. The definition was open to interpretation and it tended to exclude the lower classes. Since education was meant to form citizens and women were not citizens and the lower classes, including Indians, were seen as dangerous and often excluded from the rights of citizenship, there was no great urgency to extend to them the benefits of education. The highly influential citizen's catechism published in 1874 illustrates this attitude. The section on the sovereignty of the people defines the issue in a question and answer format:

What do we mean by "the people"?

It is a group of men that has the objective of the preservation and happiness of its members and is governed by the political institutions produced by the group itself. In this sense the people is the same as the society, which is different from the common meaning of the word in which "the people" is equivalent to the rabble. Thus, the statement "the people are sovereign" is equivalent to the less dangerous statement "the society is sovereign." (Galindo 1904, 1)

The lack of teachers, not to mention qualified ones, further limited access to education. Teacher wages were low, and thus, few stepped forward to meet the challenge. Once hired, teacher punctuality was as much of a preoccupation for local boards of education as student absenteeism. The lack of trained teachers was a persistent concern of the authorities but early efforts to establish teacher training schools failed. The first teacher training schools founded in 1858 did not last more than a year. In 1864, in a single province a third of the schools were closed for the lack of teachers. It was only until the 1870s when a normal school became a stable institution, but it was graduating only fifteen students per year.

It was hard to find any type of secondary education besides teachers' school. The first secondary school, *Colegio de la Asunción*, was established in 1841 at the same time as the *Universidad de El Salvador*. Established for the sole purpose of preparing students for the university, the Colegio's curricula and regulations were written by the same governing body that regulated the university. Secondary education was under the same regime as the university until 1885 when the Secretary of Public Instruction took over this responsibility. Conceived strictly in terms of access to the university, secondary education became reserved for a very small minority. Moreover, over time much of secondary education took place in private institutions, which further limited access to the university to the very small, well-to-do segment of the Salvadoran populace.

The elitist nature of secondary education can be observed not only in the small number of students enrolled in it, but also in the regulations of the schools. In order to limit the status competition among students caused by the "luxury that has been introduced in our society" (Gaceta de El Salvador 1858), the authorities of the main public secondary school in the capital dictated in 1858 the type and amount of clothes and supplies that the students had to bring to the boarding school. The official list included a uniform, four dark slacks, four frock coats, six white linen or cotton shirts, two white vests and two dark vests, six pieces of underwear, two black silk ties and two cotton ties, four cotton undershirts, six handkerchiefs, two pillows and four pillow covers, two bedspreads and four bed sheets, three pairs of black shoes, a Panama hat, one bed, one chair on the school's design, two regular-size trunks, and other similar items. Needless to say that in a mostly rural country like El Salvador the number of teenage boys who could afford such long list of demands was extremely small.

Private secondary schools stressed the teaching of foreign languages. No doubt they were preparing the children of the elite to take advantage of the business opportunities available thanks to the increase in exports of coffee to Europe and the United States. In general, these institutions operated without close governmental supervision, although many of them received government subsidies. In 1887, there was only one student in secondary school for every sixteen students in primary school. In the same year only three of the eighteen secondary education schools were public. In sum, the system that evolved in the nineteenth century provided educational opportunities at the secondary level only to a very small group of privileged students.

The 1885 legislation that put oversight of secondary education under the jurisdiction of the Secretary of Public Instruction was part of an effort to centralize and professionalize the system of public education. It was part and parcel of a change in a central state that was becoming stronger. We can detect a first period of centralization and professionalization in the five-and-a-half decades between the late 1870s and the early 1930s. The strengthening of the central state in El Salvador began after the middle of the nineteenth century thanks to the increasing tax revenue following the rapid growth of agricultural exports. Having more resources at its disposal, the central government began to replace the municipalities as the entities responsible for public education. A more influential and better financed Ministry of Education took over the responsibility of dictating the curriculum and began appointing school principals. Some of the initial actions the authorities took during this period included the establishment of a normal school for women in 1875 (up until then the only teachers' school was reserved for men), a new law of public instruction in 1885, and the invitation to a group of Colombian teachers to collaborate with the Secretary of Public Instruction in 1887. These teachers encouraged the abandonment of the Lancasterian system; introduced modern pedagogical ideas, particularly those of Pestalozzi; and encouraged the use of textbooks. They also advocated the strict separation of schools for boys and girls. The landmark education law passed in 1885 made school compulsory for boys between seven and fifteen years of age, but loopholes in the law made it impossible for universal schooling, even if only for boys, to become a reality. The law left the education of girls at the discretion of their parents. Moreover, children who lived more than a mile away from a school were exempt from the obligation. These exemptions, coupled with the limited funds to build schools and hire teachers, resulted in low school availability and attendance.

Beginning in 1893 it became necessary to finish six years of primary education in order to enter secondary school. Until then, it was only necessary to prove proficiency in writing and math. During this period religious orders were invited to the country to organize private schools that, although few in numbers, had a tremendous influence on the education of the children of the elite. This process started with the arrival of the nuns of the Sacred Heart (1894), and was followed by the Salesians (1897) and, somewhat later, by the Jesuits (1921), and the Marists (1924).

Secondary and higher education received a great deal of attention from the authorities. Between 1880–93 five changes in the curricula were passed as law, but that attention was based on the premise that access should be limited to the top of society. At the same time in the first decade of the century vocational education was introduced: a trade school, an agricultural school, and a painting academy.

Since the country became independent government authorities were unanimous in their rhetorical support for education, but by the end of the nineteenth century little of this rhetoric manifested as significant achievements. By 1900, no more than 5 percent of the total population was attending primary school and most students left school after the third grade. Ten years later only 12.4 percent of kids in school age attended school.

THE FIRST HALF OF THE TWENTIETH CENTURY

The arrival of a German mission to the teachers' school in 1924 introduced Johann Herbart's ideas and trained a generation of teachers who were given scholarships to go to Chile to receive further education. The main disciples of the German mission became prominent in educational policy, and they had influence on the educational reforms of 1940, 1945, and 1968. During this period new schools received names such as Froebel and Pestalozzi. Teachers began to organize and demand greater recognition. In 1930, the government gave legal standing to the *Comité Pro Día del Maestro*, a committee of teachers organized to designate an official Teachers' Day, unify the teacher corps, celebrate the memory of their deceased colleagues, give awards to distinguished teachers, organize scientific conferences, and lobby in favor of disabled colleagues. In sum, it was a group with a comprehensive program to strengthen their professional identity and lobby for their rights. The first National Pedagogic Congress that the committee organized in 1930 promoted the idea of Active Schools citing with great enthusiasm the work of the Swiss educator Adolphe Ferriere.

The printed material produced after this event provides a snapshot of the increasing and relatively new role of women as teaching professionals and the difficulties that they had making their voices heard in a still male-dominated profession. The organization listed twenty founding officers, including two women. However, when the conference was organized two years after the committee's establishment, no women were found among its officers. The proceedings of their event did not mention any participation of female teachers, even though the official photographs of the event show that at least one-fourth of the participants were women.

Between 1923 and 1931, the government engaged in the first sustained effort in the country's history to build schools. A well-publicized plan of school construction introduced a new type of solidly built school designed by an Italian architect. The plan started slowly under President Quiñonez Molina (1923–27); in that period only thirteen school buildings were erected, mostly in the capital and neighboring provinces. In the next administration, Pío Romero Bosque's (1927–31), the total number of schools increased from 808 to 1,034 but few of them were housed in adequate buildings. The limited progress made during this period came to a halt following the arrival of the Great Depression and its political consequences.

What we have called the first period of professionalization, roughly from 1871 to 1932, ended with the traumatic events that took place in January 1932. Toward the end of its term, the administration of President Pío Romero Bosque faced spiraling unemployment, growing urban unrest, numerous bank foreclosures, and widespread discontentment, as a result of the economic crisis. Romero Bosque's successor failed to deal with the situation, and a military coup d'etat ousted him. Barely weeks after coming to power, the new head of state, General Maximiliano Hernández Martínez (1931–44), brutally repressed a peasant uprising in the heavily Indian populated western region. The government characterized the uprising as communist inspired. Estimates of the victims of the repression range between ten and thirty thousand, mostly members of indigenous communities. General Hernández Martínez ruled the country as a dictator for thirteen years and forged the alliance between the military and the economic elite that continued until 1979.

One of the consequences of the uprising was a deepening in the erasure of Indian communities from the national consciousness. During the first decades of the century the ideology of *mestizaje* that purported the majority of the population was mixed blood, became popular among members of the elite. After 1932, the national census stopped asking questions about ethnic identity and the official discourse began to ignore the existence of Indian communities, which became invisible to mainstream society.

The Martínez administration introduced few changes in the educational system until 1940 when the government created a Ministry of Education (as opposed to having the education portfolio attached to another ministry) and spearheaded a reform of primary education. The 1940 reform was possible thanks to the professionalization movement of earlier decades. The four-member Coordinating Commission that conceived and implemented the reform included three teachers of the 1928 generation. They had continued their studies at the National Psychopedagogic Institute of Chile and sought the direct advice of the director of the Institute who became a virtual non-voting fifth member of the Commission.

One of the authors recognized that the reform was based on pedagogical reflection but not on an analysis of the socioeconomic needs of the country. Moreover, the changes did not emerge from a public discussion of educational policy. Instead they were conceived at the highest level and implemented without consultation of the citizenry, as could be expected of a dictatorial regime that eschewed democratic participation.

The reform consisted in the development of new curricula. Its authors claimed that it had the virtue of being based on pedagogical principles and that it offered pedagogical guidelines to teachers. These features were a significant departure from the mere laundry lists of topics that had characterized government-mandated curricula up to that point. The underlying curricular thought stressed the correlations or links between different subjects. The reform, however, did not address the problem of the limited number of schools available, particularly in rural areas. According to the new guidelines, the life of the school ought to be organized around the seven functions of the school: technical, disciplinary, social, hygienic, industrial, artistic, and sports. Besides teachers, students were also responsible in promoting each function. For the "hygienic function," for example, each grade had a committee of children responsible for the development of good hygienic habits. The guidelines stated that the guiding principles of the reform were continuity and correlation. Ironically for a school system in a dictatorship, civic education in the third grade included a "Democratic School Republic" as a civics education activity. Students organized among themselves in political parties, nominated presidential candidates, campaigned, and finally voted a citizen president of the "Republic." In another way that was more consistent with the authoritarian culture of the period, the curriculum established a rigid set of subjects and dictated the number of hours per week that each topic ought to be taught.

The school week lasted twenty-seven hours for first graders, thirty for second graders, and thirty-four from grades three to six. An American visitor described the typical schools as follows:

Very few Salvadoran schools are housed in buildings originally constructed for educational purposes. The great majority are found in former residences of the Spanish colonial type, in which the classrooms surround a patio that is used as a playground. Some are single-story buildings; some, two story. Only rarely have the old buildings been altered to meet the needs of effective education. The classrooms are generally small, badly lighted, and poorly equipped. In 90 percent of them, there is little more than a blackboard, a map of El Salvador, and a few readers. The desks are mostly old, disfigured, and inadequate in number—frequently three and four pupils are found seated in a desk intended for two. In the Ministry of Public Education it is estimated that 95 percent of the country's school buildings are inadequate for their purposes. (Ebaugh 1947, 23)

One of the problems encountered by the school reform commission was the fact that few teachers had professional training. The four public normal schools graduated only a small percentage of the teachers that the country needed, and so most teachers in the classroom had some general education but no specific training in pedagogy. In response, at the end 1939, the commission organized and taught a six-week training course for all teachers during the student's vacation time. The curriculum of the two teaching training schools (one for men and one for women) was revamped. The rewriting of the curriculum, again, was done by the Commission. They also taught the courses and seminars that were deemed necessary to retrain the people responsible for the schools. The percentage of the school-age population attending primary school, however, barely increased during this period.

If the actions to improve primary education during the Hernández Martínez regime were late and inadequate, the government initiatives at the secondary level were even less satisfactory. Inspired more by politics than by the educational needs of the country, the most perceptible change at this level was the militarization of the three public secondary schools. Principals and assistant principals of these schools received military ranks and presided over a highly regimented system that enforced a rigorous discipline. The rest of secondary schooling was carried out in twenty-four private institutions under the strict supervision of the Ministry of Education. Control from the Ministry of Education was fairly thorough. At the end of the academic year all secondary school students in the country had to take the same exam at the main public high-school, the National Institute "General Francisco Menéndez."

On the surface the curriculum was not very different from that in an American high school of the same period, but the school environment and the teaching methodology reinforced the authoritarian agenda of the regime.

An American observer described how classes were conducted in high-schools:

The teachers lecture, explain the assignment or the lesson, and then dictate a prepared summary or brief which the students enter in their notebooks. Class discussion of the materials studied is infrequent and student questions are extremely rare. (Ebaugh 1947, 39)

The lectures were not very stimulating and there was nothing else in the school environment that would spark independent thinking or intellectual curiosity. School libraries, if available, had outdated books, and students rarely used them. Laboratories, when in existence, offered demonstrations rather than hands-on experience. Private schools, which were normally superior in quality, and had better facilities, were accessible only to the children of relatively affluent parents. Most of these schools were managed by Roman Catholic religious orders.

University education received some, but largely negative, attention from the Martínez regime. In 1930, during the democratizing years of President Romero Bosque, new legislation had given the University autonomy of action. This meant that the institution could independently change its organization and its curriculum. This situation was uncomfortable for a dictatorial regime and in 1939 the University lost its autonomy and was put under the direct supervision of the Ministry of Public Education.

The Hernandez Martínez regime ended in 1944 with a coup d'etat sponsored by democratizing middle class groups and young military officers. The educational legacy of this period was meager. Government expenditures in education declined by one-third in 1933 and did not recover their 1932 levels (both in monetary terms and as percentage of the national budget) until the end of the dictatorship. By 1944, two-thirds of school-age children lived in rural areas but only 10 percent of rural children had access to education. Most of the rural schools offered only the first grade, and less than one-fifth offered the second grade. Figures from 1945 show that less than 30 percent of the primary school age population was attending any kind of school. Only 4 percent of the total school enrollment was at the secondary level. Interestingly, enrollment was fairly evenly distributed between boys and girls, 52 percent and 48 percent, respectively. The percentage of young women in secondary education is not available, but given that high school was considered a preparation for the university and in 1949 only 13.4 percent of university students were women, it can be inferred that more young men than women were enrolled in secondary education throughout the 1940s. There was, however, a vocational school for girls at the secondary level. In 1945, it had a daily attendance of less than a hundred students and the curriculum included, along with arithmetic, Spanish, and chemistry applied to industry, subjects such as flower-making, millinery, hand embroidery, cooking, and men's tailoring and pressing.

The momentum towards a greater professionalization of teachers in the 1920s had been reversed. Only 30 percent of teachers had degrees that qualified them to teach elementary school, while most teachers had six years of schooling or less. By the end of the Martínez regime the total number of students enrolled in any kind of teacher training school was 345. By this time coeducational schools were less of a rarity.

THE SECOND HALF OF THE TWENTIETH CENTURY

The group that deposed Martínez wanted to establish a clear break with the dictatorial past and portray itself as truly modernizing. They were quick to introduce new initiatives in education as soon as they gained power, if only because teachers and university students and professors had been instrumental in the movement that toppled Martínez. In the months that followed the government change teachers received a 71 percent salary increase. But the defeat of the dictatorship was not complete. Former officials of the Martínez regime regained power until 1948, but even they recognized that times had changed and were less dictatorial.

During the 1944 through 1948 transition, the government's main contribution to education was an initiative to reorganize secondary education. This time the change was made in coordination with the government of neighboring Guatemala, where a new president, himself the product of a regime change, had had a long career as an educator. El Salvador and Guatemala appointed a bilateral commission of experts to discuss the state of education in the region. They met in western El Salvador in the city of Santa Ana in 1945. The Salvadoran commission included one of the architects of the 1940 reform, Manuel Luis Escamilla. This 1945 convention stressed the three years after the sixth grade as the critical time to provide a solid core education. Based on the convention's recommendation, new legislation grouped grades seven, eight, and nine into a new level called *Plan Básico* that was earmarked to provide general education. The *Plan Básico* was followed by two years of *bachillerato* (high school) that served as either for preparation for college or for vocational training. This feature of secondary education remained in place until the 1968 reform. The participants of the convention readopted some of the discourse of the "active schools" that had started in the 1920s but was forgotten during the dictatorship. Even though the impact of the policies implemented after the gathering was limited to the junior high curriculum, the participants in the discussions made progress identifying the most pressing issues such as the weaknesses in rural education and the low levels of literacy. An innovation introduced during this period went almost unnoticed and its significance unappreciated until years later. The American School started operating in 1945; it was the first bilingual school in the country. Bilingual schools have never reached a significant percentage of students, but in the past three decades they have become very important in the training of the ruling class, providing a distinct type of education that sharpens class differences. Two of the last four Salvadoran presidents are alumni of the American School. In general, the changes in secondary education introduced during this period did not seek to increase the very limited enrollment in secondary schools. Statistics from 1951 show less than half of the school age population was matriculated in any type of school, and only one in every eighteen students attending school was in the secondary level. In 1948, the forces that had overthrown Martínez, led by junior military officers, finally returned to power. The new regime established at this time proved to be remarkably stable until 1979. The group in power portrayed itself as a modernizer and began to address the main weaknesses of the educational system. To deal with the scarcity of teachers they founded a new teachers' school, the *Escuela Normal Superior*, to train primary and secondary school teachers, and two teachers' schools targeted for rural areas. The Ministry of Culture established a new unit to address the high levels of illiteracy (1950 official documents put illiteracy in a range between 40 percent and 50 percent). The president elected in 1950, Colonel Oscar Osorio (1950–56), had lived in Mexico and sought to imitate some of the initiatives that followed the Mexican revolution. He built "revolution style" schools in urban and rural areas and instituted cultural brigades. His rhetoric was more grandiose than his achievements; in fact only two brigades ever functioned.

Attention to education was an important element of a broader effort to modernize the economy. In contrast with the previous regimes that conceived education as a tool to strengthen the political system, the governments after 1948 began to stress the economic role of education. In 1952 the country invited experts from the United Nations Educational, Scientific and Cultural Organization (UNESCO) to develop educational projects, initiating the participation of international organizations in the formulation of educational policy— a trend that would help to bring about important changes in the future. The first UNESCO mission discovered that the attendance of school-age children stood at 40 percent, the shortage of primary school teachers at 45 percent and the deficit of school buildings at 37 percent.

The first efforts in the modernization of the educational system led to an increase in primary school enrollment—an almost 50 percent increase between 1956–62—that prompted an increase in the construction of school buildings in the early 1960s. The U.S. foreign aid program, Alliance for Progress, financed 200 school buildings. Yet, official reports continued to show that most of the enrollment was concentrated in the first and second grades. Particularly worrying for economic planners was the small enrollment in secondary education and, as a consequence, the tiny enrollments in the university. They thought that the country would have great difficulty developing industry with a work force that barely had finished two years of primary school. They began to apply for foreign aid to develop vocational schools, and strengthen secondary education. At that point they began considering the use of radio and television to increase the reach of secondary education.

The improvement of education at the university level was a unique challenge. University students, although a very small percentage of the overall student population (less than 1 percent of total school enrollments as late as 1962), were very active in politics. They had been instrumental in the toppling of the Martínez dictatorship and during the writing of the 1950 constitution that gave women the right to vote. As the limits of the modernization project of the post-Martínez period became evident, university students became increasingly vocal and the government proved to be ready to repress them. On the other hand, economic modernization required a greater number of university-educated leaders. The fact that the government was aware of the need for a good university at the same time that it feared an environment of independent thinking that could challenge government policies led to contradictory policies. The autonomy of the university, lost in 1939 under the dictatorship, was restored in 1944. Plans for the construction of a new campus of the university began after 1948.

However, the political changes that took place in the world during the 1950s made the government more suspicious of university students. The 1959 Cuban Revolution was seen by left-wing university students as an example to follow and gave impetus to a movement of opposition to the government. After street demonstrations, the confrontation between them and the government became violent when government troops entered the university campus and killed a student. In 1960 President José María Lemus (1956–60) closed the public university for a few days. The situation deteriorated rapidly since the economy was doing badly and there was widespread discontent. The turmoil led to President Lemus's downfall in October.

The tension between the need for excellence in higher education and a distrust of the political activism continued. In the early 1960s a highly effective university president, Fabio Castillo, upgraded the quality of education and expanded enrollment. Under his leadership the university established tenure rules and being a college professor became a career. The fact that the university began having a stable faculty that worked full time at the institution had a positive impact on the quality of education. He also reorganized academic administration in discipline-based departments, streamlined the admissions process, and began a program of financial aid for economically disadvantaged students.

The perception of the public university as a focus of anti-government and possibly pro-communist activism opened the door for the authorization of private universities. In 1961 Catholic bishops began advocating for a Catholic university and explicitly mentioned its potential role as an instrument to stop the advance of communism. The result of their initiative was the approval in 1965 of legislation that permitted the foundation of the first private university in El Salvador, the Jesuit-run Universidad Centroamericana José Simeón Cañas.

The highest point in the modernization of the educational system was the education reform of 1968 promoted by President Fidel Sánchez Hernández (1967–72)—perhaps the period in Salvadoran history when education received the highest priority. For President Sánchez Hernández and his team, education was the key to economic growth and the industrialization of the country. To that end, they conceived educational policy as an aspect of overall economic planning. Moreover, their plans received the strong financial and technical support of the United States. From the point of view of U.S. foreign policy, the support to Salvadoran reform was part of the policy of containment of communism. President Lyndon Johnson's advisors believed that the reform could help El Salvador to move from a traditional to a modern economic and social system, and that modernization was the best antidote against the advance of communism.

The technical studies carried out to prepare for the 1968 reform provide a snapshot of the problems that lay ahead. Few students finished the second grade. Only twenty of every one hundred students that entered the first grade stayed in school until the sixth grade. Very few graduated from secondary school. The year 1962 was the first one in the country's history that more than two thousand students graduated from secondary school. At the same time the percentage of university students that were women was barely 18.7 percent.

A letter sent by the Salvadoran government to the World Bank summarizes the rationale behind the reform:

Education, at the high school and university levels, is particularly important for accelerated economic growth. It is estimated that during the next five years it will be necessary to create at least 30,000 new jobs each year. Most of these jobs will be in the commercial, industrial and service sectors, and many of them will need training at the secondary or vocational school levels. (UNESCO Archive 1964)

To them, the discrepancy between the woeful number of students enrolled in secondary education and the pressing needs of the economy called for an urgent approach.

The 1968 reform was perhaps the most comprehensive that the country ever saw. It also represented an instance when the international organizations and foreign agencies that constituted the development community (UNESCO, World Bank, and the aid agencies of the United States, Japan, and England) played a prominent role in the formulation of policies and financing of the new initiatives. The reform included:

1. Reorganization of the Ministry of Education;
2. Extensive teacher training;
3. Curriculum revision;
4. Development of new teacher's guides and student workbooks;
5. Improvement of the system of school supervision to provide "advice" instead of inspection;
6. Development of a wider diversity of technical training programs in grades ten through twelve;
7. Extensive building of new schoolrooms;
8. Elimination of tuition in grades seven, eight, and nine;
9. Use of double sessions and reduced hours to teach more pupils;
10. A new student evaluation system incorporating changes in promotion and grading policies; and
11. Installation of a national instructional television system for grades seven through nine.

The most remarkable feature of the reform was the last item: the introduction of educational television as a prominent tool. Educational authorities felt that television was an expedient way of dealing with the scarcity of teachers capable of performing at the secondary school level. In fact, they conceived of television lessons almost as a replacement of the teacher in the classroom. The introduction of television completely transformed the classroom experience for students in grades seventh to ninth. The following class observation report illustrates the impact of introducing the innovative technology in a classroom full of children in a poor community.

On May 12 [1972], the TV set from the Ministry arrived, two months late. The set had been placed in the classroom the night before; the students caught their first glimpse of it as soon as they entered the room. The reactions were varied and enthusiastic. ¡Qué galán! [How handsome!] ... ¡Qué chulo! [How cute!] ... ¡Qué grande! ... [How big!] ¡Qué bonito! ... [How pretty!] Some students simply stood in front of the set and stared. Others touched it, and one went so far as to put his arms around it lovingly. Another wrote on the board in bold letters, "Do not touch the television set." The rest of the students walked around the room selecting the best seating position to view their first lesson. (Mayo et al. 1973, i)

By the third year of the reform all the seventh-, eighth-, and ninth- grade students in the public system, and many in private schools, sat in front of TV monitors to receive their math, science, Spanish, English, and social sciences classes. The tele-teacher taught for twenty minutes and then the classroom teacher explained a few points and answered questions. Classroom teachers, considered part of a "team" with the tele-teacher, had to be retrained to adapt to the new classroom dynamics. They received courses at a new teacher's school that was opened to update their teaching techniques. The administrative organization of the Ministry of Education was also reconfigured to respond to the needs of the introduction of the new technology.

The *Plan Básico* was eliminated and now primary education went from first to ninth grade. The three subsequent years represented a period of relative specialization to satisfy the manpower needs of the economy. Besides a *bachillerato académico* for college-bound students, the new system included *bachilleratos* in areas such as industry, tourism (to staff the developing tourism industry), fishing, commerce, health sciences (to train nurses aides), and agriculture.

The government's commitment to education was rewarded with a significant increase in enrollments. The number of students attending school doubled between 1965 and 1979. But the reform was introduced in a way that caused considerable turmoil and great resistance from the part of teachers. The new teachers' school was established at the expense of closing down dozens of small institutions devoted to teacher training. The new curriculum introduced new topics such as "new math" which many did not understand and did not find useful. The fact that lessons were broadcast from a central location meant that there was no way to catch up if the class or a few students were left behind. Many teachers felt that they had been reduced to the role of assistants to an electronic box. Moreover, already unhappy with the low level of their salaries and the lack of benefits, they now experienced an increase in workload due to the higher enrollments and the rapid changes in the curriculum. They resented the fact that the government had made great investments in educational technology while their income remained constant. The result was a mobilization of teachers demanding better salaries and working conditions and growing opposition to the reform. A teachers' strike paralyzed the public school system for two months in 1971. The government's violent reaction to the strike included imprisoning teacher activists, intimidating them, and even killing them. These actions embittered the members of the union to the point that many of them became increasingly active in radical political activities. They were prominent in the anti-government forces during the eleven-year civil war that started in 1981.

Opposition to the education reform became a rallying cry for the political left which had been inspired by the Cuban Revolution and the activities of various guerrilla movements throughout the hemisphere. Both the authorities and student groups of the public university were particularly active in their opposition to the reform. They characterized it as an instrument of "Yankee imperialism" and part of the counterinsurgency program of the United States. This opposition was only part of the growing political activism of the public university and of the political polarization of the country as a whole. The government hostility towards the public university increased to the point that in July 1972 the government fired its entire leadership, suspended university autonomy, and sent troops to occupy the institution. The significant progress made in increasing the quality of education and doubling of enrollments between 1962–69 began to stymie. As a response, students enrolled in increasing numbers in private universities, despite the fact that having to pay tuition was a significant burden for most of them. The confrontation with teachers and university students that took place during the implementation of the reform was part of the increasing political polarization experienced by El Salvador during the decade of the 1970s. The victory of the left-wing Sandinista revolution in neighboring Nicaragua in 1979 accelerated the process. The authoritarian military government felt threatened by a victory of the left and radical groups felt energized. An eleven-year civil war began in January 1981. During the period of the war the government's highest priority was not education but the conduct of the war. Under those circumstances there were no innovations in the public school system. Moreover, some of the territory in the northern part of the country was controlled by rebel forces. Public schools in those areas experienced multiple problems related to the war, including the emigration of children, the difficulty of sending school supplies, abandonment of teachers of their positions, and other innumerable practical problems. Many public schools simply ceased to operate.

A new kind of school appeared in that fourth of the territory controlled by the rebels; they called them "popular schools." The schools were started by the communities that organized themselves to train teachers. They even devised a system to raise money to pay teachers by "taxing" truckers passing through the area. Popular educators were directly or indirectly influenced by the Brazilian educator Paulo Freire's ideas of education as a vehicle to liberate the poor from oppressive structures. Popular teachers had no formal textbooks to distribute and school supplies were almost nonexistent. Some popular educators used their ingenuity to develop simple educational materials, sometimes under the direction of members of the teachers' union. Following Freire's practice of using "generating words" to teach literacy, the educational material developed by popular teachers would use words such as "revolutionary" or "refugee" to start the process of teaching. Classrooms were makeshift when they existed at all. Particularly in the early years of these schools, it was not rare to have classes meeting in the open air under the shade of a big tree. These schools sought to instill the values of community and participation that inspired the fight against the government. By the end of the war about one hundred such schools were active.

The creativity shown by these communities was a response to the enormous difficulties that the school system had to face. As a result of the civil war the government diverted to the military many of the resources that had been ear-marked for education. After the implementation of the 1968 educational reform the government had continued to assign a significant amount of re-sources to education. At the eve of the Civil War the educational sector repre-sented 3.6 percent of the country's economy, but by the end of the war it was only 1.5 percent. In addition, the war caused an estimated damage to the edu-cational infrastructure of two billion dollars.

Such sharp decrease in resources caused serious harm to the system. By the end of the war three out of ten Salvadorans over the age of fourteen had never attended school and only one-third of the people in the same age group had completed more than six years of basic education. The quality of the education of those who did attend school was limited. The description of a typical class-room in 1992 was barely different from a description in the 1940s or the 1880s. A contemporary study stated that:

As a general rule children spend the school day copying verbatim from their textbooks, the blackboard or the teacher's lessons. They engage in few group activities, they are always sitting in neat rows and have little or no participation in the organization of their learning. Teacher lesson planning is rare, improvisation is common. Schools have few teaching materials, class and school libraries are practically non-existent.... The situation is worse in rural areas. (Harvard Institute for International Development 1994, iii)

However, women had achieved parity at all levels of education by 1992. They had the same access to poor quality schooling as men. The experiment with popular education lost its reason for being after the signing of the 1992 Peace Accords that ended the war, but it left a legacy. A Ministry of Education advisor visited rural areas and admired the initiative shown by communities in the organization of popular schools. She thought that the experience could be imitated in a program sponsored by the government that could help address the serious deficit of schools in the countryside. Based on her initial insight, the Ministry of Education started a program called *Educación con participación de la comunidad* (EDUCO, Education with Community Participation). The program is now in widespread use in rural areas. The first step in the organiza-tion of EDUCO schools is the training of a community organization (the Communal Association for Education, ACE in its Spanish acronym) to manage school funds and hire teachers. Once the training is completed, the Ministry of Education makes monthly transfers of funds to a bank account set up for the school, and then the ACE takes over the hiring of teachers, the improvement of school buildings, buying school materials, and the day-to-day management of the school. The Ministry sets the curriculum and supervises the teachers' academic performance. The experience with the new system has been, by and large, positive. It has been a mechanism for a rapid expansion of the educational system in rural areas, while the communities have been empowered to take over one of the most important local institutions. To be sure, the system is open to corruption and abuse, but for the moment it appears to have no greater corruption and abuse than schools run directly by the Ministry of Education.

The experimental phase of EDUCO served as the stepping-stone for an important post-Civil War educational reform aimed at confronting the educational problems created by the conflict. The reform of 1995 was an expression of the changing political atmosphere after the signing of the historic Peace Accords of 1992. It was based on a sober assessment of the educational sector led by a team of Harvard University-based researchers. The main guidelines for the reform came from a pluralistic presidential commission that included representatives from different sectors of society including a vice-rector of the Jesuit-run university, a member of the think tank of the business community, the deputy bishop, two former commanders of the guerrilla forces, business leaders, and academics. The appointment of a pluralistic commission was just a first step in the process. The Ministry of Education also engaged in a concerted effort of consultation with teachers, parents, students, Ministry staff, private schools, mayors, and private universities. Ministry representatives were dispatched to each department to hold seminars with the above mentioned groups, to listen to concerns, and to discuss the main, evolving points of the reform.

The conception of the new reform represented an important departure from the past. Late nineteenth century centralization efforts had evolved into a Ministry of Education in charge of appointing every single teacher and their duties included not only curriculum design and teaching supervision but also pencil purchases and chalk consumption monitoring. The epitome of the trend to centralization had been the educational television that made all students listen to the same teacher at the same hour and go through the school year at exactly the same pace.

The 1995 reform stressed the decentralization of school administration. With strong support from international donors and lenders, particularly the World Bank, the reforms included an effort to transfer functions from the central Ministry of Education to the schools themselves. In rural areas decentralization took place by expanding the EDUCO program. A similar, although less thorough, scheme was implemented in urban schools where school councils with representation from parents, teachers, and students received a role in school administration decisions.

Both in the EDUCO program and in the urban school councils, parents, often from very humble background, have an opportunity to participate in decisions that shape not only their children's school but also their community. Oftentimes, in the household division of labor prevalent in El Salvador, women who are in charge of the education of their children find these programs to be avenues for acquiring leadership in the schools, and that leadership is transferred to other community organizations. The active presence of parents in the schools not only brings benefits to their children but also has also served to check common abuses such as sexual harassment and racist behavior within schools.

The reform also included the introduction of new textbooks at the primary and secondary levels. The primary school textbooks encourage student interaction and more dynamic pedagogical techniques. The textbooks also give greater emphasis to the representation of images more consistent with the children's real life and occasional references to environmental and gender issues. New secondary school books were introduced for history and natural history. They made an effort to engage students in the complexities of their country's reality. They were conceived in the spirit of the "culture of peace" that was heavily promoted by UNESCO at the time of the reform. Teachers received a teacher's guide that included discussion exercises and other pedagogical innovations. These textbooks, however, have been abandoned.

The most tangible result of the 1995 reform has been a rapid expansion of the educational system. By 2000 primary school enrollment was almost universal and secondary school enrollment had risen above the 50 percent mark for the first time in history. In both educational levels there was gender parity.

The situation was more complex at the university level where the Ministry of Education had less influence. The phenomenon of massification and privatization of higher education that has characterized higher education in Latin America early in the twenty-first century had very distinctive characteristics in El Salvador due to the Civil War. Military governments always considered the public university as a hotbed of opposition, but during the Civil War distrust was turned into outright hostility. The public university was sometimes closed, occupied, and always deprived of resources. Numerous university professors were targets of death squads and were either killed or left the country. To further weaken the public university the government liberalized the rules to open new universities. Numerous private universities opened but failed to satisfy minimum standards of quality. By the end of the war, forty universities operated with very little supervision. A new law of higher education was passed in 1995 and it included a system of closer governmental supervision of colleges and universities and a system of accreditation that includes incentive mechanisms to improve the quality of education. The new system has had some success in weeding out private universities that did not meet acceptable standards of quality.

The world of schooling in El Salvador was always an accurate reflection of the violent swings of the country's turbulent history. It was affected by wars, economic crisis, and the authoritarian nature of the political system. It reflected, more than anything else, the exclusions of the political system. As long as the political culture denied large segments of the population the right to full participation in society, the state's efforts to expand the educational system were half-hearted. The signing of the Peace Accords of 1992 gave hope to those who cherish education, and the advances in school enrollments since then have been significant, but having free elections is not enough to change a culture of exclusion. The universal access to quality education is still an elusive dream in El Salvador.

A DAY IN THE LIFE

Rafael is a thirteen-year-old boy attending a rural school with educational television. This reconstruction of the typical day of a student is based on fieldwork carried out by a Stanford University research team in 1973.[1]

Rafael gets up at 4:30 AM. His first chore is to go to the fields to gather the firewood that his mother needs to prepare the warm milk and corn tortillas that he and his six siblings will have as breakfast. Their adobe hut has no running water or electricity. At around 5:15 AM, he leaves for school wearing his only uniform. The mile-and-a-half walk to school over very rugged terrain becomes lighter thanks to the company of friends that join him along the way. The rented house that serves as school sits on top of a hill; it is closed when they arrive at 6:45 AM. The kids wait until 7:00 AM when the teachers arrive to open the school. When the bell rings students rush into their classroom to make sure that they get a desk; if they are not prompt, they may end up sitting on the floor.

When the Spanish teacher arrives, the boys and girls stand up until they are given permission to sit down. At the end of the class, at 8:00 AM, all students leave the room to pass inspection. The teachers check the cleanliness of hair, nails, shoes, and make sure that the boys are wearing ties and have a handkerchief.

The second class, social studies, is taught with the help of educational television. The teacher turns the television on, the students watch the clock on the screen until the tele-teacher appears at ten past the hour. The twenty-minute lesson is about the pre-Columbian period. After the tele-teacher finishes the lecture, the classroom teacher asks review questions for another twenty minutes until recess.

At 9:00 AM, all kids run to the grounds for recess. Those who can afford candy buy it at the student-run store. Science is next. Again the lesson is televised, this time followed by a very simple demonstration experiment carried out by the classroom teacher. The math teacher arrives after a ten-minute break. Her class has no help from television; she explains the difference between positive and negative numbers and gives exercises for the pupils to understand the concept.

The school day ends with the English class—the students' favorite. The tele-teacher is engaging and his lesson is accompanied by background music from the Beatles (the song *Yesterday*). The entertaining tele-class is followed by repetition exercises that the class finds very boring. By noon, the lesson is over and the boys and girls are dismissed for the day.

The downhill walk back home is easier, but Rafael is tired. As soon as he gets home, he eats the corn tortillas, rice, and beans that his mother has prepared. He cannot afford to play with his brothers for too long. Unless he starts doing his homework in the middle of the afternoon, he will not have enough daylight to finish. After the sun sets, the only light in the hut is provided by the fire.

TIMELINE

1778   Spanish colonial authorities decree the establishment of schools in Indian towns to be financed by the communities themselves. Teaching had to be in Spanish.

1821   Central America becomes independent form Spain and forms a Federation.

1827   The legislature passes a decree establishing schools for boys and girls.

1832   The State of San Salvador approves the first Primary Education regulations.

1833   The first school that applies the Lancasterian method opens.

1839   The Federation ends.

1841   Foundation of the *University of El Salvador* and the first secondary school, the *Colegio de La Asunción*.

1858   The first teachers' school opens. It is short lived.

1875   Opening of a teachers' school for women.

1885   Opening of the *Instituto Nacional*, the leading public institution of secondary education to this day. A new law puts oversight of secondary education under the jurisdiction of the Secretariat of Public Instruction.

1887   Arrival of a group of Colombian teachers that has a profound influence on the professionalization of the system of education.

1893   First pedagogical conference of Central America.

1924   The government puts a group of German educators in charge of the men's teachers school.

1930   The first teachers' association, *Comité Pro Día del Maestro*, receives legal standing. First national pedagogical conference.

1939   The University of El Salvador looses its autonomy until 1944.

1940   First modern education reform updates the curriculum of primary schools.

1945   Meeting of Salvadoran and Guatemalan educational authorities leads to the creation of *Plan Básico*, a general education curriculum for the three grades after primary school.

1952   Arrival of first UNESCO mission marks the beginning of the influence of international development organizations on educational policy.

1958   Street demonstrations mark the beginnings of modern teacher organizations.

1963   Fabio Castillo reforms the University of El Salvador. He leads the University until 1967.

1965   The legislature passes a law authorizing the opening of private universities. Foundation of *Asociación Nacional de Educadores* (ANDES), the teachers' union (June 21).

1968	Fidel Sánchez Hernández's administration begins a profound education reform that includes the use of educational television.
1971	ANDES organizes a massive strike to protest against working conditions and the education reform of President Sánchez Hernández.
1981	A civil war begins. Popular schools begin to operate in areas controlled by the guerrilla movement.
1992	The civil war ends with the Peace Accords.
1995	A new education reform seeks to reconstruct an educational system devastated by war.

NOTE

1. The pupil's name is fictional. The fieldwork was carried out by Yolanda Ingle, the results of her work are John K. Mayo, Robert C. Hornik, et al. "Television and Educational Reform in El Salvador: Report on the Fourth Year of Research." (Stanford University. Institute for Communications Research, 1973), 68–81. US Agency for International Development, *U.S. Overseas Loans and Grants* (Washington, DC: USAID), Order No. PN-AAB-410-A1.

BIBLIOGRAPHY

Books

Aguilar Avilés, Gilberto and Héctor Lindo-Fuentes. 1998. *Un vistazo al pasado de la educación en El Salvador*. San Salvador: FEPADE.

Anaya Montes, Mélida. 1972. *La segunda gran batalla de ANDES*. San Salvador: Editorial Universitaria.

Beirne, Charles J. S.I. 1996. *Jesuit Education and Social Change in El Salvador*. New York: Garland Publishing.

Cañas-Dinarte, Carlos, ed. 1998. *José María Cáceres: Un docente, una época*. San Salvador: Fepade.

Ebaugh, Cameron D. 1947. *Education in El Salvador*. Washington, D.C.: Government Printing Office.

Escamilla, Manuel Luis. 1981. *Reformas educativas; Historia contemporánea de la educación formal en El Salvador*. San Salvador: Dirección de Publicaciones.

Espinosa, Francisco. 1998. *La escuela salvadoreña*. San Salvador: FEPADE.

Galindo, Francisco E. 1874. *Cartilla del ciudadano*. 1st ed. San Salvador: Imprenta Nacional, 1904.

Hammond, John L. 1998. *Fighting to Learn: Popular Education and Guerrilla War in El Salvador*. New Brunswick: Rutgers University Press.

Lindo-Fuentes, Héctor. 2001. *Comunidad, participación y escuelas en El Salvador*. San Salvador: FLACSO-Ministerio de Educación.

Mayo, John K., Robert C. Hornik, and Emile G. McAnany. 1976. *Educational Reform with Television: The El Salvador Experience*. Stanford: Stanford University Press.

Purcell-Gates, Victoria and Robin A. Waterman. 2000. *Now We Read, We See, We Speak: Portrait of Literacy Development in an Adult Freiran-Based Class*. Mahwah, NJ: Lawrence Erlbaum Associates, Publishers.

Universidad Autónoma de El Salvador. 1949. *Guión histórico de la Universidad Autónoma de El Salvador.* San Salvador: Editorial Ahora.

Van Oss, Adriaan C. 1986. *Catholic Colonialism.* Cambridge: Cambridge University Press.

Waggoner, George R. and Barbara Ashton Waggoner. 1971. *Education in Central America.* Lawrence: The University Press of Kansas.

Articles and Chapters

Cuellar-Marchelli, Helga. "Decentralization and Privatization of Education in El Salvador: Assessing the Experience." *International Journal of Educational Development* 23, no. 2 (2003): 145–66.

Ingle, Henry. "Behavioral Objectives and the Evaluation of Educational Reform in El Salvador." *Educational Broadcasting International* 6, no. 2 (1973): 91–97.

Lindo-Fuentes, Héctor. 2005. "La televisión educativa en El Salvador como proyecto de la Teoría de la Modernización." In *Memoria del primer encuentro de historia de El Salvador.* San Salvador: Dirección de Publicaciones e Impresos.

Newspapers

Gaceta de El Salvador. 1858. San Salvador, November 13, 1858.

Reports and Other Non-print Sources

Archivo Municipal de Sonsonate. 1853. Junta de instrucción pública papers. Nahuizalco teacher to Alcalde Primero de Sonsonate, April 12, 1853.

Emerson, L. H. S., Guilhermo Dutra da Fonseca, J. A. Laing, and Maya J. Paez. 1965. "Educational Priority Projects for Development: El Salvador—Mission." UNESCO document.

Harvard Institute for International Development con la colaboración de Fundación Empresarial para el Desarrollo Educativo y la Universidad Centroamericana José Simeón Cañas. 1994. "Diagnóstico del sistema de desarrollo de recursos humanos de El Salvador." Chap. 4. Working document, San Salvador.

Kilgo, Reese Danley. 1966. "The Development of Education in El Salvador." PhD diss., University of Texas.

Mayo, John K., Robert C. Hornik, et al. 1973. "Television and Educational Reform in El Salvador: Report on the Fourth Year of Research." Stanford University. Institute for Communications Research, 1973. USAID. *U.S. Overseas Loans and Grants.* Order No. PN-AAB-410-A1. Washington, DC: USAID.

Secco, Luis, and M. Dino Carelli. 1983. "El Salvador: Completion report, Second Education Project." UNESCO document.

UNESCO Archive. 1964. Reg. X07.21 (728.4) Relations with El Salvador—Official. Borja Nathan to Orvis Schmidt, Director of Operations, World Bank. June 25, 1964.

Chapter 10

SCHOOLING IN MEXICO

Aurora Loyo Brambila

INTRODUCTION

In the following pages we will take off on a journey that will take us from the *telpochcalli* and the *calmecac,* where Aztec teenagers in Tenochtitlán were brought up during the Spanish arrival, to modern Mexico's broad education system. We will be able to visit just a few places and stop in certain episodes; the intention is to provide a panoramic view that will provide incentive to the reader's curiosity and will motivate him/her to study the history of education in this country more in-depth, with results almost as uneven as its orography.

The mixture of ethnicities is Mexico's main singularity. This mixture began through physical violence, endured, and became more thorough through an ambitious linguistic, religious, cultural, and educative venture. Two of the most important contemporary writers, Octavio Paz and Carlos Fuentes, have been able to give light to the complexities of this process. The Mexican population has exceeded one-hundred million inhabitants, representing the most important Hispanic-speaking nucleus in the world; it is also a predominantly Catholic country. But the originality of its culture, which manifests itself through arts and crafts, cooking, the way people have of relating themselves with others, the parties and celebrations—the Day of the Dead, among others—rests on the persistence of Mesoamerican cultural features. During the three centuries of Spanish domination, these features were assimilated and transformed, and the Spanish many times thought that they could eliminate them. Nowadays, the Mexican culture assimilates other influences, too, and, like in the past, transforms and molds them, giving them a special kind of rhythm and color.

From a cultural point of view, the family and school are privileged spheres through which Mexico's historic density can be penetrated. A strong sense of belonging, great respect towards ancestors, traditions, and rites, repeated constriction of individuality in the name of the collective, a certain consent to exceedingly unjust situations are interrupted throughout Mexico's history by violent shocks, moments of rupture, times of hope for change, and anarchic phases.

To guide our steps in this journey, we must emphasize the role school has played in the construction of Mexico as a nation, in the modern sense of the term. This is why we will limit ourselves to a few paint strokes to describe Aztec school establishments in central Mexico prior to the conqueror's arrival, we will stress some milestones which happened during the three centuries of colonial history, and we will look out for more precise approaches from the beginning of Mexico's independent life to the present. The potentiality but also serious deficiencies perceived in the education system may be fully understood and its accomplishments better evaluated after joining us on the journey we will now begin.

EDUCATION IN THE GREAT TENOCHTITLÁN

During the beginning of the sixteenth century, the territory known today as the Republic of Mexico was inhabited by different native groups that had both splendid and decadent moments, in cycles that nowadays are a matter of discussion between specialists. There are more certainties about the social and political life of the Aztecs and Mexicas. These were indigenous groups that at the time of the Spanish conquest had their political and religious center in the lake city of Tenochtitlán, a portion of land that belongs to Mexico City in the present. How were Aztec children and teenagers educated? Taking the Mendoza Codex as main source, Jacques Soustelle offers us a vivid painting of the children and teenager's life. The difference between the two types of school, the *calmecac* and the *telpochcalli*, is quite comprehensible taking in account the fact that the society was arranged under a strong hierarchical order.

The parents were the ones in charge of teaching their children about practical tasks during their childhood; this socialization was taken care of with great strictness, and parents were inclined to physically punish their children if they did not behave adequately. The lazy child would be scratched with maguey thorns by his parents, or would be forced to breathe the smoke of a fire that would have red chili peppers burning in it. There is no agreement about the age at which children entered school. However, it can be stated that priests and officials were formed in the *calmecac*, and that it was mainly open for dignitary's children although there were exceptional cases where young children from merchant or commoner families were admitted. Everyone had to be submitted to very rigid rules and was taught the value of discipline, to bear fasting and self-control in general terms. On the other hand, the *telpochcalli* was in charge of bringing up all the other children and was less severe and emphasized on the training for battle. The educational duality was also reflected on the patron gods: while at the *colmecac* the students devoted themselves to

Quetzalcóatl, the god of books, the calendar, and the arts, the *telpochcalli* was under the influence of its enemy, Tezcatlipoca, a young warrior who made use of enchantments.

Women had a subordinate role in this warrior society and assisted other schools. A selected group of girls was educated for priesthood; the rest of the young girls had an education based on practical skills and were held within schools until the day they were married. Jacques Soustelle emphasizes that the fact that every young person went to school before the Spanish arrival is quite remarkable, even though the intellectual instruction only existed at the *calmecac*, where they were taught the reading and writing of pictographic characters, divination, chronology, poetry, and rhetoric.

THE COLONIAL PERIOD

Mexican historiography has been developed on the basis of a debate concerning the way in which the Conquest and the colonial period are interpreted. The "hispanist" side highlights the positive aspects of the Spanish contribution to Mexican culture, such as the Catholic religion and the Spanish language, which was disseminated by the members of the religious orders that crossed the Atlantic Ocean to "save souls" and to "civilize the savages." On the other end, the "indigenist" side has emphasized the violence and cruelty of the Conquest, and the colonial domination; the prototypical images are the Conqueror who imposes his law through the sword and the settler who ruthlessly exploits the natives.

Through the study of a great variety of sources, modern historiography has fortunately been able to capture shades of meaning, the great social, ethnic, and regional diversity within the *Virreinato* (Viceroyalty) and has been able to identify moments of change throughout the colonial period. It would be convenient to stress the education work carried out during the first half of the sixteenth century by the Franciscans who arrived around 1523. Catechesis constituted the foundations where the education work was built. It was profoundly imbued in a hierarchical view of society, but also in the utopia of being able to return to Christianity's ideals in the New World. In this way, they established two clearly differentiated types of instruction for the natives. Monks congregated the *macehualtin*, natives who belonged to the lower social stratum, on the churches' atrium to transmit to them the rudiments of the Catholic doctrine and, at the same time, induce them as much as possible to abandon their customs and their ways of relating themselves with their families, at their work and within the community. On the other extreme of society, monks founded convent-like boarding schools for the children who came from prominent native families, where they could learn to speak and write in Spanish, as well as learn some Latin. The academic teachings that included grammar and had a broad humanistic orientation only existed in a couple of institutions from which the *Colegio de Santa Cruz* from *Tlatelolco* stood out.

Towards the second half of the sixteenth century, colonial education shifted away from the humanities and from the interest in finding new ways of educating the natives, like Don Vasco de Quiroga had done in the hospitals in the town of *Santa Fe* and the *Colegio de San Nicolás*. In the new phase that would extend itself until the mid-eighteenth century, the Spanish Crown's interest limited itself to making sure that the inhabitants of their lands were submissive enough to be able to extract as much wealth as possible from their work and territories to compensate for the Royal Treasury's bankruptcy. Laws and regulations destined to make the education institutions come close together with the Church's dogma and with the rules established by the Spanish institutions were multiplied to this effect. In this way, as the *Virreinato de la Nueva España* (Viceroyalty of the New Spain) was being consolidated, a much more worldly aim was added to the so called "spiritual conquest" (which itself did not disappear). The idea was to keep a constant and suffice supply of native labor to work in rural areas, in mines, and as the domestic service. In this new vision, the schooling of the natives no longer came up as an important necessity. At the same time, natives were permitted to keep their custom about having respect for the older members of the group, in other words, to be submissive towards the authority. This rite was very propitious to ensure order within families and communities.

The Spanish and the Creoles' *(criollos)* education was in charge of the Jesuits who did their best to establish discipline and demanded a rigorous use of the time at their schools. Their cultural and education work was interrupted by their expulsion in 1767, but left a trace in the Mexican "high culture."

The Spanish Enlightenment did not stand out in its philosophical developments or its radicalism. The disastrous economical and administrative situation of the Kingdom was the main concern, which was expressed in a series of political and administrative reforms. Nevertheless, the education field responded to the new scientific developments, and the experimentation of students was promoted, partly replacing the traditional method of memorization that had been used. After the closing of Jesuit schools, other religious orders became in charge of education in the New Spain. The academic reform was much more limited than in the metropolis, and the new times brought a greater awareness among the creoles about the privileges that were reserved only for the Spanish in terms of access to high ranked civil or ecclesiastic posts, but also, and very importantly, in the education field. The defense of Creole wit was essential in awakening *criollismo*, which would later become a central factor in the birth of the Independence movement.

THE COLONIAL PACT RUPTURE AND THE MISFORTUNES OF THE NINETEENTH CENTURY

The history of the nineteenth century is covered in events and vicissitudes that ended up leading the way to the loss of over half of the national territory after an uneven war with the United States. Although this complex event will not be approached in this chapter, it would be useful to distinguish two great periods that, put together, give shape to the political history of Mexico in the nineteenth century. The first one begins in 1810 with the Independence War and, passing through the insurgent triumph in 1821, extends itself to the beginning of General Porfirio Díaz's presidency in 1876. The second period is precisely what is know as the *porfiriato*, in which the General Díaz, succeeded in the presidential seat by many of his unconditional men, controlled every detail of the national political life. This second period ends in 1910 with the protest movement led by Francisco Madero, that unleashed the Mexican Revolution.

In the education arena, there are four features that best define the predominant tendencies in the nineteenth century: the secularization of society and its effects on education, the continuous and intentional backwardness of rural and native education, the restricted implementation of new pedagogical models, and the developments in the organization of schooling that tended towards the establishment of a modern education system.

The Church's predominant role in education matters was not eliminated with independence and although the growing secularization meant greater responsibilities for the State, the political elites never made an attempt to eliminate the private and predominantly Catholic education. Between 1786–1817, a couple of decrees were issued that demanded the Church fulfill its obligation of opening schools of first letters also called "pious schools." The town councils were in charge of the schools. The project to establish a general regulation of public education in 1823 stated that every citizen had the faculty to create particular establishments of education in all of the arts and sciences, and for all occupations, but the State reserved its authority to supervise and make sure that the teachers in these schools had the required aptitudes and training for teaching.

Once liberalism triumphed, important advances were obtained in the secularization process. Private Catholic schools were located in cities and found their juridical support in the freedom to teach that both liberals and conservatives accepted. Nonetheless, a number of reforms affected the power of clergymen. On the other hand, the achievements in the organization of public education were quite limited but proved to be the best way towards a gradual secularization of the Mexican society. However, when Porfirio Díaz became president there was an important change: although he formally kept in effect the liberal Constitution of 1857, he gave multiple concessions to the Church. The influence of Catholic schools was strengthened in this context, and new religious orders arrived to the country to create new schools. As it will be seen further on, liberalism once again took up its thrust with the triumph of the Mexican Revolution, making anti-clergy passions grow, but mainly reducing the role of religious congregations in education.

The constant disputes between liberal and conservative ideas during the nineteenth century constituted the background to the education debates of the time. But something that is not always taken into account when analyzing this period of Mexican history is that beyond these political conflicts, the school, understood as an institution that works normally, is a part of a well structured system, it possesses a physical space that is adequate to teach, a fixed timetable and calendar, and a trained teacher who receives a regular pay, was the exception rather than the rule in the first century of independent life. The modern school requires certain stability that a tempestuous environment such as the one produced by the political and military events during the nineteenth century hardly permitted. It also requires certain homogeneity that the social inequalities inherited by the colonial period made unfeasible. There were some pedagogical advances, but they were restricted to the cities. In the rural areas and places where the native population was a majority, ignorance remained intact. The few luminous spots found in the cities, as well as the progressive ideas that were expressed in the Third Article of the Constitution of 1857, constituted a legacy that would only be fruitful in the twentieth century.

The exclusion of the native population from schools was not changed during the *porfiriato*. In a context in which public resources were chronically scarce, there were deprivations in education matters, and there was an inherited prejudice against indigenous people, it is comprehensible that education in the cities was thought of as a priority. It was almost normal to think that the education for the rural or native population didn't have the same requirements or demands. As in the colonial period, it was thought that teaching Spanish and rudimentary knowledge was more than enough for this population.

In the cities, Lancastrian schools appeared around 1820 and kept their influence until 1890. Although they were private associations that offered free education in the beginning, they obtained governmental support through the *Dirección General de Instrucción Primaria* (General Direction of Primary Instruction) and state sub-directors in 1842 onwards. The Lancastrian method, based on Joseph Lancaster's work (1778–1838), involved the utilization of the most advanced students to help their classmates and included a semicircle formation of children in wide and well ventilated classrooms, where they carried out reading or calculus exercises. These schools had a fixed timetable, morning and afternoon, which included an hour for lunch at midday.

The other great pedagogic influence of the time was August Comte, but it was mainly directed at the high school level. Gabino Abrreda introduced Comte's positivist ideas at the *Escuela Nacional Preparatoria*, making only a few changes in their conceptions. Finally, it is important to mention the influence of Froebel's ideas that gave way to the establishing of the first kindergartens. These and other pedagogical innovations permitted some partial and discontinuous advances, but constituted the bases over which the national education system would be built in the twentieth century.

The most significant innovations in terms of organization of the system were established in the *Congreso de Instrucción* of 1889. In this event, the possibility of establishing a national system of education that would give uniformity to the primary education was discussed. It was also decided that, following the Constitution, schools within this system should be secular, free of charge for students, and compulsory. Another conclusion of the event was that primary education should have a basic length of four years, including children between six and twelve years of age. In this direction, it was decided that there should be a general and integral program for a basic primary education.

AN OVERTURN IN HISTORY

Even though the "Revolutionary Political Party," which remained in power from 1921 to 2000, declared that education was central in the revolutionary movement that was initiated in 1910, the only important document which articulated proposals for the "improvement and promotion of education" was the Liberal party's program. These proposals were based on the education thesis that had been previously outlined by Dr. Mora and Justo Sierra. In this way, the issue of education—that had been eclipsed during the armed phase that happened with the uprising of the rural masses who called for a land reform and the democratic demands made by the middle classes—gained a privileged place in the political debate in 1916. The temporary triumph of one of the revolutionary factions made the installation of the Constitutional Convention possible. In this debate, two factions were opposed: liberals and Jacobins. The passionate controversies were centered on two much related points: the degree of control that the state should have in education matters, and how the principle of secularization of the education system should be interpreted in practice.

The liberal project, presented by President Venustiano Carranza, was moderate with respect to state control, and emphasized the freedom to teach, already established by the 1917 Constitution. Carranza suggested that the obligation of a nonreligious education should only be demanded from public schools. Thus, the only innovation in his project was the proposal of making public schools free of charge for students and their families, but the possibility of having Catholic private schools was left untouched.

However, in the debates that took place in the Constitutional Convention, Carranza's position was rejected. The new project argued that President Carranza's position proclaimed an unlimited freedom to teach. On the contrary, this project suggested that it was perfectly fair to restrict a natural right whenever its free exercise could affect the conservation of society or obstruct its development. Alfonso Romero presented an alternative text to the Third Article written by the Commission, which established that education had to be secular not only in public schools, but also in private ones. It also prohibited any religious order to establish or direct primary schools. He additionally demanded that private primary schools should be subject to official vigilance. The vote favored this last project with ninety-nine votes against fifty-eight that defended Carranza's position. A Third Article in education matters had been added to the

Mexican Constitution and its contents would have deep implications for the direction that the Mexican education system would take. The new country that was emerging from armed conflicts was already showing signs of its path towards the building of a strong and controlling state. From then on, the state assumed the responsibility for education as an important source of legitimacy, but the education system also became once again an arena for political struggles, just like in the nineteenth century.

THE LAST CAUDILLO,[1] A CULTURAL AND EDUCATION PROMOTER

The general Álvaro Obregón, great general and true revolutionary *caudillo*, successfully revolted against President Carranza. In 1921, due to a request made by José Vasconcelos, he created the Secretaría de Educación Pública (SEP—Secretariat of Public Education). Counting on the president's unlimited support, Vasconcelos himself took up the Secretariat and began his work with amazing energy. In Vasconcelos's view, education and culture could be articulated through certain actions and oeuvres. For example, he saw mural paintings as a contribution of the artists to the mission of inculcating amongst the people the love for the *Patria* (motherland) and the consciousness about the Mexican historic struggles. Another way in which the new Secretariat carried out its education mission was through the editing and distribution of classic books throughout the Republic, reaching even the most far-off places in the country. However, the two innovations that gave a particular hallmark to Mexican education in this historic period were the Cultural Missions and the Rural School.

The idea of the Cultural Missions came up from the work made by Spanish missioners during the colonial period. Vasconcelos designed a model that included the coordinated action of a group of teachers that would usually consist of a supervisor, a social worker, an expert in hygiene, pediatrics, and first aid, a physical education teacher, and a manual arts specialist, and a person who would be in charge of the school's organization and the teaching methods. The Rural School, on the other hand, was aimed at educating farm laborers and their children, so that they could improve their life conditions by means of a better and more rational use of farming and the small related industries. At the same time farmers and their children learned the rudiments of reading and writing. Rural teachers were also in charge of the difficult mission of struggling against alcoholism and premature sexual relations and to look for greater solidarity among natives and *mestizos* (persons with mixed European and indigenous ethnicities) through the generalized use of the Spanish language.

EDUCATION AS A POLITICAL ARENA

During General Plutarco Elías Calles's presidency (1924–28), support to rural schools was kept and further innovations were introduced in other levels within the education system. In keeping with the increase in industrial and commercial activities, as a result of a certain pacification to the country, the government was showing its modern view by giving resources to technical schools, creating middle schools, and proceeding to a reorganization of the *Escuela Nacional de Maestros* (National School for Teachers). Nonetheless, this constructive labor darkened by the confrontation between the Church and the State with respect to the fulfillment of the Third Article of the Mexican Constitution.

In 1926, the country's Catholic bishops and some Catholic organizations undertook a campaign to reform the constitutional articles which opposed their interests. Even though the attempt to reform the Constitution failed, it was not possible for the State to avoid what is known as the "*cristero* uprising," led by armed farm laborers and middle classes of the central region of the country who counted with the initial support of the clergy. These groups that professed a devoted Catholicism refused to accept what had been established by law in relation to the prohibitions and limitations to religious education and priesthood activities. Calles's government was able to find a negotiated way out, but it was ephemeral. A few years later, *Cristiada* expanded and made way for violent actions from the Federal Army and the revolutionary groups. Finally in 1932, another negotiation took place with the participation of the high hierarchy of the Mexican Catholic Church. As a consequence of this arrangement, the successive governments allowed private Catholic schools to teach religion. However, the legislation was not modified. It was an arrangement in which the colonial tradition of accepting the transgression of valid juridical rules was reaffirmed.

Beyond these difficulties, State control over education was being strengthened. The focuses of resistance were marginal and no longer constituted a real threat for the government. From then on the source of conflict shifted. Debate and the struggles would be based on the aim of different political groups of imposing their points of view in the definition of the general objectives that would guide primary and middle school education. Secular education established in the 1917 Constitutional Convention did not provide clear guidelines. Two political groups dominated the debate: one led by the former president Calles and the other by the supporters of the future president, General Lázaro Cárdenas.

Cárdenas's supporters did not have a unified conception about what the school should be, but they wanted to oppose the conservative ideas of Calles, and they intended to impose what they defined as a "socialist education." They succeeded. On December 5, 1933, during the Convention of the *Partido Nacional Revolucionario* (the antecedent of the Partido Revolucionario Institucional—PRI) it was decided that the Party would propose a reform of the Third Article of the Constitution to replace the principle of secular education with the concept of "socialist education." The only point in which there was consensus within the Party was that education had to become an effective instrument to support the social reforms that were to come.

The new growing political group led by General Lázaro Cárdenas, president between 1934 and 1940, emphasized the benefits that farm laborers and urban workers would receive from education. The distinctive tone in Cárdenas was the view that education would make people more conscious about their responsibilities towards society as a whole, and in that way it would also give them the better resources to defend their class interests through worker's and farmer's organizations. In his speeches as president, Cárdenas would insist on the need to develop nationalist feelings on children. In his view, that would later translate into a permanent attitude of defense of national sovereignty. Another important component of this non-aggressive nationalism was a certain exaltation of the legacy of pre-Hispanic cultures. These elements, together with the promotion of cooperation, were in the center of *socialist education,* which never intended to attack private property.

THE MEXICAN SCHOOL AND THE CURRENT EDUCATION SYSTEM'S INSTITUTIONAL BASES

The main reforms made by Cárdenas—oil expropriation, agrarian reform, and in a smaller scale, *socialist education*—generated a growing polarization in the Mexican society. The candidate for the *Partido de la Revolución Mexicana* (PRM), new denomination for the party in power, was General Manuel Ávila Camacho. When he became president, he immediately declared that he was not a socialist but a democrat, and that he considered that giving confidence to Mexican and foreign investors was of major importance. He then added that he was a Catholic believer by birth and feeling. The international context did not totally determine this change of tone, but it favored it. During 1940, his first year of presidency, the effects of the World War II started to be felt in Mexico: it was an unusually good opportunity for the growth and diversification of the national industry.

This favorable climate was perfect for an ideological change, and the government promoted the so-called "policy of national unification." It was expected that the individual interests should be sacrificed in the name of the nation. In the education sphere, these ideas were not easily accepted. Many teachers were still faithful to Cárdenas and his view of education. Several ministers passed through the Ministry of Education, but the conflicts with the teachers' unions did not stop. Finally, President Ávila Camacho decided to put Jaime Torres Bodet, a prestigious writer, in charge of the Ministry. Bodet's ideas also moved away from the vindictive and popular tone that dominated education discourse in the 1930s, but in a more subtle way. He thought that the principles of education should develop those qualities that a child would need later as a grownup and citizen: patriotism, the love for work, the brotherhood among social classes, and social justice.

Once again, the text of the Third Article of the Constitution was not followed in practice: *socialist education* had been excluded from education discourse and action by Ávila Camacho's government officials. However, having defeated the stronger centers of left-wing resistance, it was not until the last part of this government in December 1945, that an initiative to reform the Third Article was presented aiming at a return to the liberal line that had been partially abandoned with the establishment of the principle of *socialist education*.

This reform was a real piece of engineering work. Secularity and the limitations established since 1917 for religious corporations were preserved. State control over private education was also kept, although slightly attenuated. The most important thing was that the socialist nature of education, included in 1934, was eliminated to establish a much clearer and precise orientation for education. Especially interesting are the Third Article's sections that refer to the criteria that will guide education. The democratic criterion is established in the first section, "considering a democracy not only as a juridical structure and political regime, but also as a way of life rooted in the constant economical, social and political improvement of the masses." A second criterion is the emphasis on "nationhood," which indicates that "without hostilities or exclusiveness, education will attend to the comprehension of our problems, the use of our natural resources, the defense of our economic independence, and the continuity and growth of our culture." The direction that basic education has taken has varied very little since then and the spirit of the 1946 text is kept.

Another event that structured the national education system took place in 1943, when the government achieved the unification of different teacher organizations into only one union, the *Sindicato Nacional de Trabajadores de la Educación* (SNTE—National Union of Education Workers). This organization has been a privileged actor in the sphere of education policies for kindergarten, primary, middle school, and teacher education ever since.

Consequently, when General Manuel Ávila Camacho's presidency was finished, the bases of the actual Mexican education system were already established. We will now explore two topics that will provide the reader with a complete view of the patterns that have shaped the actual Mexican education system. In the first place we will refer to the expansion of the education system and to the modalities adopted in this expansion, and in the second place, to the system's decentralization.

THE EXPANSION OF THE SYSTEM

There was an optimistic atmosphere in the country when World War II was over. In December, 1946, Miguel Alemán became president of the Republic. The Generals' era had finished. Alemán was a young lawyer who was interested in business and in giving a "modern" look to the country, fortifying the bond with North American investors. One of his government's icons would be the University Campus, located at the south of the Federal District: the Universidad Nacional Autónoma de México's (UNAM) new building. Its architecture combined modern criteria of functionality with artistic nationalism that gave its particular features to the walls of the main building. The lively atmosphere of the university that had brightened up the streets of the Historic Centre in the City of Mexico since the colonial period began its exodus to new neighborhoods and new ways of life.

In 1952, Adolfo Ruiz Cortines succeeded Miguel Alemán in the presidency of the Republic. The country's economic conditions did not seem too promising by this time and there was a hard devaluation of the national currency in 1954. The number of public schools continued to grow and once again there was an attempt to promote technical education. The *Centro de Investigación y Estudios Avanzados del Instituto Politécnico Nacional* (CINVESTAV—Center of Research and Advanced Studies of the National Polytechnic Institute) was founded and is currently considered one of the most important scientific institutions in the country. Enrollments continued to grow in primary and secondary education and so did the number of teachers. United in the SNTE, teachers were considered strategic allies of the regime and assumed additional tasks besides teaching, such as participating in campaigns for the prevention of diseases, negotiating social services for communities, and organizing local and federal elections. With the exception of a few groups, teachers were part of the PRI, the governmental party that substituted the PRM with another name. This party stayed in power until 2000.

In 1958, in the capital city, teachers began a strike demanding for the democratization of the Union, and for a rise in salaries. This was one of the first cracks in the interior of the corporative system, in which the teachers, organized in a single and national union, had won labor stability but at the same time had lost ground in terms of professional and political autonomy.

President Adolfo López Mateos, who assumed power in December 1958, appointed Jaime Torres Bodet to Secretary of Education. He had already been in that position a decade before. On the basis of his national and international experience, the Secretary developed what is known as the *eleven-year plan* in which he committed the government to the fulfillment of the constitutional precept that established that primary education was compulsory. This meant that the government had to satisfy the education demands on that level. In the same direction, the government initiated the policy of free textbooks for primary schools. This was one of the most important measures of the time because of its relevance in the education system. Since then and up to the present, the SEP, based on the education programs that are applied in the whole country, elaborates millions of textbooks every year, distributing them for free to all primary students. The content of textbooks has changed in different times, and these transformations have given place to passionate controversies, especially around what the contents in history textbooks should be. Besides, there have always been critics that considered that the freedom to teach was limited by the fact all students had to use the same textbook. Other critics considered that the free textbook policy constituted a disloyal competition towards private textbook editors or represented an instrument of ideological control. Nonetheless, it can not be denied that these books have been one of the greatest educational supports, considering the impoverished condition in which a large percentage of the population lived.

The anniversary of the fiftieth Mexican Revolution was celebrated in 1960. The rhythm at which school enrollments, at every level and modality, and social security services were growing allowed the government to present an encouraging picture. However, in this decade, new criticisms were directed at the social deficits of the "revolutionary regimes." In education matters, it was signaled that although enrollments had grown, the number of illiterates and the number of children and young people that did not finish the primary or secondary school were increasing, too. Given the growth in population during that time, the economic resources that the Mexican society destined to education were not enough to reduce the education deficit.

On the other hand, the urban middle classes began to feel that the existing political system which was almost based on a single party, left them with quite narrow margins of action. In 1968, some students from the UNAM and the *Instituto Politécnico Nacional* (National Polytechnic Institute) confronted the regime on the streets, and the army suppressed a manifestation that was being held on the Tlatelolco Park on the day before the Olympics began, leaving an undetermined number of dead and injured people. Something had changed in Mexican society, and the regime's will to survive was expressed in the following administration under the name of *apertura democrática* (*democratic liberalization*); and, in the education system, this change resulted in a significant rise in the resources destined to education.

The government led by Luis Echeverría (1970–76) was characterized by its intense activity and for a change in the rhetoric where nationalism was now closely related to the defense of the *Third World*. This rhetoric went side by side to solidarity support actions towards the victims of the coup d'état perpetuated by General Augusto Pinochet in Chile as well as the victims of the military dictatorship in Argentina. However, the regime's authoritarian features continued. Once again, students that were taking part in a manifestation were brutally assaulted by a paramilitary group in June 1971. There were also various guerrilla groups that were eliminated by illegal means, including assassinations and disappearance. This was, however, a localized repression that did not permeate public opinion because it happened in poorer and isolated areas. In compensation, the urban university sectors benefited in different ways. The government honored the intellectuals, sponsored the creation of a new public university in the City of Mexico—the *Universidad Autónoma Metropolitana* (UAM)—provided resources to create and expand the state universities, increased the teachers' salaries, and promoted a new statutory law derived from the Third Article of the Constitution: the Federal Law of Education.

Víctor Bravo Ahuja was the Secretary of Education and was part of the team of specialists that was in charge of updating the free textbooks. The *Consejo*

Nacional de Fomento Educativo (CONAFE—National Council for the Promotion of Education) was formed to find solutions for the educational problems of the poorer groups in the country. As enrollments in basic education grew, there was also an increase in the number of students in teacher education. The SNTE continued strengthening its political power and kept its unconditional support to the regime. President Echeverría also promoted new leaders in the union by promoting a teacher called Carlos Jonguitud to the post of General Secretary. He would later take up different political posts, and he was even Governor of his natal state. Jonguitud would keep the Union's control until 1989. The political alliance of the government with the SNTE also had an influence in the expansion of teacher education: in 1970, there were 56,000 students in normal schools and in 1976, the number had grown up to 136,000. Overall, in this expansion quality was sacrificed in the name of quantity, and the imposition of the Union's criteria was placed over professional and academic criteria. An example of this was the conquest that the union made of the *double post,* allowing the same teacher to take two positions, mornings and afternoons, which would substantially improve their income, but that would have negative effects on the quality of a teacher's work in the long run.

Luis Echeverría's sixth year ended with a financial crisis and a great political polarization. His successor, José López Portillo, who had been the secretary of the Treasury, gave a great importance to planning and named Fernando Solana to the SEP. With excellent training in public administration, the new Secretary took important steps towards the beginning of the process of decentralization. The expansion of the education system continued into the following decade, but a new cycle had begun where the main focus was put on the decentralization of the system.

THE LONG WAY TOWARDS DECENTRALIZATION AND THE EFFECTS OF THE SIX-YEAR CRISIS

Why did decentralization become such an important issue at the end of the seventies? The main reason was that the SEP could not efficiently govern an education system that had grown in great proportions. The system was structured in such a way that every decision was centralized at the SEP and the teachers' union had a very strong influence on these decisions. This made planning or any attempt to innovate an improbable success.

The aims that were pursued by Solana's team turned out to be much more difficult to reach than it had been expected. On the one hand, education planning and more rationalized administrative practices were included in the SEP but the introduction of these practices was very slow. At the same time, the ephemeral prosperity in public finances that received an unexpected flow of foreign currency due to oil exportations allowed for some developments in the fulfillment of the goals contained in the *Plan Nacional de Educación* (National Plan for Education) and especially in the *Education for All* program.

Among the most interesting innovations in those years was the creation of the *Universidad Pedagógica Nacional* (National Pedagogic University), initially conceived as an excellence center that would aim at improving teacher education and at the same time reducing the Union's influence in this field. The University was founded and considerable resources were provided for it; however, the initial project could not be sustained mainly because of the Union's strong opposition.

Regarding decentralization, the Secretary tried to create special units in the states that would directly obey to his command. Once again, the Union articulated a belligerent response that produced the forced resignation of many of these government officials. Nonetheless, the first step towards decentralization had been taken. Also, some limits were set to the absolute power that the hegemonic union, the *Vanguardia Revolucionaria* (VR—Revolutionary Vanguard) led by Carlos Jonguitud, had over all of the country's unions. The birth of the *Coordinadora Nacional de Trabajadores de la Educación* (CNTE—National Coordinating Committee of Education Workers) in 1979 was a great contribution to this because it united the efforts made by the dissident groups of teachers that, without abandoning the SNTE, were able to fight against VR's control.

Once more, José López Portillo's government ended with a serious economic crisis that led him to make a desperate decision: to nationalize the banks. Miguel de la Madrid Hurtado was elected in this critical situation in 1982. The effects of the crisis clearly marked a breaking point in expansion of the education system. The State had deep economic problems and the budget for education was severely reduced. The salaries of teachers got to the lowest levels ever, generating new and stronger teacher protest movements. The struggle between the SEP and the Union were held on the same lines as the previous six years. The authorities tried to weaken the Union and it was established that teacher education would be upgraded to the level of a bachelor degree. Consequently, the new incoming students needed to have a baccalaureate high school degree to be accepted into teacher education. As a result of these measures and the meager salaries of teachers, enrollment in normal schools descended drastically.

Finally, the advances in decentralization were very limited, and the struggles with the Union ended with a transitory truce promoted by the governmental necessity of counting with the support of the SNTE in the federal elections of 1988.

The PRI's candidate for the presidency was Carlos Salinas de Gortari, economist with postgraduate studies in Harvard and the son of a former minister. The electoral process had some irregularities. In this context in which his legitimacy was doubted, Salinas decided to take fast and convincing actions as soon as he was in the presidency. The measure that had immediate effects on the education field was the removal of the "moral leader" Carlos Jonguitud from the SNTE. On April 24, 1989, he was substituted by Elba Esther Gordillo, who has been the real leader in the Union since that date.

The Secretary of Education in the new government was Manuel Bartlett. He persisted in a frontal struggle against the Union, while at the same time he negotiated with the governors in order for them to accept their new role of being in charge of schools in their respective States. His persistence was successful in the negotiations with the governors. Meanwhile, to defeat the Union's resistance, he carried out a broad media campaign. The conflict grew day by day until the president decided to put one of his most trusted men, Ernesto Zedillo, in Bartlett's place. After a short while, the leaders of the Union accepted that decentralization would take place in the end, and that it was possible to reach an agreement with the government that would protect their integrity as a national organization.

THE CONTENTS IN THE AGREEMENT

The document under the name *Acuerdo Nacional para la Modernización de la Educación Básica* (ANMEB—National Agreement for the Modernization of Basic Education) pointed out that its main purpose was to improve the quality of education.

The responsibilities that would correspond to each governmental level were also established in this document. The Federation kept the responsibility for establishing the general regulations of the system, formulating plans and programs, and evaluating the education system. Each State was put in charge of the teacher's salaries and would be able to propose *regional contents* in order for them to be included in the education programs. The municipalities were put in charge of the equipment and maintenance of schools. Another important point in the new outline was that it promoted *social participation*.

A second aspect of the Agreement was the *Reformulation of education contents and materials*, which included the renewal of the free textbooks for primary education and the reintroduction of civic education in the middle school. An in-service program for teachers was also organized. The fourth point was the so-called *revalorization of the Teaching Career* through which an incentive system called the Teaching Career was instituted. Thus, the decentralization framework that was implemented in Mexico transferred the responsibility for paying and negotiating with teachers and other employees of the education sector from the federal to the state level.

Fifteen years have gone by since the signing of the ANMEB, and there are significant differences in the rhythm at which each state has developed and consolidated its education system, and some financial and technical capacity of some states is highly dependant on the collaboration of the Federal State.

THE LAST LEGISLATIVE CHANGES IN EDUCATION MATTERS

The economic and political model that was promoted by Carlos Salinas's government required some changes in some of the most important articles of the Constitution. Once again, the Third Article was subject to reforms. Actually, there were two reforms of this article in this six-year period, in a process that ended up with the approval of the General Law of Education that substituted the Federal Law of Education of 1973.

The first reform in 1992 had the aim of suppressing the prohibition of religious orders or priests to teach in basic education. This reform was simultaneous with the reform of article 5 (monastic orders), 24 (freedom of belief), and 130 (state-church relations). The second modification removed the restrictions that existed for private institutions to offer education services. In addition, the reform made secondary education compulsory. The main actors in these initiatives had been the Federal Government and the Catholic Church. It was clear that the aim of the government was establishing a broad alliance with the *Partido Acción Nacional* (National Action Party), the Catholic Church, and with the organizations that had traditionally been opposed to the revolutionary regimes.

After the signing of the ANMEBs, and the modification of the Constitution, the next step was to replace the Federal Law of Education of 1973, to adapt the regulation of the system to the new legal order. A *Ley General de Educación* (LGE) was sanctioned in 1993. This law reaffirmed the distribution of power between the different levels of the state, regulated recognition of private schools, incorporated a special chapter for educational equity, established the public nature of evaluations of the education system, and gave way to the creation of organizations for social participation.

The last reform that is worth mentioning in this historical account is the extension of compulsory education for three more years. This reform took place during Vicente Fox's government (2000–2006) and resulted in Mexico's current twelve years of compulsory education. This is a goal that will take some time before it is fully accomplished. Some of the data mentioned below are indicative of this assertion.

INTERROGATING THE DATA: THE CURRENT SITUATION AND FUTURE PERSPECTIVES

We currently have access to more detailed and complete information about the education system. Additionally, as an indirect effect of globalization, a great interest has been aroused among experts, the media, and in public opinion to compare education indicators, and especially results of standardized evaluations with other countries. What can we make from this enormous amount of information?

- The Mexican education system is one of the largest in the world. The country does not only find itself among the most populated (103 million inhabitants in 2005), but also has a high proportion of children of school age. For all this, the educational challenge is formidable. According to the *Instituto Nacional de Evaluación Educativa*

(National Institute of Educational Evaluation), at the beginning of school year 2004–5, the education system served a total of 35,817,000 students, 90 percent of them in traditional schools and 10 percent of them in alternative systems.

- The figure of almost 6 *million illiterate girls* recognized by year 2000 official statistics was very discouraging. It is true that the proportion of illiterate girls decreased during the twentieth century. Since 1970, this trend stabilized; however, a cohort monitoring that was made public by the *Consejo Nacional de Población* (National Council of Population) showed that this improvement has not been a result of the mediocre literacy campaigns—it has simply been the result of increased schooling services in the new generations. Older adults and indigenous people, and especially indigenous women, continue to be victims of a great indifference in almost every aspect, including the possibilities of learning how to read and write. A census sample showed for year 2000 that out of 473,173 native women of more than 65 years of age, the immense majority (303,458) were illiterate. This is the social group with the highest rate of education exclusion.

- The educational lag, including illiteracy, is still marked by a strongly sexist and patriarchal society. In the rural areas, male and female illiteracy rates in the year 2000 for young people—between fifteen and nineteen years old—were practically identical: 3.64 percent and 3.7 percent, but in adults aged thirty-five to thirty-nine, the gap is considerable because the illiteracy rate for women is 13.4 percent and for men is 7.68 percent. The rates for forty-five to forty-nine-year-olds show that the disadvantage for women increases because their illiteracy reaches a rate of 22.7 percent while for men it is 11.9 percent.

- The advances in the participation of women in education have been spectacular. The average number of school years in the year 2000 was around 7.6 for women and 8.1 percent for men. In middle-to-high school levels, there is almost the same proportion of entering men (64.5 percent) and women (65 percent). Additionally, a better performance and permanence of women in schools determines that in general terms, out of each cohort of eighteen-year-olds, approximately four women finish middle school for every three men.

- Primary school is the level where the largest number of enrollments is concentrated. It was the best-attended level in the last decades, influenced without a doubt by the international organizations' recommendations, and especially by the World Bank. This general orientation has been kept although it has been combined with a recent interest in the improvement of preschool and middle school. Currently, almost fifteen million children attend primary school, representing 60 percent of school's population registered in the basic level. Even though the net coverage is over 99 percent and the graduation rate of this level is estimated to be in 91.8 percent, there are still 1.4 million children left out—most of them belong to indigenous ethnic groups, living in disperse houses or the sons and daughters of unskilled laborers.

- Among the programs that are increasing the coverage of the system, diminishing dropouts, and improving graduation rates, are compensatory programs for groups that live in extreme poverty. These programs include scholarships to avoid dropouts, especially from girls. During Vicente Fox's government, *Enciclomedia* and *Escuelas de Calidad* (Quality Schools) were put in place with the aim of improving the quality of education through a change in management practices, providing new equipment, or using new technologies and didactic material. However, these programs were only applied in a limited proportion of the country's schools and there is no certainty about their continuity. Before this, in the 1990s, a couple of reform plans of primary education were carried out, and new and better free textbooks were edited and distributed. The *Carrera Magisterial* was implemented, establishing economic incentives based on indicators which considered the professional training of teachers and their performance. This program does not seem to have accomplished its objectives and it is currently going through a process of review.

- A constitutional reform was recently approved (November 2002) to include three years of kindergarten in the basic education cycle, making it compulsory. This reform was very controversial because it was considered that only one compulsory kindergarten year would have been enough. This constitutional change gave more power to the already extremely powerful SNTE, because preschool educators are part of this union, and large amounts of funds will be needed for the expansion of this level. In this context, the challenge is trying to avoid that the extension of preschool education becomes an addition to inequalities in education: the service will expand in a gradual manner and will probably reach the less favored sectors of society with delay. The current enrollment is around four million children, but it is possible to predict that the expansion of this level in the next few years will be very fast.

- Middle school is an education level that presents a mixed diagnosis. In the last decade, enrollments in this level increased significantly: from 82.3 percent in 1990 to 93.4 percent in the year 2000 due to the constitutional reform that made it compulsory. Nonetheless, there are still too many young people that do not enter into this level, and there are high failing and dropout rates. All of this led to the establishment of the "Middle School Reform" in 2005 that reduced the number of subjects and aimed at improving the quality of education offered in this level. Estimates conducted using the census data indicate that in the year 2000, only 57.3 percent of sixteen-year-olds completed middle school.

- Both the national and the international evaluations have shown very low learning levels in Mexican schools, placing educational quality at the center of the political agenda. The Program for International Student Assessment of the OECD (PISA) for the year 2003, focused on mathematics, established six performance levels–65 percent of the Mexican students were on level one or below the minimal score. Even more alarming are the indicators related with internal inequalities within the Mexican education system: 94 percent of the students that come from *Telesecundarias*, schools that attend the rural population and very marginal sectors, obtained results that correspond to the lowest levels of the scale on the exam. On the other hand, within the 10 percent of best qualified Mexican students, 85 percent came from private schools and presumably from a middle class or high socioeconomic status.

- Education is a public good. However, we can distinguish two big sectors through the school's sources of maintenance: the public and the private sectors. The private sector's participation is heterogeneous regarding the different school cycles and their geographic location. In basic cycle levels, private participation is low and it increases considerably in the post-basic levels. In kindergarten, the percentage of students attended by the private sector is of 13 percent. In primary schools, the proportion decreases to 8 percent and 7 percent in middle school. In high school private schools are in charge of 20.5 percent of the students and in vocational education the private sector represents 38 percent of enrollments. In higher education, the total coverage for people between twenty to twenty-four years of age is only 22 percent where the private sector only provides services to 17 percent. However, if we analyze enrollments in the undergraduate level in universities, the dynamism of private universities is surprising: if in 1980 they attended to 13.51 percent of total enrollments, in 2003 they took up 33.26 percent of students. It is important to point out that this is a sustained tendency and that in middle-sized to big cities is where this expansion is mostly concentrated.

- In the near future, demographic trends indicate that enrollments in high schools and higher education will account for a much bigger proportion of students with respect to total enrollments. Prospective studies indicate for year 2030, the volume of population in between the ages of six to eleven that corresponds to primary education will drop by 23.4 percent with respect to the same age group in the year 2000. Similarly, in 2007–8 the population that is old enough to go to middle school begins to decrease, but given that a considerable increase in the middle school coverage is also expected, the combined effects will determine an increase in enrollments in middle and high schools.

CONCLUSIONS

Once again, as in the beginning of its independent life, political and intellectuals groups agree on the importance of education as an instrument to carry the Mexican population to a more satisfying level in all the dimensions of their individual and collective lives. The roads they suggest have been divided, although it is important to specify that there are today more convergences than before; convergences that can be explained by the intensification of the global relations which, on the education field, have given place to the mirage of a common agenda.

This expected common education agenda, in Latin America's case, consists of a limited number of general ideas that are elaborated daily in the multilateral organizations and in many other agencies, such as governmental offices, universities, foundations, academic associations, and specialized journals. They are part of an *education discourse* from which it is practically impossible to escape. Nonetheless, this is manifested in a clear way throughout the different contributions that constitute this volume, the convergence of the most popular themes, as well as the pretended common agenda, both contrast with very different national realities. Decentralization, educational quality and coverage, privatization and social participation, acquire tones, and various and even opposed meanings according to the particular features of each nation. Within this perspective, and as a conclusion to our essay, we now propose, without the intension of being exhaustive, ten aspects that help us characterize the Mexican education system.

1. A remarkable institutional continuity that can be seen in the capacity that the SEP had since 1921 to establish education plans and programs which all the normal and basic education schools must follow without exceptions. Decentralization, called

educational federalism in Mexico, transferred administrative responsibilities to the state authorities, but the normative aspects were firmly kept in the hands of the federal government through the SEP. Meanwhile the influence of municipalities in education matters is minimum.

2. Mexico has the strongest and biggest teacher union in Latin America, with more than two million members. In spite of the decentralization of the system established in 1992 and the political downfall of the party to which it was attached, the SNTE kept its national character and its decisive influence in education policies. On the other hand, and although in ascent, the real influence of private groups, nongovernmental organizations, and the Church is considerably smaller than in other countries in the region

3. Some marked educational inequalities are still very notorious even though the profound vindictive tone that the 1910 Revolution gave to education as an essential component for the struggle towards *social justice*. A few years from celebrating the centenary of the beginning of that social movement, education is no longer viewed as a privileged sphere for the struggle of different social collectives for the construction of a more fair society.

4. The tendencies towards education growth are accompanied by a tendency towards the segmentation of the school populations, mainly dependent upon socioeconomic origins. In addition, a greater dynamism has been observed in the last years in the base and the top of the socio-educational pyramid. In the base, as a consequence of the amplified coverage of kindergarten and primary education. It is important to emphasize also the benefits obtained from the impact of the social policy programs focused on supporting the most marginalized and poor populations. There is a great dynamism at the top of the system due to the relative boom of postgraduate and research programs mostly financed by the State, but also due to the rise in enrollments in private universities that are still much smaller than in public institutions.

5. There are very few educational innovations in a very bureaucratic education system. Organizations of "social participation" have been created, but in reality they have carried out works that do not correspond with the functions to which they have been assigned. Also, special programs like *Escuelas de calidad* only attend to a limited proportion of education institutions.

6. There is much backwardness in teacher education, and a lack of clear regulations for hiring of teachers, with the persistence of political "clientelism" practices, and a weak professional culture among teachers.

7. A notable lack of articulation between education policies and more broad cultural policies.

8. There has been a quick incorporation of girls and young women to education institutions, together with an improvement of their performance at school.

9. There are still persistence deficiencies in the coverage and quality of the education services for indigenous populations, and the quality of education in the rural and marginal urban areas is very low. Very high dropout rates and failings can be seen in middle school.

10. A remarkable lack of attention has been given to the high school level, and it has been very difficult to establish a national system of higher education that is compatible with the autonomy that benefits large public universities. On the other hand there is a clear deficit in the regulation of the new private institutions.

The difficulties can seem to be the product of a pessimistic or unhopeful view. However, it is nothing like that. I have tried to give a synthetic view, not a simplistic one of Mexico's education, and tried to share with the reader the educational contrasts and paradoxes that this country presents. The political and cultural elites have suggested explications about our educational and social backwardness, some of which have been particularly attractive and even beautiful. Likewise, since the beginning of our independent life, a great amount of ideas and programs that would put an end to the education problems and put the country "on the vanguard of the world" have been put forward. Maybe the moment has come for us to change our view to see the horizon of the future years to come with greater realism. This necessarily implies the renunciation to evoke these spectacular takeoffs, these true "education revolutions" that vanish as soon as the popular discourse is worn out, for us to keep ourselves close to an ethic of responsibility from now on, to the compromise of achieving modest but solid and sustained advances. This requires, as a first step, to get to know and admit our own backwardness and the limited resources we have to face it.

A DAY IN THE LIFE

Vanessa is a pretty girl with big black eyes. In fact, she looks very much like the children Diego Rivera drew in his murals. She is ten years old and is in fifth grade. She lives in Jiutepec, in Morelos State. Jiutepec looks like a town. It has a sixteenth-century church, a very lively, although somewhat dirty, central park, and a multicolored market. But it is so close to Cuernavaca, the state's capital, that it has practically converted itself into a suburb of that city. Jiutepec is one of the municipalities with greater growth in the country; this growth has happened due to the industrial belt that has been settled there and many people from other states, mainly from the neighboring Guerrero state, have come to look for better life conditions—among them is Vanessa's father. His name is Mateo and he earns his living as a gardener and a plumber, he is very lively and communicative. Her mother, Abigail, spends lots of her time with her religious group, the *Jehovah's Witnesses*. She is serious and very tranquil. Vanessa has a younger brother that goes to "kinder."

Her school day begins at 7:00 AM, when she wakes up with the television. Her mother takes her to school. They walk for twenty minutes with extreme care because cars pass by very fast. Vanessa wears a school uniform. When she wakes up late she doesn't have time to eat breakfast. Anyway, she knows she won't be hungry because she takes a bean cake and fruit juice for break time. Her teacher is "a little bit angry." In her class there are more girls than boys, and according to Vanessa, the boys are the ones who make the teacher angry. When this happens, he punishes them by making them stand in a corner or "no break."

She shows me her backpack: she carries a *Larousse* dictionary covered in plastic and six free textbooks: geography, mathematics, natural sciences, history, and civics and two for Spanish, the reading textbook and the exercise book; she also has four copybooks and a pencil case.

When they arrive at school, everyone enters the class, and while they stand, say, "Good morning, Teacher." The teacher tells them to sit down and calls roll to see who didn't show up. They take out their books to see what subject is coming up and they "put on the video" right away. (Vanessa here refers to the *Enciclomedia,* a software program that was one of President Fox's most important innovations.) Vanessa enjoys it very much. She says it is fun and they work with it until 1 PM, when they leave school. The teacher uses the computer and the class has an interactive white board. She likes "the video" so much that she says she is happier this year at school than the last.

On the other hand, her mother has a complaint: this year the fourth-grade children have had their computer class suspended. This was due to the fact that the school bought more computers. There were ten at school and now there are twenty. But the electric system in the school can't take that voltage and that is why the computers are not being used at all. There is only one person who is in charge of turning them "on" everyday "to make sure they don't go to waste."

Vanessa informs me that her teacher gives her homework around three times a week. She needs more or less half an hour in order to complete it. She also watches TV in the afternoons, plays with her brother, and takes a bath at night whenever the weather is too hot. She would like it if the school organized more field trips: last year, they went to Mexico City to visit the *Papalote* (Kite) Museum, two museums in Cuernavaca, and the botanical gardens. There is always a special preparation for five dates: Mother's Day, the Day of the Dead, Children's Day, the "parade" for Independence Day (September 16), and a Nativity play.

One last comment: Vanessa wears glasses although they are broken. At school, all children went through a vision test and school officials realized that she does not see well. She also mentions that they have put fluorine on her teeth and administered vaccine shots.

TIMELINE

1543	Vasco de Quiroga establishes the *Escuela de San Nicolás* in Pátzcuaro.
1551	*Real y Pontíficia Universidad* is founded.
1820	Lancastrian schools are founded.
1823	The creation of basic education schools for girls and adults is decreed.
1857	Reform Laws. Secular education is established.
1865	Public Education Law eliminates the legal impediments that prevented women from registering in the *Escuela Nacional Preparatoria*.
1867	Middle school for women.
1878	Regulations that establish the *Escuelas Primarias Nacionales*.
1884	First private schools for preschoolers.
1887	The first woman doctor's professional exam.

1889–90   *Primer Congreso Pedagógico* (First Pedagogical Convention).
1900   Forty-five Normal Schools are counted in the country.
1904   The first public kindergartens for children are established.
1908   The degree of educator (for preschoolers) is created.
           Ley de Educación Primaria (Law for Primary Education) for the Distrito Federal and federal territories.
1917   Constitution of 1917. Third Article establishes secular education in all the private and public primary schools.
1921   The *Secretaría de Educación Pública* (SEP) is created.
1924   Rural education project.
1925   Foundation of the *Escuela Normal para Maestros* (Normal School for Teachers).
1934   Third Article's reform. Socialist education.
1944   The *Instituto Federal de Capacitación del Magisterio* is established.
1946   Third Article reform establishes that education will be democratic and nationalistic.
1958   The *Comisión Nacional del Libro de Texto Gratuito* (National Commission for the Free Textbook) is created.
1972   Free textbooks reform according to new pedagogical theories.
1973   *Ley Federal de Educación* (Federal Law of Education).
1981   *Instituto Nacional de Educación para Adultos* (INEA—National Institute for Adult Education) creation.
1992   *Acuerdo Nacional para la Modernización de la Educación Básica* (National Agreement for the Modernization of Basic Education).
           Third Article Reform. The prohibition that prevents religious corporations and cult ministers to intervene in private schools of Basic Education is eliminated.
1993   Third Article Reform. The restrictions that prevented particulars from providing education service is eliminated.
           Ley Genral de Educación.
2002   *Instituto Nacional de Evaluación Educativa* (INEE—National Institute of Educative Evaluation) is created.
2004   *Encyclomedia,* a multimedia program is distributed and put in place in all the public primary schools.

NOTE

1. Term used to refer to charismatic populist leaders among the people.

BIBLIOGRAPHY

Books

Cook, Maria Lorena. 1996. *Organizing Dissent. Unions, the State, and the Democratic Teachers Movement in Mexico.* University Park, Pennsylvania: The Pennsylvania State University Press.

Emery, Sarah. 1984. *Centralized Education in Mexico—Unification Through Standardization: An Annotated Bibliography.* Monicello, IL: Vance Bibliographies.

Frost, Elsa Cecilia. 2005. *Los colegios jesuitas*. Fondo de Cultura Económica, El Colegio de México, México D.F.

Gonzalvo, Pilar. 1990. Historia de la educación en la época colonial; La educación de los criollos y la vida urbana. El Colegio de México, México D.F.

Instituto Nacional de Estadística, Geografía e Informática (INEGI). 1994. *El rezago educativo en la población Mexicana*. Aguascalientes: Ags.

Latapí, Pablo. 2004. *La SEP por dentro: las políticas de la Secretaría de Educación Pública comentadas por cuatro de sus secretarios (1992–04)*. Fondo de Cultura Económica, México D.F.

Latapí, Pablo, ed. 1998. *Un Siglo de Educación en México*, 2 vols. Biblioteca Mexicana, Fondo de Cultura Económica, Méxio D.F.

Lorey, David. 1994. *The Rise of the Professions in Twentieth-Century Mexico: University Graduates and Occupational Change Since 1929*. Los Angeles: UCLA Latin American Center Publications.

Martin, Cristopher. 1994. *Schooling in Mexico: Staying in or Dropping Out*. Aldershot: Ashgate Publishing.

Meneses Morales, Ernesto. 1998. *Tendencias educativas oficiales en México, 1821–1911*. 2nd ed. Centro de Estudios Educativos, Universidad Iberoamericana, México D.F.

Ornelas, Carlos. 1995. *El sistema educativo mexicano; La transición de fin de siglo*. Mexico: CIDE-FCE-Nafin.

Secretaría de Educación Pública. 2005. *Equidad, calidad e innovacion en el desarollo educativo nacional*. Fondo de Cultura Económica. Colección Editorial del Gobierno del Cambio, México.

Soustelle, Jacques. 1970. *Daily Life of the Aztecs: on the Eve of the Spanish Conquest*. Stanford, Calif.: Stanford University.

Staples, Anne. 2005. *Recuento de una batalla inconclusa: la educacion mexicana de Iturbide a Juarez*. El Colegio de México, México.

Vaughan, Mary K. 1997. *Cultural politics in revolution: teachers, peasants and schools in Mexico 1930–40*. University of Arizona, Tucson.

Zegarra, H. 1998. *Decentralization and Autonomy in Chiapas, Mexico: 1994–98. A Case Study of Cultural-Educational Change*. Pittsburgh: University of Pittsburgh.

Chapters and Articles

Cortina, Regina. 1992. "Gender and Power in the Teachers' Union of Mexico." In *Women and Education in Latin America, Knowledge, Power and Change*. Edited by: N. Stromquist. London: Lynne Rienner.

Martin, C. J. and C. Solórzano. "Mass Education, Privatization, Compensation and Diversification: Issues on the Future of Public Education in Mexico. *Compare* 33, no. 1 (2003): 15–30.

Schmelkes, Silvia. 2000. "Education and Indian Peoples in Mexico." *Unequal Schools, Unequal Chances*. Edited by F. Reimers, 319–33. Cambridge, Massachusetts: Harvard University Press.

Printed Material

Guichard, Stéphanie. 2005. *The Education Challenge in Mexico: Delivering Good Quality Education to All*. Organisation de Coopération et de Développement

Economiques. *Economics Department Working Papers*, No. 447, ECO/WKP 34 (2005): 32.

López-Azevedo, Gladys. 2002. *Teachers' Incentives and Professional Development in Schools in Mexico*. The World Bank Latin America and the Caribbean Region, Poverty Reduction and Economic Management Sector Unit, Policy Research Working Paper 2777.

Tatto, M. T. 1999. *Improving Teacher Education in Rural Mexico: The Challenges and Tensions of Constructivist Reform. Mexico*. World Bank. 1998. Mexico: Advancing Educational Equity in the Context of Descentralization, Phase I Report. Washington, DC: World Bank.

Web Sites

Diccionario de historia de la educación, CONACYT, CIESAS, Coordinadora: Dra. Luz Elena Galván Lafarga. http://biblioweb.dgsca.unam.mx/diccionario/.

Secretaría de Educación Pública: www.sep.gob.mx.

Chapter 11

SCHOOLING IN NICARAGUA

Robert F. Arnove, David C. Edgerton, Guillermo A. Martínez, Isolda Rodríguez Rosales, and Raúl Ruiz Carrión

DAILY LIFE IN NICARAGUAN SCHOOLS

Nicaragua's schools are as varied as the country's regions and landscape. There are tiny rural schools with one teacher, a single classroom, and twenty or thirty students who walk to school along paths through coffee plantations or lowland rainforests or along country roads past cane fields and small farms. In Managua, the capital, there are huge, overcrowded urban schools where as many as 4,000 students attend school in morning, afternoon, and evening shifts, sometimes sixty or more students to a room. On Nicaragua's marshy Atlantic coast, separated from the cities of the central and Pacific regions by several hundred miles of sparsely populated woodlands and savannas, the language of instruction in many schools is not Spanish but Creole, Miskitu, or other minority languages, and in some places students travel to school in small boats through mangrove forests or along seasonal waterways.

In spite of this diversity, unifying characteristics can be found throughout the Nicaraguan education system. One of the most important of these is community participation in support of schools. Local community activism is a strong characteristic of Nicaraguan culture. Under Nicaragua's recently decentralized education system, the locally elected School Council and the Student Government both have significant decision-making authority. In many towns and rural areas, parents are frequent presences in classrooms and on the school grounds, making repairs, providing the mid-morning snack, or serving as classroom assistants; students, parents, and community members work together to maintain and improve their schools. This section looks at the daily lives of three students in three such schools: a small rural school, a large urban school on the Pacific side of Nicaragua, and a school in Nicaragua's South Atlantic Autonomous Region that serves a community on the shore of a lagoon.

A Small Rural School

El Arenal Primary School is a blue and white poured-concrete rectangle with half-walls, louvered windows, and a red sheet-metal roof. Two teachers teach grades one through six to about one hundred students in the little school's two rooms.

El Arenal ("expanse of sand" in Spanish) stands at the crest of a rise on an unpaved country road. Beyond the school, rolling hills recede into the distance—stands of tropical hardwoods, orange and avocado trees, and upland tropical pine interspersed with hillside coffee groves and open patches where cattle graze. Coffee is the main commercial crop in Nicaragua's north-central highlands. Coffee prices are in decline, and in spite of the beauty and fertility of the landscape, the rural community served by El Arenal School is impoverished.

Anabel Gómez is vice-president of the Student Government. Anabel is ten years old and in the fourth grade. Her father, Hector Gómez, is on the School Council. Don Hector is an agricultural laborer. When Don Hector is not working at a nearby coffee plantation, he often walks with Anabel and her brother a mile and a half (2.4 kilometers) from their house to school, and stays for a while to help out.

Most of Nicaragua's rural multigrade schools (schools with more than one grade in a single room) use an open-classroom active learning system, where students spend much of the school day studying together in small groups, using self-study guides. School starts at 8:30 AM and ends at 1:00 PM. Today *Profesora* Rosalina divides the fourth graders into two groups and starts one working on *cívica* (civics) and the other on reading. *Profesora* Rosalina appoints Anabel as group leader for today's *cívica* study. To facilitate small-group work, the classroom is furnished not with individual desks but with small wooden tables that can accommodate up to six students. Two tables can be pushed together for larger groups. While the fourth graders work on reading and *cívica*, *Profesora* Rosalina is at the blackboard at the front of the room, leading the fifth and sixth graders in a mental-calculation math drill.

By 10:15, the two fourth-grade study groups have switched tasks, the fifth and sixth graders are also studying in small groups, and *Profesora* Rosalina is working with a couple of students who need extra help with reading. A group of visitors appears at the school gate. Anabel and *Profesora* Rosalina both look up at the sound of the metal gate latch opening. Visitors are always received at the school gate by members of the Student Government. The *Profesora* nods at Anabel, and her friend Guillermo, a sixth grader and the Student Government President, excuse themselves from their study groups and go out to greet the visitors.

On the front patio, a School Council mother is stirring up a batch of *pinolillo*, a traditional Nicaraguan drink made of toasted corn meal. *Recreo* (recess) is at 10:30, and the *pinolillo* will be today's *recreo* treat. At the front gate,

Anabel recites a little poem she recently composed for greeting visitors. The visitors are the district technical coordinator from the Ministry of Education, and a new teacher from a nearby school who has come to observe. Anabel and Guillermo usher the visitors to the shade of the covered patio. Guillermo arranges a circle of straight-backed chairs on the patio, the mother hands each guest a well-worn plastic glass full of pinolillo, and Anabel and Guillermo sit down with their guests to tell them about El Arenal School. They are both confident, well-spoken children. As Student Government President, it is Guillermo's place to begin: "Welcome to *El Arenal* Rural Multi-grade School. We have two teachers and one hundred students." Vice-president Anabel takes up the narrative: "We study together in small groups ... today in Fourth Grade, we studied *cívica* and reading."

A Large Urban School

An hour's distance northeast of *El Arenal* is the city of Matagalpa, one of Nicaragua's major urban areas and a regional hub for coffee production and textile manufacture. *El Progreso* Urban School serves 1,100 students in two shifts, morning and afternoon. An evening continuing education program for adults also meets at the school. Class sizes are large, averaging forty students per room. The school is located in the busy heart of town and occupies a city block. Classrooms surround a central yard with two basketball courts and a playground. Concrete steps rim the yard on all four sides, leading up to covered walkways and the rows of classrooms. Snacks and soft drinks are for sale at a kiosk beside the front gate. A eucalyptus tree near the kiosk and the gate shades that corner of the otherwise barren yard.

Marlon Zamora is a small, slender thirteen-year-old. He is in sixth grade. He hopes to finish high school, but he hasn't yet reached middle school (*Educación Media*) because he has had to drop out of school twice to work full-time for part of the year; both times, he had to repeat the whole year when he went back. Every morning, Marlon rises at first light, helps his mother prepare breakfast for the family, walks to a warehouse near their two-room shed-roofed house, and spends the morning hours cleaning and sorting coffee beans. It is technically illegal for a child his age to hold regular employment, but it is common knowledge that children often work to help support their families and keep themselves in school. With few exceptions, Nicaraguan schools require school uniforms. Some of Marlon's earnings go to pay for his school uniform and a school materials fee. The rest is for the family; he has two younger sisters, and his mother is single. Marlon is a serious boy and a good student. Like Rosalina and Guillermo at *El Arenal*, he is a member of the Student Government, and it is a point of pride for him to dress as neatly as he can.

Afternoon shift starts at 1:00 PM and ends at 5:30. Today, a group of parents is gathered in the school media center, which doubles as a meeting room. The parents are expressing concern about growing security and traffic safety problems near the school. During afternoon break, Marlon and two other Student Government members join *Profesora* Silvia Casco Zamora, *El Progreso*'s Principal, to participate in the conversation with the concerned parents.

At 5:30, Marlon goes back to the media center, finds the center's single computer unoccupied, and takes the opportunity to practice his computing skills. He has been thinking recently that someday he might like to be a programmer or a computer engineer. Also, he is waiting today for some older boys from his neighborhood who have stayed on after school for a game of pickup basketball, so he can walk home with them when they finish their game. The streets are indeed less safe than they once were in this provincial capital. As Marlon willingly explained to the concerned parents when he met with them at mid-afternoon, his own solution to the problem is to walk home with some "big guys."

It's dusk by the time Marlon gets home, walking through streets lined with warehouses, fried food stands, and *pulperías* (little street-front grocery shops). He does his homework after dark at the kitchen table by the light of a single bulb dangling at the end of an electric cord. Then, he joins his sisters and his mother, who are already asleep in the other room. Marlon needs his rest. Tomorrow, the early dawn light will wake him for another day of labor and study.

An Atlantic Coast Multilingual School

Four hundred miles east of Matagalpa and *El Progreso* School, on Nicaragua's Atlantic Coast, *Beulah Lightburn* School stands on a bluff overlooking the community of Pearl Lagoon. The best way to get to Pearl Lagoon is from the coastal town of Bluefields. To arrive by mid-morning, you set out at first light in a *panga* (a flat-bottomed river craft with an outboard motor) and travel north along a series of channels through mangrove forest kept dredged by the Nicaraguan Army. *Beulah Lightburn* is a large school by coastal standards, serving over 600 primary and secondary school students from the municipality that comprises Pearl Lagoon and surrounding communities.

Yolanda Slate is a tall, lean seventeen-year-old, in her final year of *Educación Secundaria* (high school) at *Beulah Lightburn* School. She lives with her large family in the nearby fishing community of Marshall Point. Marshall Point has an elementary school but no high school. In dry weather, she can walk to school in forty-five minutes. Today, she caught a ride to school with her father, a fisherman, in his handmade fourteen-foot sailboat.

Yolanda is a star centerfielder and power hitter on the *Beaulah Lightburn* girls' softball team. She recently accepted an athletic scholarship for next year to play on the varsity women's team at one of Nicaragua's public universities, "the UCA" (*Universidad Centroamericana*, Central American University), in Managua.

Yolanda is quadrilingual, in Spanish, standard English, the Miskitu indigenous language, and her mother tongue, an English-based Creole spoken by the majority Afro-Caribbean population of Nicaragua's South Atlantic Autonomous Region. Today after school, Yolanda goes to the teachers' lounge, where she often works for an hour or so as a volunteer tutor, until softball practice starts at 3:30. This year has seen an influx of new children in the elementary grades who are monolingual speakers of Mayangna, another indigenous language. Yolanda is helping a dozen Mayangna children with beginning reading, a task so complicated that the effort makes her feel giddy. Yolanda speaks Miskitu but not Mayangna so to speak to the children at all, she must rely on a bilingual Miskitu-Mayangna mother to interpret for her. There are no reading texts and few texts of any kind in Mayangna, aside from the Bible, so Yolanda is trying to teach these children to read in Spanish, a language they do not speak. She does the best she can, using the old fashioned phonic-syllabic reading method by which she learned to read herself. She works with the children on the classic Spanish basic reader sentence "*Mamá me mima*" ("Mommy hugs me"), filtering it word by word through three languages, trying to teach the children to sound it out, first a letter and then a syllable at a time. After an hour of this, she looks up and sees that Lissa Powell, *Beulah Lightburn*'s Principal, has come in and is watching her work. "You're doing fine, Yolie," Profesora Lissa says. "I'm going down to Bluefields tomorrow. Maybe I can find something in Mayangna at the college. Meanwhile, maybe we should try the Bible."

By the time softball practice is over, it's nearly seven. As Yolanda leaves the school grounds, she sees her father tied off down at the municipal dock, unloading a good catch of what looks like flounder or red snapper. She knows he'll need to light the lantern and use the outboard motor to get home. She starts down the long hill. Halfway down, she pauses. She thinks for a moment about leaving next year, starting at the university, living in Managua, a big, distant city. She wants to be a teacher and a coach, and she knows she must go; but she knows she will miss this lovely, tranquil place. She will miss it terribly.

HISTORY OF NICARAGUAN EDUCATION

The three schools described at the beginning of this chapter reflect the historical forces that have shaped Nicaraguan education over more than two centuries. These forces have included different forms of colonialism as well as internal conflicts between contending political parties and social groupings. Our historical review indicates that despite countless efforts over the centuries to expand educational opportunity, inequalities have persisted between rural and urban areas, as well as between powerful elites and the vast majority of the population. We have divided the history of Nicaraguan education into the following periods:

- colonial;
- post-independence;
- liberal;

- the Conservative Restoration and U.S. intervention;
- Somoza dynastic dictatorship;
- Sandinista;
- post-Sandinista; and
- contemporary.

Colonial Period (1536–1821)

Education in Nicaragua dates back to the very beginning of the Spanish conquest. At that time Rodrigo de Contreras, governor of the province of Nicaragua, made every effort to carry out the wishes of the King of Spain (Molina 1953, 27). Among other things, the King demanded that the indigenous people be educated in the Catholic religion. On May 26, 1536, a law was passed, giving Governor Contreras authority over the education of the Indians in matters of faith. In 1537, Contreras received another Royal Mandate encouraging him to build schools where children of indigenous people were taught industrial arts. Subsequently, Contreras visited each village of the Nicaraguan province and ordered the building of churches and placed the parish priests in charge of teaching the people in Christian doctrine.

The two most important concerns of the Spanish conquerors were to maintain possession of the new land to exploit its natural resources and, secondly, to spread Christianity. To achieve these priorities, the Spaniards employed the following strategy: they built cities close to indigenous villages—for example, Granada near to Xalteva, and León next to Subtiava—which provided the Spaniards with a conveniently located work force. Because slavery was forbidden, the Spaniards created an alternative working arrangement called "*encomiendas*," a grant of land or other privileges for purposes of both use and care. Indigenous people were given to Spaniards in the form of an *encomienda*. In return for the use of the Indians as laborers, the Spaniards were obligated not only to put the Indians to work, but also to make sure they studied Catholic doctrine and the industrial arts needed, for example, to exploit the gold mines and to harvest crops.

By contrast, education for the sons of the Spanish elites prepared them for positions of rule and privilege. Their education had a strong scholastic orientation. The curriculum consisted of the study of Latin grammar, theology, morality, philosophy, arithmetic, algebra, geometry, and physics. Higher education was sought at the University of San Carlos in what to become neighboring Guatemala.

Independence and the Post-Independence Period (1821–1893)

Nicaragua's emergence as an independent nation resulted from protracted political turmoil and regional warfare over the first third of the nineteenth century. On September 15, 1821, the Captaincy General of Guatemala, which included Nicaragua, declared independence from Spain. Two years later, in 1822, Central America was annexed by the Mexican Empire. There was strong resistance to Mexican rule throughout the Central American region. Five provinces— Nicaragua, Guatemala, Costa Rica, El Salvador, and Honduras—declared independence from Mexico in 1823. Each of the five established an independent internal administration under a weak central authority. Fourteen years of regional strife followed, ending in the dissolution of the Central American Federation in 1837. Nicaragua's status as an independent nation was formalized by a Constituent Assembly the following year.

These conflicts constituted a major obstacle to the institutionalization and strengthening of Nicaragua's educational system. There were, however, initiatives at the local level to offer basic education as well as establish important higher level education until 1818, when the University of León was created. By 1826, for example, education had become the responsibility of municipalities, which had to pay teachers' salaries. In 1846, Public Instruction Promotional Committees were established to promote education, oversee educational centers, and hire teachers. In that year, classes were reopened at the University of León, which had been closed because of wide scale armed conflict. University classes were taught in Latin grammar, philosophy, cannon law, moral theology, and rhetoric—reflecting a strong scholastic heritage, despite separation from Spain.

By the mid-nineteenth century, basic education was reaching only a limited number of students (2,800 out of a population of between 200,000–300,000 inhabitants). These students were taught reading and some arithmetic, but not how to write because basic materials such as pencils and paper were so expensive.

The first attempt to reorder the education system took place in 1868, with the publication of the Statutes of Primary Instruction. These statutes established systematized public education: they specified that education should be divided into primary and intermediate levels, with primary education the responsibility of a Board of Public Instruction. Similarly, they determined that primary education should consist mainly of reading, writing, arithmetic, Christian doctrine, moral principles, virtue, and etiquette. Intermediate education had three subject areas:

- philosophy and humanities, the study of Castilian, Latin, French, psychology, logic, metaphysics, and morality;
- geography, ancient and modern history, Nicaraguan history, and literature; and
- mathematics and physical sciences, including arithmetic, algebra, elemental geometry, rectilinear trigonometry, geometry, cosmography, physics, zoology, botany, mineralogy, and geology.

There is no way of verifying if this overloaded curriculum was ever implemented. However, some inspectors' reports from later years indicated that only those subjects directors considered convenient were taught.

During the second half of the nineteenth century several important post-primary institutions were established. In 1874, the *Colegio de Granada* was founded with educators from Spain (from the Free Teaching Institute, *Instituto Libre de Enseñanza*) who introduced progressive curricular and pedagogical ideas, including separation of church and state. In 1882, the first women's college was opened, staffed by lay North American teachers. This center produced graduates who became notable female educators, including Josefa Toledo, Maria Medina, Isabel Espinoza, and Guadalupe Montes de Oca. In 1884, the Eastern and Western National Institutes (*Instituto Nacional de Oriente* and *Instituto Nacional de Occidente*) were founded.

In 1888, the first school census was conducted that counted 39,359 boys and girls of school age, of whom only 19,160 were enrolled and only 14,890 regularly attended school. At that time, there were 320 elementary schools, attended to by 375 teachers, of whom only 23 were graduates of teacher education.

Liberal Period (1893–1910)

The implementation of progressive reform would have to wait for the Liberal revolution led by José Santos Zelaya (1893–1909). Among the more liberal currents influencing Nicaraguan education were those coming from Chilean educators. The liberal government focused on primary education, which they proposed to extend to the most remote rural areas. For the first time, the 1893 Constitution established compulsory, free, and secular education. It created a school inspectorate to ensure compliance with the 1894 Fundamental Law of Public Instruction. Two significant curricular changes (1901 and 1906) introduced a utilitarian orientation that further attempted to eliminate the colonial scholastic inheritance. These reforms were modeled on the ideas advocated by French and Prussian educators. Among the liberal reforms introduced were night schools for workers and artisans, educational centers for army officials and soldiers, and previously excluded populations. Technical schools were opened to prepare qualified laborers for the burgeoning coffee industry and other sectors of the modernizing economy.

A census (1906) revealed a school population of 64,733 boys and 62,536 girls, of whom only 20,840 were enrolled. Of this number, 15,644 attended school regularly (about 13 percent of the school-age population). Poor enrollment figures, however, do not reveal the fact that the Liberal government had created at least 450 new schools. In 1907, to improve the quality of education, the Teaching School for Girls was created. Three teaching schools functioned at the time, in León, Managua, and Bluefields, the latter having as its objective the preparation of indigenous educators.

At the higher education level, universities were reformed in accordance with the French Napoleonic model, consisting of specialized schools offering careers in, for example, law, medicine, and pharmacy. As in France, only societal elites had access to post-secondary education.

The Conservative Restoration and U.S. Intervention (1910 to mid-1930s)

The Liberal government was overthrown in 1910 under pressure from the U.S. government, which had cut diplomatic relations with Nicaragua during the Zelaya Period. When José Dolores Estrada assumed power, he re-established diplomatic relations with the United States. In doing so, he was forced to accept onerous loans (under the so-called Dawson Pacts) resulting in a debt of 1.5 million pesos. The most significant curricular change involved a reemphasis on religious education. The 1919 reform of the Constitution established Roman Catholicism as the national religion, despite the 1893 constitutional separation of church and state. Equally significant was the U.S. Marine occupation of the country for most of the period between 1909–32, the insurrection headed by Augusto César Sandino (1927–33), and the worldwide Depression that caused a drop in the prices of coffee and wood. The economic downturn was so great that there often was no money to pay teachers. Finally, as against imposition of Catholicism as a state religion during this period, a countercurrent of secular North American cultural influence resulted from the presence of U.S. troops.

Due to the armed conflict and sociopolitical instability of the period, the illiteracy rate exceeded 75 percent. In 1928, only 14 percent of the school-age population was enrolled. In 1930, 277 schools were closed due to instability in the countryside occasioned by the Sandino-led revolt against U.S. forces. Many schools were used as refuges and hospitals. During these years, education took place mainly in religious centers, which catered mostly to the elite. Simultaneously, there were efforts by more liberal groups to reintroduce a secular, humanistic education. Progressive developments also were occurring in the universities of Managua and Granada, which opened new schools, including dentistry and obstetrics. Another advance was the publication of national textbooks and educational journals.

Education during the Somoza Period, 1937–1979

From the period that Anastasio Somoza García, commander of the Nicaraguan National Guard, seized power and become president of the country in 1937, he and his family directly or indirectly ruled the country for forty-two years. The economic policies of the Somoza regime in conjunction with international capital had a profound influence on the content, forms, and scope of education programs in the country. The expansion and direction of the education system largely followed the booms and busts in the economy. When the economy grew rapidly in the 1950s and 1960s, the education systems expanded accordingly. Fueling the growth of these years, was the modernization of rural infrastructure to facilitate the export of cotton during the Korean War, the infusion of capital as part of the Alliance for Progress[1] following Fidel

Castro's rise to power in Cuba in 1959, and the creation of the Central American Common Market. In the 1970s, with the economic downturn, illiteracy rates rose, the rate of school expansion declined, and investments in higher education were dramatically reduced. The overall development policies of the country, according to Petras (1979), might be described as "rapid growth from above ... made possible by the autocratic dictatorship and its 'free market' and repressive labor policies—a pattern not unknown to other Latin American countries." He goes on to note that the "'autocratic development-from-above-and-outside' model prevented sustained and consequential *democratization*. Rather, the pattern was one of selective and time-bound *liberalization*— modification of dictatorial policies—followed by widespread and systematic repression" (Petras 1979, 3–4).

Despite the rhetoric of the Somoza regime, and the 1974 Constitution which declared free and compulsory primary education to be a state obligation, the education system in 1979 was extremely underdeveloped and characterized by gross inequities. The illiteracy rate was slight over half (50.35 percent) of the population with more than three-fourths (76 percent) of the rural population unable to read or write. There were under 25,000 students enrolled in adult education programs, the great majority the responsibility of the private sector and church groups. Primary education reached only 65 percent of the relevant age group; pre-primary programs were available to 5.3 percent of children, mostly in private, fee-paying centers; and special education enrolled a mere 355 students. Of those entering the school system, only 22 percent completed the sixth grade—34 percent in urban areas and 6 percent in rural areas. A principal reason for such low completion rates in the countryside was that the vast majority of rural schools consisted of only one or two grades and a single teacher.

Only 15 percent of the relevant age group attended secondary education. Approximately 70 percent of secondary schools were private, although they enrolled fewer than half (about 40 percent) of secondary education students. Fees in these schools might be as high as US$100 in a country in which, according to Kraft, an estimated 50 percent of the popular earned less than US$210 per year, and 77 percent of the rural population had never produced annual per capita cash incomes of over US$120 (Kraft 1983, 89). In a country in which 45 percent of the population was employed in agriculture and agricultural exports accounted for the lion's share of foreign earnings, less than 1 percent of students were enrolled in agriculture studies, while 87 percent were either in pre-university academic programs or in commercial studies. The classic secondary school, *bachillerato,* which was encyclopedic in nature, as well as verbalistic and memoristic, prepared students for the next step on the education ladder.

The higher education system, which had expanded considerably during the economic boom years, by the mid-1970s, enrolled 5.38 students per 1,000 (about 8 percent of the age group). According to the *Encyclopedia of the Third*

World (Kurian 1978, 1065), Nicaragua, in 1976, ranked 86 among nations in adjusted school enrollments for primary and secondary education, but 61 in per-capita university enrollments. Like other Latin American countries, Nicaragua under Somoza provided extensive education at public expense to urban elites, but it failed to provide primary education or even basic literacy to a majority of its citizens.

The majority of higher education students were not enrolled in technical fields or careers related directly to production. More than half of university students enrolled in courses connected with the tertiary sector while only 1 percent followed courses linked with the primary sector, particularly farming. Of the 27,000 tertiary-level students in 1979, for example, only 497 were in agricultural, forestry, and fishery studies, but as many as 4,168 were in commercial and business administration.

The following information is indicative of the qualitative limitations of the pre-1979 school system at all levels. In higher education, most teachers were part-time. A number of instructors supplemented their incomes by teaching in high schools, where as many as 68 percent of the teachers were not certified. At the primary school level, as many as 73 percent of the teachers were unqualified.

The poverty of the country alone does not suffice to explain the underdeveloped state of the education system, which had been shaped and distorted to serve the special interests of the rural Somoza family and external funders, principally in the United States. According to Kraft (1978, 85):

During the Somoza era[,] education was seen as a tool to train a technical cadre to run the family enterprises and state bureaucracies, with the emphasis generally in that order. With all important decisions being made by the president, the centralized educational system responded to his general direction.... The level of interest by the president and the cabinet tended to be in direct proportion to the loans and grants being given by U.S. and international lending agencies which were leading influences over the direction of education in the country.

This was the general situation of the country in July 1979, when the Somoza dynastic dictatorship was overthrown by a broad coalition of forces led by the *Frente Sandinista de Liberación Nacional* (the Sandinista National Liberation Front, FSLN).

Education during the Sandinista Period, 1979–1990

The revolution catapulted Nicaragua onto the world stage. Although disagreement exists over the revolution's precise nature, in particular over the socialist intension of the FSLN, most observers would agree that it was nationalist, populist, and anti-imperialist. The unique features of the revolutionary regime included a commitment to a mixed economy, political pluralism, and a nonaligned foreign policy. Among the Sandinista government's major commitments and achievements were the provision of land, health care, and education to the vast majority of the population.

Education was called on to play a key role in promoting social change in Nicaragua. Toward that end, the education system was expected to foster the development of a "new person," a more critically conscious and participatory citizen motivated by collective goals, and also to promote the transmission of the skills and knowledge necessary to overcome decades of underdevelopment and set the nation on the path of self-sustaining growth. In shaping the education system to be an integral component of the revolution, the leadership of the Ministry of Education (MED) envisioned the expansion, improvement, and transformation of education as contributing, respectively, to the democratization of basic social services, the independence of the Nicaraguan economy from foreign domination, and the development of a new model of capital accumulation based on different social relations of production and forms of public and cooperative ownership.

The revolution's very first year was declared the "Year of Literacy" as a massive national literacy campaign was undertaken between March and August 1980 to democratize education and mobilize the population around the revolution's goal. The literacy "crusade" was followed by a campaign in the native languages of the Atlantic Coast region and an innovative program of adult basic education that reached over 180,000 youths and adults in a country of 2.4 million.

During the revolution's first five years, enrollments expanded significantly at all levels of formal education, including the previously neglected areas of preschool and special education. Between 1979–84, pre-university education grew from 540,688 to 758,203. By 1984, approximately one-third of the total population was participating in some form of systematic education, while the teaching force had risen from 17,346 during the revolution's first year to 46,683 (including volunteer adult educators). The national educational budget grew during that period from 2.9 percent of gross domestic product (GDP) to 6 percent. The increased allocations led to the construction of schools in previously neglected areas, as well as additions to existing facilities in the form of libraries, laboratories, and workshops.

Among the major improvements were the establishment of a national textbook industry, the revision of curricula, and the introduction of new instructional methods, particularly in the language arts. Organizationally, the MED in Managua assumed a more decisive role in long-range planning and in the formulation of more coherent policies for the entire system.

Transformations in learning processes centered on fostering more collective, participatory, inquiry-oriented, and work-related methods. Major steps were undertaken to involve schools more directly in the activities of their surrounding communities and in the resolution of national problems. In higher education, the most striking transformations involved the close integration of admissions policies and faculty and curriculum development with national economic plans, and the inclusion of a significant work component in all study plans.

Despite these accomplishments, nearly a decade of warfare, natural disasters, and economic decline hindered sustainable gains in education. The Sandinista social experiment was never able to be fully tested or come to fruition-largely because of the U.S.-organized and financed counterrevolution and economic embargo of Nicaragua. Nearly ten years of fighting produced more than 50,000 casualties, hundreds of thousands of displaced people, and over US$15 billion in direct and indirect damage to the economy. The progress of the education system was inextricably linked to the fate of the revolution. Over time, the 1979 Government of National Reconstruction shifted its priorities from education and production to defense and, finally, to national survival.

By the end of the 1980s, many of the same education problems the FSLN had encountered and set out to overcome a decade earlier still plagued the MED leadership. Enrollments had been expanded, but more than 150,000 school-age children remained outside the education system. Approximately 22 percent of students who started first grade completed the sixth year of primary school; less than 10 percent of rural children did so. Despite systematic efforts to expand the number of teacher-training institutions and upgrade the qualification of in-service teachers, more than 60 percent of teachers were *empíricos* (uncertified). Turnover was also high due to the inability of teachers to live on their salaries, whose real value had been reduced by more than three-fourths by hyperinflation. School facilities were badly damaged, libraries and equipment were scarce and in disrepair, and textbooks almost nonexistent in the rural areas. With the lion's share of the national budget going to defense, funds for the social sector were cut in half. Despite many attempts to introduce innovative pedagogy, most classroom instruction was still teacher-centered and traditional. Secondary education continued to be heavily academic and geared toward entering the university. At the university level, while more students were enrolled in fields related to national priorities, constant mobilizations of the university community for defense and production activities and inadequate funding all contributed to deterioration in the quality of education. In addition, the close linkages between the university community and the Sandinista revolution had reduced the political space for dialogue and dissenting points of view.

The Central American peace process that was initiated in Esquipulus, Guatemala, in 1987, culminated in national elections in Nicaragua in February 1990. Rejecting years of warfare and economic hardship, the Nicaraguan population voted for a change of government. A broad coalition of fourteen political parties and factions—ranging from the far left to the far right—defeated the FSLN. The victorious National Opposition Union (*Unión Nacional Opositora*, UNO) led by Violeta Barrios de Chamorro promised national reconciliation, access to international credit and investment, and greater prosperity than was possible under the FSLN.

Period of "Liberal" Governments and "Neo-Liberal" Policies, 1990–2006

Despite its diversity, the UNO coalition's political orientation was essentially right of center. The dominant group that emerged included modernizing industrial, commercial, and financial elites as well as technocrats oriented toward reintegrating the country into the global economy. Among the country's principal problems were hyperinflation, fiscal deficits, and a staggering foreign debt that had grown from US$1.6 billion in 1979 to approximately US$10 billion in 1990. To gain access to capital and foreign capital and markets, the country sought the assistance of the International Monetary Fund (IMF) and the World Bank as well as national technical assistance agencies such as the U.S. Agency for International Development (USAID). But to secure such aid, the Nicaraguan government also had to agree to the fiscal austerity and economic adjustment policies recommended by these agencies. These policies led to a drastic reduction in the State's role in social spending, deregulation of the economy, and liberalization of import policies. The education counterparts of these policies included moves to decentralize and privatize the public school system.

Another central thrust of the incoming government was an initiative to reassert traditional Christian values. Selection of the MED's leadership was entrusted to Cardinal Miguel Obando y Bravo, the country's leading religious authority, and to the Council of Bishops (*Conferencia Episcopal*). The cardinal had been the single most formidable opponent of the Sandinista regime during the 1980s, and the individuals he handpicked to lead the MED were among the leading conservative Catholic ideologues who had opposed FSLN educational policy.

Along with initiatives to reverse Sandinista social and economic policies, the new Government of National Salvation also set out to dismantle the educational system erected by the FSLN. The 1980 national literacy campaign, programs of adult popular education, and the entire system of publicly financed and regulated schooling (primary through higher education) were viewed by the incoming government as instruments of state indoctrination to win youth to the Sandinista's revolutionary cause. In 1990, the education system, as much occurred in 1979, was to be reshaped in accordance with Nicaragua's new realities.

The new agenda called for a major educational restructuring. The state's central role in administration of education was to be diminished: (since 1994, a central component of reform efforts has been a "school autonomy" project) political content was to be excised from the curriculum; traditional values were to be reintroduced; the power of Sandinista-affiliated mass organizations, such as the National Association of Nicaraguan Educators (ANDEN) and the Federation of Secondary Education Students (FES) was to be reduced; the role of parents in school decision-making was to be increased; and the costs of education were to be borne by its users, particularly at the university level.

Thus the stage was set for those who had championed and benefited most from educational reforms and those who viewed these initiatives as destructive of the educational system and harmful to the society. In much the same way as the Sandinistas had used education as a state apparatus to legitimize the revolutionary order of the 1980s, the conservative coalition that had defeated the FSLN in 1990 set out to use education to consolidate its vision of the society and its historical project to accord priority to market mechanisms, traditional values, and parliamentary—rather than mass-based—forms of democracy. The logic of the majority was to be replaced by the logic of the market, and values with a socialist orientation by Christian-inspired principles. In these circumstances, schools inevitably became sites of contestation of educational governance, financing, curriculum, and pedagogical methods.

Persisting Problems and Challenges (1990–2006 and On)

Over fifteen years of Liberal party rule by Arnoldo Alemán (1996–2001) and Enrique Bolaños (2001–6) as well as neoliberal economic policies, the education system confronted the same challenges posed during the 1980s. Although enrollments have expanded, many students still repeat grades, do not attend school regularly, or drop out entirely. Those who remain in school often receive an education of mediocre quality. Funding for education in Nicaragua is inadequate, even with significant continuing support from international donors. The teacher force is troubled: teachers' salaries are dismal, turnover is high, and many teachers are uncertified or under-qualified. Adult illiteracy continues to grow. The results of administrative reform efforts are mixed. There are serious gaps in educational access and quality between rural and urban areas and between public and elite, private schools.

Access

The population of Nicaragua is among the youngest in the hemisphere. The average age of a Nicaraguan citizen is 24: 2,350,000 citizens—42 percent of Nicaragua's total population of 5.5 million are between three and eighteen years of age. Of these, in the year 2005, 830,000—22 percent of children and adolescents between seven and seventeen years of age were outside the education system, a figure that has remained about the same since the mid-1990s. The most seriously marginalized Nicaraguan social sector, the rural poor, have the least access. Only one in ten rural dwellers ever completes high school (compared to four out of ten in urban areas). In the poorest area of Nicaragua, the North Atlantic Autonomous Region, only 5 percent of the high-school age population ever even enrolls in secondary school. Failure to attend school is highly associated with persisting high levels of illiteracy.

Illiteracy

Illiteracy is a good indicator of broader inequities in the education system, since there is always more illiteracy in areas of extreme poverty. As discussed in the previous section, one of the single achievements of the Sandinista period was a massive literacy campaign that treated illiteracy as a national emergency and enjoyed strong popular support. Literacy efforts subsequently languished in the late 1980s and early 1990s. In 1997, the Ministry initiated a national literacy program that currently uses "literacy specialists" attached to Nicaragua's 153 Municipal Education Offices. The "specialists" organize and lead local beginning-reading "literacy circles" for teens and adults in schools and private homes. Neither effort has had much permanent impact on illiteracy, which according to the most conservative estimates has hovered for years at about 20 percent.

Bilingual Education

The eastern half of Nicaragua's land mass consists of two administratively semi-autonomous regions (*Regiones Autónomas del Atlántico Norte y Sur*). The inhabitants of the Autonomous Regions comprise only 10 percent of Nicaragua's population. Most are non-Spanish speakers. The Miskitu indigenous language predominates in the Northern Region. A majority of the inhabitants of the Southern Region speak an English-based Creole.

A major contribution of the Sandinista government to educational equity was a 1987 constitutional amendment specifying the right of Nicaraguan linguistic minorities to receive instruction in their native languages. Bilingual education programs are expensive and complex, and theory and practice in the field of bilingual education are rife with controversy. Also, in spite of ongoing good intentions regarding education opportunities for language minorities, bilingual education offerings in schools in the autonomous regions are spotty, underfunded, and of varying quality. The Ministry houses a small Office of Bilingual-Intercultural Education (*Oficina de Educación Intercultural-Bilingüe*) currently responsible for providing technical services to about one-hundred Autonomous Region schools that offer bilingual education programs.

Efficiency of the School System

Educators and policymakers commonly measure the efficiency of a school system by looking at how many graduates the system produces, and how long that takes; in other words, how many students repeat grades, how many first graders eventually complete sixth grade, and how many entering high school students go on to graduate from high school.

Repetition. High levels of grade repetition in the primary grades have been characteristic of education throughout Latin America for generations. An important reason for this is a longstanding traditional view, common among parents and community members as well as teachers, that children should not advance past first grade until they have demonstrably mastered basic reading and math skills. Given this view, together with the obstacles to learning that have long affected primary schools in Nicaragua—lack of learning materials, ineffective teaching methods, high absenteeism—many children repeat grades, never advancing past first grade or the first few grades. Sixty percent of Nicaraguan primary-school children repeat one or more grades, and 26 percent drop out before they complete sixth grade.

To address these problems, the Ministry, in the late 1990s, implemented a policy requiring automatic promotion through third grade. In the first years of this policy, primary repetition rates dropped dramatically, from 14.8 percent in 1995 to 5.1 percent in 2000. Teacher and community resistance to the automatic promotion policy was strong, however, administration and enforcement were spotty, and by 2004 the primary-school repetition rate had risen again to 10.5 percent.

Absenteeism and Dropout. The current total dropout rate for Nicaragua, secondary as well as primary, is 41 percent. Studies conducted by Nicaragua's Ministry of Education, Culture and Sports (MECD, renamed in 1998) show that the most common reasons why students are absent or drop out of school are economic: for the poorest families to survive, everyone must work. In rural areas, young people often enter the agricultural work force full-time by early adolescence.

The quality and relevance of schooling is another reason why students drop out of school. Economically hard-pressed Nicaraguan parents are not likely to accept the additional expense of keeping their children in school if they see that their children are not learning or if what their children learn in school is of little apparent use.

Completion. Universal sixth-grade education is a standard goal in many developing countries. Education through sixth grade has long been compulsory in Nicaragua. Nevertheless, in 1990, only 44 percent of primary-grade students completed sixth grade. The percentage rose steadily over the 1990s and by 2004 had reached 74 percent.

High rates of grade failure combine with low graduation rates to further reduce the efficiency of the education system, especially in the primary grades. In 2004, it took the Nicaraguan school system an average of 10.5 years to produce a sixth-grade graduate. Of every hundred students who started first grade in Nicaragua in the year 2000, only forty reached sixth grade on time in 2005, without repeating a grade.

Quality of Instruction

Until recently in many Latin American nations, an important cause of diminished educational quality and effectiveness has been teachers' use of antiquated, ineffectual classroom methods. Even where classrooms are badly overcrowded, and even in conditions of extreme poverty, reform programs that focus on improving classroom methodologies can strengthen the quality of primary education. Beginning in the early 1990s, with assistance from several international development agencies, the Ministry undertook a massive effort to train all of

Nicaragua's primary school teachers in the use of "active learning" classroom methods and techniques which are the standard methods for teaching young children in use throughout most of the industrialized world.

This effort was largely successful in changing the perspectives and practices of Nicaragua's primary school teachers. By 2003, most Nicaraguan primary teachers could articulate the reasoning behind active, learner-centered teaching methods, and many were using active-learning methods in their classrooms. To date, however, teaching in the middle and secondary grades appears to have been less affected by Ministry efforts to modernize classroom teaching. In the secondary grades, many Nicaraguan teachers still teach entirely by lecture while students passively copy lecture material into their notebooks.

Teacher Salaries and Qualifications

In spite of persistent Ministry training and certification efforts, 30 percent of primary teachers and 50 percent of secondary teachers are uncertified. The percentage of uncertified teachers has been rising in recent years, most precipitously in the years between 1998–2002, when it rose from 15.7 percent to 28.9 percent (primary and secondary combined). Low teacher salaries are the most obvious reason why the school system has trouble recruiting and keeping qualified teachers. Teacher salaries have risen modestly in recent years, but are still too low for a teacher to live on and support a family. As of 2004, the average monthly teacher salary was $123 (U.S. dollars)—20 percent below the 2004 *canasta básica* ("basic breadbasket"), the economic threshold for family survival set annually by the Nicaraguan government.

Academic Achievement, Academic Standards, and Standardized Testing

Although the Ministry's methodological reform efforts had a measurable impact on how Nicaraguan teachers teach in the primary grades, to date there is no evidence that improved teaching methods have resulted in improved student academic achievement. The Ministry began reworking the primary curriculum in the late 1990s with a view to developing a standardized testing system based on consistent academic standards for the primary grades. Pilot-standardized third and sixth grade reading and mathematics tests were administered nationwide in 2002. The tests were criterion-referenced to existing Central American regional academic standards.

To date, the testing has not been repeated, so there is no comparison across years, to try to detect any changes in academic achievement over time. The Ministry did not report the test score results or result percentages outright, but instead set test score cutoff points, used those cutoff points to group test results into three levels of proficiency, labeled "basic," "intermediate," and "proficient," and reported those percentages. A large majority of Nicaragua's students fell into the "basic" category—in other words, did poorly on the tests—in both Spanish and mathematics, in both third and sixth grades, including 61.7 percent "basic" in third grade mathematics; 71.2 percent in third grade Spanish; 88.1 percent in sixth grade mathematics, and 69.7 percent in sixth grade Spanish.

In 2005, the Ministry began an ambitious multi-year curriculum reform (*transformación curricular*) expansion effort to promote the use of competency-based curricula in all schools nationwide. The Ministry plans call for 50 percent of secondary schools and 40 percent of primary schools to use competency-based curricula by 2007, and full national use to be in place by 2008.

Unsurprisingly, the nationwide percentages of private-school students classified as "proficient" in reading and mathematics were dramatically higher than those of students in the public schools, and many more public school students got low test scores than did students in Nicaragua's private schools. Nicaragua's first experience with national standardized testing served to confirm the obvious: students whose families can afford to send them to private schools learn better than students in the severely underfunded public system.

Educational Organization and Administration

Nicaragua's education system is presently organized into three administrative divisions: General Basic Education, Technical Education, and Higher Education. MECD is the entity in charge of pre-primary, primary, and secondary education. The pre-primary educational offering is a three-year program that accepts children from ages three to six. (The pre-primary program is relatively small, presently serving about 100,000 children.) Primary education (*Educación Primaria*) includes grades one through six, serving an intended age range of seven through twelve (many primary students are in fact older then twelve, because of high grade repetition). Secondary education (*Educación Media*) usually consists of five years, and is further sub-divided into "general education" (the first three years), and the "diversified cycle" (*Ciclo Diversificado*, the last two years). Nicaragua's eight normal schools, responsible for training teachers, offer an additional sixth year of teacher preparation.

A separate public entity, the National Technical Institute (*Instituto Nacional Tecnológico*, INATEC) is responsible for Nicaragua's technical-vocational schools and curricula. INATEC operates vocational training centers in each of Nicaragua's eighteen Departments and in the two Atlantic Coast Autonomous Regions. INATEC operations are funded largely through a 2 percent corporate tax on Nicaraguan industries.

The government relinquished much of its direct administrative control over higher education in 1990. Although only eight specially designated universities receive public funding (see further discussion under "Funding for Education," below), all are administered by independently elected or appointed boards of directors, operating under the general aegis of an autonomous National University Council (*Consejo Nacional de Universidades*, CNU).

Administrative Decentralization

In 1993, the Ministry began shifting administrative responsibility to Regional and Departmental Education Offices, marking the beginning of a broad-based, long-term effort to decentralize education in Nicaragua. By the mid-1990s, eight Regional Education Offices were in operation, as well as Departmental Offices in all fifteen of Nicaragua's administrative Departments. From 2001–3, the Ministry undertook a further step, phasing out the Regional Offices and shifting significant administrative responsibility to 153 small, municipal-level local education offices.

Decentralizing educational administration is widely viewed as a sound measure for developing countries to take in the interests of administrative efficiency and transparency. There was resistance to decentralization, especially in the early years of the decentralization process, among some central Ministry personnel based at MECD headquarters in Managua; nevertheless, the process proceeded steadily, and is now largely complete. There have been concerns that full decentralization to the municipal level could leave schools vulnerable to local politics, including teacher and *director* (school principal) appointments based on political party affiliations; but similar arguments can be made regarding the vulnerabilities of schools to political considerations when education is tightly controlled by central authorities.

School Autonomy

Simultaneous with administrative decentralization, the Ministry also undertook a school autonomy initiative. According to the MECD, by 2004, over 4,000 schools—62 percent of Nicaragua's institutions of public education, serving 79 percent of the public school student population—were participants in the autonomy program.

Nicaragua's is one of the most radical school autonomy programs in the world at present, and has proven considerably more controversial than administrative decentralization. The program was undertaken largely at the urging of the World Bank, which heavily underwrites the Nicaraguan public school system through long-term loans. Under the program, an elected School Council consisting of parents and community members administers most of the school's operating budget, which is transferred from the central Ministry into a local account managed by the School Council. Together with financial responsibility for managing the school, the School Council also, in theory, exercises administrative authority that extends to hiring and firing teachers and school administrators.

In practice, the extent to which the School Council actually manages the school appears to vary considerably. In some cases, the local School Council is indeed the entity that controls virtually every aspect of the school. In others, local entities or individuals—the mayor's office, the church, local business people—gain control of the School Council and run the school. In still others, the School Council turns to the Central Ministry in Managua for guidance in administering the school, essentially returning to the centralized form of administrative authority that existed before the autonomy program.

By far, the most controversial aspect of the school autonomy program is school fees. The Autonomous School Councils have the authority to charge fees, and most do so. Nicaragua's constitution specifies that education shall be free, as well as mandatory, through sixth grade. All school fee assessments include the specification that parents who cannot afford the fees are not required to pay them. In a few instances, the central Ministry has taken School Councils to task and ordered the dismissal of local school administrators found to have kept children out of school when their parents could not pay the fees. There is obviously social pressure on poor families to find money for fees, and families and children who plead impoverishment are stigmatized.

With continuing incremental implementation of the autonomy program, school fees are now widespread in Nicaragua. The autonomy program as a whole is viewed by many Nicaraguans as a pretext for charging fees—as a ploy, in effect, for privatizing education. The main counter argument—that Nicaragua is simply too poor as a nation to fund education entirely out of public revenues—satisfies few critics, and the debate is certain to continue.

Community Participation

Controversial as the school autonomy program may be, there is general agreement that the promotion of empowered, locally active School Councils has had the beneficial effect of encouraging greater participation by parents and community members not just in local school administration, but also in support of school quality. There is strong evidence that increased local participation by parents in school life can markedly improve the quality of a school. With some technical support and modest seed money from international donors, growing numbers of schools, particularly in rural areas, are benefiting from the presence of parents and community members at school, participating in school repair projects, helping with sports and field trips, and serving as classroom assistants.

Legislative Reform

Following decades of debate and indecision, in March 2006 the Nicaraguan legislature finally passed a sweeping set of laws affecting government oversight of the education system. The General Education Law (*Ley General de Educación*) replaced confused and outdated legislation, some fully a century old, with new provisions intended to modernize and consolidate government oversight of the education system. The General Education Law importantly includes the establishment of a permanent National Commission of Evaluation and Accreditation, responsible for developing and administering uniform national standards for school accreditation and teacher certification.

Funding for Education

A rule of thumb in development is that, in order to grow economically, a developing country should invest at least 5 percent of its GDP in education. Nicaragua's GDP investment in education has hovered just below 3 percent for years, rising to 3.1 percent in 2005. Expressed as a percentage of Nicaragua's annual budget, in recent years the education investment has stood at approximately 13 percent (13.3 percent in 2005). Expressed as a dollar amount per student per year, Nicaragua's education investment rose above US$100 for the first time in 2005—to US$101. A comparison with other countries is instructive. The industrialized nations of the Organization for Economic Cooperation and Development (OECD) average $4,850 per primary and secondary student. In comparison to Nicaragua's 3.1 percent GDP expenditure, neighboring Costa Rica spent 4.9 percent of its GDP on education in 2004; Colombia, 4.9 percent; the Dominican Republic, 5 percent; Bolivia, 6.4 percent.

An unusual and controversial influence on the allocation of funds within Nicaragua's total public education expenditure is Public Law 89, a law famous among Nicaraguans, passed in 1990, in the last days of the Sandinista government. Public Law 89 requires that 6 percent of the national budget be allocated to Nicaragua's public institutions of higher education. Nicaraguans simply refer to Law 89 as "*el seis porciento*" ("the 6 percent"). With annual total funding for education at around 13 percent, the effect of Law 89 is that each year nearly half of the public funds available for education go to Nicaragua's universities. Nicaragua, a highly indebted poor country (HIPC), 40 percent of its population without a sixth grade education, spends more per student in real dollar amounts on higher education than Mexico, Italy, Portugal, and Spain.

The argument in favor of "*el seis porciento*" is that Nicaragua has a long, distinguished intellectual tradition, protected, and maintained by its universities, and that Nicaragua's present and future professionals and intelligentsia deserve the institutional support that only a robust domestic higher education system can provide. In addition to the obvious counter-argument that the law hampers Nicaragua's development by drawing scarce funds away from basic education, counter arguments also often include the charge that the Sandinistas passed the law in their final hours specifically for the purpose of establishing permanent sinecures inside the universities for Sandinista party functionaries. Whatever the merits of each case, Law 89 is perennially among the most inflammatory issues in Nicaraguan education, and is likely to remain so for as long as it remains on the books.

Dependence on International Aid

Dependence on international sources to supplement funding for education from the public treasury has diminished somewhat in Nicaragua over the past decade. In 2000, 37 percent of Nicaragua's education budget came from international donors and development bank loans. By 2003, the portion of the budget from international loans and donations was down to 20 percent (13 percent of that was from a single source, the World Bank). Although World Bank support is vital to the survival of public education, Nicaragua's already towering national debt has grown correspondingly with each Bank loan. In 2005 and 2006, all of the textbooks and much of the furniture for Nicaragua's schools were provided by the World Bank's *APRENDE* ("learn") project. Nicaragua's dependency on foreign aid would be significantly reduced, if not eliminated, if it were to raise the public investment in education to at least 5 percent of GDP, and to concentrate that investment on strengthening basic and intermediate education.

CHANGE OF GOVERNMENT: IMPLICATIONS FOR EDUCATION

In November 2006, Daniel Ortega, the leader of Nicaragua's Sandinista Party, was reelected President of Nicaragua. The return to power of Ortega (President, 1984–90) and the Sandinistas is likely to prove a critical moment for Nicaragua's education system. Historically, during transitions of government in Latin America, new authorities have often been inclined to reject wholesale the education sector policies and accomplishments of the previous government, using education as a means of distinguishing itself from its political rivals. Much has been accomplished in education since the Sandinistas left power in 1990; and many of those accomplishments were in fact built on the Sandinistas' own education initiatives during the 1980s. It would be an unfortunate irony if the new Sandinista government decided to erase that progress.

The new Sandinista government is promoting increased equity of educational opportunities by strengthening policies and programs in areas such as literacy and rural education. Initiatives of the new government include a large-scale literacy campaign, with Venezuelan financial backing and technical support provided by Cuban specialists and teachers. It is to be hoped that the new government will maintain the many policies and programs developed over the last fifteen years that are in keeping with progressive and democratic ideals and have demonstrably improved the education system, including active-learning methodologies, administrative decentralization, and community participation in support of schools, while revisiting the failed and controversial changes of the 1990s, such as the assessment of school fees.

Unfortunately, the evidence as of this writing suggests otherwise. The newly-appointed Minister of Education recently announced a "National Public School Crusade" (*Nuevo Diario*, 2007), one of the purposes of which is to dismantle the Autonomous Schools effort and the various privatization initiatives undertaken over the previous sixteen years of neoliberal government. The stage has thus been set for the education system once again to become the site of conflicting projects based on ideology, and the further polarization of Nicaraguan society.

TIMELINE

1536   The King of Spain orders Governor Contreras to educate the indigenous people.
1621   First high school opens in El Realejo but closes shortly after its founding.
1680   First institution of higher education, San Ramon Seminary, opens in León.
1803   The King of Spain allows San Ramon Seminary to confer titles.
1812   Municipal schools are created by the Constitution of Cadiz.
1818   The University of Leon opens.
1821   Independence of the Province from Spain on September 15.
1824   State of Nicaragua Constitution (April 8).
        Central America Federal Constitution (November 22).
1846   Boards of Public Instruction created to promote education, oversee centers, and contract teachers.
1868   First attempt to reorder educational system by publishing the Statutes of Primary Instruction.
1874   The Colegio de Granada opens with teachers from Spain.
1877   Presidential Legislative Ordinance establishes free and compulsory education for children of both sexes from ages five to fourteen.
1882   First woman's college opens with North American secular teachers.
1893   The Liberal Revolution (1893–1910) promotes major reforms inspired by Chilean professors.
1894   The Fundamental Law of Public Instruction clearly defines the character of education.
1910   Overthrow of Liberal Government by Conservatives; the Conservative period begins.
1912–28 Conservative Restoration Period.
1918   Constitutional Reform establishes Catholicism as the official religion.
1930   Dramatic decrease in schools, particularly in the northern zone of Nicaragua, due to Sandino's guerrillas.
1937   Somoza Period: autocratic regime, free market, repressive labor policies, many inequities in education.
1979   Sandinista Regime: Literacy Crusade, educational policies strive for universal access, improvement, and transformation.
1990   First Neoliberal Regime: Government of Violeta Barrios de Chamorro. General Education Guideline: School Autonomy.
1996   Second Neoliberal Regime: Government of Arnoldo Alemán—National Plan for Sustainable Development.
2001   Third Neoliberal Regime: Government of Enrique Bolaños. National Plan of Education (2001–5): General Law of Education.
2002   Higher Education Institutional Evaluation.
2006   General Law of Education: Sandinista Front wins presidential election.

NOTE

1. The Alliance for Progress, launched by the Kennedy administration in 1961, was a massive foreign-assistance program for Latin America intended to counter the perceived influence of leftist revolutionary movements in the Hemisphere, in particular the Castro regime in Cuba.

BIBLIOGRAPHY

Historical Sources (Colonial through Neoliberal)

Books

Arnove, Robert F. 1986. *Education and Revolution in Nicaragua*. Westport, CT: Praeger.

Arnove, Robert F. 1994. *Education as Contested Terrain*. Boulder, CO: Westview Press.

Molina Arguello, Carlos. 1953. *La enseñanza de la historia en Nicaragua*. México: Instituto Panamericano de Geografía e Historia.

Nielsen, H. Dean and William K. Cummings, eds. 1997. *Quality Education for All: Community-Oriented Approaches*. New York and London: Garland.

Rodríguez Rosales, Isolda. 1998. *La educación durante el liberalismo. Nicaragua: 1893–1909*. Managua: Editorial Hispamer,

Rodríguez Rosales, Isolda. 2004. *Historia de la educación en Nicaragua. Restauración Conservadora, 1910–30*. Managua: Editorial Hispamer.

Articles and Chapters

Kraft, Richard J. 1983. "Nicaragua: Educational Opportunity under Pre- and Post-Revolutionary Conditions." In *Politics and Education: Cases from Eleven Nations*. Edited by Murray Thomas, 79–103. New York: Pergamon Press.

Petras, James. "Whither the Nicaraguan Revolution?" *Monthly Review* 31 (October 1979): 1–22.

Persisting Problems and Challenges—Sources

Reports

Arcia, Gustavo, and Humberto Belli. 1999. "Rebuilding the Social Contract: School Autonomy in Nicaragua." New York and Washington, D.C.: World Bank Publications.

Castillo, Melba, Vanesa Castro, Ana Patricia Elvir, and Josefina Viril. 2006. "Siete prioridades de la educación nicaragüense para el período 2007–12." Centro de Investigación y Acción Educativa Social [CIASES]. Managua, Nicaragua: CIASES.

Edgerton, David C. 2005. "Schools, Communities, Democracy: The Nicaragua BASE Project." Washington, D.C.: Academy for Educational Development (AED).

Gershberg, Alec Ian. 2001. "Empowering Parents While Making Them Pay: Autonomous Schools in Nicaragua." New York: Milano School of Management and Urban Policy, New School University.

Kaestner, Robert, and Alec Gershberg. 2002. "Lessons Learned from Nicaragua's School Autonomy Reform: A Review of Research by the Nicaragua Reform Evaluation Team of the World Bank." New York and Washington, D.C.: World Bank Documents & Reports.

King, Elizabeth M., et al. 1999. "Nicaragua's School Autonomy Reform: Fact or Fiction?" New York and Washington, D.C.: World Bank Documents & Reports.

Ministry of Education, Culture and Sports (*Ministerio de Educación, Cultura y Deportes*). 2004. "Estado del Sistema de Educación Básica y Media." Managua, Nicaragua: MECD.

UNESCO. 2004. "Education for All Global Monitoring Report 2005." Paris: UNESCO.

U.S. Department of Education. 2006. "International Comparisons of Expenditures for Education." Washington, D.C.: U.S. Department of Education, National Center for Education Statistics.

U.S. Department of Education, National Center for Education Statistics. 1999. "Educational Indicators: An International Perspective."

U.S. Department of Education, National Center for Education Statistics. 2006. "International Comparisons of Expenditures for Education."

Web Sites

Academy for Educational Development (AED) (reports on educational development in Nicaragua under "International Education"): http://www.aed.org/Toolsand Publications/.

Nicaragua Ministry of Education, Culture and Sports (*Ministerio de Educación, Cultura y Deportes*): http://www.mecd.gob.ni/.

Nuevo Diario on-line: http://www.elnuevodiario.com.ni/.

United Nations Educational Cultural, and Scientific Organization (UNESCO) (Education): http://portal.unesco.org/education/.

United States Agency for International Development (USAID) online Development Experience Clearinghouse: http://dec.usaid.gov/default.cfm.

World Bank (education statistics): http://devdata.worldbank.org/edstats/.

Chapter 12

SCHOOLING IN PARAGUAY

Rodolfo Elías

This study provides a general overview of the Paraguayan education system, beginning with a description of its historical development and concluding with an analysis of the current situation. Special attention is given to bilingual education, since one distinctive characteristic of Paraguayan society is that the indigenous Guaraní language is used by the vast majority of the people, while in the rest of Latin America the language of the colonizers—Spanish and Portuguese—predominate.

A BRIEF REVIEW OF THE PARAGUAYAN HISTORY

Paraguay, a mediterranean country in the heart of South America, has a population of 6,347,884 (2005), and a surface of 406,752 square kilometers; 57 percent of the population live in urban areas; 43 percent live in rural areas. The main economic activities are agriculture and livestock. Paraguay's main export products are: cotton, soja bean, wood, and bovine meat.

There are different periods in Paraguay's history: the pre-colonial period (before 1524, when the first Spanish group explored the present Paraguayan territory); the colonial period (from 1524–1811); independence (1811–70); post-war (1870–1954); the Stroessner dictatorship period (1954–89); and democratic transition (1989 to the present).

During the pre-colonial period there were several indigenous nations living in the present Paraguayan territory with their culture and political organizations. Particularly important was the Guaraní nation, the predominant group in the region. The relationship between the Guarani and the European colonizers was a key factor in the construction of Paraguay as a nation, with its own cultural identity.

During the conquest and the colonial period (1524–1811), the Spaniards initiated the exploration of the territory, the concentration and foundations of towns, and the development of social and political institutions. The fort of *Nuestra Señora de la Asunción* (actual city of Asunción, capital of Paraguay) was founded in 1537 by Juan de Salazar y Espinoza and the first Governor of the Province of Paraguay was Domingo Martínez de Irala (during the period from 1539–56). The Catholic Church was an important influence, especially of Jesuits. This religious order created the Reductions (*Reducciones*), in which they developed a model of political and social organization. The Jesuits systematized the Guaraní language, which was used in the evangelization and in the education of the indigenous population.

Independence from the Spanish Crown initiated a new phase in Paraguayan history. After the revolution (May 1811), a collegiate government (*Junta Superior Gubernativa*) was installed but, after a short period of time, dictatorship became the predominant form of government. The dictator, Dr. Gaspar Rodriguez de Francia, ruled the country for a long period (from 1814–40). The Dr. Francia's government was responsible for the country's significant economic growth and defended Paraguay from its neighbors (Argentina and Brazil), which had expansionist intentions during this time. After Dr. Francia's death, Carlos Antonio López was elected as the first President of the Republic of Paraguay (1844). Carlos Antonio López maintained strong control of political power, promoting cultural, technological, and economic development of the country. After Carlos Antonio López's death, his son Francisco Solano López assumed the presidency of the country. During his time, Paraguay sustained a long, defensive, and devastating war against the "Triple Alliance" of Argentina, Brazil, and Uruguay (1865–70). As a result of this war, Paraguay lost almost half of its population, most of its resources, and an important part of its territory.

During the postwar period (1870–1954) the country was reorganized, and new political and social institutions were created. There was a liberal period where traditional political parties were founded; authorities approved the first National Constitution of the country (1870); presidential elections occurred; and the State created a Congress and a Judicial System. During this period, Paraguay faced another international war against Bolivia (1932–35) due to problems with territorial limits between these countries. In 1954, after a period of political instability, General Alfredo Stroessner, occupied the presidency in a military coup d'etat, and gradually controlled and shaped military and political power. With the support of the Colorado party, the army, and in the context of the Cold War and the Alliance for Progress ideology, Stroessner exercised a right wing dictatorship, the longest in the region.

On February 3, 1989, a coup led by General Andrés Rodríguez drove Alfredo Stroessner out of power and initiated the transition to democracy. During his transitional period, the policymaking process initially operated under the existing rules, but with new leadership. However, in 1992, a new

Constitution was adopted and several new governors were chosen in national elections. There have been important advances in terms of strengthening the democratic institutions, the development of citizenship, and respect for human rights. On the other hand, the country is still facing economic difficulties and high levels of inequity, which endanger the consolidation of democracy and social development.

THE DEVELOPMENT OF THE EDUCATION SECTOR

The Colonial Period

There are news reports and official records from the colonial period which refer to the first government efforts to institute an education system, which mainly benefited the sons of Spaniards and of the mixed-blood population that was taking shape in the new settlements in Paraguayan territory.

In 1556, the government of Domingo Martínez de Irala established a primary school that had two teachers and more than two thousand people in attendance. Another reference from the colonial period is a resolution by the *Cabildo* (town council) of Asunción in 1596, which stated that Lázaro López would assume responsibility for basic instruction and give classes in a house near the main church. Nevertheless, it was not until the second half of the eighteenth century that public education spread throughout the Paraguayan territory, although even then that level of instruction continued to be very basic.

During the last years of the colonial period, rural communities sprang up around country chapels and small urban centers. At the initiative of the inhabitants of these rural communities, teachers were nominated by the *Cabildo* and the bishop of the diocese. The level of education continued to be very basic in reading, writing, arithmetic, and rudimentary Christian doctrine. Instruction was reserved almost exclusively for the sons of Spanish and Creole families. By a royal decree on August 2, 1776, the San Carlos Royal College Seminary, the first institution of higher learning, was founded. This seminary remained in existence until 1823, when it was definitively closed by one of its former instructors, the dictator Dr. José G. Rodríguez de Francia.

The Catholic Church exercised considerable cultural and educational influence during the colonial period. Various religious orders worked to evangelize the population and introduce formal education. The contribution that Jesuits made to education was especially important. They took great interest in the study of indigenous languages and systemized the Guaraní language, codifying the grammatical rules that are accepted today. The most distinguished linguist of that time was Antonio Ruiz de Montoya, a priest and author of the book *Treasure of the Guaraní Language*, which was published in Spain in 1639. In addition to its work in the missions, the Company of Jesus maintained the College of Asunción founded in 1609 and seven other schools in the Province of Paraguay.

The Period of Independence

Beginning in 1811, the year in which Paraguay became independent from the Spanish crown, successive governments took an interest in the issue of public education. The first form of management in the area of education was collegial in nature, inasmuch as the *Junta Superior Gubernativa*, the governing council that was created at independence, took charge of promoting the training of teachers in reading, writing, and arithmetic.

In 1812, *the Junta Superior Gubernativa* began to carry out a radical reform, the liberalization and modernization of public instruction. The *Junta*'s main achievements in the field of education were: the Edict of January 6, 1812, which made reference to the importance of public education; the Edict of February 7, 1812, which approved instructions for schoolmasters (73 articles); and two printed volumes on rules for reading and writing.

Between 1814–40, the dominant figure in Paraguay was Dr. José G. Rodríguez de Francia, dictator for life. Throughout all of Dr. Francia's dictatorship, elementary education was promoted, and there were schoolmasters who gave elementary classes in settlements in the countryside. In 1828, secondary education was declared mandatory and education was the State's responsibility.[1] Dr. Francia's successors put greater effort into expanding primary education and restoring higher education. According to the report given by President Carlos Antonio López in his Message of 1857, 16,755 children were attending 408 elementary schools maintained by the State and parents. There were reports that in 1862, 435 schools were in operation with 24,524 students and approximately 70 teachers. With regard to secondary education, the National Congress of 1841 called for the creation of a high school, and to carry out this resolution, the government decreed the establishment of the Literary Academy.

During his stay in Europe, General Francisco Solano López, (son and future political heir of then President Carlos Antonio López), hired the Spanish journalist and writer Ildefonso Antonio Bermejo to teach and promote cultural activities in Paraguay. Bermejo founded a normal school and later, the Hall of Philosophy. As president of the republic, Carlos Antonio López personally presided over the first public exams held at the Hall of Philosophy, accompanied by the bishop, ministers, and the highest civil and military authorities. From that class, five distinguished students were given scholarships to study in Great Britain, some of whom returned to Paraguay in 1863. During Carlos Antonio López's government, fifty-six Paraguayan youths were sent to Europe to advance their knowledge, in accordance with a resolution approved by the National Congress in March 1844.

After the War of the Triple Alliance, the situation in Paraguay was desperate in every respect. Approximately 80 percent of the male population and a good part of the female population had perished in the difficult years from 1864–70. In the Constitution of 1870, it was stipulated that primary education was mandatory and that the government and the Congress would give preferential attention to education. Article 8 stated: "Primary education will be mandatory and the subject of Government's special attention, and the Congress will hear reports of the minister from this branch annually, in order to promote by all possible means the instruction of citizens."

Beginning in 1870, there were a number of elementary schools operating in the capital and in the interior that were private, and many of those were religious, such as the *Colegio de la Providencia*, founded in 1883 by the San Vicente sisters and the *Colegio Monseñor Lasagna*, run by the Salesian brothers. In 1874, the number of elementary schools reached 80 for boys and 25 for girls. The High Council on Education was created in 1887, to which the Superintendency of Public Education was added as an executive body, and the whole entity was transformed into the General Department of Schools in 1900. In 1890, there were 252 elementary schools in operation (173 public and 79 private) with a total of 15,569 students—10,057 boys and 5,512 girls.

In 1872, the National College (a high school) opened; in 1882, the School of Law was established; and in 1889, the national University of Asunción was created. A few years later, normal schools were opened for teaching personnel training. Twenty teacher training schools were inaugurated: three in the capital and the remaining seventeen in the most important settlements and towns.

Education during 1900–1935

This period was characterized by sustained growth in enrollments and a better organization of the education system. During this time important contributions were also made by various educators, such as Ramón Indalecio Cardozo, who introduced new perspectives in the field of pedagogy. The system of training teachers in special schools in which they earned degrees, or which recognized training obtained elsewhere, began to displace the earlier system of one-room schools supervised by improvised tutors with no pedagogical training. Thus, trained teaching personnel began to graduate from the normal schools that were being opened throughout the country.

In 1901, there were 25,137 students enrolled in the schools throughout the Republic. In 1910, there were 52,000 and in 1930, 108,222. The National Education Council and the Law on Mandatory Education of 1909 had a positive impact on this process. At the same time, the new system of teacher training was gradually spreading to the interior, and by 1920, there were normal schools in Villarica, Pilar, Concepción, Encarnación, Barrero Grande, and San Juan Bautista de las Misiones. All of these schools had one or two complete primary school sections attached to them; these functioned as a site for practice-based instruction. "Model lessons" were taught by the most capable teachers. The organization of teaching methodology used in primary education, which had been established in 1896, was reformed in 1915 and 1922. In 1992, the procedures for teacher training were also revised.

Education Reforms of the Twentieth Century

Beginning in the twentieth century, various reforms reshaped education in Paraguay. There were partial reforms, which affected education to some extent (the reforms of 1904 and 1931) and other more integrated ones which restructured the whole national education system (the reforms of 1924, 1957, and 1973).

Reform of 1904

In December 1904, the Franco Plan went into effect. This plan outlined a six-year Study Plan for the High School Degree, which was intended to teach the student what a "well educated and cultured man should know" and emphasized quality above quantity of knowledge.

In 1909, the Law on Mandatory Education was passed, which established that children from ages seven to fourteen were to receive primary education in state-run or private schools, or in their own homes. In addition, public leaders were required to take an annual census of school-aged children in their jurisdictions and pass on to the school authorities data for their possible attention.

Reform of 1924

The reform carried out in 1924 was the work of Prof. Ramón Indalecio Cardozo, who formulated the first integrated reform of basic and normal education according to the criteria of functional teaching based on basic socioeconomic activities, and on the ideals of liberty, progress, rectitude, and the common good. The basic cycle was reduced to six years of schooling with five grades: lower first, upper first, second, third, and fourth and fifth, with emphasis on basic subjects, crafts, agricultural skills, livestock-raising, and homemaking.

Reform of 1957

The Reform of 1957 introduced important changes in the structure and organization of the country's education system, based on the advice of specialists from UNESCO and the American Cooperative Education Service. The education system proposed was organized according to the 6-3-3 sequence: six primary grades, three basic courses, and three diversified courses leading to a bachelor's degree.

The Reform of 1957 included the development of programs and study plans for all levels of formal education. Regarding teacher training, a study plan was approved for normal schools throughout the country, and rural and urban normal schools were created. Through an agreement between the governments of Paraguay and the United States, the headquarters of the Experimental Rural School was created in the city of San Lorenzo. This school became a pilot institution that provided five years of professional training and led to a rural teacher diploma.

The Reform of 1973

The Reform of 1973 (Educational Innovations) was the culmination of a process which began with the promulgation of the National Constitution of 1967, and was followed by an assessment of the education system carried out in 1968, the First National Seminar on Education Development held in 1970, the formation of a commission charged with drawing up the education innovations project in 1971, and the creation of the Technical Team for Curriculum and Education Administration. Finally, in 1973 the new plan and its corresponding programs were gradually introduced at the primary level in some institutions around the country.

Among the positive aspects of this reform were:

- It generated great national interest and debate on education issues.
- A great effort was made to update and improve the formal education system and to extend the opportunity to participate in an organized school system to the whole country.
- Innovative pedagogical arrangements were introduced in an adequate way in some institutions.
- Diversified bachelor's degree programs were created.
- Emphasis was placed on teacher training.
- Evaluations of the program were carried out, and revisions and adjustments were made.
- New technologies were incorporated.

Among the negative aspects were:

- The program did not escape the government's ideological influence and political practices.
- The pedagogical model, with its technological and hierarchical orientation, had its limitations.
- No analysis was made of the local culture prior to developing programs of study.
- The reform was carried out in a hierarchical, vertical, and centralized way with little participation by the different sectors of society.

The reform of 1973 remained in effect until the end Alfredo Stroessner's government (1989) and was revised at the beginning of the democratic transition. The sociologist Domingo Rivarola points out that these latter reforms in 1957 and 1973 were predicated on the political and ideological situation that dominated the country at the time. Given its importance as a tool for ideological indoctrination, education was a matter of concern to the government and kept under its control. Thus, notwithstanding the pedagogical and educational innovations they enunciated, these reforms were limited by internal controls, propaganda to legitimize the regime, and the fear of repression.

Bilingual Spanish-Guaraní Education: A Central Aspect of Formal Education in Paraguay

Paraguay is a bilingual country, in which the majority of the population uses the Guaraní language. According to data from the 2002 National Census, the language usually spoken in the great majority of homes is Guaraní (59 percent) followed by Spanish (36 percent), and other languages that together represent 5 percent. Nevertheless, in Paraguay, as in other Latin American countries, the official language policy was Hispanization, which was primarily carried out through the education system. The linguist Bartomeu Melià mentions the following chronicle written in 1796 by the Governor Lázaro de Rivera, which is a clear expression of this policy during the colonial period:

At the time of the expulsion of the Jesuits, and in accordance with the law, primary schools were established in the towns with the important objective of teaching the natives Christian doctrine and the Spanish language, and how to read, write and count. But what have we achieved in 28 years of labor? Nothing more than the loss of more than one hundred thousand pesos that have gone to endow some useless, if not harmful, schoolmasters. The Indians continue in absolute ignorance of our language, and since it is impossible to explain the eternal truths of our religion well in their language, which is known as Guaraní, the spiritual well-being of these unfortunate people is enveloped in the shadows of ignorance and, sometimes, error.

This policy of Hispanization in education continued from the time of independence practically up until the present day. The historian Juan Speratti came across an interesting story about the education provided in the school of Master Quintana at the time of Carlos Antonio López, as told by Juan Crisóstomo Centurión in his *Memoirs*:

It was prohibited to speak in Guaraní during classroom hours, and in order to make this prohibition effective, there had been distributed to the citizens or supervisors a number of bronze rings which they would hand out to the first one they caught conversing in Guaraní. This person would pass them to the next who was discovered in the same error, and so it continued throughout the week until Saturday, when the presentation of these rings was requested, and each person who had a ring, being one who had entered into crime, received the punishment of five lashes to the shoulders from his schoolmates.

It is difficult to explain why the Guaraní language not only survived but grew stronger. Perhaps one of the main factors was the influence of the Jesuit missions, where Guaraní was used as the language of instruction and where the first texts in this language were written.

During the last thirty years, Guaraní has been incorporated into the official program of study. As part of the education reform of 1973, Guaraní was introduced as a subject in all teaching institutions in the country. In addition, in recognition of the fact that language is an important factor in scholastic success, the Ministry of Education implemented an experimental program of bilingual education in some schools in 1978. Aimed at monolingual Guaraní-speaking children, the program is based on a *transition* model in which the child gradually passes from being monolingual and Guaraní-speaking to bilingual Guaraní/Spanish-speaking. However, there is no research or reports available that might permit an evaluation of this experiment in bilingual education.

The Program of Bilingual Education started to go into effect in 1994, along with the introduction of the curricular reform in the first grade. Current bilingual education is understood as a planned process of teaching in two languages, meaning that bilingual education is not limited to teaching both languages (languages taught) but implies the use of both languages as vehicles for teaching other areas of knowledge (languages of instruction). The native language (L1) is understood as the one in which the child has greater oral competency upon entering school, while the second language (L2) is the one in which the child has less competency.

The model of bilingual education that is being implemented today is one of *maintenance*; that is, its objective is to train coordinated bilingual individuals, with high levels of proficiency in both Guaraní and Spanish. This differs from previous approaches in which a *transition* bilingual model was used. This program aims to produce coordinated bilingual students by the end of primary school. Beyond that, its objective is to reach secondary education (humanities and technical) and the tertiary, or university, level.

The Current Situation in the Education System

In 1994, the Education Reform began in the first grade of Basic School Education (EEB) and thereafter it was gradually extended to higher grades, which are structured in three cycles of three years each to meet the educational requirements of boys and girls of ages six to fourteen. In 2002, the reform reached the last year of secondary school, which serves fifteen- to seventeen-year-olds.

Education reform has been a central theme in Paraguay's democratization agenda since the beginning of the post-authoritarian period in 1989. Despite the political changes that have occurred since that time, and some ups and downs in the education area, education reform has been one of the government initiatives with the greatest continuity during this period.

Education reform during this period has been the result of a process which included the establishment in 1990 of a National Commission for Reform whose mandate was to draw up an integrated reform of the Paraguayan education system based on a comprehensive analysis of the existing system and proposals to overcome its deficiencies (CARE, 1992). Thereafter, the Commission set up the Advisory Board for Education Reform (CARE), which in turn set out the objectives of the Education Reform and submitted them for national consultation during 1992 and 1993 (MEC 1995). As part of the national consultation, nineteen regional congresses and two national congresses were held, one on primary education (December 1992) and the other on secondary education (July 1993). The various sectors involved in education participated in these congresses.

These consultations showed that the need for reform was widely recognized among the different sectors involved in education. In particular, it was recognized that the existing education model had serious deficiencies and needed to be adapted to the democratic transition that the country was experiencing. It was also proposed that the national education reform take account of the linguistic and cultural characteristics of Paraguay's multicultural society, as well as the new proposals for political and economic integration with other countries in the region. In the documents that came out of the work of CARE, education reform was defined as a permanent, participatory, and open process that should involve all sectors of society.

Reform began with the design of programs for primary and secondary school education, based on the policy directions outlined by CARE and the national consultations. The Education Reform is a process which continues up until the present with the support of international aid organizations and a consensus among government authorities and the public on its basic principles.

Basic Principles of Education Reform

Education reform is a permanent, participatory, and open process which involves all the spheres of official management, institutions, and related groups—from the family and the neighborhood to the municipality and the State. The reform proposes a change in the education system from which other social and cultural changes are expected to ensue. The reform seeks to make fully effective the concept of the education community as a system which involves and commits everyone in the process of change.

With regard to the goals of Paraguayan education, the reform seeks to train girls and boys who, by developing their own personalities, achieve sufficient human maturity to be able to relate to others and to God in a comprehending, natural way and in accordance with the principles and values on which society is based.

By guaranteeing equal opportunities, education seeks to have boys and girls, at different levels, and according to their individual potential, develop professional qualifications so that through their work can contribute to improvements in the standard and quality of life of all of the inhabitants of the country. The reform also mentions the need to affirm the identity of the Paraguayan nation and its cultures, as well as the need for understanding, the ability to live together, and solidarity among nations.

The document *The Education Challenge: A Proposal for Dialogue on Educational Opportunities in Paraguay* outlines a strategic plan based on two main objectives: strengthening the ability to live together in a democratic society and increasing the competitiveness of the Paraguayan labor force to reduce poverty. To achieve these objectives, it sets out five proposals:

1. Promote the participation of Paraguayan society in the development of a collaborative plan for the Education Reform.
2. Reinforce social integration, reduce poverty, and promote effective general education.
3. Increase the productivity of human resources in general.
4. Reduce the misallocations in the labor market caused by MERCOSUR.[2]
5. Promote creativity, innovation, and personal initiative.

The legal framework for education is set out in Articles 73–80, and 85 of the National Constitution and includes the General Law on Education, the Code on Children and Adolescents, and the Statute on Educators. In Article 73, the National Constitution establishes "that every person has the right to an integrated and permanent education and the elimination of discriminatory educational content. In addition, the eradication of illiteracy and the promotion of job training are two permanent objectives of the educational system."

The General Law on Education (1998) assigns education a privileged role in consolidating democracy, reducing indices of poverty and marginalization, and opening new opportunities for all of the inhabitants of the country. In addition, it explicitly ensures equal opportunity in obtaining the benefits of culture and education and eliminates all obstacles to working as a teacher. At the same time, it establishes the general principles of education.

The Coverage, Quality, and Equality of Education in Paraguay

With regard to the *coverage of education*, the first and second cycles of basic education (EEB), which correspond to the first through the sixth grades, has had universal coverage since the 1990s. The expansion of coverage has taken place in the third cycle of the EEB (seventh to ninth grades), as a result of the incorporation of this cycle in free and mandatory education, and at the preschool level.

The fact that the third cycle is mandatory has meant that sectors of the population who previously did not attend school at this level, either for reasons of supply (that is, the lack of institutions) especially in rural areas or because of the cost implied in continuing their studies, now have access to this level of education and are continuing their studies.

According to official data from the Department of Educational and Cultural Planning of the Ministry of Education, the different levels in the education system have the following net enrollment rates:[3]

- 2 percent of the population of five-year-olds is enrolled in preschool.
- 97 percent of six- to eleven-year-olds are enrolled in the first and second cycles of the EEB.

- 54 percent of twelve- to fourteen-year-olds are enrolled in the third cycle of the EEB.
- 36 percent of sixteen- to eighteen-year-olds are enrolled in secondary school.

According to the most recent National Census, the rate of illiteracy among the population aged fifteen or older is 7.1 percent.

As far as the *quality of education* is concerned, data from the National Evaluation System for the Education Process indicate that results on national tests at the different cycles of education continue to be low. By such measures, the results obtained by students in the third grade on tests given in 2001 averaged less than 60 percent, while test results for sixth graders in 1997 averaged less than 50 percent. At the same time, a study of education in Latin America placed Paraguay among the countries with slightly lower results than the regional average.

The quality of teacher training institutes is also low. The majority of teacher trainers lack both academic knowledge in their areas and pedagogical skills. Measures of academic performance in basic areas carried out in the Institutes for Teacher Training indicate that the students who are finishing their teacher-training year have low performance, both in their minimal conceptual grasp of basic subjects and in their knowledge of teaching methodologies.

As far as the *efficiency of the education system* is concerned, there continue to be high rates of grade repetition, especially in the first cycle of the EEB (11 percent). In first grade, repetition is 15 percent. The highest rate of school drop out occurs in the third cycle of the EEB (7.8 percent) and in high school (12.7 percent). The principal reason that students drop out of school is economic (57 percent).

With regard to the *equity of the education system*, education policies have not had a significant impact in reversing the disadvantages and educational inequality facing some social sectors (for example, *campesinos*, the urban poor, women, and indigenous people). Given this situation, the Ministry of Education is implementing programs to meet the educational needs of these groups. However, there is no data as yet to evaluate the impact of these programs.

As for education in rural areas, there is still a gap in coverage, especially in the third cycle of primary school, where net enrollment is 30 percent in rural areas versus 70 percent in urban areas. Likewise, there is a large gap between secondary school enrollment rates, with 12 percent and 49 percent enrollment in rural and urban areas, respectively. There are also gaps in quality, since students in rural areas show lower academic achievement than their peers in urban areas, and in efficiency, since there are higher rates of grade repetition and drop out in rural areas than in urban areas, irrespective of grade level and cycle. One program aimed at improving the quality of rural schools is *Escuela Viva Heko-katuva*, which operates in 1,000 high-risk rural schools and 150 schools in marginal urban areas.

A bilingual education policy (mentioned above) is currently being implemented. This program has received favorable evaluations but requires more follow-up. At the same time, actions with broader scope should be undertaken, since the majority of children, especially those in rural areas, enter school speaking mainly Guaraní but have to learn to read and write in Spanish. This factor would partly explain the high levels of grade repetition in the first cycle of primary education in rural areas.

With respect to gender, the data indicate that there are no differences between boys and girls insofar as their enrollment and academic performance are concerned. Nevertheless, schools still promote the images and values of a patriarchal society. The Ministry of Education, along with the Secretariat for Women, promoted the creation of the Program on Equality of Opportunity and Results for Women in Education. This program has carried out teacher training and participated in the development of school textbooks.

Another area of great importance in promoting greater equity and equality of opportunities in education is the strengthening of preschool and early childhood education. Traditionally, preschool education in Paraguay has been limited to the middle and upper economic classes living in urban areas. In recent years, the Ministry of Education has given great impetus to increasing the coverage of preschool education, and indeed, this level of education has seen the greatest increase in enrollments. It has also developed a National Plan for Early Childhood Education, and sizeable investments have been made in its implementation. Nevertheless, programs for early childhood education are still lacking, especially for the first years of life. In addition, data is needed on the quality of the preschool education currently provided throughout the country.

Education of indigenous people is another area that requires greater attention given their cultural and linguistic diversity, which requires different educational approaches. In addition, the living conditions in indigenous communities are characterized by poverty and basic services are inadequate. The Ministry of Education currently has some initiatives underway on behalf of the indigenous population, which seek to increase the coverage of these populations and, at the same time, promote educational experiences that incorporate the languages and cultures of the different indigenous groups.

FINAL CONSIDERATIONS

The history of education in Paraguay shows that efforts have been made since the colonial period to create and sustain an education system. Nevertheless, education during the colonial period and the first years of independence was limited to basic instruction. During the colonial period, the most significant action was the educational and cultural work of the religious orders, especially the Franciscans and the Jesuits. The Jesuits used the indigenous languages and systematized the grammatical rules of Guaraní in their missions, which is probably one of the main reasons why the language has remained.

After independence, the *Junta Superior Gubernativa* and the National Congresses, such as the ones in 1841 (after the Dr. Francia's dictatorship) and 1870 (at the end of the War of the Triple Alliance), promulgated laws and defined actions to promote basic education. The work of President Carlos Antonio López was also very important in promoting higher education among youth who subsequently provided distinguished service both during and after the war.

From 1900 to 1935, the education system grew and became more organized and institutionalized, thanks to the creation of the National Education Board and the Law on Mandatory Education of 1909. From 1900 on, there were a number of education reforms in Paraguay. Various educators contributed to these reforms to build an education model based on the trends and breakthroughs in pedagogy and the sciences related to education. One of the main thinkers and administrators of Paraguayan education during this period was Professor Ramón Indalecio Cardozo, the principal author of the Reform of 1924.

The reforms of 1957 and 1973 brought important innovations in the structure of the education system, the program of studies, and teacher training. Nevertheless, these reforms were limited by the context in which they were carried out: a dictatorial regime which considered education an ideological tool and an instrument for indoctrination.

With the fall of General Stroessner's dictatorship and the beginning of democratic transition, various social sectors thought it necessary to carry out a profound transformation of the education system. This transformation began with education reform.

Important advances have been made in the framework of this reform, such as the creation of the Advisory Board on Education Reform, which has brought together important figures in Paraguayan culture and education, promoted the analysis of education issues, and generated the theoretical basis for education policies. In addition, the Ministry of Education has promoted various programs in response to specific national educational challenges. These programs are being implemented with the support of various international organizations and the participation of government and nongovernmental sectors.

The results indicate that there has been increased coverage by the education system and increased access of certain social groups that previously had been excluded from formal education. There have also been advances in the organization of the Ministry of Education and in the collection of data for evaluating the state of education in the country (Department of Planning and Statistics, National System for the Evaluation of Educational Progress).

Nevertheless, advances are still needed with regard to the quality of education, since, on average, students do not achieve the expected educational results. At the same time, much remains to be done to redress the education inequality facing certain social groups, such as people who live in rural areas, people whose primary language is Guaraní, and indigenous people.

A DAY IN THE LIFE

Juanita is an eight-year-old girl who resides in a poor urban community in Asunción. She lives with her mother, her grandmother, two sisters, and one brother. Juanita speaks Guaraní and Spanish. With her mother and grandmother, she usually uses Guaraní, and with her sisters and classmates, speaks in Spanish. Her mother and grandmother work at the market selling fruits and Juanita usually helps them at the market and with house chores—taking care of her smaller sisters and brother, cleaning the small house, and preparing meals.

Juanita goes to a public school in Asunción. She is in the third grade. She went to preschool and the first grade in the same school, near her house. Most of the children in her community go to this school.

Juanita wakes up at 6:00 AM and gets ready for school. She also prepares breakfast for her sisters: milk with *cocido* (infusion of yerba mate), and a piece of bread. She walks to school with her brother, who is in the first grade. Classes start at 7:00.

At 7:00 AM, a bell rings. All the students, from different grades stand in line in the yard of the school. The director announces some messages: she remembers the day of independence and speaks of what happened in May 1811. Afterwards, Juanita and her classmates go into the classroom. The class is part of an old building. The furniture is in bad condition and each student shares a desk with another classmate. All the desks are lined up to face the front of the room where there is a large blackboard. On the wall, there are some maps of Paraguay, the alphabet, and some religious images. In Juanita's classroom, there are thirty students and one teacher, Prof. Graciela.

The teacher is already inside the classroom. When everybody is at their desks, she begins roll call. After that, Prof. Graciela begins natural science class in Spanish. She refers to the invertebrate animals and dictates a definition, a classification of insects, and some morphological characteristics. All the students copy in their workbooks in silence. When the teacher finishes the dictation, she tells the students that they must memorize this text for the exam. Prof. Graciela writes questions on the blackboard and each student must find the answer in the text they copied and write it in their workbooks.

At 9:00 AM, the bell rings and all students go to the yard for a recess. Most of the boys play soccer. Girls usually stay in groups talking. Juanita looks for her brother and gives him an *empanada* (a fried dough of flour stuffed with meat) that she bought from the *cantina* (snack bar). At 9:20, the bell rings and all the students run to their rooms. When everybody is in their place, the class continues. The teacher starts mathematics class. First, they practice multiplication tables for twos, threes, and fours. Everybody repeats in unison two by one, two; two by two, four; two by three, six. After finishing, Prof. Graciela asks some students to walk in front of the class and repeat the multiplication table. Juanita stands and repeats the table of threes correctly and Prof. Graciela congratulates her.

The teacher writes some multiplication exercises on the blackboard and each student has to answer in silence in their workbooks. Some boys who sit in the back of the class make some jokes and Prof. Graciela warns them to be quiet or they must leave the class. The teacher writes some extra exercises for homework and says that everybody must bring the answers to school the following day.

At 11:00 AM, the bell rings and the students place all of their books and materials on their back and stand near their desk. They say goodbye and leave the class. When Juanita arrives home, she helps her grandmother prepare a meal (rice with meat). After finishing lunch, she cleans everything and has a siesta with her sisters and brother. During the afternoon, Juanita helps her mother at the market (selling fruits) and when she returns in the evening, tries to do her homework but she is very tired and wants to watch her favorite TV program at Lucia's house (her neighbor).

TIMELINE

1537   The Fort of Nuestra Señora de la Asunción (actual city of Asunción, capital of Paraguay) was founded by Juan de Salazar y Espinoza.

1556   Domingo Martínez de Irala, first Governor of Paraguay, established a primary school which had two teachers and more than two thousand people in attendance.

1693   The most distinguished linguist of the day, Antonio Ruiz de Montoya, published *Treasure of the Guaraní Language*, in Spain.

1776   The San Carlos Royal College Seminary, the first institution of higher learning, was founded by a royal decree. This seminary remained in existence until 1823.

1811   Paraguay became independent from Spain.

1812   The *Junta Superior Gubernativa* promulgated the edict which approved instructions for schoolmasters and two printed volumes on rules for reading and writing.

1828   During the dictatorship of *Gaspar Rodríguez de Francia*, primary education was declared mandatory and education was a responsibility of the State.

1841   The National Congress called for the creation of a secondary school; to carry out this resolution, the government decreed the establishment of the Literary Academy.

1870   End of the War of the Triple Alliance: the situation in the country was desperate in every respect. Approximately 80 percent of the male population and a good part of the female population had perished in the difficult years, 1864–70.
       First National Constitution of the country.
       There were a number of elementary schools operating in the capital and the interior of the country that were private, and many of those were religious, such as the *Colegio de la Providencia*, founded in 1883 by the Vicente sisters, and the *Colegio Monseñor Lasagna*, run by the Salesian brothers.

1889   The National University of Asunción was created.

1904   First education reform: This reform outlined a six-year Study Plan for the Bachelor's Degree, which was intended to teach the student what "a cultured man should know" and emphasized quality above quantity of knowledge.

1909   The Law on Mandatory Education was passed, which established that children from ages seven to fourteen were to receive primary education in state-run or private schools, or in their own homes. Additionally, public leaders were required to take an annual census of school-aged children in their jurisdictions and pass the data on to the school authorities for their possible attention.

1924   Education reform was carried out by Ramón Indalecio Cardozo, who formulated the first integrated reform of basic and normal education according to the criteria of functional teaching based on basic socioeconomic activities, and on the ideals of liberty, progress, rectitude, and the common good.

1957   The Education Reform introduces important changes in the structure and organization of the education system, based on the advice of specialists from UNESCO and the American Cooperative Education Service. The education system proposed was organized according to the 6-3-3 sequence: six primary grades, three basic courses, and three diversified courses leading to a bachelor's degree.

1973   A new education reform (Educational Innovations), that was the culmination of a process which began with the promulgation of the National Constitution of 1967, and its corresponding programs were gradually introduced at the primary level in some institutions around the country.

1989   The fall of General Alfredo Stroessner's dictatorship and the beginning of democratic transition.

1994   Education Reform began in the first grade of Basic School Education and thereafter it was gradually extended to higher grades, which are structured in three cycles of three years, each to meet the educational requirements of boys and girls of ages six to fourteen. The Program of Bilingual Education went into effect, along with the introduction of the curricular reform in the first grade.

1998   The General Law on Education was approved. This law assigns education a privileged role in consolidating democracy, reducing poverty and marginalization, and opening new opportunities for all of the residents of the country.

2002   Education reform reached the last year of secondary school.

NOTES

I would like to express my gratitude to José Molinas for his support for the preparation of this chapter. I am also grateful for the contributions of Carolina Acosta, Eleonora Cebotarev, and Liz Hansen.

1. Juan Speratti documents the debate among historians and intellectuals concerning Dr. Francia's contibution to education. Many believe that what had been achieved in the field of education up until that time, especially by the *Junta Superior Gubernativa*, was lost during the dictatorship of Dr. Francia. Further, many consider that all initiatives to develop institutions of higher learning were blocked due to Dr. Francia's confrontations with the Catholic Church, which had had a leading role in education and Paraguayan culture since colonial times. Nevertheless, other authors see Dr. Francia as a great promoter of elementary education throughout the country. What is certain is that during this period formal education was limited to basic instruction.

2. The *Mercado Común del Sur* or MERCOSUR is a comercial block integrated by Argentina, Brasil, Paraguay, and Uruguay.

3. The net enrollment rate is the percentage of the population in the specified age group that is enrolled at the level specified for that age group.

BIBLIOGRAPHY

Books

Acosta González, C. 1996. "Reforma Educacional de 1957." In *Las raíces de la educación Paraguaya*. Edited by Melquiades Alonso, 65–74. Aregua: Gobernación del Departamento Central.

Alonso, M., D.C. Debulpaep, E. Delgado, R. Elías, and V. Kanonnikoff. 2002. *Diseño de la escuela comunitaria*. Asunción: A.M.A.R.

Cadogan, M. 1996. "Innovaciones educacionales." In *Las raíces de la educación Paraguaya*. Edited by Melquiades Alonso, 75–93. Aregua: Gobernación del Departamento Central.

Centro Paraguayo de Estudios Sociológicos (CPES). 1998. *Estudio sobre bilingüismo en el marco de la reforma educativa*. Asunción: Ministerio de Educación y Cultura (MEC), Programa de Mejoramiento de la Calidad de la Educación Secundaria (MECES).

Consejo Asesor de la Reforma Educativa (CARE). 1992. *Reforma educativa, compromiso de todos*. Asunción: Ministerio de Educación y Cultura (MEC).

Consejo Asesor de la Reforma Educativa (CARE). 1996. *El Desafío Educativo: Una propuesta para el diálogo sobre las oportunidades educativas en el Paraguay*. Asunción: Ministerio de Educación y Cultura (MEC).

Consejo Asesor de la Reforma Educativa (CARE). 1996b. *Paraguay 2020: Enfrentemos juntos el desafío educativo, plan estratégico de la reforma educativa*. Asunción: Ministerio de Educación y Cultura (MEC).

Consejo Asesor de la Reforma Educativa (CARE). 1998. *Avances de la reforma educativa*. Asunción: Ministerio de Educación y Cultura (MEC).

Consejo Nacional de Educación y Cultura (CONEC). 2002. *Situación de la educación en el Paraguay*. Asunción: CONEC.

Dirección General de Estadística, Encuestas y Censos (DGEEC). 2002. *Censo indígena 2002*. Asunción: DGEEC.

Dirección General de Estadística, Encuestas y Censos (DGEEC). 2002b. *Encuesta integrada de hogares 2000–01*. Asunción: DGEEC.

Dirección General de Planificación Educativa y Cultura (DGPEC). 2000. *Anuarios estadísticos 1980–2001*. Asunción: Ministerio de Educación y Cultura (MEC).

Dirección General de Estadística, Encuestas y Censos (DGEEC). 2003. *Principales resultados del censo 2002. Vivienda y población*. Asunción: DGEEC.

Dirección General de Planificación Educativa y Cultura (DGPEC). 2003. *Situación de la educación en Paraguay*. Asunción: Ministerio de Educación y Cultura (MEC).

Dirección General de Planificación Educativa y Cultura (DGPEC). 2004. *Análisis cuantitativo de la evolución educativa 1990–2001*. Asunción: Ministerio de Educación y Cultura (MEC).

Dirección General de Planificación Educativa y Cultura (DGPEC). 2005. *Situación de la educación en Paraguay*. Asunción, Ministerio de Educación y Cultura (MEC).

Melià, B. 1992. *La lengua guaraní del Paraguay: Historia, sociedad y literatura*. Madrid: MAPFRE.

Melià, B. 1996. "Un sistema paraguayo de educación: el guaraní." In *Las raíces de la educación Paraguaya*. Edited by Melquiades Alonso. Aregua, 15–25. Aregua: Gobernación del Departamento Central.

Ministerio de Educación y Cultura. 2000. *Educación para todos, evaluación año 2000.* Asunción: Ministerio de Educación y Cultura (MEC).

Molinas, J. 2002. "Los determinantes del rendimiento educativo en América Latina y el Paraguay." In *Las reformas educativas en acción: Eficiencia, equidad y calidad en el sistema educativo de la República Dominicana y América Latina.* Edited by A. Medina, 61–91. Santo Domingo: Banco Interamericano de Desarrollo (BID)-Instituto Interamericano para el Desarrollo Social (INDES)-Instituto Tecnológico de Santo Domingo (INTEC).

Molinas, J., R. Elías, and M. Vera. 2004. *Estudio y análisis del sector educativo en Paraguay.* Asunción: Instituto Desarrollo and Japan International Cooperation Agency (JICA).

Oficina Regional de Educación para América Latina y el Caribe (OREALC). 1998. *Primer estudio internacional comparativo sobre lenguaje, matemáticas y factores asociados en tercero y cuarto grado. Laboratorio Latinoamericano de evaluación de la calidad de la educación.* Santiago: UNESCO.

Pangrazio, M.A. 2005. *Las constituciones del Paraguay.* Asunción: Intercontinental Editora.

Quintana de Hórak, C. (1996). *La educación escolar en el Paraguay: Apuntes para una historia.* Asunción: Serie Educación (CEPAG, Sumando, Fundación en Alianza).

Sistema Nacional de Evaluación del Proceso Educativo (SNEPE). 2001. *Informe de las pruebas nacionales.* Asunción: Ministerio de Educación y Cultura (MEC).

Sottoli, S. and R. Elías. 2001. *Mejorando la educación de las niñas en Paraguay.* Asunción: UNICEF.

Speratti, J. 1996. *Historia de la educación en Paraguay 1812–1932.* Asunción: Biblioteca de Estudios Paraguayos.

Velázquez, E. 1999. *Breve historia cultural de Paraguay.* 12th ed. Asunción: Universidad Católica Nuestra Señora de la Asunción.

Periodicals

Elías, R. "Fundamentos de la educación bilingüe y sus implicancias en la práctica docente." *Revista UMBRAL* 7 (2001). REDUC: www.reduc.cl.

Rivarola, D. "La reforma educativa en el Paraguay." *Serie políticas sociales* 4 (2000). Santiago: CEPAL.

Web Sites

Dirección General de Estadística, Encuestas y Censos: www.dgeec.gov.py.

Ministerio de Educación y Cultura: http://www.mec.gov.py/.

Música paraguaya: www.musicaparaguaya.org.py.

Paraguay (review of the country history, politics leaders, and international organizations and treaties): www.worldstatesmen.org/Paraguay.html.

Presidencia de la República de Paraguay: www.presidencia.gov.py.

Republic of Paraguay, Political Constitution of 1992: http://pdba.georgetown.edu/Constitutions/Paraguay/para1992.html.

Seretaría Nacional de Turismo: http://www.senatur.gov.py.

Chapter 13

SCHOOLING IN PERU

María Balarin

INTRODUCTION

The development of schooling in Peru is closely related to the country's history, particularly to its colonial past and post-colonial state development efforts. What is now the Peruvian territory is well known for having been the center of the Inca Empire, one of the most important pre-Columbian cultures in the American continent, which extended to large parts of what are now Bolivia, Ecuador, Chile, and Argentina. But even before this, what is now known as Peru was the stage for the development of several pre-Inca cultures, some of which were conquered by the Incas, and which included, among others, the Moches, whose importance is somewhat less known but often compared to that of the Mexican Mayas. Beginning approximately during the twelfth century AD, the Inca Empire lasted until the time of the Spanish conquest and later colonization, which started in the sixteenth century AD. Colonial rule would last until 1924.

Education, in more or less formal ways, was already existent during the Inca Empire, but with the advent of colonization, some more explicit educational aims appeared in relation to the spread of the Spanish language, Catholic religion values, and submission to Spanish rule. The education model in the colonies, however, was explicitly set to maintain colonial domination and thus was highly exclusive, particularly of the local population. While independence meant the establishment of important changes, it was a process largely led by Spanish descendent elites, and thus, for a long time, did not entail radical changes in the direction of a more egalitarian social and political organization. Educational developments were largely functional to the prevalent exclusionary social practices and often helped maintain the existing social divisions.

The early years of the Republic were marked by permanent turmoil and the succession of various military leaders in power. While some agreement was reached at the end of the nineteenth century, the country long maintained its agrarian economic base and a considerably feudal-like form of social organization. Several attempts to change this took place in the early 1900s, but it was not until the later half of that century that serious modifications began to take place in the country's social and economic structure. Led by demographic changes first, and then by some only partially successful state-led policies, the country moved along towards the development of a somewhat more modern economy. Social changes, however, did not follow, and strong levels of inequality as well as considerable barriers to social mobility soon led to an outburst of political violence that jeopardized the country's stability during most of the 1980s. The decade following this saw the rise of a government which managed to stop terrorist violence and gave way to a series of neo-liberal economic reforms under the auspices of international organizations such as the World Bank and the International Monetary Fund. While the face of the country has changed radically in the past three decades, the historical problems of inequality and exclusion still prevail, and are undeniably underwritten by educational developments.

It is in this sense that the history of education in Peru can be said to have been dominated by contradictory dynamics. On one hand, increasing educational expansion, especially during the second half of the twentieth century, has been associated with an extension of social opportunities. On the other hand, the education system, since its inception, has been linked to exclusionary dynamics that have often curtailed the possibilities of personal and social advancement through education. Schools have thus played a paradoxical role. While being associated with the spread of knowledge and therefore of opportunities, they have, at the same time, contributed to exclude vast majorities of the population. The exclusions that operated through the education system, first by limiting access and more recently by providing an education that is highly deficient in quality, are undeniable. However, it is also patent that education has helped to open up opportunities for all. The following pages will offer an analysis of the historical development of the Peruvian education system with an emphasis on these contradictory dynamics and on the changes that education has been related to.

EDUCATION BEFORE AND DURING COLONIAL TIMES

Although the idea of schooling is often associated to the establishment of massive education systems, and thus with the rise of the modern nation state, it is clear that other forms of educational activity, often formal as well, existed before the latter. In the case of Peru, formal education dates back at least to the time of the Incas. The expansion of the Inca Empire is known to have been based on a collective form of organization that was closely dependent on the spread of cultural and political values: a common language among the peoples of the empire, a (coerced) disposition to submit to the authoritarian power of the Inca and to participate in the established forms of communal work. The Inca Empire, then, had an explicitly educational mission (see Valcárcel 1961, 1975).

The latter became particularly explicit during the time of Inca Roca, who, initiating a new dynasty embarked on a reorganization of the empire that included a specific educational dimension. Among his actions was the creation of the Yachaywasis, a form of school aimed at educating the nobility and the higher castes of the empire. The famous *amautas* (the Quechua word for sage or teacher) were in charge of teaching—particularly in relation to the art of government, war, religion, language, and the use of *quipus*.[1]

Although the Inca Empire had an implicit educational mission, the elitist nature of its more formal education system was evident. Evangelina Antay, a Peruvian teacher writing in the beginning of the twentieth century, recalls that according to Inca Roca, "It was not convenient for the children of common people to learn the sciences, which belong only to noblemen, lest they become arrogant and bring turmoil to the Empire" (Antay 1930, 106). This situation changed to some extent during the times of Inca Pachacutec, who, apart from considerably expanding the empire through massive conquests, extended educational activities to the "inferior" castes (see Valcárcel 1975).

Teaching in Incan times was mainly carried out orally—as they did not have a written form of language—and it was associated with the practical aims of the empire, such as those related to the different areas of economic activity. As Valcárcel (1975) suggests, the individual was first educated to "serve the collective" (as a political subject, as a warrior, as a religious person, etc.), but there was always "the purpose of achieving a practical efficiency. However, as the empire advanced, different forms of providing an education became associated with the different castes.

With the advent of colonialism, the Inca educational organization was completely dismantled and replaced with a series of educational efforts that aimed at the acculturation of the colonial peoples. The colonial powers sought to reeducate and indoctrinate the Indian population into the Spanish language, Catholic religion, and the principles of European social life, all with a clear objective of keeping them subjugated. The first document organizing colonial education was the *Capitulación de Toledo* in 1529, which, among other issues, established regulations for the education of the native population. The document mandated that members of the Catholic Church should be taken to the colonies to educate and catechize the locals.

Although targeting the whole of the Indian population, the scope of teachings varied according to social hierarchies. Thus, the lower castes received only a limited education, while the former members of the nobility—increasingly seen as crucial allies for the political aims of the colonies—received a much more complete instruction through the *Colegio de Caciques* that was specifically created for their education.

Valcárcel (1975) emphasizes the importance of the first *Concilio Limeño* carried out between 1551 and 1552, which declared that it was compulsory to educate the Indian population. Primary education was mainly made available to them. Before Sunday mass, they would listen to the lessons "sitting on the floor." The priest would impart a teaching in both Quechua and Spanish and then they would all say it out loud (Valcárcel 1975, 79). According to Valcárcel, during the early eighteenth century, there were twelve free primary schools with teachers paid by the Viceroy, and the student population totaled about 1,000 people. During this time, "Instruction Commissars" also existed who were in charge of inspecting schools.

The case of secondary and higher education was different. Existing intermediate education institutions only allowed entry to Spanish descendents, and some accommodated mixed race people. In the case of universities, entry was exclusive to members of the aristocracy: Antay (1930) refers to Viceroy Count of Castelar's prohibition that people from "inferior classes" (usually indigenous or mixed race people) should have access to universities. Here it is worth mentioning that the University of San Marcos—one of the first universities in the Americas—was founded in Peru in 1551.

According to Peruvian historian Carlos Wiesse, the exclusive nature of providing an education responded to the fact that "the majority of the people of some position and of the people in charge of some areas of public administration in the American colonies saw a social danger in the spread of teaching and knowledge ... to those individuals who lacked fortune and who were destined, because of their poverty conditions, to manual work." This was alleged to be "for their best interest and for the sake of social peace" (quoted in Antay 1930, 106).

Such discriminatory practices strengthened as colonial times advanced. In many schools, teachers began requiring that students contribute to their education with some form of payment (either in money or goods). While the education system had considerably expanded by the late eighteenth century, it did not favor the Indian population, whose access was impeded either through such economic requirements, or by more explicit entry barriers.

This can be understood as a consequence of the prevalence of a feudal type of political and economic organization in the colonies, which was largely dependent on the existence of uneducated masses that could dedicate themselves to manual work. The prevalence of such a feudal structure hindered some incipient attempts at industrialization during the late eighteenth and early nineteen centuries, which, in terms of education, had begun to produce a certain interest in more practical—and less scholastic—educational options. As Macera (1977) reminds us, "While the discovery of America was one of the factors that accelerated the economic and social 'modernization' of Europe, this meant at the same time a 're-archaization'" of America (Macera 1977, 142). It is evident that such a strategy had definitive consequences for the region's educational developments.

EDUCATION DURING REPUBLICAN TIMES

This was the context in which Peruvian education initiated its Republican history in 1821. The years of the struggle for independence had seriously curtailed educational developments, but since the beginning of the Republic a clear commitment to the spread of knowledge through education appeared. In a public speech, liberator Don José de San Martín made it clear that one of the central columns of the Spanish domination had been the state of ignorance in which they kept the colonial peoples (Valcárcel 1975, 139). In accordance, he thus introduced free public education for all.

In spite of this initial democratizing élan, the heritage of colonial times was to linger way into the Republic, with its feudal and aristocratic form of social organization that was strengthened and reproduced by the exclusive character of available education. It might be useful to remember that the independence movement in Peru and other colonies was not led by the local peoples, but rather by Spanish descendent elites, partly in reaction to the neo-absolutist policies of the Bourbon dynasty in Spain, which was reestablished in power in the early nineteenth century and strongly opposed to any liberal political trends. Colonial emancipation was not, thus, a popular movement, and although liberation was achieved vis-à-vis the colonial power, a new form of internal colonialism came to replace it (see Quijano 2000). The Republic, then, was still very much based on a feudal political and economic organization that was against the more democratic ideas that had been associated to the independence movement (Macera 1977).

These contradictions—between the modernizing and democratizing ideas of the Republican project and the feudal structure of the country—were to linger way into the twentieth century, and had a definitive impact on educational developments. Until the 1940s, Peruvian education consisted of a limited primary school, and a secondary education level that was very reduced in scope, with only very few national schools mainly attended by middle class children, while the lower classes and especially the rural population were largely excluded from access to education.

In terms of educational expansions, the limitations experienced during the first decades of the Republic were clearly related to the prevailing feudal organization of the country and the domination of an aristocracy opposed to offering social opportunities. On the other hand, this was also related to the political turmoil experienced during the nineteenth century, which was associated with the civil war first and later with the war against Chile (1879), and the predominance of military governments that considerably slowed down the pace of development.

During these early Republican years, however, some progress was made towards the expansion of educational access. In 1850, for instance, the government of Ramon Castilla passed an Instruction Regulation (*Reglamento de Instrucción*) that considerably reorganized the chaotic administration of the education system and was, in practice, the first education law in the country. The document established the organization of the education system into three levels—primary, secondary, and special or higher education—which has prevailed until now. In 1875, under Manuel Pardo's government, a Public Instruction Law was passed that promoted access to primary education to people from all social classes. Advancements made during this time were curtailed by the advent of the war with Chile, which considerably reduced the state's capacities to fund educational expansion—it was during the aftermath of the war that school administration was transferred to the local councils, precisely because of the central government's funding problems. After the war, some recovery was made in terms of educational expansion. Under Nicolás de Piérola's government, the state once more assumed central control over the education system, and a Normal Teachers' School was created to strengthen the basis of primary schooling.

The turn of the century gave rise to more political stability as well as to new political trends. However, in terms of education, the twentieth century can be seen as an example of the contradictions that were experienced by the state more generally.[2] On one hand, the initially slow but then more rapid opening of educational opportunities, helped to spread what some have called "the myth of education" (Ansión 1995), which suggested that opportunities for personal and social advancement could be achieved through access to education. At the same time, this was accompanied by a pervasive resistance on the part of existing elites to democratize educational access, as the latter was seen as a conduit for the introduction of changes to the dominant forms of social organization.

These contradictory trends have given rise to equally conflicting results, as the evident flexibilization of the social structure that has taken place during the century—particularly in its second half—has not helped overcome existing social inequalities, but has rather transformed them into new shapes. As will be discussed in more detail later, in terms of the education system, the original problems that were experienced in terms of access have given way to problems in terms of quality and the divisions between public/private and urban/rural education.

Two central trends can be identified in educational developments during the first half of the twentieth century and that, at an ideological level, are associated with the "Civilist" and the "Indigenist" movements. The former, which translated into a political option by the same name (the Civilist Party), dominated the early decades of the twentieth century with the two governments of José Pardo and the two governments of Augusto B. Leguía. It is associated with the liberal democratic and positivistic ideals of modernity and progress. The latter is linked to the ideas of thinkers like José Carlos Mariátegui and the critiques of the existing socioeconomic and political order that kept the masses of indigenous people oppressed and in a state of servility towards large landowners. Both trends, although for different reasons, were committed to increase access to education. In the case of the Civilist movement, it was associated with a civilizing effort that was to spread the ideals of progress and modernity; while in the case of the Indigenist movement, it was more associated with a commitment to social justice.

Manuel Vicente Villarán was the Civilist Party's ideologue for educational proposals and incarnated the new modernizing spirit associated with a trend towards the formation of a capitalist nation and the consequent expansion of liberal democratic ideals. During the first years of the twentieth century, he engaged in a historical debate with Alejandro Deustua, who defended the educational ideals of the old aristocracy and was against any considerable expansion of educational access. In 1905, under the influence of Civilist ideals, a new Public Instruction Law was passed, which almost doubled the number of primary schools from 1,445 to 2,500, and moved the system towards an explicitly North American (that is, United States) model for education with a more practical and vocational orientation than the rather academic French models on which the educational system had previously been based (Antay 1930).

The efforts to democratize education that took place during the first decades of the twentieth century had a definitive impact on the country's educational and social organization. In spite of this, however, the strong opposition exerted by members of socioeconomic elites that wanted to maintain the existing status quo considerably limited the scope of such changes.

LEGUÍA AND THE "CIVILIST" REFORM OF THE 1920s

In 1919, Augusto B. Leguía won the presidency for a second period that was to last eleven years. Like in his first government, he again faced the limitations of trying to modernize the state while the country's organization was still strongly feudal. The central character behind the civilist educational reform was, once again, Manuel Vicente Villarán, a believer in the ideals of positivism and their association with the aims of modernization. The educational reform he promoted can be more clearly qualified as a bourgeois reform, although it also had an explicit intention of including the popular masses.

Although some of the changes introduced would have clearly positive effects on the establishment of a more open education system, the Civilist movement faced strong opposition from the dominant elites that were associated with the feudal-like economy of large land tenure. Education reforms also faced opposition, particularly in rural areas, where the "clientelistic" and patriarchal social relations made peasants as well as landowners resist changes. As some have suggested, this appeared to be too progressive a reform for the socioeconomic relations that prevailed across the country, and which exerted strong resistance to the proposed changes.

Basadre (1963), however, suggests that the failure of the reform was also related with the lack of a clear idea of what to do. This can be seen in the continuous attempts to legislate education changes, which had a strong influence from North American experts, but were not adapted to the reality of the country, and were therefore largely unsuccessful.

In terms of education changes, historian Jorge Basadre (quoted in Morillo 2002) thus explains the failure of the Civilist reform:

the agrarian and mercantilist characteristics of Peruvian society led it to maintain the old educational model of a free primary education but of only limited access to the rural classes and with a markedly middle-class character. A secondary level with lower rates of enrollment that was the preface to a higher education level that was mainly oriented, in a democratic sense, to the liberal professions, without a concern for industrialization and economic development.

Antay (1930) also refers to the prevailing colonial organization of the country as one of the main limitations of the reform. She also points to the fact that the reform was very strongly based on the ideas of American rather than local specialists, and states that the whole attempt at changing the education system remained at a theoretical rather than practical level.

THE 1940s

During the 1940s, some small progress was made towards the development of a more inclusive education system. In 1941, during the government of Manuel Prado (1939–45) a new Organic Law of Education was approved, introducing some profound changes in the education system. Strongly influenced by the spirit of positivism and modernity, the government and the law stressed the importance of science and technology for social and economic development. The following government of Bustamante y Rivero (1945–48) introduced the provision of free secondary education for children from state schools, which constitutes a considerable step forward in the provision of more inclusive education.

It was probably the military government of Manuel Odría (1948–56) that introduced some of the most important changes in education, although like the preceding policies of the decade, they did not amount to a proper reform of the education system. In 1948, a national education fund was created and in 1950, the government published a National Education Plan that dealt with a range of issues from pedagogical methods to school organization and teacher training and set the basis for educational planning in Peru (Morillo 2002).

In spite of these and previous educational changes, there were still very serious problems in terms of service provision and system wide inequalities. Until the 1950s, most of the country's population lived in rural areas (two-thirds of the whole population). The difficulties that this created for the provision of education—especially when we consider the ruggedness and inaccessibility of much of the Peruvian territory—together with a lack of commitment towards popular education meant that school was very much an elite business, with only one in three children getting enrolled in primary education. Those left behind were mostly in rural areas, partly also because schooling took place in Spanish—35 percent of the country's population (settled mostly in the rural highlands) spoke only Quechua or Aymara—a situation that also rendered illiteracy rates extremely high. Exclusion was also skewed to the detriment of girls, who were seen by many families as naturally destined for house and agricultural work, rather than school (King and Bellew 1989).

THE 1950s AND EARLY 1960s: EDUCATIONAL EXPANSION

The 1950s can be seen as the beginning of some of the deepest transformations that were to take place in Peru's Republican history. It was not until two decades later, with Juan Velasco Alvarado's military government, that the land property regime was reformed, thus putting an end to the oligarchic form of socioeconomic organization that had prevailed during most of the twentieth century. However, the 1950s saw the beginning of popular movements that were to change the face of the country; in particular, a migration process from rural to urban areas that has continued until the present, and experienced its highest point during the 1980s due to the prevalence of terrorist violence in the Peruvian highlands. Migration has been generally associated with the centralized structure of the country's political and economic system, where Lima and a few other urban centers—and to a large extent still do—concentrate most economic, employment, and educational opportunities. By the early 1970s, a large proportion of the rural population had migrated mainly to Lima and some other coastal cities, making the country urban by 60 percent.

In terms of education, and associated with the increasing urbanization resulting from migratory processes, the 1950s saw the biggest increase in school enrollment rates both for males and females. However, this expansion included urban children more than rural children (only 63 percent of rural children were enrolled in primary education, compared to about 90 percent of those living in urban areas (King and Bellew 1989)), a trend that deepened when it came to secondary schooling, mainly due to the lack of provision of this level in rural areas. However in urban areas, secondary education began to expand, especially in association with the creation of the first large schools, often known as "Large Education Units" (*Grandes Unidades Escolares*), because of their size, which permitted the entrance of large masses of pupils into the education system. All these changes meant that between 1940–81, the proportion of the population who had never attended school dropped from 58 percent to only 16 percent.

The particularly high levels of expansion of school provision and enrollment rates during the 1950s and early 1960s coincided with the governments of Presidents Prado (1956–62) and Belaúnde (1963–68). Both administrations had a strong commitment towards modernization processes, and although in the latter case, expected social changes were not achieved (thus giving way to the military dictatorship of the 1970s), there was an emphasis on expanding schooling through more investment in education and the creation of more opportunities. "Between 1955 and 1965, the number of primary schools rose from just 12,000 to 18,500 and the number of teachers nearly doubled" (King and Bellew 1989, 6). During this time, Peruvian children's enrollment in school "far exceeded participation rates in the average Latin American country" (King and Bellew 1989, 7). All this was possible thanks to the economic prosperity of the decade, which allowed for the availability of more funds to be invested in social services. During this time, investment in education rose from only 14 percent of the national budget in 1950 to 23 percent in 1968, which represented 1.6 percent and 5 percent of GDP respectively.

Belaúnde's government in particular put a lot of emphasis on education as the key for national development. Increased investment was particularly geared towards achieving universal primary education, and also aimed at "expanding universities and improving the quality of instruction" (King and Bellew 1989, 8). It also raised teachers' salaries and engaged in attempts at developing bilingual education programs as a way of creating more inclusive alternatives for all the population.

Such reforms were not very far-fledged, largely because of economic problems which made it difficult for the government to keep up with the compromises it had assumed in terms of teachers' salaries and educational investment in general. Also, the divide between rural and urban areas had not decreased through the introduction of such reforms, so the strongest inequalities in the system remained constant. Apart from these problems, the lack of economic dynamism meant that educational expansion was not accompanied by an expansion in the labor market, and thus school graduates were in many cases unable to find suitable employment according to the skills they had gained. However, by the end of this period, school retention levels had increased, which meant that students were staying in school—drop-out rates went from 85 percent in 1943 to 60 percent in 1968 (still high, but showing some definite improvement).

THE 1970s AND THE REVOLUTIONARY EDUCATION REFORM OF THE MILITARY GOVERNMENT

In 1968, a military coup led by General Juan Velasco Alvarado put an end to Belaúnde's government. The dictatorship that followed lasted for twelve years. It was led by Velasco himself until 1975, and then by his successor General Morales Bermudez. Acknowledging the problems with Belaúnde's government, which were reflected in the social unrest that gave rise to a guerrilla movement in the second half of the 1960s, Velasco's government conceived itself as a revolutionary one and was tied to socialist aims of creating more equality among the country's citizens. Thus, it embarked on a series of deep reforms that aimed to radically alter the country's social and economic structures. The key element of these goals was agrarian reform that put a definitive end to the domination of the oligarchy by expropriating big land tenures and distributing it among the peasants. The counterpart of this reform was state-led industrialization. Changes were also accompanied by massive expropriations of private businesses that were generally tied to foreign capital, thus maintaining what was described as a dependency model that limited the country's economic development (see Stepan 1978).

The strongly ideological nature of the government's revolutionary project made educational reform one of its central aims, since changing people's social representations was seen as important as putting an end to the agrarian and exploitative basis of the economy. Many authors blame the failure of the reform precisely on its excessive ideological and messianic content (Palomino Thompson 1993; Haddad 1994).

In 1972, a new General Law of Education was passed. It was the result of the Reform Commission's analysis, led by philosopher Augusto Salazar Bondy, and published in a famous "Blue Report," setting the basis for the reform. The analysis stated that the reform had to relate education with careers in the labor force and for national development; that education had to serve the purpose of achieving a structural transformation of society; and that it had to promote the self-affirmation and the independence of the Peruvian nation (Ministry of Education of Peru 1970). The new Law followed the Report's prescriptions very closely. It thus placed special importance on technical and professional education, it promoted community participation in education as a means for extending changes beyond the school, and it aimed at permanently getting rid of "negative values such as profit-making and inequality" (Palomino Thompson 1993, 66).

The report also placed strong emphasis on the ways in which the educational system had excluded children from less well-off backgrounds who tended to fail in the early years and often dropped out from school. The Law also established automatic grade promotion. However, as Palomino (1993) suggests, creating social awareness about the need for more equal relations was the main aim of the reform. At a more specific level, the law promoted the formation of school networks to improve the provision of services, and it also regulated private educational activities. Private schools were a strong source of opposition to the reform because the Law impeded schools from operating as for-profit organizations; it established that private schools should follow the national curriculum, provide scholarships for less advantaged children, make their infrastructure available for use by children from public schools, and require that school teachers be Peruvian (a measure explicitly set to change the administration of international schools).

Velasco's government also changed the structure of the education system integrating the vocational and academic strands that had been previously available during the late stages of secondary schooling into just one alternative. The previous six years of primary education followed by five of secondary education, were replaced by a nine-year "basic education" that would then be followed either by university or by the newly introduced Schools of Professional Higher Education (*Escuelas Superiores de Educación Profesional—ESEP*). The aim was to homogenize school provision as a way of promoting equality among students. In this sense, a somewhat anecdotal, but no less important feature of the educational reform, was the introduction of a single school uniform for all schools in the country—both private and public.

Although enrollment rates kept rising during these years, the school system in general did not expand as fast as in the previous decades. The government did not place much emphasis on educational infrastructure nor in promoting access, but concentrated on changing the nature of educational institutions. "Rather than building more schools, multigrade teaching was introduced in incomplete schools, and all schools, including private ones, were required to make their facilities available to the community for evening adult education programs" (King and Bellew 1989, 9). Bilingual education was also included for children from monolingual Quechua and Aymara populations, and there was an emphasis on the provision of educational materials. Some of these reforms were especially geared to promote inclusion in rural areas.

Even though the reform's initial élan was very strong, it was not very successful. This was due in part with the slow pace at which implementation took place because of the emphasis put on detailed planning. Opposition from private schools was also strong. However, as mentioned above, the main reason for the reform's failure was, according to various analysts, its excessive ideological nature. Additionally, it was a very vertical reform, planned wholly from above, and did not include schools and teachers in conceiving the desired changes.

Adding to this, the country's economy, which by the end of the 1970s had considerably weakened and had serious debt problems, made the application of many of the reform policies impossible. By the end of the military government, investment in education fell again to only 13 percent of the national budget, which represented 3.1 percent of GDP (King and Bellew 1989).

With the advent of General Morales Bermudez in power, the revolutionary project of Velasco, including its educational branch, was slowly dismantled. This went on until the end of the decade. In 1979, the government called a Constituent Assembly to rewrite the country's constitution and finally gave way to a new democratic election in 1980.

EDUCATION DURING THE 1980s: ECONOMIC CRISIS AND THE RISE OF POLITICAL VIOLENCE

Although the military reform project definitively altered the face of the country, especially through agrarian reform, it failed to accomplish the promise of social change. The revolutionary ideas that had already been present before the military coup of 1968 were revived, but this time with a more violent spirit that gave rise to *Sendero Luminoso*, the Maoist-Leninist terrorist movement that jeopardized the country's internal security for over a decade.

In 1980, Fernando Belaúnde was reelected; previously, he had been ousted in the 1968 military coup. His government rose to power amidst a serious economic crisis, partly led by the heavy weight placed on the country for international loan repayments. In a process that, as will be seen later, is very similar to what has taken place in more recent years in the transition between the government of Alberto Fujimori and that of Alejandro Toledo, the newly-elected democratic government of Belaúnde built its legitimacy partly in contraposition to the authoritarian characteristics of the preceding government. Therefore, his government found it necessary to put an end to the reform processes the previous government had begun. The dismantling which had already begun during the late years of the military government therefore was completed.

The 1979 Constitution had opened the way for rethinking the educational legal framework. Belaúnde's government thus embarked on the process of preparing a new General Law of Education that was passed in 1982. Through this legislative change, the structural changes introduced during the 1970s were reversed, thus going back to a system with six years of primary education and five years of secondary education—rather than the nine years basic education proposed by the military. This change also entailed the disarticulation of the ESEPs created by Velasco, which now became a post-secondary (rather than an intermediate) level and included a name change to Higher Technological Institutes (*Institutos Superiores Tecnológicos*).

Apart from these changes, the law gave a "much better treatment to private schools" and it was "much shorter and therefore much more flexible" than the preceding one (Palomino Thompson 1993, 94). Although this was quite a change compared to the previous law and its strong emphasis on legislating every aspect of school practices, the regulation of the law that came in the following years tended increasingly to enhance the vertical control of schools by the Ministry of Education.

The return to democratic government in the 1980s was initially accompanied by a shift towards a market economy that replaced the "organic statism" (Stepan 1978) of the military years. The government's liberal project experienced serious limitations due its difficulties in balancing internal demands for better redistributive policies with external demands from multilateral agencies for debt repayment—discipline to repay the debt led the government to commit 43 percent of the fiscal budget (Lopez 1997, 286), considerably reducing its capacity for internal investment. Additionally, a particularly strong *El Niño* phenomenon occurred in 1983 with devastating floods in the north and droughts in the south of the country, which ended up weakening the national economy and any possibility of consolidating the political and economic changes that the government wanted to promote.

At the start of his presidential mandate, Belaúnde declared that his would be an "Educational Period" ("*El quinquenio de la educación*"). In practice, this translated into a considerable increase in school enrollment, which jumped from 5,449,800 to 6,588,400 and meant that in primary education, 95 percent of the corresponding age group was being provided for. The secondary and higher education levels also experienced a considerable expansion. However, this growth was not coupled with budgetary increases. Quite the opposite, economic problems during this period led to a reduction in the education budget.

The second half of the 1980s saw the return of populism, thus confirming the trend described by Gonzales de Olarte and Samamé (1991) as the "Peruvian pendulum"—a trend which according to the authors has characterized the Peruvian political economy since the early 1960s, and in which the failure to establish liberal economic regimes due to an incapacity to balance internal and external demands, has generally led to the installation of populist governments that aim to respond to popular demands with unsustainable state investment that leads to inflation and thus, again, to the deployment of more orthodox corrective economic measures. In 1985, Alan Garcia was elected president, and in contrast to his predecessor, who had responded mainly to external demands for loan repayment, chose to focus on internal pressures for better redistribution—committing only 10 percent of export value to debt repayment—not only through social programs, but through import-substitution to promote industrial growth. After an initial economic boost, Garcia's project was soon to face strong limitations when the state's subsidiary policies led to hyperinflation.

The collapse of Garcia's economic model and the deep fiscal crisis, together with the rise of terrorist violence, led to the increasing paralysis of the state's functions and institutions. In terms of state development, the 1980s were thus a "lost decade" in which neither the liberal nor the populist model managed to modernize and strengthen the state apparatus. On the contrary, there was an almost complete disappearance of state institutions, while simultaneous expressions for social demands on the state were contained due to the presence of extreme political violence (that is, terrorism). This is not to say that there was a social paralysis. Quite the opposite, the 1980s gave rise to a series of social movements—seen for instance in the rise of an informal economy (De Soto 1987) and for popular support organizations—through which citizens partly took over the state's responsibility to respond to social needs.

In terms of the education system, Garcia's government had disastrous consequences, especially due to the economic situation, but also due to the government's tendency towards a minute regulation of every educational aspect. In this respect, Palomino (1993) remembers that regulations arrived to the quite ridiculous point of establishing that people serving in school kiosks could not have a moustache. Besides its anecdotal character, this demonstrates the excessive influence of the state in all school matters, which to a large extent breached the constitutional right to "freedom of teaching." This extreme regulation also extended to school plans and programs which dictated not only the basic contents to be taught in each course, but also determined the sequencing of contents and the pace at which they should be covered. This regulating tendency was accompanied by unprecedented growth of the state bureaucracy that followed from the government's general tendency to fill public posts with its party members. During this period, the government also made attempts to promote a new law of education. This initiative, however, was not taken up by parliament, which had only recently approved the Law prepared by Belaúnde's government.

A discussion of the educational developments of the 1980s cannot leave untouched the relationship between education and the rise of terrorist violence in the country. After the failed attempt in the 1970s to promote a more inclusive society through state intervention, the 1980s gave rise to an explosion of popular processes (Matos Mar 2004) that was accompanied also by a rise in terrorist violence associated with the problems of social exclusion. A clear link exists in the rise of *Sendero Luminoso*, the main terrorist movement, with the failure of the state to expand opportunities and, more specifically, the failure of education to do so (Ansión 1995). The rise of *Sendero Luminoso* is linked both to a social agenda that aimed to put the masses of excluded population at the center of political action, and to the vertical and authoritarian mode of education that prevailed in most national schools, and which facilitated the appropriation of a dogmatic and radical discourse.

But the links between *Sendero Luminoso* and the school system went beyond this. Many of the movement's leaders were part of provincial intellectual elites, linked to local universities. Additionally, *Sendero*'s strategy explicitly included the indoctrination of young people through schools and universities. The increasing presence of *Sendero*'s ideas among university teachers meant that the development of school teachers would become increasingly charged with the movement's radical ideology. Although *Sendero Luminoso* was dismembered in the early 1990s, the influence of such radical leftist ideas is still present in some factions of the Teachers' Union, specifically one linked to the communist party *Patria Roja*.

The links between teachers and the terrorist movement, and especially the consequences of an education system that has not only a vertical approach to educational administration but also to knowledge, have been the subject of much debate. Criticisms of such a vertical model are at the basis of many of the proposals that appeared in the 1990s, with their emphasis on active learning and on making learning, rather than teaching, the center of educational aims.

EDUCATION DURING AND AFTER THE 1990s: LIBERALIZATION, QUALITY REFORMS, AND POLICY DISCONTINUITIES

After the economic disaster experienced during Alan Garcia's government, the 1990s opened up to a new reformist spirit. Alberto Fujimori, a Japanese descendent and recently naturalized as a Japanese citizen, and the leader of an independent movement won the elections, and was to last in power for ten years. Soon after his government began, Peru was readmitted into the international funding community from which it was expelled after Alan Garcia refused to pay international loan agreements. This readmittance was conditional on the application of a structural adjustment program of a neo-liberal nature that was to be carried out under the auspice of the International Monetary Fund and the World Bank (similar to many countries in the region). The World Bank, in particular, stressed the need to develop education reform, which was seen as the fundamental correlate of the structural adjustments carried out in the country and involved flexibility in the economy to promote private investment, the privatization of public sector enterprises, and a general reorganization and reduction of the state bureaucracy.

In the education system some related attempts were made at the beginning of the 1990s that involved a move to incorporate school choice mechanisms for parents and the municipalization of educational administration—in a similar vein as the reforms carried out in the neighboring country Chile. These reform attempts faced strong opposition from both the Teachers' Union and the parents, who claimed that the gratuity of education would be lost; these reforms were eventually dismissed by the government.

In the mid-1990s, Fujimori's government embarked on a series of new reforms, although these reforms were less concerned with administrative changes and more focused specifically on changes in the structure of the system as well as on issues of pedagogy. In 1996, the government passed a law that liberalized investment in education (D.L. 882)—thus allowing educational institutions (from schools to universities) to operate as for-profit businesses—and gave rise to a proliferation of schools, higher education institutes, and universities all over the country.[3] The policies introduced as part of the reform program, and which were associated with the slogan of "educational modernization," were directed to generate changes in school practices. Among other things, they involved a curricular reform, production of school materials, construction of schools, and the training of teachers. At the curricular and pedagogical level, there was a strong emphasis on changing school practices and on shifting the current teacher-centered model of education, with its authoritarian and vertical approach to knowledge and teaching, to a student-centered model with a much more horizontal orientation.

Many of the reforms set in motion during these years were discontinued with the change of government in 2001. Fujimori's regime, although democratically elected, had become largely authoritarian over the years—the president closed and reorganized Congress in 1993 and then embarked on a second unconstitutional reelection process that led him to win the presidency for a third consecutive time in a flawed election process—and had lost legitimacy with the more democratic political factions.

When Fujimori fled the country after very explicit evidence of deep corruption in his government,[4] a one-year transition government followed and led to a new election process. In education, the new government's representatives felt compelled to discontinue the reforms under claims that they had been initiated in an undemocratic context. Despite the difficulties that such discontinuities create for assessing the quality of the 1990s reforms, many analysts have suggested that they were misled and that they failed to tackle some of the central educational problems, such as those related to the teaching profession. Although evidence already existed of insufficiencies in classroom practices, new evidence from national assessments cast light on the links between student achievement and teachers' subject knowledge, leading to an awareness of the limitations of current teacher education and selection criteria (Unidad de Medición de la Calidad Educativa 2005). In light of these new findings, the effort and money invested during Fujimori's government seems to have been lost, as it focused more on the relational and pedagogical elements of teaching— proposing a transformation of the teaching paradigm and the introduction of more "active" teaching methodologies—when it should have emphasized teachers' knowledge of the areas in which they teach. By emphasizing teachers' practices, the 1990s reforms seem to have contributed to an even deeper lack of concern with the knowledge being learned in schools.

Whether these critiques are right or wrong, other problems have risen from the policy changes introduced since 2001. Curricular policies have kept changing continuously, and in 2005, after almost ten years of various experimentations, a new curriculum that articulates primary and secondary education has been approved. The constant changes in curricular proposals, however, have created strong confusion among the teachers. In recent years, it has become increasingly clear that although there is a new discourse among the teachers that is more focused on children's learning, there are serious misunderstandings as to the aims of classroom practices—teachers can often be found who say that curricular contents are not important, for instance.

In accordance with the general decentralization process that the country is undergoing, the emphasis of educational policies in recent years has also moved strongly towards the aim of decentralizing educational administration. Although decentralization was initially set to devolve powers to the regional administration, there has been a recent attempt by Alan Garcia's newly-appointed government (reelected in 2006) to devolve powers to the local councils (*Municipalidades*). This change has come about without much consultation or providing reasons to the public, and has elicited strong resistance from the Teachers' Union—in a similar way as it did in the early 1990s when Fujimori attempted to municipalize education.

THE CURRENT SITUATION

Having reached the end of this historical account, we will close the chapter with some reflections about the current problems that the Peruvian education system is facing. As we have seen, Peru's educational system has experienced constant growth, especially since the second half of the twentieth century. The problems of access, which used to be the main source of educational exclusion, have thus given way to new concerns about the quality of educational services provided in the country. Since the early 1990s, it has become increasingly clear that educational growth has not been coupled with budgetary increases, thus leading to serious problems in quality (Ministry of Education of Peru 2000; Bing Wu 2001).

This has given rise to a wave of "quality reforms"—a term applicable to the regional education policy trends in general. During the early 1990s, when these reforms began, it had become evident that problems were systemwide. School infrastructure was deficient and there was barely any supply of teaching materials for schools. The teaching profession had particularly suffered from the expansion: as the demand for educational services increased, the standards for entering the teaching profession were lowered, thus admitting professionals who were not well prepared for the task. Additionally, the lack of sufficient economic resources to fund educational expansion also meant that teachers were increasingly under-paid—a situation that contributed to attract less-prepared professionals for teaching posts—and that they had few opportunities for in-service training.

Apart from this, the educational administration had grown increasingly ineffi-cient due to the expansion of the bureaucracy and the exaggerated tendency to regulate every aspect of school practices, which blocked particular initiatives and increased red tape. This also had an impact on learning, as school practices had become increasingly vertical and driven by memorization methods. The high dropout and repetition rates, especially among children from rural areas, had led to an increasing awareness not only about the system's inefficiency, but also about the disconnectedness of school practices and many children's reality.

After more than a decade of quality reforms, many of these problems still linger (see PREAL 2003). Recent data shows that enrollment rates are high, but considerably eschewed in favor of urban over rural populations, and also to the detriment of the poorest. There are also differences according to gender; males have somewhat higher enrollment rates than females (see figures 13.1 and 13.2). School infrastructure and access to education materials have improved, and there has been considerable advancement in the production of information about children's achievement, which facilitates monitoring of policy outcomes. However, problems in the teaching profession and those related to school practices are still deeply entrenched. Although pay raises for teachers were approved during the Toledo government, teachers' remunera-tions are still very meager. Such pay raises have not been linked to changes in the regulations, which are fundamental for changing conditions under which teachers enter and are promoted in the system and for making demands for better quality of teaching.

At the classroom level, problems are still persistent, and through participa-tion in national and international assessments, it has become increasingly clear that Peruvian children are performing well below expected levels (UNESCO 2003). This can be explained partly as a consequence of the persistence of obsolete teaching practices in schools for which 1990s reforms and their emphasis on active learning have not been able to modify adequately.

National assessment results have also cast light on the inequalities between urban and rural areas and between private and public education. The following

Figure 13.1
Net Coverage Rates in Primary Education According to Gender, Residence Area, and Poverty Level, 2003

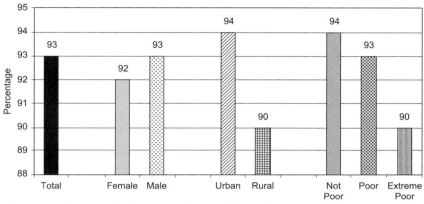

Elaborated by: Ministerio de Edcuación del Perú—Unidad de Estadística Educativa.
Source: Instituto Nacional de Estadística—Encuesta Nacional de Hogares 2003.

Figure 13.2
Net Coverage Rates in Secondary Education According to Gender, Residence Area, and Poverty Level, 2003

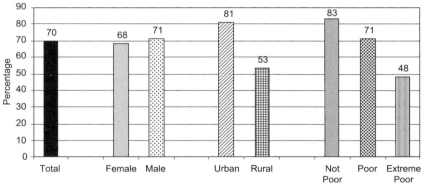

Elaborated by: Ministerio de Edcuación del Perú—Unidad de Estadística Educativa.
Source: Instituto Nacional de Estadística—Encuesta Nacional de Hogares 2003.

four graphs show the results in national achievement tests of students who have concluded their primary education. The general trend shows that only 24 percent of the total national cohort that was assessed achieved basic or sufficient levels in communication skills, while the achievement of 77 percent of cohorts was below the basic level. While differences between males and females in this area are not very strong, when it comes to comparing public and private schools, the differences are markedly in favor of the latter. While 81 percent of children in public schools achieved below the basic level, only 39 percent of those in private schools did so (still considerable, but much lower than in the case of public schools). The percentage of those reaching the sufficient level is much higher in private schools. The last two bars in figures 13.3 and 13.4 show achievement by students from public schools according to whether they attend single or multiple-teacher schools. The former, it must be highlighted, tend to be in rural areas, so the data shows that rural students achieve less than their peers in urban areas. The trend in math as shown in figure 13.4 is somewhat more positive, with more students achieving at the basic or sufficient level. The differences between public/private and rural/urban schools, however, are still marked. As mentioned above, the more recent national assessments (Unidad de Medición de la Calidad Educativa 2005), while showing the persistence of these trends, have also highlighted the strong correlation between teachers subject knowledge and student achievement.

The rural education programs that were supposed to tackle one part of these problems have been largely inefficient, especially due to constant discontinuities in educational policies and discourses.[5] However, the 1990s have shown the increase in bilingual and multicultural education programs, which aim at

Figure 13.3
Achievement in Communication of Students that Conclude Primary Education, According to Gender, Form of Administration, and School Type, 2001

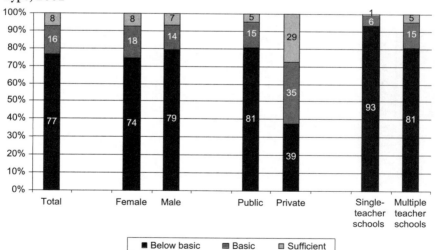

Note: The single-teacher category includes multigrade schools with more than one teacher. In both cases they are publicly administered schools.
Elaborated by: Ministerio de Educación del Perú—Unidad de Estadística Educativa.
Source: Ministerio de Educación del Perú—National Student Achievement Assessment 2001.

Figure 13.4
Achievement in Math among Students that Conclude Primary Education,
According to Gender, Form of Administration, and School Type, 2001

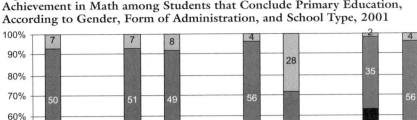

Note: The single-teacher category includes multigrade schools with more than one teacher. In both cases they are publicly administered schools.
Elaborated by: Ministerio de Educación del Perú—Unidad de Estadística Educativa.
Source: Ministerio de Educación del Perú—National Student Achievement Assessment 2001.

tackling the problems of exclusion by bringing the cultural and linguistic reality of the school closer to the everyday realities of rural children. While educational services provided in rural areas were usually associated with primary education—and especially with multigrade teaching (Ames 2003)—in recent years, there has been an expansion of secondary schools in rural areas. Although increasingly becoming incorporated into the mainstream state-run system, the rise of rural secondary schools has been largely associated with community initiatives, thus testifying to the importance that rural communities undertake education as a means for accessing better social opportunities.

Since Peru's reentry into the international community in the early 1990—and its consequent participation in international education conferences such as *Jomtien* and agreements such as those of Education for All—issues related to gender and education have become increasingly present in the policy discourse. This has been especially true since the early years of the 2000 decade, particularly after the New Law of Education was passed. As various authors show (Ames 2006; Muñoz 2006), however, there are still strong limitations in the way in which gender issues have been treated by policymakers and schools. This is because the general trend has been to conflate gender with sex, and to treat inequalities in relation to these criteria in terms of inclusion. Given the high rates of enrollment of both boys and girls, particularly in primary education, there seems to be a widespread idea that the gender inequality is not a problem in Peruvian education or, if it is, it is restricted to vulnerable populations such as rural women. Of course, such a view overlooks the sociocultural dimensions of gender, and the ways in which gender relations within schools "might help reproduce existing hierarchies and inequalities" (Muñoz 2006, 393).

These reflections about the current inequalities that pervade the education system lead us to some final remarks. Peruvian social scientists have long linked the phenomenon of school expansion with what has been described as "the myth of education." This idea refers to the widespread expectation among the popular and indigenous classes that better opportunities for social advancement could be reached through access to education—thus, the presence of education demands among indigenous movements (Ansión, Gorriti, Montoya, and Valderrama 1987) and the increasing demand for educational services more generally linked to the growth of the education system.

The enthusiasm about the opportunities provided by education has often not been matched by the actual possibilities for improving well-being through access to better employment and better economic conditions. This has to do partly with the economic problems that the country has faced during most of its Republican history and with the limitations of attempts at modernization and industrialization vis-à-vis the lengthy predominance of feudal forms of economic organization. But some suggest that the failure of the education system has to do with the remaining strong prevalence of discriminatory practices in schools, especially those in rural areas, which benefit one form of language acquisition over others, for instance, and have a vertical approach to knowledge that is disconnected from the cultural realities of many children.

As we have seen, the more traditional concerns with issues of access to educational services have now been replaced by a preoccupation with the quality of educational services and their capacity, or not, to provide people with adequate means for personal advancement. Thus, the "myth of education" has come into question. However, the enthusiasm people place on the possibilities offered by education is still very strong. In coming years, we must see whether these trends can be reversed and whether a more inclusive education system— and more inclusive society in general—can be achieved. As positive as the macroeconomic bonanza of recent years might be in this respect, the history of Peruvian education clearly shows that more than economic resources is needed to bring about desired changes.

A DAY IN THE LIFE

Paola wakes up at 6:00 AM every morning. She is ten years old and lives with her mother, an older sister, and three younger siblings in a marginal neighborhood on the outskirts of Lima. Her parents split up a few years ago and she has not heard from her father ever since. Her mother and older sister go out very early every day to work at the local market where they have a food stall. Paola stays in charge of the younger siblings. After washing herself, she makes breakfast and gets them ready for school. They all go out together and she drops them off at their school before entering hers at 7:30 AM. She will spend five hours there. The use (or misuse) of time in Peruvian schools is a widespread problem. Out of these five hours, almost two get spent in breaks and delays in starting class. The day starts with a language class where the kids have to fill in some exercises in a spreadsheet handed out by the teacher. There is also a lot of copying from the blackboard. After an hour-and-a-half period, there is a first break and then a history lesson. The teacher is telling them about the history of the Incas. Only the teacher speaks, while the children listen silently and make notes in their copybooks. The class finishes without much discussion about the learned issues. Another break follows, this time a longer one that goes on for almost an hour. Then, there is a final math period before the kids return home.

On the way back Paola picks up her younger siblings. They stop at the communal kitchen to pick up their lunch. There will be no one else at home when they get there, so Paola is in charge. She and her siblings have lunch and then she has to clear everything up, wash the dishes, and tidy up the house—which she did not get to do in the morning. She has to make the beds and pick up the stuff that her younger brothers and sisters have left lying around the house. Once she is finished, she gets to do her homework. There is no one at home to help her with this, so if there is something she does not understand, she has to sort it out herself by going to a friend and discussing what to do.

At about nine, and after watching one or two hours of TV, she and her siblings go to bed. Her mother and older sister arrive shortly afterwards.

TIMELINE

1529   *Capitulaciones de Toledo*, which mandated that colonized peoples should be educated and that priests should be taken to the colonies to carry out that mission.

1821   The year of independence from the colonial powers saw the creation of a free national education system.

1822   A legal decree establishes the creation of free primary schools in all regular convents of the country; the first normal teaching school is created in the country.

1850   The government of Ramon Castilla passes the new "Instruction Regulation" (*Reglamento de Instrucción*), which, in practice, was to work as the first education law in the country. The regulation considerably reorganized the chaotic administration of the educational system.

1875   The government of Manuel Pardo passes the first Public Instruction Law, which aimed at expanding access to primary education to all social classes.

1905   A new Law of School Instruction (*Ley de Instrucción*) is passed and the number of primary schools rises from only 1,425 to 2,500.

1920–31	The Civilist government of Augusto B. Leguía sets in motion a series of educational reforms that aim at modernizing the education system and expanding access.
1936	The government of Oscar R. Benavides creates the Ministry of Education— before this, education issues were dealt with by other areas of public administration.
1950s	Period of large expansion of education in the country.
1972	New Law of Education approved by the military government of Juan Velasco Alvarado sets the basis for the revolutionary education reform project.
1979	A new Constitution is approved and gives way to a new democratic election in the country.
1982	Belaúnde's government approves a new General Law of Education (Number 23384), which was in accordance with the 1979 Constitution and put a definitive end to military education reform.
Late 1980s	The second half of the 1980s is characterized by terrorist violence and severe economic crisis that lead to a paralysis of the state apparatus—education included.
Early 1990s	The new government of Alebrto Fujimori makes several attempts at changing the education administration by way of legal reforms. The latter points towards granting municipalities control of educational administration. After eliciting strong opposition are abandoned by the government.
1996	The government gets the D.L. 882 for "Promoting Investment in Education" approved by Congress. The latter liberalizes educational investment allowing educational institutions to work as for-profit businesses. It also reduces the requirements for the creations of new schools and higher education institutions.
2003	The New General Law of Education is approved by Congress. It has a very strong emphasis on decentralizing the educational system and on promoting parental and community participation in school matters.

NOTES

1. An Inca devise consisting of threads on which knots were made to keep track of ideas and matters concerning public administration.

2. Here it is worth mentioning Roger Dale's (1989) idea that the contradictions at the heart of education systems can, to a large extent, be read as reflecting the contradictions at the heart of the state.

3. This liberalization has not been accompanied by supervisory mechanisms to help ensure the quality of the services provided by these new educational institutions, so the quality of the services provided by them is highly questionable.

4. An enormous amount of leaked videos showed the president's close collaborator bribing all sorts of figures that ranged from media tycoons, congressional representatives, and business owners for political support.

5. Fujimori's government was due to launch a distance education program for rural areas, but it was never fully applied and later discontinued by the succeeding government. Additionally, the Ministry of Education has been working in the formulation of a rural education project which was deemed unsuccessful before its application was

realized and that now has given rise to a new program that aims to tackle rural education problems through the creation of school networks.

BIBLIOGRAPHY

Books

Ames, P. 2006. *Las brechas invisibles: desafíos para una equidad de género en la educación*. Lima: Instituto de Estudios Peruanos.

Ames, P. 2003. *Multigrade Schools in Context: Literacy in the Community, the Home and the School in the Peruvian Amazon*. London: University of London.

Ames, P. 2000. "La escuela es progreso? Antropología y educación en el Perú." In *No hay país más diverso*. Edited by C. I. Degregori. Lima: Red para el desarrollo de las ciencias sociales en el Perú.

Ansión, J. 1995. "Del mito de la educación al proyecto educativo. In *El Perú frente al siglo XXI*. Edited by G. Portocarrero and M. Valcárcel. Lima: Fondo Editorial Pontificia Universidad Católica del Perú.

Arregui, P., M. Benavides, S. Cueto, J. Saavedra, and B. Hunt. 2004. *¿Es posible mejorar la educación peruana? Evidencias y posibilidades*. Lima: Grade.

Basadre, J. 1963. *Historia de la República del Perú*. Lima: Ediciones "Historia."

Benavides, M., S. Azañedo, S. Cueto, J. León, E. Neira, M. Mena, I. Olivera, C. Ramirez, J. L. Rosales, and P. Ruiz Bravo. 2006. *Los desafíos de la escolaridad en el Perú: Estudios sobre los procesos pedagógicos, los saberes previos y el rol de las familias* Lima: Grade.

Bing Wu, K., P. McLauchlan de Arregui, P. Goldschmidt, A. Miranda, and J. Saavedra. 2000. "Education and Poverty in Peru." In *Unequal Schools, Unequal Chances: The Challenges to Equal Opportunity in the Americas*. Edited by F. Reimers. Cambridge, Mass.: The David Rockefeller Center Series on Latin American Studies and Harvard University Press.

Dale, R. 1989. *The State and Education Policy*. Milton Keynes, Philadelphia: Open University Press.

De Soto, H. 1987. *El otro sendero: la revolución informal [The Other Path: The Economic Answer to Terrorism]*. Lima: Instituto de Libertad y Democracia.

Ferrer, G. 2004. *Las reformas curriculares de Perú, Colombia, Chile y Argentina: ¿Quién responde por los resultados?* Lima: Grupo de Análisis para el Desarrollo (GRADE).

Hunt, B. 2004. "La educación primaria Peruana: aún necesita mejorarse." In *¿Es posible mejorar la educación peruana?* Edited by P. Arregui, M. Benavides and S. Cueto. Lima: Grupo de Análisis para el Desarrollo (GRADE).

Macera, P. 1977. *Trabajos de historia*. Lima: Instituto Nacional de Cultura.

Matos Mar, J. 2004. *Desborde popular y crisis del estado: veinte años después*. Lima: Ediciones del Congreso del Perú.

Muñoz, F. *Caminos cruzados: género en las políticas educativas en el Perú en los últimos diez años*. 2006.

Palomino Thompson, E. 1993. *Educación Peruana: historia, análisis y propuestas*. Lima: Consorcio de Centros Educativos Católicos del Perú.

Saavedra, J. and P. Suárez, P. 2002. *El Financiamiento de la educación en el Perú: el rol de las familias*. Lima: GRADE.

Stepan, A. 1978. *The State and Society: Peru in Comparative Perspective.* New Jersey, Surrey: Princeton University Press.
Valcárcel, C. D. 1975. *Breve historia de la educación peruana.* Lima: Editorial Educación.
Valcárcel, C. D. 1961. *Historia de la educación incaica.* Lima: Editorial Educación.

Articles

Ansión, J., L.C. Gorriti, R. Montoya, and M. Valderrama. "La escuela rural: mito, realidad y perspectivas." *Debate agrario* 1 (1987): 77–95.
Antay, E. "La educación en el Perú." *Hispania* 13, no. 2 (1930): 105–116.
Arregui, P. "Las políticas educativas durante los noventa en el Perú: resultados y pendientes." *Tarea: Revista de educación y cultura* 46 (2000): 7–11.
Benavides, M. "Cuando los extremos no se encuentran: un análisis de la movilidad social e igualdad de oportunidades en el Perú contemporáneo." *Bulletin de l'Institut Francais d'Etudes Andines* 31, no. 3 (2002): 473–94.
Crum, S. J. "Colleges Before Columbus: Mayans, Aztecs and Incas Offered Advanced Education Long Before the Arrival of Europeans." *Tribal College Journal of American Higher Education* 3, no. 2 (1991).
Hazen, D. "The Politics of Schooling in the Nonliterate Third World: The Case of Peru." *History of Education Quarterly* 18, no. 4 (1978).
Quijano, A. "Coloniality of Power and Eurocentrism in Latin America." *International Sociology* 15, no. 2 (2000): 215–32.

Reports

Benavides, M. and Rodriguez, J. 2006. *Políticas de educación básica 2006–11.* Lima: CIES-GRADE.
Bing Wu, K. and W. B. 2001. *Peru—Education at a Crossroads: Challenges and Opportunities for the 21st Century.* Washington, D.C.: World Bank.
Congreso de la República del Perú. 2003. *Ley general de educación.* Lima: Congreso de la República del Perú.
Du Bois, F. 2004. *Programas sociales, salud y educación en el Perú: un balance de las políticas sociales.* Lima: Instituto Peruano de Economía Social de Mercado, Fundación Konrad Adenauer.
Haddad, W. 1994. *The Dynamics of Education Policymaking: Case Studies of Burkina Faso, Jordan, Peru, and Thailand.* Washington, D.C.: Economic Development Institute of the World Bank.
King, E. and Bellew, R. 1989. *The Effects of Peru's Push to Improve Education.* The World Bank.
Ministry of Education of Peru. 2000. *Educación para todos 2000—Perú: informe nacional de evaluación (Education for All 2000—Peru: National Assessment Report).* Lima: Comisión Peruana de Cooperación con la UNESCO/Oficina de Planificación Estratégica y Medición de la Calidad Educativa del Ministerio de Educación.
Ministry of Education of Peru. 1970. *Informe general de la reforma de la educación Peruana.* Lima: Ministry of Education of Peru.
PREAL. 2003. *Informe de Progreso Educativo.* Perú: PREAL.
Unidad de Medición de la Calidad Educativa. 2005. *Presentación de los resultados de la evaluación nacional del 2004.* Lima: Ministerio de Educación del Perú.

Web Sites

The Association for Educational Publications TAREA (most publications are in Spanish): www.tarea.org.pe.

Escale is particularly relevant for those interested in further researching Peruvian education. It provides user-friendly information (including graphs and tables) on enrollment, repetition, and drop-out rates, as well as information on student achievement and more general statistical data. See statistics section: http://escale .minedu.gob.pe/escale/.

Foro Educativo, the education discussion forum also provides a publications area (they tend to be in Spanish): www.foroeducativo.org.

The Group for the Analysis of Development (GRADE) has an important education research area, and provides some resources in English: www.grade.org.pe.

Ministry of Education of Peru provides a good amount of materials: www.minedu .gob.pe.

Ministry of Education of Peru's Assessment Unit (UMC) provides information on achievement issues. It includes reports on all national and international educational assessments that Peru has participated in during recent years. (Most of the information is in Spanish.) Visit: http://www.minedu.gob.pe/umc/.

Morillo, E. 2002. *Reformas educativas en el Perú del siglo XX*: http://www.campus-oei.org/revista/deloslectores/233Morillo.PDF.

UNESCO. 2003. OECD/UNESCO study identifies regional disparities in student performance: http://portal.unesco.org/en (verified 2003).

Chapter 14

SCHOOLING IN URUGUAY

María Ester Mancebo

INTRODUCTION

Uruguay is a small country in the southern cone of Latin America, with an area of 176,215 square kilometres and around 3,300,000 people (Instituto Nacional de Estadística (INE) 2006). It occupies a good position in country rankings in the Human Development Index (HDI) elaborated by UNDP.[1] Uruguay is considered to have high level of education development due to its minimum rates of illiteracy, universal enrollment in primary education, expansion of secondary education, and good quality of university studies.

Uruguay obtained its independence from Spain in 1825 after a revolutionary war that began in 1811 under José Gervasio Artigas's leadership. During the nineteenth century, civil wars were frequent and the State's capacity was not solid enough to rule effectively all over the country. In this context, education reform that José Pedro Varela (considered to be the founder of the Uruguayan education system) initiated in the 1870s laid the foundations for republicanism, on the one hand, and contributed to the creation of a democratic society, on the other.

During the twentieth century, education opportunities expanded gradually in terms of access to primary and secondary education. Presently, around 720,000 children and adolescents attend primary, secondary, or vocational schools and there are more than 100,000 students in university courses. The education system has also been a successful channel to achieve gender equity. However, serious inequalities persist between social classes, private and public schools, rural and urban areas—with great disparities in access, completion, and performance. At present, equity and quality have become key issues in the education agenda.

The Uruguayan education system is characterized by a state-centred matrix: over 80 percent of the students in all educational levels attend state-run schools. The State has a leading role in the regulation of private education. Uruguayan education administration is original and complex in comparative perspective, with a high degree of autonomy from political power. This chapter on the history of Uruguayan education is divided into five sections:

1. Colonial times and period of national organization corresponding to the nineteenth century;
2. Expansion of education in the twentieth century centered on its first six decades;
3. Social crisis and the reign of authoritarianism, referring to education during the breakdown of democracy and emergence of a military government;
4. From restoration to debate in the education field, referring to the period from 1985 to the present;
5. Current situation and future perspectives with a review of the main challenges that Uruguay faces today in the education field.

COLONIAL TIMES AND PERIOD OF NATIONAL ORGANIZATION

During colonial times, the so-called *Banda Oriental* was a marginal territory for the Spaniards: political authority was located in Buenos Aires, not in Montevideo, and the land was considered poor since it did not have gold or silver. In this context, social and educational development was slow. There were only a few elementary schools that taught reading, writing, math, and religion using boring methodologies based on memory and physical punishment; also, there was no middle or higher education at all.

The independence revolution (1811–25) brought about two interesting experiences in education. On the one hand, Artigas founded the so-called *Escuelas de la Patria* in Montevideo and Purificación (1815) with a clear emphasis on republicanism, citizenship, and equality among social classes and races. On the other, a Lancaster school worked in Montevideo from 1821–25, applying the monitor methodology.

Both of these experiences were short-lived and, by the middle of the century, the state of education in Uruguay was very poor. According to a report written by Palomeque (Secretary of Public Instruction), only 899 students attended the thirty schools spread out in the country, where nonqualified and isolated teachers taught elementary writing, reading, math, and religion without any support and/or supervision from the education authorities. On the basis of this assessment, Palomeque suggested the adoption of a set of policy lines that could promote education development (increase in funding for education, establishment of compulsory education and teacher education). However, none of these measures were carried out in the first decades of the nineteenth century.

In 1868, José Pedro Varela (1845–79), together with a group of intellectuals, created the *Sociedad de Amigos de la Educación Popular* (Friends of Popular Education Society-SAEP) to promote education reform following the ideas introduced by Horace Mann and Domingo Faustino Sarmiento in the

United States and Argentina, respectively. SAEP gained great recognition in Uruguay and also in other countries of the region (Argentina, Chile, Paraguay, Brazil, and Perú) through its model school (*Elbio Fernández* School), creation of an important library, publication of pedagogical books, and organization of conferences and teaching courses.

Varela's educational philosophy is contained in *La Educación del Pueblo* and *De la Legislación Escolar*, in which he dealt with a wide variety of education topics ranging from its goals, the relation between school and democracy, methodology, school organization, discipline, school premises, and didactic materials. In particular, Varela emphasized that progress in education required qualified teachers and, following Friedrich Froebel's experience and methodology, promoted preschool education for kids under six years of age. In his view, education had to be compulsory, free, and no religious contents should be taught in schools. Education was the keystone of democratic government since a universal ballot required all citizens to be educated. Ignorance should be considered an abuse on behalf of the State. Therefore, students should not pay any tuition at all.

In this context, a major reform took place in the 1870s when Varela was appointed Secretary of Instruction in President Latorre's authoritarian government and prepared a bill of education on the ground of his innovative ideas. A law (*Ley de Educación Común*) was passed in 1877 and primary education became compulsory and free for all citizens. Even though laicism was not included in the reform and Catholicism continued being taught in public schools, children could skip it if their parents preferred. Furthermore, the law established a highly centralized education system, directed by a Council composed of seven members appointed by the executive branch of the government.

Varela's ideas raised opposition among Catholic authorities and the reform was deeply criticized by political parties that considered it illegitimate because of the dictatorial tone of Latorre's government. Varela argued that popular education was the main instrument to fight authoritarianism and create a solid basis for democracy. In his own words:

If education is important for all human beings and all human societies, it has utmost importance for those people like ours that have adopted the democratic-republican form of government.... Universal ballot requires universal education: without it, human beings are not conscious of their acts ... all Republican requirements have only one means of realization: educate, educate, always educate.... School is the base of the Republic, education is indispensable to citizenship. (Varela, La Educación del Pueblo 1874)

In spite of the initial resistance, Varela's reform became a milestone in the history of Uruguayan education with the passing of time.

During the nineteenth century, most public efforts were concentrated on primary education and there were only a few policy actions in other education levels. The *Universidad de la República* (UdelaR) was founded in 1849 with limited material and human resources. University studies were not only expensive but also restricted to law. In this context, the creation of a School of Medicine in 1875 and a School of Math in 1885 were considered indicators of modernization.

For three decades, UdelaR had competence over all levels of public education, from primary to tertiary education. In fact, primary school gained autonomy with Varela's Reform in 1877 but secondary education remained part of UdelaR until 1935. By the end of the nineteenth century, secondary education was viewed as a preparation for university studies. In particular, a law passed in 1885 (*Ley Orgánica de la Universidad*) established that the goals of secondary school were to complete basic education and prepare students for the tertiary level.

EXPANSION OF EDUCATION IN THE TWENTIETH CENTURY

During the first half of the twentieth century, there was a significant growth of enrollment in primary and secondary studies: students in both levels totaled 25,485 in 1875 and increased to 390,305 in 1963—equivalent to 6 percent and 15 percent of the population, respectively. (See Table 14.1.)

By 1963, more than 90 percent of ten-year-old students attended regular classes at school. Primary education did not only grow in numbers but also developed new modalities. In the 1910s, authorities created an institute for the education of deaf-mute children, a school for blind children, an "open air" school for those children who suffered from tuberculosis, and special schools for children with learning disabilities. From 1908 on, adults could attend regular classes in free courses taught in public schools spread throughout the country. The exception was rural education, which did not succeed in the fight against illiteracy despite curricular changes introduced in 1927 and 1949.

Secondary education also expanded in the second decade of the century: several high schools were opened all over the country (not only in the capital

Table 14.1
Evolution of Enrollment in Primary School (1880–1965)

Year	Students	Schools	Teachers
1880	24,785	310	610
1890	38,747	470	831
1900	52,474	571	1,131
1910	74,717	793	1,502
1920	102,880	1,005	2,155
1933	160,421	——	——
1940	192,057	——	——
1965	290,795	——	——

Source: Bralich 1996.

Table 14.2
Evolution of Enrollment in Secondary Education (1890–1963)

Year	Students
1890	500
1931	11,360
1942	19,309
1950	30,000
1963	79,510

Source: Rodriguez et al., 1984.

city) and a high school for women was created in Montevideo.[2] As a result, the number of students grew from 500 in the 1890s to 11,360 in 1931. The expansion continued in the following decades: 30,000 students in 1950, and 79,510 in 1963. According to the curricula approved in 1910 and reformed in 1941 and 1963, secondary studies were organized in two cycles of four and two years respectively, and were considered as a step to the university. (See Table 14.2.)

In the field of vocational education, an Arts and Crafts School had been working as a boarding school since 1879. It enrolled around two-hundred students aged thirteen to eighteen who were taught arts and crafts with strict military discipline. This orientation changed radically when Pedro Figari (lawyer and artist) was appointed Director of Technical Education (1915–17) since he conceived the goal of the school should not be limited to the training of workers and should teach a combination of science, crafts, and arts in a free educational environment. Technical skills were to be considered a means to a superior end: the development of students' competencies.

Figari's ideas had great impact on the evolution of this school, which received the name and status of Labor University (*Universidad del Trabajo del Uruguay*—UTU) in 1942, in a clear effort to reinforce its social legitimacy. In 1939, the institution had 9,000 students and by the 1960s, it had 20,000 students in ninety-five schools spread all over the country.

SOCIAL CRISIS AND THE REIGN OF AUTHORITARIANISM

In the 1960s and 1970s, Uruguay went through a severe socioeconomic crisis. In education, the status of the crisis elaborated by CIDE[3] (1965) pointed out several structural problems: universal completion of primary education was far from being achieved; repetition and drop out were extensive in middle and high school; preschool education only benefited a small proportion of Uruguayans; and there was a limited number of trained teachers for secondary school. To resolve these problems, CIDE proposed a variety of measures such as the extension of pedagogical time, improvement of teacher education, diversification of didactic methods, and the introduction of compensatory programs. Few of these policy lines were implemented in the 1970s or 1980s but in the

1990s, Germán Rama, one of the authors of the CIDE report, made most of them the core of his education reform.

In June 1973, after four decades of political stability, Uruguayan democracy broke down and a military government took over. Some months earlier, in January 1973, a controversial Law of Education (Number 14,101) was passed during a climate of social and political tension. The law aimed at restoring order and discipline in education; to do so, it made the education administrations dependant on political authorities, putting an end to the autonomy that the education system had enjoyed for a long time. Furthermore, the new legislation established nine years of compulsory education. Therefore, in 1976, the seventh, eighth, and ninth grades were grouped into a new level called *Ciclo Básico* (Basic Cycle) that was organized to provide general education. *Ciclo Básico* was followed by three years of *bachillerato* (high school), which served as preparation for university studies.

During the dictatorial regime (1973–84), authoritarianism reigned in education: hundreds of teachers who opposed the government were dismissed, school meetings were forbidden, communication was controlled, discipline was strict, certain books were banned, and the curricula was changed to avoid the spread of ideas considered leftist or revolutionary. Military authorities identified education as a main battleground where ideological victory had to be gained.

FROM RESTORATION TO DEBATE IN THE EDUCATION FIELD

After the return of a democratic government in 1985, five stages in education policies become apparent.

Restoration (1985–1990)

During this stage, when the National Administration of Public Education (ANEP) was led by Professor Juan Pivel Devoto, prodigious efforts were made to reinstitutionalize the education system, which had been strongly affected by the de facto regime. A Law of Education was passed as a matter of emergency, specifically establishing that:

pupils' independence of moral and civic conscience is fully guaranteed ... official pronouncements made by directing or consulting organs shall not obstruct functionaries' or pupils' right to petition nor their exercise of freedom of thought.... Teaching-learning shall be carried forward without impositions limiting right of access to all sources of culture.

Additionally, in order to re-democratize the education system, people who had been dismissed from the different sub-systems (primary, secondary, vocational, and teacher training) were rehired, competitions and elections for positions were reestablished, and Teaching-Technical Assemblies (ATDs) were brought back to represent the interests of primary and secondary school teachers. As in many other areas of national life, the thrust was for the restoration of the rules for democratic coexistence in force before the 1973 coup d'etat.

At the pedagogical level, the Single Basic Cycle (CBU) was established in middle school. This three-year cycle replaced the 1976 Common Basic Cycle (CBC), and was part of a long list of successive attempts to make effective the nine-year obligatory schooling established in the 1973 Law of Education. This law was "in the van" (on the vanguard)—in Latin American terms—but proved extremely hard to put into practice. Additionally, the notion of compensatory education made its appearance in the field of education policy (for instance, the 1986 Plan for compensation courses designed to support pupils with difficulties in different areas).

Evaluation of the Education System (1990–1995)

There were two notorious characteristics to this period: the positioning of ATDs as a relevant actor in education policy design, and the implementation of external evaluations, which showed all too clearly the shortfall in quality and equity in primary and middle schools nationwide. The wide circulation of these evaluations, which were respected and propitiated by the ANEP Authorities under Juan Gabito Zóboli's leadership, led to the optimal positioning of education on the public agenda and prepared the political scenario for education reform. In particular, the following education problems were brought up by the evaluations:

- shortfall in quality, measured by means of the first standardized primary and middle school learning tests ever carried out in Uruguay;
- education inequity, and strong linkage of education results and students' social backgrounds;
- difficulties in education management, at both the pedagogical and administrative levels; and
- insufficient training of middle school teaching staff.

Reform (1995–2000)

After the 1994 national election campaign (in which education enjoyed a central position and every political party vowed publicly to work intensely in this field) and during the 1995–2000 period, reform was carried out under the stern leadership of Germán Rama as President of ANEP.

ANEP reinforced the State's pedagogical role and carried forward a full repertoire of education policy lines. Chief among them were the expansion of pre-school education,[4] an increase in the number of full-time schools, implementation of a new syllabus for the basic cycle of middle school (the 1996 Plan), implementation of baccalaureates in technology within the sphere of vocational education, creation of a new model for initial teacher training for the middle school in six Regional Teacher Training Centres (CERPs), policies in connection with textbooks and didactic materials, and establishing a system for the assessment of learning.

From the procedural point of view, it was a rationalist, top-down reform seeking to strengthen existing institutions in a fashion that would allow actors adequate functions within the framework of a "classic" model of education policy. According to this model, policies derive their legitimacy from the democratic nature of education authorities, who are responsible for establishing education policies and organizing services, while teachers position themselves as "producers" of the service and students as its "receivers."

Opposition to Rama's reform was strong: it was considered authoritarian and was deeply criticized for the lack of teachers' participation. This resistance accounts for the difficulties in the institutionalization of most of its policy lines and also explains the emphasis future administrations would put on education dialogue.

Increased Damping Action (2000–2005)

During the period from 2000 to 2005, Javier Bonilla's administration mostly kept to the 1995–2000 platform and lost the capability of fostering innovation. This damper-like effect on the pace of educational change stemmed from factors both within and outside the education system. Of the former was the unrelenting opposition encountered by the reform, which considered authoritarian and undeliberated. A second factor was Bonilla's leadership style, which leaned towards an incrementalist design of policy. The main factor outside the education system was the economic crisis that came to a critical stage in 2002, leading to a serious lack of funds which played havoc with the day-to-day business of education.

Within the framework of this increasing damper-like effect, the main effort was centered on the consolidation of policy lines initiated between 1995–99: pre-school education, full-time schools, the 1996 Plan in the Basic Cycle, vocational baccalaureates, assessment of learning, and CERPs. Noteworthy innovations were reform in the second cycle of middle school, a plan for distance qualification of middle school teachers upcountry, and the design of a new plan for training primary school teachers, which became effective in 2005.

Education Debate (2005–2006)

In November 2004, for the first time in Uruguayan history a leftist party, the *Frente Amplio*, won the national elections. This change has affected education to a very great degree as, under the new government which came into power in March 2005, a process of wide-ranging education debate started, led by the Ministry of Education and Culture (MEC) and accompanied by ANEP authorities under Luis Yarzábal's leadership.

This debate may provide a preamble to the passing of a new education law to replace the existing one, which has been in force as emergency legislation since 1985. That said, the intention is for it to become a tonic for wide reflection on the present and future situation of national education. To this end, all citizens have been invited to participate, as well as social organizations, NGOs, trade unions, and the media. In the words of the ANEP president:

I firmly believe in the transformation of the national education system into a matter of such general importance that it cannot be left exclusively in the hands of the authorities, teachers, students, educational workers. Rather than this, modifications must be tackled by society in general. I thus invite all those present to stimulate the participation of fathers and mothers, neighbours of educational premises, so the process is plural, democratic and sustainable.[5]

There have been three structuring elements in the process:

- Creation of an Organizing Commission for Education Debate (CODE), an independent committee appointed by the Minister of Education in an agreement endorsed by the Educational Coordinating Commission, which consists of twenty-two members who act on their own behalf and who were proposed by ANEP, the State University (UdelaR), private educational centers, political parties, and education trade unions.
- MEC drafted a basic document[6] with five items for collective reflection: Education for All, Education and Citizenship, Education in the Model for National Development, Uruguayan Education in the Knowledge Society, and the Organization of a National Education system.
- Defining a work methodology to organize the debate in three stages: first, a stage where Territorial Assemblies are held upcountry, Zone Assemblies in the capital city of Montevideo, and Sector Assemblies all over the country (April–September 2006); second, committee work (September–November 2006) to process all the information gathered in the Assemblies; third, the National Congress for Education in December 2006. The Final Report will be submitted to Parliament, ANEP, UdelaR, and private education centers.

Inertia, Restoration, or Innovation over Two Decades of Educational Policies?

The answer to this question makes it necessary to distinguish three dimensions of education policies as public policies:

- The *content* of the policy; that is, its lines of action oriented by certain fundamental principles.
- The policy's *process*, history, and cycle.
- *Institutions* included in the framework of the policy in question—the main focus of this article.

These are three complementary dimensions that allow us to sketch out the following interpretation of the 1985 to 2005 period:

- During the first post-dictatorship administration, emphasis was placed on the reinstallment of the education system embracing democratic rules and functioning. This can be understood as the institutional and procedural restoration of a democratic past torn asunder during the 1973–84 de facto government. Regarding content, there is evidence to some degree of pedagogic innovation in the design of the 1986 Plan for the basic cycle of middle education.

- Between 1990 and 1995, there was innovation in the very centerpiece of the processes. On the one hand, diagnosis of educational situation was incorporated as a first-line factor in establishing an educational agenda, and on the other, teachers were widely involved in establishing policy, through the ATDs. However, regarding the dimensions of content and institutions, preservation of what already existed was predominant.
- The Reform period had dual characteristics: enormous impulse for change in the content of educational policies, and inertia in the procedural and institutional spheres. As an indication of this duality, we would mention that, unlike what happened in most Latin American countries, Uruguay developed its education reform without passing a new education law to replace the emergency law of 1985.
- Even though some new courses of action were designed at the time, the first five years of this century showed no progress in all dimensions of education policies, for reasons both endogenous and exogenous to the education system.
- Finally, in the two years since the present administration came to power (2005 and 2006), policy process has taken center stage in the authorities' agenda. This is clearly an innovation for processing education policies since 1985. With more than half of the present government's term of office (2005–) yet to go, it is still not possible to clearly establish the degrees of inertia, restoration, or innovation in the three dimensions. In fact, differing indicators can be identified in the areas of content and institutions. For example, there has been a restoration of the 1986 Plan in the basic cycle of middle education, whereas, at the same time, there is outstanding innovation in the Community Teachers' Program in primary education.

CURRENT SITUATION AND FUTURE PERSPECTIVES

State-centered Matrix

The Uruguayan education system is characterized by a state-centered educational matrix: in 2004, 87.8 percent of primary school students attended state schools as did 86.0 percent of middle school pupils, 89.0 percent of those in secondary, 100 percent of teachers training course participants, and 88.1 percent of university students.

Returning to a long-standing tradition initiated in the second half of the nineteenth century with José Pedro Varela's reform fostering free compulsory schooling, during the late 1990s the predominance of State education became even greater. This was the combined effect of two factors: increased State education offered due to education reform led by Rama, and a drop in the demand for private education services stemming from the economic crisis Uruguay suffered after 1999.

The great majority of private primary and secondary schools apply the syllabus established by the State and take advantage of their autonomy at times and in areas complementary to those that are officially regulated.

Education and Social Class

In the first half of the twentieth century, Uruguayan society was highly integrated, with education playing a key role in the process of social integration. However, as of 1960, a weak model for development together with feeble social policies led to high levels of poverty and social exclusion that are still present today.

According to data gathered by the National Institute of Statistics in 2006, 27.4 percent of the general population was living under the poverty line. This proportion was even higher among children and adolescents due to a regressive pattern of social protection: 49.6 percent of children under six, 48.4 percent of six- to twelve-year-olds, and 41.1 percent of adolescents.

More than 60 percent of students attending state primary schools and about 50 percent of those in state high schools are members of poor families. The education system has not been able to overcome the pedagogical difficulties associated with this social legacy and results indicate serious stratification of students' achievements. In PISA 2004, 15 percent to 30 percent of the students obtained very poor results and 5 percent of the best students exhibited reading skills three times superior to those of the bottom 5 percent. Students attending private-sector high schools did better that those in state high schools, and their performance was better than that of vocational school pupils. This is evidence that Uruguay's education system is deeply segmented.

Access to Education

Compared to other countries in the region, Uruguay was very much a pioneer. Law Number 14,101, passed in 1973, calls for nine years of compulsory education (six years of primary education and three years of middle school—the "basic cycle").

Twenty-five years later, Law Number 17,015 (passed in 1998) called for one additional year of compulsory education, at the pre-primary level. In 2002, ANEP reported that universal education of five-year-olds had been achieved. In fact, between 1995–2000, pre-primary enrollment increased almost 100 percent (46,618 pupils in 1995 compared to 87,607 in 2000). Educational expansion at the pre\school level is deemed one of the most important social policies implemented in the last few decades.

Educational access is guaranteed for all Uruguayans, male or female, at the primary and secondary levels. However, universalization has been achieved in primary but not in secondary education. Rama's reform included several measures promoting expansion of this education level (a new syllabus for middle school, extension of pedagogical time in most high schools, creation of new models of the basic cycle for rural areas) but results have been poor.

According to 2005 data, 155,665 children under five received preschool education (out of a total number of 294,117 children under five—53 percent) and 354,777 children attended primary school (94 percent of children between six and twelve years old). Finally, 331,684 students attend middle, high school, or vocation schools while children aged thirteen to seventeen increases to 260,539; these figures points out a serious problem of inefficiency at this educational level (see below).

Efficiency of the School System

Children and adolescents attend school from March to December and have a long vacation from early December until the end of February. Within this school calendar, pedagogical time is short compared to developed countries (around 800 hours a year).

In Uruguay, the democratization of access to education was not accompanied by democratization of completion of compulsory education (a total of ten years: one pre-primary, six primary, and three middle school). This inefficiency stems from high rates of repetition, falling behind in primary schools, and dropping out in secondary schools.

For over two decades, Uruguay has enjoyed practically universal access and completion rates in primary education. The net rate of schooling is about 95 percent. Nevertheless, high repetition rates persist, especially in first grade. This leads to late completion of the cycle. In the 1990s, the repetition rate for first to sixth grade was 10 percent while the rate for first grade alone was 20 percent. Repetition is heavily concentrated in the first grade of primary schools and in schools with a high proportion of pupils from deprived families.

It is true that as of 2000 the repetition rate has been decreasing. This is due to the creation of full-time schools and the expansion of initial education coverage: the repetition rate for first to sixth grade has dropped from 10.3 to 8.1 percent, and the rate for first grade alone has dropped from 20.4 to 16.1 percent. Nonetheless, high repetition rates lead to a significant increase in the average time to finish primary school. The rate for on-time completion of primary school has been around the 70 percent mark for the last fifteen years. Access to middle education has also reached levels approaching universality, but there is a high number of pupils falling behind or dropping out. The theoretical age for completion of the basic cycle is fifteen, but only 40 percent of state high school pupils manage to finish on time. In the same vein, the theoretical age for completion of the second cycle of middle education is eighteen, but only 20 percent of those students of each age-cohort complete on time. In summary, while on-time completion of primary school is a fundamental challenge, at the middle education level the battle against dropping out and falling behind is central.

Academic Achievement, Academic Standards, and Standardized Testing

Simultaneous with the inclusion of standardized systems to assess students' learning in the rest of Latin America, ANEP set up an education evaluation unit in the 1990s. This unit has gradually grown stronger, reaching a satisfactory level of institutionalization.

On the one hand, the national assessment system has strengthened the concentration of authority at the central level. The Educational Results Measurement Unit (UMRE) has become the actor with the greatest responsibility for assessing educational performance, thus reinforcing the model with ANEP as the main regulator, provider, and evaluator of the country's educational services. This system, which also evaluates private schools, has chosen to restrict the availability of information about education results at school levels, attaching greater importance to analysis of socioeconomic factors influencing student performance. No clear link between results and incentives or compensatory mechanisms has been established.

Of the forty-one countries that took part in PISA 2004, Uruguay was thirty-fourth in reading skills, thirty-fifth in science, and thirty-sixth in math. This performance was better than other Latin American nations but is well behind those of the best-placed countries (Finland and South Korea).

Teachers' Qualifications

There are clear differences between primary and post-primary education with regard to teachers' qualifications. At the primary level, all teachers are appropriately trained and hold teaching credentials. However, in secondary schools this figure stands at roughly 47 percent, dropping to 30 percent in vocational schools, with 20 percent of teachers lacking a degree.

University Studies

The official *Universidad de la República* (UdelaR) held a monopoly on university studies until 1985 when the government authorized a private university, *Universidad Católica del Uruguay.* According to 2004 data, there are 103,160 students at the tertiary level, including university and non-university careers. Public education predominates over private: UdelaR has 70,156 students and ANEP has 20,958 students in teaching education. Even though enrollment in private universities has had a steady growth in the last decade, at present 9,494 students attend classes at the *Universidad Católica, ORT,* and *Universidad de Montevideo.* Tertiary education is concentrated in the capital city: more that 80 percent of enrollment is located in Montevideo.

Institutional Setting

Several organizations are involved in regulating education:

- The National Administration of Public Education (ANEP) was established in 1985. It is an autonomous body independent from the executive branch, covering primary, secondary, and vocational education as well as teacher training.

- The University of the Republic (UdelaR) is also autonomous and independent from the Department of Education, and is responsible for state university education.
- The Department of Education (Ministry of Education and Culture, MEC) is a part of the executive branch. Its responsibility is limited to the regulation of private preschool and university education.

In comparison with other systems, the Uruguayan institutional setting is both unique and complex due to four factors:

- First, ANEP and UdelaR are headed by plural collegiate bodies: a five-member central council plus three councils of three members each for primary, secondary, and vocational education in the case of ANEP, and a twenty-five-member central council in the case of UdelaR.
- Second, ANEP and UdelaR enjoy technical and administrative independence from political power and the executive branch.
- Third, MEC is not a central actor in the design, implementation, or evaluation of policies at most education levels: basic education, secondary, vocational, teacher training, and university.
- Fourth, the mechanism for the appointment of ANEP and UdelaR education authorities affords them great stability in their positions, as opposed to the rest of Latin America where ministers of education average roughly two years on the job.

Organization and School Autonomy

Unlike other Latin American countries, Uruguay did not develop a decentralization process in the last decade of the twentieth century. Since the transition back to democracy in 1985, there have been several timid drives to extend decentralization, but most have come to nothing.

The model adopted for state schools was the French system, and the structure of the Uruguayan education system is centralized and hierarchical. The central authorities of ANEP, based in Montevideo, make most relevant education decisions, which are later applied throughout the country. In fact, Rama's reform (1995–2000) reinforced the state's role in all phases of education policy: design, implementation, and evaluation. All decisions made in the capital city and uniformly enforced throughout the country: curricular framework, planning, assessment of students' performance, teacher evaluation, and management of human and financial resources.

There are a few extremely limited instances of organizational decentralization or institutional autonomy. This centralized model has been dubbed "de-localization" since the national government retained all administrative, management, and financial matters. This model explains why Uruguayan public schools are homogeneous throughout the country. They may vary in size: in Montevideo, the capital city, there are huge, overcrowded urban schools whereas there are very small schools in the rural areas. But all schools carry out the same curriculum and have the same organization, rules, and procedures.

Community Participation

Teachers can participate in education decisions through their unions, which advocate for their interests as workers, and the so-called Teaching-Technical Assemblies (ATDs). These are deliberative bodies that are usually consulted by the educational authorities, and can also submit technical initiatives. Of the post-dictatorship periods of educational policies, it was during the Gabito Administration (1990–95) when the ATDs became most relevant in policy design, participating in task forces discussing a variety of pedagogic subjects.[7] At the time of the Reform (1995–2000), the ATDs mostly addressed education authorities, and lost their characteristic of being an interlocutor with the government. As of 2003, the Bonilla Administration (2000–2005), with its purely incrementalist nature, added the task of designing the Transformation of Superior Middle Education (TEMS) to the ATDs' duties.

Conversely, mechanisms to promote the participation of students, parents, and local communities are feeble. In fact, "Fostering Committees" in primary schools and "Associations of Parents and Friends" in high schools have been limited to fundraising. A review of experiences associated with the participation of external actors in education institutions exhibits two main levels:

- Participation in case-by-case support (attending meetings, answering queries, contributions of cash, materials, or time).
- Participation in the process of decision-making at the management level (assessment and supervision, problem analysis, planning, execution).

During the wave of education reforms in the 1990s, Latin American countries experimented with different modes of parent and general community participation in education, ranging from decisions regarding the use of services (for instance, the parents' selection of subsidized private schools in Chile), funding and approval of outlay for facilities and maintenance (Bolivia, Brazil, and Colombia), to full-school administration (specific programs in Guatemala, Honduras, Nicaragua, and El Salvador). To these ends, the countries concerned set up school councils, school committees, or parents' associations, which imply a major redefinition of educational-centered micro-politics.

This is practically an untouched area in Uruguay, where specific institutional arrangements would be required to make any development possible. The Community Teacher Programme (PMC), which is co-executed by ANEP and the Ministry of Social Development (MIDES), with the technical assistance of the NGO *El Abrojo*, has been attempting since 2005 to weaken the rigid boundaries separating school and family, by means of parents' participation in school activities, or by community teachers' work in students' homes.

Building an Intelligent Teacher-State

The story of Uruguayan education is that of the gradual consolidation of a teacher-state, which can be understood as the major presence of the State as a direct provider of educational services. At this level, it is a challenge for Uruguay to construct an intelligent teacher-state, while substantially strengthening the following:

- Decision-making capability stemming from institutional design. As stated earlier, the complexity of educational institutionalization—particularly regarding the twin heads constituted by ANEP and MEC, and the collegiate character of ANEP organizations—entails the risk of decision blocks, which might be avoided with different institutional arrangements.
- Institutional coordination. In its role as principal provider of educational services, ANEP must improve its channels of communication with the rest of the bodies responsible for social policies. In the face of the crumbling "architecture of social welfare" that Uruguay is encountering, mere sectorial responses are not enough.
- The ability to plan, monitor, and evaluate education policies, programs, and projects. The intelligent teacher-state requires sound planning skills, as well as the capability to follow up and evaluate policies, programs, and projects. The former will allow for early awareness of any deviation from what is planned, while the latter will make it possible to compare the program being evaluated with a preestablished criteria or model (for instance, quality of education, equitableness, transparency).

DAY IN THE LIFE

Leaving aside differences in size, Uruguayan schools are homogeneous throughout the country: they all apply the same curriculum, use the same books, and follow the same rules decided in Montevideo. However, there is an important gap between primary and secondary level.

Primary School

Sofía is an eleven-year-old girl who attends an urban public school in Manga, a poor neighborhood in the capital city, Montevideo. She gets up at 7:00 AM, has breakfast with her mother and puts on her white tunic and blue bow, symbols of Uruguayan public education. She walks about eight blocks to arrive at her school before 8:00 AM when the bell rings and all students arrive in their classrooms.

Susan, Sofía's teacher, applies a variety of classic methods to teach math, Spanish, science, and social studies to her forty students class, but she seldom uses new technologies in her daily lessons because they are not available at the school. Her students do not take music or physical education classes because neither the school nor the parents can afford the teachers' salaries.

At 10:00 AM, all kids run to the grounds for a twenty-minute recess while teachers supervise, discipline, and talk about personal and professional issues.

At the end of the class, at 12:00 PM, Sofía has a free lunch at school before she returns home. In the afternoon, she will spend about an hour doing some homework Susan asked her to. She will do it by herself because her parents will be working until 8:00 PM. She would like to learn English to understand movies and songs that she loves but her parents do not have enough money to pay for private lessons—English is not part of her compulsory primary school curriculum.

Secondary School

Federico is a sixteen-year-old student in a high school located downtown in Salto, one of the most important cities in the country. He used to be a good student when he was at the primary level but now his performance is rather poor. Transition to middle school has not been easy for him: he still misses his sixth grade teacher and finds it very difficult to understand the teaching methods of his ten teachers as their criteria vary a lot. Besides, he does not have all of the required books since his parents could not afford them and the school library only has a few copies.

He definitely is not fond of school these days. He has to attend a lot of classes of a fragmented curriculum: math, literature, English, French, history, geography, drawing, biology, physics, and chemistry. He loves music, computing, and physical education, but they represent a small part of his school schedule. Besides, he is very fond of his classmates but sometimes he is afraid of the violence shown by some of them.

As a result, Federico is thinking of getting a regular job and dropping out of school. This is a hard decision for him and for his family: they know he should complete his tertiary studies so that he can find a good job when he becomes an adult but they need the money now and feel Federico is wasting his time at school.

TIMELINE

1811   Independence revolution started with José Gervasio Artigas's leadership.

1815   *Escuelas de la Patria* were opened in Montevideo and Purificación.

1821   Opening of a school using Lancaster method in Montevideo.

1825   Uruguay became independent from Spain.

1830   Uruguay passed its first Constitution.

1849   Foundation of *Universidad de la República*.

1868   José Pedro Varela created *Sociedad de Amigos de la Educación Popular*.

1877   Varela's Reform: primary education became compulsory and free for all Uruguayan citizens. Primary education gained autonomy when it was separated from *Universidad de la República*.

1882   Primary teachers' education started (*Instituto Normal de Varones Joaquín Sánchez e Instituto Normal de Señoritas María Stagnero de Munar*).

1910s Expansion of primary and secondary education.

1915   José Batlle y Ordoñez laid the foundations for Uruguayan Welfare State.
       Reform of vocational education under Figari's administration.

1935   Secondary education gained autonomy when it was separated from *Universidad de la República*. Two primary teachers' schools were united into one institution.

1949   Secondary teachers' education started (*Instituto de Profesores Artigas*, IPA).
1965   Diagnosis of state of Uruguayan education by *Comisión de Inversión y Desarrollo Económico* (CIDE).
1973   Deep social and political crisis led to authoritarianism.
        Parliament passed controversial Law of Education.
        Military coup d'etat.
1976   Creation of a Basic Cycle for middle school (seventh, eighth, and ninth grades).
1985   Democratic restoration. New Law of Education was passed by Parliament.
        First private University opened (*Universidad Católica del Uruguay*).
1995   Rama's reform carried out to promote quality and equity in education.
2005   Leftist party (*Frente Amplio*) won national elections for the first time in Uruguayan history.
2006   National debate on education in process.

NOTES

1. United Nations Development Program, UNDP. Uruguay occupies position number 46 in a list of 177 countries. The value of Uruguayan IDH is 0.840 (2005).

2. Even though secondary education was not legally forbidden for women, cultural factors limit their attendance in high school and, therefore, in universities.

3. Comisión de Inversión y Desarrollo Económico (CIDE).

4. Preschool education had an early start in Uruguayan education history. In 1892, Enriqueta Compte y Riqué opened a kindergarten for children of ages three, four, and five. However, the growth of this level was very slow until the 1990s when it became a key point of Rama's reform.

5. Speech calling for debate on education, delivered by ANEP President L. Yarzábal in the city of Young (Rio Negro, Uruguay) on August 15, 2006.

6. MEC (2005).

7. For example, the revision of 1986 Plan basic cycle programs.

BIBLIOGRAPHY

Books

Ardao, María Julia. 1962. *La creación de la sección de enseñanza secundaria y preparatoria para mujeres en 1912.*
Bralich, Jorge. 1986. *Una historia de la educación en el Uruguay; Del Padre Astete a las computadoras.* Montevideo: Fundación de Cultura Universitaria.
Bralich, Jorge. 1987. *Breve historia de la educación en el Uruguay.* Montevideo: CIEP-Ediciones del Nuevo Mundo.
Comisión de Inversiones y Desarrollo Económico (CIDE). 1965. *Informe sobre el Estado de la educación en el Uruguay, plan de desarrollo educativo.* Montevideo.
Rodriguez de Artucio, Elia, Ma. Luisa Rampini, Carmen Tornaría, Alex Mazzei, Ernesto Rodríguez, and Pablo da Silveira. 1984. *El proceso educativo uruguayo: del modelo democrático al intento autoritario; Apogeo y crisis de la educación uruguaya.* Montevideo: Fondo de Cultura Universitaria.
Traversoni, Alfredo and Diosma Piotti. 1984. *Nuestro sistema educativo hoy.* Montevideo: Ed. Banda Oriental.

Articles and Chapters

Amarante, Verónica and Andrea Vigorito. 2006. "Pobreza y desigualdad en Uruguay 2006." Uruguay: INE.

ANEP-TEMS. 2003. "Trayectoria educativa de los jóvenes: el problema de la deserción." *Serie Aportes para la Reflexión y la Transformación de la Educación Media Superior, Cuaderno de Trabajo no. 20.* Montevideo: MEMFOD.

Appratto, Carmen and Lucila Artagaveytia. 2004. "La educación." In *El Uruguay de la dictadura (1973–1985).* Edited by Benjamín Nahum. Montevideo: Banda Oriental.

Bernasconi, Gabriela and Mónica Maronna. 2002. "Itinerario histórico; Un siglo de educación pública 1975–85." www.anep.edu.uy/ANEP/historico.

Mancebo, María Ester. 1999. "Las políticas educativas uruguayas en el contexto latinoamericano (1985–94)." *Revista Uruguaya de Ciencia Política* no. 10. Montevideo: ICP.

Mancebo, María Ester. 2002. "La 'larga marcha' de una reforma 'exitosa': de la formulación a la implementación de políticas educativas." In *Uruguay: la reforma del estado y las políticas públicas en la democracia restaurada.* Compiled by Mancebo-Narbondo-Ramos. Montevideo: Banda Oriental-ICP.

Mancebo, María Ester. 2006. *La educación uruguaya en una encrucijada: entre la inercia, la restauración y la innovación.* Montevideo: MEC.

Opertti, Renato. 2005. "Educación: una historia de luces y sombras con debes importantes." In Gerardo Caetano, *20 años de democracia; Uruguay 1985–2005: miradas múltiples.* Montevideo: Ed. Taurus.

Web Sites

Administración Nacional de Educación Pública: www.anep.edu.uy.

Instituto Nacional de Estadística: www.ine.gub.uy.

Museo Pedagógico José Pedro Varela: www.crnti.edu.uy/museo/.

Red Académica Uruguaya: www.rau.edu.uy.

United Nations Educational Cultural, and Scientific Organization (UNESCO) (education web page): http://portal.unesco.org/education/.

World Bank education statistics online database: http://devdata.worldbank.org/edstats/.

BIBLIOGRAPHY

BOOKS

Applebaum, N.P. 2003. *Muddied Waters: Race, Region and Local History in Colombia, 1846–1948*. Durham: Duke University Press.

Biermayr-Jenzano, Patricia. 2001. *Intercultural Education for Quechua Women: A Participatory Study on Gender Relations, Cultural Preservation and Identity Formation in Rural Bolivia*. Doctoral dissertation. Cornell University.

Braslavsky, C. 2000 *The Secondary Education Curriculum in Latin America: New Tendencies and Changes*. Geneva: International Bureau of Education.

Brock, C. and Schwartzman, S., eds. 2004. *The Challenges of Education in Brazil*. Didcot: Oxford Studies in Comparative Education/Symposium Books.

Carnoy, M. 2007. *Cuba's Academic Advantage: Why Students in Cuba Do Better in School*. Stanford: Stanford University Press.

CSUTCB (Confederación Sindical Única de Trabajadores Campesinos de Bolivia). 2001. *Voices and Processes Toward Pluralism: Indigenous Education in Bolivia*. No. 9. New Education Division Documents. Stockholm: SIDA. (Originally published in Spanish under the title *Voces y procesos desde la pluralidad; La educación indígena en Bolivia*. La Paz, Bolivia: Plural Editores.)

De Moura Castro, C. and D. C Levy. 2000. *Myth, Reality and Reform: Higher Education Policy in Latin America*. Washington, DC: Inter-American Development Bank.

Freire, P. 1996. *Pedagogy of the Oppressed*. London: Penguin.

Gale, L. 1969. *Education and Development in Latin America with Special Reference to Colombia and Some Comparison with Guayane, South America*. London: Routledge and Kegan Paul.

Gershberg, Alec Ian. 2001. *Empowering Parents While Making Them Pay: Autonomous Schools in Nicaragua*. New York: Milano School of Management and Urban Policy, New School University.

Gustafson, Bret. 2002. *Native Languages and Hybrid States. A Political Ethnography of Guarani Engagement with Bilingual Education Reform in Bolivia, 1988–99.* Doctoral dissertation. Harvard University.

Gvirtz, S., Ball S., and G. Fischman. 2003. *Crisis and Hope: The Educational Hopscotch of Latin America.* London: Routledge Falmer.

Hanson, M. 1986. *Educational Reform and Administrative Development: The Cases of Colombia and Venezuela.* Stanford, CA: Hoover Institutional Press.

Kaestner, Robert and Alec Gershberg. 2002. *Lessons Learned from Nicaragua's School Autonomy Reform: A Review of Research by the Nicaragua Reform Evaluation Team of the World Bank.* New York: World Bank Documents and Reports.

King, Elizabeth M., et al. 1999. *Nicaragua's School Autonomy Reform: Fact or Fiction?* New York and Washington: World Bank Documents and Reports.

Klein, Herbert. 1982. *Bolivia: The Evolution of a Multi-Ethnic Society.* New York: Oxford University Press.

Luykx, A. 1999. *The Citizen Factory: Schooling and Cultural Production in Bolivia.* Albany: State University of New York Press.

Maier, J. and R. Weatherhead. 1979. *The Latin American University.* Albuquerque: University of New Mexico Press.

Nobrega, Manuel da. 1954. *Diálogo sobre a conversão do gentio* (1559). Lisboa: Edição comemorativa do IV Centenário de São Paulo.

Post, D. 2001. *Children's Work, Schooling, and Welfare in Latin America: Chile, Peru, and Mexico Compared.* Boulder: Westview Press.

Randall, L. and J. B. Anderson, eds. 1999. *Schooling for Success: Preventing Repetition and Dropout in Latin American Primary Schools.* New York and London: M. E. Sharpe.

Rappaport, J. 2005. *Intercultural Utopias: Cultural Experimentation and Ethnic Dialogue in Colombia.* Durham: Duke University Press, 2005.

Reimers, F. 2001. *Unequal Schools, Unequal Chances. The Challenges to Equal Opportunity in the Americas.* Boston: Harvard University.

Rein, M. E. 1998. *Politics and Education in Argentina, 1946–62.* New York, Armonk: M.E. Sharpe.

Safford, Frank, and Marcos Palacios. 2000. *Fragmented Land, Divided Society: Colombia.* Oxford, University Press.

Stepan, A. 1978. *The State and Society: Peru in Comparative Perspective.* New Jersey, Surrey: Princeton University Press.

Stromquist, N., ed. 1992. *Women and Education in Latin America, Knowledge, Power and Change.* London: Lynne Rienner.

Tedesco, Juan Carlos. 2003. *Educación y sociedad en la Argentina (1880–1945).* Buenos Aires: Ediciones Solar.

Torres, C. A. and A. Puiggrós, eds. 1997. *Latin American Education: Comparative Perspectives.* Boulder, Colorado: Westview Press.

Vaughan, Mary K. 1997. *Cultural Politics in Revolution: Teachers, Peasants and Schools in Mexico 1930–40.* University of Arizona, Tucson.

Waggoner, George R. and Barbara Ashton Waggoner. 1971. *Education in Central America.* Lawrence: The University Press of Kansas.

Weinberg, Gregorio. 1987. *Modelos Educativos en la Historia de América Latina.* Buenos Aires: Kapelusz.

Zegarra, H. 1998. *Decentralization and Autonomy in Chiapas, Mexico: 1994–98. A Case Study of Cultural-Educational Change.* Pittsburgh: University of Pittsburgh.

ARTICLES AND BOOK CHAPTERS

Beech, J. 2006. "The Institutionalization of Education in Latin America: Loci of Attraction and Mechanisms of Diffusion." In *The Impact of Comparative Education Research on Institutional Theory.* Edited by David P. Baker and Alexander W. Wiseman. Oxford: Elsevier Science Ltd.

Bing Wu, K., P. McLauchlan de Arregui, P. Goldschmidt, A. Miranda, and J. Saavedra. 2000. "Education and Poverty in Peru." In *Unequal Schools, Unequal Chances: The Challenges to Equal Opportunity in the Americas.* Edited by F. Reimers. Cambridge, Massachusetts: The David Rockefeller Center Series on Latin American Studies and Harvard University Press.

Bushnell, D. 1969. "Education in Colombia." In *History of Latin American Civilization 2.* Edited by Lewis Hanke, 26–63. London.

Cortina, Regina. 1992. "Gender and Power in the Teachers' Union of Mexico." In *Women and Education in Latin America, Knowledge, Power and Change.* Edited by Stromquist. London: Lynne Rienner.

Cox, C. 2000. "The Chilean Secondary Education Quality and Equity Improvement Program 1995–2000." Unpublished paper presented at the Organizations of Eastern Caribbean States Workshop organized by the World Bank on June 19–21, 2000. http://www1.worldbank.org/education/secondary/documents/CHILE'SM-eng.pdf.

Cox, C. 2002. "Citizenship Education in Curriculum Reforms of the 1990s in Latin America: Context, Contents, and Orientations." In *Education et vivre ensemble* [Education and living together]. Edited by Francois Audigier and Norberto Bottani. Geneva: Service de la Recherche en Education.

Cuellar-Marchelli, Helga. "Decentralization and Privatization of Education in El Salvador: Assessing the Experience." *International Journal of Educational Development* 23, no. 2 (2003): 145–66.

Dussel, Inés. 2001. "School Uniforms and the Disciplining of Appearances: Towards a History of the Regulation of Bodies in Modern Educational Systems." In *Cultural History and Education: Critical Essays on Knowledge and Schooling.* Edited by Thomas S. Popkewitz, Barry M. Franklin, and Miguel A. Pereyra, 207–41. New York: Routledgefalmer.

Faria Filho, L.M. and Vidal. "History of Brazilian Urban Education: Space and Time in Primary Schools." In *The International Handbook on Urban Education.* Organized by W. Pink and G. Noblit. Dordrecht: Springer (forthcoming).

Fischman and Gvirtz. "An Overview of Educational Policies in the Countries of Latin America during the 1990s." *Journal of Education Policy* 16, no. 6 (2001).

Gvirtz, S. "Curricular Reforms in Latin America with Special Emphasis on the Argentine Case." *Comparative Educación* 38, no. 4 (2002).

Gvirtz, Silvina. "Recent Educational Reforms in Latin America with Special Reference to Argentina." *The Alumni Association Bulletin* (The Institute of Education, University of London) no. 4 (Aug. 2000).

Gvirtz, S. and J. Beech. 2007. "The Internationalisation of Education Policy in Latin America." In M. Hayden, J. Levy, and J. Thompson, *Handbook of Research in International Education*. London: Sage.

Gvirtz, S. and J. Beech. "From the Intended to the Implemented Curriculum in Argentina: Exploring the Relation Between Regulation and Practice." In *Prospects* 34, no. 3 (2004).

Gvirtz, S. and G. Fischman. "An Overview of Educational Policies in the Countries of Latin America during the 1990s." *Journal of Education Policy* (England) vol. 16, no. 6 (2001).

Gvirtz S. and S. Larripa. December 2002. "Reforming School Curricula in Latin America: a Focus on Argentina." In *Curriculum Change and Social Inclusion: Perspectives from the Baltic and Scandinavian Countries.* Edited by S. Tawil. IBE-UNESCO.

Hazen, D. "The Politics of Schooling in the Nonliterate Third World: The Case of Peru." *History of Education Quarterly* 18, no. 4 (1978).

Hornberger, Nancy and Luís Enrique López. 1998. "Policy, Possibility, and Paradox: Indigenous Multilingualism and Education in Peru and Bolivia." In *Beyond Bilingualism: Multilingualism and Multiculturalism in Education.* Edited by J. Cenoz and F. Genesee, 206–42. London: Multilingual Matters.

Kraft, Richard J. 1983. "Nicaragua: Educational Opportunity under Pre- and Post-Revolutionary Conditions." In *Politics and Education: Cases from Eleven Nations.* Edited by Murray Thomas, 79–103. New York: Pergamon Press.

Levinson, Bradley A. U. "Hopes and Challenges for the New Civic Education in Mexico: Toward a Democratic Citizen without Adjectives." *International Journal of Educational Development* 24, no. 3 (2004): 269–82.

López, Luis Enrique. "Top-down and Bottom-up: Counterpoised Visions of Bilingual Intercultural Education in Latin America." In *Can Schools Revitalize Languages?* Edited by Nancy Hornberger. New York: Palgrave-Macmillan, forthcoming.

Luykx, A., N. H. Quiroga, A. M. Gottret, I. Velarde, and V. H. Arrázola. 2001. "Education of Indigenous Adults in Bolivia: A National Study." In *Adult Education in Africa and Latin America: Intercultural Experience in a Multicultural Encounter.* Edited by Wolfgang Küper and Teresa Valiente-Catter, 347–90. Lima, Peru: GTZ.

Martin, C. J. and C. Solórzano. 2003. "Mass Education, Privatization, Compensation and Diversification: Issues on the Future of Public Education in Mexico." *Compare* 33, no. 1 (2003): 15–30.

Mayo, John K., Robert C. Hornik, et al. 1973. "Television and Educational Reform in El Salvador: Report on the Fourth Year of Research." Stanford University. Institute for Communications Research, 1973. USAID. *U.S. Overseas Loans and Grants.* Order No. PN-AAB-410-A1. Washington, DC: USAID.

Narodowski, M. and M. Andrada. 2001. "The Privatisation of Education in Argentina." *Journal of Education Policy* 16, no. 6 (2001): 585–95.

Narodowski, M. & L. Manolakis. "Defending the 'Argentine Way of Life.' The State and the School in Argentina (1884–1984)." *Paedagogica Historica. International Journal of History of Education* (2002).

Rhoten, Diana. "Education Decentralization in Argentina: A 'Global-Local Conditions of Possibility' Approach to State, Market, and Society Change." *Journal of Educational Policy* 15, no. 6 (2000): 593–619.

Schmelkes, Silvia. 2000. "Education and Indian Peoples in Mexico." *Women and Education in Latin America, Knowledge, Power and Change.* Edited by Stromquist. London: Lynne Rienner.

Taylor, Solange. 2004. *Intercultural and Bilingual Education in Bolivia: The Challenge of Ethnic Diversity and National Identity.* (Instituto de Investigaciones Socio Económicas Working Paper Number 01/04). La Paz: Universidad Católica Boliviana.

JOURNALS

Cowen, Robert, ed. "Special Issue on Latin America and Educational Transfer." *Cowen Comparative Education* 38, no. 4 (2002).

Fishman, Gustavo and Silvina Gvirtz, eds. "Special Issue on Latin America." *Journal of Education Policy* 16, no. 6 (2001).

INDEX

ABOUT THE EDITORS
AND CONTRIBUTORS

Robert F. Arnove, Chancellor Professor Emeritus of Education at Indiana University/Bloomington, is an Honorary Fellow and past president of the Comparative and International Education Society (CIES). He has written extensively on educational and social change in Latin America, with numerous articles and two books on the recent history of Nicaragua.

María Balarin is postdoctoral fellow at the Department of Education of the University of Bath where, in 2006, she obtained a PhD in Education. She has previously worked as an education researcher at the Group for the Analysis of Development (GRADE—Peru) and in the Ministry of Education of Peru. Her interests focus on the politics of education policy making, the sociology of education policies, and relationships between education and citizenship formation, particularly in Peru and Latin America.

Jason Beech is Director of the BA in Education at the Universidad de San Andrés in Buenos Aires, Argentina, where he also teaches Comparative Education. He has a PhD in Comparative Education from the Institute of Education, University of London. He is also a consultant for the IIPE-UNESCO, Buenos Aires. His main interests are the transfer of specialized knowledge about education in the global education field and conditions of reception in different local contexts. He has published several articles and book chapters in Argentina, Brazil, Denmark, Spain, Switzerland, the United Kingdom, and the United States. Some of his latest publications are: "The Internationalisation of education policy in Latin America" in M. Hayden, J. Levy, and J. Thompson, eds., *Handbook of Research in International Education* (2007, with Silvina Gvirtz), and "The Institutionalization of Education in Latin America: Loci of Attraction and Mechanisms of Diffusion," in David P. Baker and Alexander W. Wiseman, eds., *The Impact of Comparative Education Research on Institutional Theory* (2006).

David C. Edgerton, worked for the Academy for Educational Development (AED) for twenty-two years, until his retirement in 2004. He directed long-term educational development projects funded by the U.S. Agency for International Development (USAID) in the Dominican Republic, Honduras, Guatemala, and Nicaragua. Before joining AED, he taught English and American literature at a regional campus of the University of Puerto Rico, and was a staff writer with the Agency for Instructional Technologies (AIT) in Bloomington, Indiana. He continues working as a consultant in educational development. He holds BA and MA degrees from Indiana University.

Rodolfo Elías, has a master's degree in Applied Social Psychology and courses in the PhD Program (University of Guelph, Canada), courses of the Master's Program in Educational Policy (Universidad Alberto Hurtado, Santiago, Chile), and a BA in Psychology (Universidad Católica, Asunción, Paraguay). Currently, he is working as coordinator of the national program of evaluation of preschool education in Paraguay in the Ministry of Education of Paraguay (MEC) and as researcher at the Instituto Desarrollo, Capacitación y Ciudadanía (Paraguay).

Diana Gonçalves Vidal is Professor of History of Education in the Faculty of Education of the University of Sao Paulo, where she coordinates the Interdisciplinary Nucleus of Studies and Research in History of Education (NIEPHE). She is a researcher at the CNP and currently is the President of the Brazilian Society of History of Education. Her latest publication is the book "Culturas escolares" (school cultures), edited by Autores Associados in 2005.

Silvina Gvirtz holds a PhD in Education. She is the Director of the School of Education at the Universidad de San Andrés and Researcher of the CONICET (National Council for Scientific and Technical Research). In 2003, she was awarded the John Simon Guggenheim Fellowship for the project "A comparison of models of school governance in Argentina, Brazil, and Nicaragua," and in 2004 she was awarded the Twentieth Anniversary Prize of the National Academy of Education of Argentina for her book, "*De la tragedia a la esperanza. Hacia un sistema educativo justo, democrático y de calidad.*" She has published twelve books; the latest is *La Educación ayer, hoy y mañana. El ABC de la pedagogía* (2007). She has also published more than twenty articles in refereed journals of different countries, such as England, Germany, Portugal, Australia, Israel, Venezuela, and Belgium. She is Director of the Educational Series of Granica Publishing, and Director of the Yearbook of the Argentine Society of the History of Education.

Yamilet Hernández-Galano has a BA in History from the University of La Havana. She works in the Department of History of Cuba in that University, where she is a professor and the Director of the "Cátedra de República." Currently, she is completing her Master's studies in Interdisciplinary Studies for Latin America, the Caribbean, and Cuba. She specializes in Gender Studies and the History of Women.

Héctor Lindo-Fuentes is Professor of History at Fordham University. Author of *Remembering a Massacre in El Salvador: The Insurrection of 1932, Roque Dalton, and the Politics of Historical Memory* (2007, with Erik Ching and Rafael Lara-Martínez); *La economía de El Salvador en el siglo XIX* (2003); *Comunidad, participación y escuelas en El Salvador* (2001); *Central America 1821–71: Liberalism Before Reform* (1995, with Lowell Gudmundson); and *Weak Foundations: The Economy of El Salvador in the Nineteenth Century* (1990). He is member of the national commission for accreditation of higher education institutions of El Salvador and of the Ford Foundation advisory group for the advancement of the social sciences in Central America. He is also past president of the Board of Trustees of the Center for Regional Research of Mesoamerica (1998–2002).

Luís Enrique López holds a PhD in sociolinguistics from the University of Lancaster (UK). He has taught at the Universidad Católica in Lima and also at the Facultad Latinoamericana de Ciencias Sociales (FLACSO) in Ecuador. He was the founding director both of the Programa de Postgrado en Lingüística Andina y Educación de la Universidad Nacional del Altiplano (in Puno, Peru), and subsequently of the Programa de Formación en Educación Intercultural Bilingüe para los Paises Andinos (PROEIB Andes). He has worked with UNESCO, UNICEF, the European Union, and the Harvard Institute for International Development, and has been a consultant to indigenous education programs in Ecuador, Guatemala, Nicaragua, Peru, and Bolivia. Between 1993–96, he was principal consultant to Bolivia's Ministry of Education as it implemented its nationwide educational reform. Currently, he is assisting in the establishment of bilingual education programs in Paraguay.

Aurora Loyo Brambila works as a researcher in the Institute of Social Research of the Unviersidad Nacional Autónoma de México, where she is also a Professor in the Department of Social and Political Sciences. She is a sociologist, and did her postgraduate studies in the Sorbonne and in the Colegio de México. Her main research interests are based on the themes of social actors and education policy, teacher unions, and basic education. She has published several books, and she regularly publishes in academic journals, especially in the *Revista Mexicana de Sociología* (Mexican Journal of Sociology). She is interested in contributing to the informed debate about education themes in her country and currently she participates fundamentally through the *Observatorio Ciudadano de la Educación* (Citizen Observatory of Education).

Aurolyn Luykx, is a joint associate professor of Anthropology and Teacher Education at the University of Texas-El Paso. After completing her PhD in linguistic and educational anthropology (UT-Austin, 1993), she spent several years training Bolivian educators in the implementation of that country's nationwide school reform, and was a founding faculty member of the Programa de Formación en Educación Intercultural Bilingüe para los Paises Andinos (PROEIB Andes). She is the author of *The Citizen Factory: Schooling and Cultural Production in Bolivia,* as well as numerous articles on schooling among culturally and linguistically diverse populations.

María Ester Mancebo, Doctor in Humanities (Option: Education), Universidad Católica del Uruguay. Master in Political Science, FLACSO-Argentina. History Teacher, Instituto de Profesores Artigas-Uruguay. Currently, she teaches "Education Policy" at the Universidad de la República and is Director of the Area of Monitoring and Evaluation at the Program Infamilia, Ministry of Social Development in Uruguay.

Guillermo A. Martínez is currently Vice President of the National Council of Evaluation and Accreditation of the Nicaraguan Educational System. He has been teaching since 1962 at secondary and university levels. He has also occupied positions as Director of the Center for Research and Social Action Juan XXIII at the Central American University (UCA) and as a member of the Center for Socio-Educational Research at the National Autonomous University of Nicaragua (UNAN-Managua). He holds Master's and PhD degrees from Indiana University School of Education, Bloomington.

Alejandrina Mata Segreda is the Vice Minister of Education of Costa Rica. She has been a teacher for all her professional life, first as an elementary and preschool educator, and until the present time as a professor at the University of Costa Rica. Also she studied counseling, adult education, and comparative education with an emphasis in evaluation of educational systems. Among her academic works, she has done research in environmental education, comparative studies of the Central American region, and continuing education for teachers.

Luciano Mendes de Faria Filho, is a Pedagogue, and holds a doctorate in History of Education from the University of Sao Paulo. He is Professor of History of Education in the Federal University of Minas Gerais. He researches the spread of schooling in Brazil and currently coordinates the Project "Thinking Education, Thinking Brazil: 1822–2022." He published, together with Diana Goncalves Vidal, *As Lentes da História* (2005), and edited the book

Pensadores Sociais e História da Educação (2006). Currently (2007), he is Vice President of the Brazilian Society of History of Education.

Angela Oría is project leader in IIPE/UNESCO Buenos Aires and teaches History of Argentine and Latin American Education at the Universidad de San Andres in Buenos Aires. She is also a PhD student at the Institute of Education, University of London, School of Educational Foundations and Policy Studies. Her main focus is in the field of history of education, but she also works on policy sociology and educational policy, having published a paper (in collaboration with Stephen Ball) in the *Journal of Education Policy* titled "Urban Education, the Middle Classes and their Dilemmas of School Choice."

Rolando Poblete Melis, has a degree in philosophy and a master's degree in social policies from different Chilean universities. He has a PhD in social and cultural anthropology at the Universidad Autónoma de Barcelona, Spain. He has done research on intercultural education in Chilean schools with indigenous and immigrant enrollment. He has worked as consultant on education for international organizations like ECLAC and IIPE UNESCO, Buenos Aires. Currently he is a teacher for the master's program in Social Policies of Arcis University, Santiago, Chile.

Isolda Rodríguez is a literary critic, researcher, and teacher. One of her important areas of specialization is the history of education in Nicaragua (for example, *Education during the Liberal Period, Nicaragua: 1983–2009*; *The History of Education in Nicaragua: Conservative Restoration, 1910–30*; and *The History of Education in Nicaragua: 50 years in the educational system, 1929–79*, in press). As a graduate in administrative education, she has also had the opportunity to direct educational processes.

Lyding R. Rodríguez Fuentes has a BA in history from the University of La Havana. She works in the *Casa de Altos Estudios Don Fernando Ortiz* of the University of La Havana. Currently she is doing her master's studies in interdisciplinary studies for Latin America, the Caribbean, and Cuba. She specializes in ecclesiastical studies in colonial Cuba.

Raúl Ruiz Carrión, is a full-time Professor of Education at the National Autonomous University of Nicaragua (UNAN-Managua). Since 1987, he has observed and taught courses concerning Nicaraguan educational systems under different national administrations. He has conducted and/or directed more than thirty national and international studies on different aspects of Nicaraguan and Central American education at primary, secondary, and tertiary levels. Currently, he is a member of the Centre for Socio-Educational Research at the National Autonomous University of Nicaragua (UNAN-Managua). He holds a master's degree from Indiana University, Bloomington.

Javier Sáenz Obregón is Professor at the Department of Sociology and the Cultural Studies program at the Universidad Nacional de Colombia. His research interests are in the fields of philosophy of education, the history of pedagogical practices, and the contemporary forms of self-creation. The themes of his most recent publications include the examination of philosophy as pedagogy, the appropriation of Dewey's pedagogy in Colombia, the impact of the birth of the Human Sciences on pedagogical practices, and the educational uses of Foucault.

Oscar Saldarriaga Vélez is a Historian of the University of Antioquia (Medellín-Colombia), and has a PhD in History and Philosophy from the Université Catholique de Louvain in Belgium. He is Director of the History Department of the *Pontifica Univeridad Javeriana*, Bogotá-Colombia, a founding member of the research group "History of Pedagogical Practices in Colombia," and director of the group "Knowledge, power and cultures in Colombia." He is the author of the book *Del oficio de maestro. Prácticas y teorías de la pedagogía moderna en Colombia* (2003); and co-author of the book *Mirar la infancia. Pedagogía, moral y modernidad en Colombia, 1903–46* (1997).